# A Pilgrimage Of Faith

The Mennonite Brethren Church
in Russia and North America
1860 - 1990

*Perspectives on Mennonite Life and Thought* is a series joinlly published between Kindred Press, the Historical Commission of the General Conference of Mennonite Brethren Churches and the Center for Mennonite Brethren Studies of Winnipeg, Manitoba, Fresno, California and Hillsboro, Kansas.*

1. Paul Toews, ed., *Pilgrims and Strangers: Essays in Mennonite Brethren History* (1977)
2. Abraham Friesen ed., *P.M. Friesen and His History: Understanding Mennonite Brethren Beginnings* (1979)
3. David Ewert, ed., *Called to Teach* (1979)
4. Heinrich Wölk and Gerhard Wölk, *Die Mennoniten Bruedergemeinde in Russland, 1925-1980; Ein Beitrag zur Geschichte* (1981)
5. John B. Toews, *Perilous Journey: The Mennonite Brethren in Russia 1860-1910* (1988)
6. Aaron A. Toews, *Mennonite Martyrs: People Who Suffered for Their Faith 1920-1940*, translated by John B. Toews (1990)
7. Paul Toews, ed., *Mennonites and Baptists: A Continung Conversation* (1993)
8. J.B. Toews, *A Pilgrimage Of Faith: The Mennonite Brethren Church in Russia and North America 1860-1990* (1993)

*Volumes 1-4 were published by the Center for Mennonite Brethren Studies (Fresno)

# A Pilgrimage Of Faith

The Mennonite Brethren Church in Russia and North America
1860 - 1990

**J.B. TOEWS**

WINNIPEG, MB CANADA    **Kindred Press**    HILLSBORO, KS USA

**A PILGRIMAGE OF FAITH**
**The Mennonite Brethren Church
in Russia and North America 1860 - 1990**

Copyright © 1993 by the Centers for Mennonite Brethren Studies, Fresno, CA; Winnipeg, MB and Hillsboro, KS.

All rights reserved. With the exception of brief excerpts for reviews, no part of this book may be reproduced without written permission of the publisher.

---

**Canadian Cataloguing in Publication Data**
    Toews, John B.
    A pilgrimage of faith
    Includes bibliographical references.
    ISBN 0-921788-17-7

    1. Mennonite Brethren Church - History. 2. Mennonites - Russia - History. 3. Mennonites - Canada - History. I. Title.

    BX8115.T64 1993   289.7'09   C93-098095-6

---

Published simultaneously by Kindred Press, Winnipeg, MB R2L 2E5 and Kindred Press, Hillsboro, KS 67063

Cover design by Gerry Unrau McKay Goettler, Saskatoon, Saskatchewan.

Book design by Fred Koop, Winnipeg, MB

Printed in Canada by Christian Press, Winnipeg, MB

International Standard Book Number: 0-921788-17-7

# Contents

Preface   iii
Foreward   vii

**SECTION 1**
**Historical Background**

1   The Mennonite Brethren: A Phenomenon of Renewal   1

**SECTION 2**
**The Early Mennonite Brethren Church, 1860-1915**

2   A People of Bibliocentric Faith   17
3   The Mennonite Brethren Understanding of Salvation and Baptism   29
4   The Mennonite Brethren Understanding of a New Testament Church   39
5   Leadership and the Teaching Ministry   53
6   In The World But Not Of The World   69
7   A Missionary Movement   81
8   Early Mennonite Brethren Missionaries   95
9   Eschatology: Not With One Voice   107
10   Mennonite Brethren at the Turn of the Century   115
11   Summary Observations of Parts One and Two   133

**SECTION 3**
**A Time Of Transition**

12   The Shadow of the Russian Revolution   139
13   Mennonite Immigration from Russia to Canada in the 1920s (Implications for the Mennonite Brethren Church)   155
14.   Mennonite Brethren Education   167
15.   Identity and Diversity   189

## SECTION 4
## The Mennonite Brethren
## Church in the Context of Modernity

| | | |
|---|---|---|
| 16 | Wrestling with Modernity | 205 |
| 17 | How Shall We Then Be Led? | 217 |
| 18 | Mennonite Brethren Evangelism | 239 |
| 19 | Missions in Context of Change | 261 |
| 20 | Faith in Tension | 281 |
| 21 | A Call To Commitment | 299 |
| 22 | "The Race That Is Set Before Us" (Hebrews 12:1) | 323 |
| Endnotes | | 329 |

# Preface

This book seeks to provide a biblical and theological framework for the Mennonite Brethren search for identity amidst the blinding cultural changes of the late twentieth century.

Typical of pilgrims, the Mennonite Brethren have experienced much movement–spiritually, geographically and culturally. In periods of great social change there is energy and exhilaration, as well as anxiety and fear. There is a determination to preserve the old ways, and an equal desire to embrace the new.

The search for a place for the current church to stand is done through a selective invocation of the past. In writing this book I have brought to bear not only historical research but also my personal observations from a lifetime of ministry and my experiences of working closely, as a young teacher and preacher, with leaders whose own ministries had overlapped with the founders of the Mennonite Brethren Church. The story of the Mennonite Brethren is told under four broad categories: Historical Background (Part I); the Early Mennonite Brethren Church (Part II); Mennonite Brethren in Transition (Part III); and Mennonite Brethren in the Context of Modernity (Part IV).

The quest for Mennonite Brethren spiritual integrity in matters of faith, polity and lifestyle became most pronounced in the period following the Second World War, 1945-1970. The fact that no fewer than fifteen study conferences were held during these twenty-five years bears witness to this concern.

The findings of the 1972 inter-Mennonite church membership profile, subsequently published as *Anabaptists Four*

*Centuries Later: A Profile of Five Mennonite and Brethren in Christ Denominations* (1975), were unsettling to Mennonite Brethren. The profile showed vividly that major cultural changes had adversely impacted the life of the church. The jolting movement from a rural, ethnically homogeneous people to a new environment of individualism and modernity produced sobering changes that raised many alarms.

The committees of reference and counsel of the Canadian, U.S. and bi-national conferences suggested a need to replicate the Kauffman and Harder study a decade later to test the trends indicated in the 1972 profile. The 1982 profile, administered only to Mennonite Brethren, provided strong proof of the accuracy of the earlier survey. The second inter-Mennonite profile of 1989, published as *The Mennonite Mosaic: Identity and Modernization* (1991), further confirmed the 1972 and the 1982 data.

The response of the Historical Commission of the General Conference of Mennonite Brethren Churches to the findings of the profiles provided the incentive to undertake this research related to the faith and life of the Mennonite Brethren Church.

Unless indicated otherwise, all Scripture references used in this book are from the King James Version. This translation was used when the 1903 Mennonite Brethren Confession of Faith was translated into English.

Many people subsequently assisted with the research. The task could not have been accomplished without the participation of teachers from our institutions, pastors, missiologists, missionaries and individual church members. Each chapter was read by three people who had special competence in the topic under review. Their contributions and critiques are part of the final manuscript.

Special recognition must be given to former *Mennonite Brethren Herald* editors Herb Kopp (Edmonton) and Harold Jantz (Winnipeg) who read the full manuscript and offered suggestions and corrections.

Former *Christian Leader* editor Wally Kroeker, now editor of *The Marketplace* in Winnipeg, undertook the task of editing the manuscript. I remain his debtor for this labor of love. Kevin Enns-Rempel, Archivist of the Center for Mennonite Brethren Studies (Fresno), and student assistants Rhonda (Warkentin) Langley and Joanne Klassen, worked to systematize the documentation.

The years of research and final publication of this volume were made possible through the financial resources provided by the Kroeker Foundation of Winkler, Manitoba, and the continuous encouragement of Walter E. Kroeker, for many years the secretary of the foundation. A second source of financial help was the William Dyck Corporation in Fresno. We remain indebted to these persons who made the project and its completion financially possible.

Last but not least I must express my deep indebtedness to Laurene Peters who has labored with me through the original typing and many subsequent editorial changes. Her patience and efficiency in the process was a contribution essential to the publication of this book.

To all the participants in the preparation of the manuscript I hereby extend my deep appreciation. Acknowledging them, however, does not absolve me from the final responsibility for the content of the book.

The process brought me both enrichment and pain. The enrichment came as I was able to immerse myself in the spiritual pilgrimage of my own people, and to see it as a testimony of God's mercy and grace. Psalm 103 contains a fitting postscript to this period of our history: "For he knoweth our frame; he remembereth that we are dust" (Ps. 103:14). The pain was felt deeply in the recognition of our imperfections and weaknesses. My conclusion to the years of research into the past and present of the Mennonite Brethren is best expressed in the words of Paul: "Being confident of this very thing, that he which hath begun a good work in you will perform it until the day of Jesus Christ" (Phil. 1:6).

# Foreward

When Eusebius, bishop of Cesarea and apologist for Emperor Constantine, wrote his *Ecclesiastical History* in the fourth century, he launched a new historical genre. Written under the impression of the church's "victory' under Constantine, Eusebius described the rise and spread of Christianity against incredible odds. When Rufinus translated Eusebius into Latin nearly a century later, he felt compelled to delete the last chapter of the *Ecclesiastical History* and replace it with two of his own that dealt with the problems created in the church by the Arian heresy. Thus, rather than conclude in triumph, Rufinus concluded with internal conflict in an age when the church had peace. Changing conditions had produced a new interpretation of church history. Had he written his own history of the church, Rufinus might well have interpreted the church's entire history quite differently than had Eusebius.

Although opposition to the triumphant Roman Catholic Church in the West led, on occasion, to an attempt to rewrite that church history - the most noteworthy example is that of Joachim of Fiore - it was not until the Reformation of the sixteenth century, with its creation of alternate expressions of the Christian faith, that another investigation of church history was launched; this time, however, not from within the church but from without. Begun by Humanists of the renaissance, who regarded "beginnings" as the purest expression of a movement, Protestants could see the "development" of the church only in terms of decline and corruption. From that point onward, church history has, as often as not, been used to justify the historian's own branch of the Christian church as to attack and seek to undermine all others. As Anabaptists/Mennonites, the latter was our lot - with a few notable exceptions - well into the twentieth century. Only infrequently have "insiders" of these churches had the courage to take a critical look at their own church history. In the German Lutheran tradition, Johann Arndt, in his *Wahres Christentum*, and Philip Jakob Spener, in his *Pia Desideria*, did so. Out of their critical reconstructions of the past grew the Pietistic revivals in the Lutheran Church that have had a profound impact in the history of the Christian church in the eighteenth and nineteenth centuries.

Church history is therefore a somewhat different entity than secular history and to a certain extent at least, pursues different purposes. One of these purposes is to trace the degree to which the church, in its various branches, has lived up to the ideals enunciated in the New Testament and embodied in the earliest church as portrayed in the Acts of the Apostles. This "primitivist" thrust was particularly characteristic of the Anabaptist movement. Subsequent renewal movements within the Mennonite Church have therefore struggled with the problem of this dual origin: their own and that of the Apostolic Church. It is for this reason that Menno and the New Testament play the role they do in the birth of the Mennonite Brethren Church in Russia. By returning - or at least attempting to do so - to this dual beginning, renewal movements of necessity become critics of their contemporaries. This lies in the very nature of their enterprise.

It is now one hundred and thirty three years since the birth of the Mennonite Brethren Church, and therefore time for someone in that church to take a backward glance to see how we have done. Who better to do this than J.B. Toews whose life spans well over half of those years and who has experienced much of what he writes about in the following pages. He is our Johann Arndt, our Philip Jakob Spener, who desires to call us to reflection, spiritual awareness, and ultimately to repentance and renewal. May God grant that we heed his call.

Abraham Friesen
Chair, Historical Commission of the
General Conference of Mennonite Brethren Churches

CHAPTER 1

# The Mennonite Brethren: A Phenomenon of Renewal

**INTRODUCTION**

The story of God redeeming a fallen human race is a story of actual events happening to real people. In other words, it is given to us in the context of history. The Old and the New Testaments are the records of the divine revelations of God to people not much different from ourselves, culminating with the ultimate personal revelation—Jesus Christ. The biblical figures of the past, though long dead, still speak to us through their faith (Heb. 11:4). Through the language of history they speak to us today as we "remember." The word "remember" serves as a continuous exhortation to review the past so we can understand the present.[1]

A French statesman, philosopher and orator coined the phrase: "take from the past the fire: not the ashes."[2] Today's generation has a tendency to distance itself from the lessons of history, preferring instead to seek inspiration in slogans for the future. The interrelationship of the present with both the past and the future receives marginal attention.

Biblical history is different. The people of God, future-oriented as they are, "remember the works of the Lord" (Ps. 77:11) to equip them for the challenges of the present and the hope of the future. In that vein a group of evangelical church leaders, pastors, and professors felt called to issue "An Appeal to Evangelicals", which reads as follows:

> We confess that we have lost the fullness of our Christian heritage, too readily assuming that the Scripture and the Spirit make us independent of the past. In so doing, we have become theologically shallow, spiritually weak, blind to the work of God in others, and married to our culture.[3]

Amid the swirling change of the late twentieth century we need to hear the exhortation of Robert Schrag, editor of *Mennonite Weekly Review*, calling us to a stronger sense of history:

> Cultivate a sense of history. The ideas and events that shaped the present came out of the past. To really know your own identity, you need to examine the roots from which you came. The lessons of history are a valuable resource for intelligent living today and in the future. Consider, too, that Christianity is an historical religion. Our faith is based on actual historical events, as God worked through a chosen people, then decisively broke into history to redeem mankind through Christ. Today, as God's instruments in the present, we can place ourselves in this long procession and look ahead to the culmination of history in the Lord's coming again.[4]

To understand the Mennonite Brethren theological and spiritual pilgrimage requires a grasp of its historical background.[5] Mennonite Brethren belong to a dynamic Anabaptist movement that emphasized the Bible as the Word of God for faith and life, the experiential reality of a New Testament conversion, the church as an interdependent fellowship, a life of rigorous discipleship, and the church as a witnessing community in evangelism and mission. Our forebears demonstrated their faith by translating biblical teachings into life and relationships, not by apologetics or creedal dogmatism. Being "born again" meant there was a recognizable difference between the "old" and the "new." A holy lifestyle of self-denial and a sacrificial ministry for others were hallmarks of discipleship, for Jesus had said: "If any man will come after me, let him deny himself, and take up his cross, and follow me" (Mt. 16:24).

To understand the increasing contrast between past and present, we must be open to seeing ourselves in the context of history. We cannot idealize our past. Rather, we must note how God, in spite of our many weaknesses and failures, was long-suffering and merciful to make us a dynamic missionary conference whose influence has circled the globe.

A careful study of our history helps us understand the phenomenon of repeated revivals, many conversions and church growth, as well as times of inward emptiness, legalism and apostasy. Only as we examine our pilgrimage can we account for these ups and downs in spiritual vitality.

To idealize our past without an increasing concern for the present is idolatry. Israel was guilty of this sin. People may seek escape from the responsibilities of the present by brooding over the past; but the opposite–degrading our history–is also a sin. We need to know and face our past to understand our present and clarify our mission for the future.

## THE PHENOMENON OF RENEWAL

Human history is a story of change, a rhythmic cycle of ascent and decline that ebbs and flows almost like the seasons. Civilizations rise to a level of glory only to decline, fade into antiquity and are replaced by an emerging new era of progress and expansion. Each epoch has its specific strength, be it art, literature, prosperity, intellectual achievement, or technology. There is a resurgence of life, a leap forward, and then weakening and recession.

Biblical history appears to be no exception. The Old Testament too records spiritual ascensions and decline.[6] People responded to the purposes of God, accepted their dependence on the Almighty, then weakened in their commitment as self-fulfillment regained priority.

Natural humanity does not have the volitional ability for a life of continued dependence on the supernatural. A sustaining relationship with God requires the continuous nurture of renewal. Some find it in the symbolism of the Old Testament Mosaic institutions, others in the New Testament provision of "abiding in Christ." In the Pauline epistles the need for such continuous inward renewal appears to be almost a law of life.[7] As with Old Testament Israel, so the history of Christianity illustrates the continuing process of God faithfully bringing renewal to his people and his church.[8]

The Mennonite church, heir of the Anabaptists who were known as the left wing of the Reformation, is no exception.[9] Its story is not merely one of social, cultural and economic factors, but rather a story of spiritual faithfulness and life-giving renewal. As John A. Toews has written, "Church renewal and new life movements cannot be explained simply in terms of an historic framework of cause and effect."[10] Religious history demands the recognition of the gracious sovereignty of God who guides and intervenes in the affairs of his people.

The story of the Mennonites in Russia–their Dutch origin and migration from the Netherlands to Prussia (1530s and following), and then to Russia (1789 and following)–is well documented in numerous publications.[11] A brief review of the spiritual conditions within the Mennonite church in the decades preceding the birth of the Mennonite Brethren reveals the shadows and light which characterized the formation and the continuing pilgrimage of the new movement.

## THE MENNONITE CHURCH IN RUSSIA
## IN THE FIRST HALF OF THE NINETEENTH CENTURY

The story of the Mennonite church in Russia, beginning with the early immigrants in 1788, reveals that spiritual life had sunk to a low ebb and ethical practices had seriously declined.[12] The Mennonite community of that era, according to historian Robert Kreider, exhibited many of the characteristics of the *Volkskirche*, or what in English is termed the parish pattern of the church.[13] Historian Gerhard Lohrenz wrote of "a slow stagnation that crept into the intellectual and spiritual life of the group." When missionary David Schatter visited the colonies in 1835 he reported that the church had "lost its salt," but the spiritual life would sink even lower during the next two decades.[14] The diary of David Epp, minister in Chortitza, reflected a deep anxiety over the loss of ethical and moral values among the Mennonites. His entries in 1837 and 1838 pointed to a breakdown in morality in the church community.[15] Jacob P. Bekker, one of the signers of the Mennonite Brethren secession document, reported in his memoirs that taverns existed in virtually every village.

> The ministers were struck with blindness and did not realize that the establishment of distilleries and saloons within the colonies would be harmful to the entire church community. At times some of the drunkards would lie in a drunken stupor and nearly unclothed, in the streets, causing the horses of passing vehicles to shy away from them. Several persons died as the result of liquor burns to their throats. The ministers were aware of these drunkards, yet the offenders were allowed to remain members of the church and were admitted to partake of the Lord's Supper.[16]

The spiritual poverty of the Mennonite church by 1860 was further reflected in the diary of a minister in the Ohrloff church, quoted by Peter M. Friesen:

> I pondered the condition of the Mennonite brethren [he means all Mennonites here]; and behold, it is even worse than the departed brethren describe it [in the secession document of the Brethren]. There is no fear of God, no

faithfulness or honesty in the land, everyone must beware of his fellow man, his own brother, and those who still repent of anything repent the fact that they cannot cheat their fellow man any worse than they already do. And those who boast, boast of their roguery and revelry, as a hero of drunkenness, as a ruffian and the like. The keepers of Zion see it and remain silent. Or should they not be able to see? Are all the keepers blind? And are they what the prophet describes further on? Do they hate discipline and order? Then it says: "Why do you take my covenant in your mouth?" The most chilling threats of God's Word then apply to them, and it may have occurred to those who left: "Let them go their way, for they are blind leaders!"[17]

The condition of the Mennonite church in Russia during this time cannot be isolated from the spiritual poverty of the mother church in Prussia. P.M. Friesen described the rural congregations as "left with an ecclesiastical, doctrinally correct, moral formalism (always, however, with the exception of 'Elijah's 7000'). Correct doctrine and morality had replaced true faith. The good house of Menno had become practically desolate and empty and was about to collapse."[18]

A major factor in the spiritual decline of the church in Russia was lack of adequate leadership. For the most part, the educated leaders in the Prussian Mennonite community did not migrate to Russia. Of their unwillingness to move with the pioneer settlements John B. Toews, historian of the Russian experience, wrote: "They knew that the practice of their art was not an option. They could not expose their modest treasures to the cross winds of a new language and new culture. The intellectual had too much to lose."[19] As a result, the cultural leadership became largely the responsibility of the church elders, most of whom were uneducated and ill equipped for the task. Peter M. Friesen likened their incompetent leadership to "a blind leader of the blind, void of any apparent education or theological knowledge as well as any spiritual life emanating from God."[20]

Mennonites in Russia–geographically isolated, intellectually anemic and spiritually impoverished–"had become a society to themselves. Religion and politics had intermingled, church and state had become one."[21] The church had become spiritually impotent. When the light that is in the church is darkness, then how great is that darkness.

Historian John A. Toews aptly stated the issue: "A river cannot rise higher than its source. But for the grace of God, a people can rise no higher than their heritage and their leadership."[22] In the midst of the generally incompetent leadership were exceptions like Bernhard Harder (1832-1884). Cornelius Krahn described him as following an "independent, warmly evangelistic course within the entire brotherhood, aiming to lift its spiritual and cultural aspects, thus making a singular contribution comparable to that of Johann Cornies in the economic realm."[23] In a letter to the periodical *Mennonitische Blätter*, dated July 28, 1862, he expressed deep pain about the conditions of the church of which he was a part:

> Friend! brother! father! or whatever else you wish to be to me who am as yet a very inexperienced person in the service of the Word and the ways of God, I cast myself on your breast and weep, for things look very sad in our midst and yet I love our people with the passion of a first love. Is there any way in which you could add to the fervor of prayer, or to the fervor of admonition to prayer through your sermons and publications? In any case, the time has come to lift up the tired hands and strengthen the weak knees. Like a woman in birth pangs, we should labor for the new birth of our people. Is the Lord's hand shortened? Has His ear become hard of hearing? Or has His blood, the precious blood of Jesus, now lost its power

and validity? O, what is lacking? We—the witnesses and watchmen—we are lacking. A large number of us lack the beginning letter of the alphabet, the capital "A" of Christianity: "Wake up, o man, from the sleep of sin, etc."

This is not due to our lack of learning—though it were desirable that matters stood differently among us even in this regard—it is due to our emptiness and estrangement from God. . . . If only we shepherds were alive, then the sheep would hear our voice, and the awakening life would flow beautifully and appropriately within the guidelines of our confession. But now it is breaking out of the decayed forms, is flattening the rotten pillars that we are, and is working its own way, as it were, over our dead bodies, to freedom. There it now crests and flows in unbridled power until the Lord of the church will finally succeed in containing it, and we will be left with a dry form, with a husk lacking the seed, with a church lacking living members. That is what it looks like here. Anything that begins to live wants to escape, as though we were doomed to die.[24]

**INFLUENCES TOWARDS REVIVAL**

The course of history demonstrates that God from time to time visits his people anew with a gracious movement of the Spirit. First, a period of gloom sets in and weariness invades the hearts of men and women. Then, sick in soul, they seek after God. The human spirit cannot rest until it finds peace in God. This search for renewal in the life of the Mennonite church in Russia emerged in several forms.

One of the earliest was the birth of the *Kleine Gemeinde* (small congregation)(1812-1819). This renewal movement, led by Klaas Reimer (1770-1837), was the result of small prayer circles of those who were discontented with conditions in the larger church. Reimer was concerned to reform the Russian Mennonites in accord with the traditions of the sixteenth-century Anabaptist church and the writings of Menno Simons, Dirk Philips and Peter Peters.[25]

The formation of the *Kleine Gemeinde* did not calm the turbulence as clashes continued between the old guard and more progressive Mennonites who were open to deeper piety, education and missionary endeavors. At one point the tension expressed itself in the forced resignation of elders Cornelius Warkentin and Heinrich Wiens over the issue of suppression of change.[26] Further controversy surrounded Bernhard Fast (1821-1860), elder of the large Ohrloff congregation. His association with evangelical believers and his endorsement of the Russian Bible Society for Scripture distribution resulted in a split, with the larger part of the congregation selecting new leadership.[27]

Another expression of a growing new mood was the Ohrloff School Society, which established a private school in the early 1820s to bolster education among Russian Mennonites. Founded under the leadership of Tobias Voth, this school became a preparatory chapter for the emergence of the Mennonite Brethren Church in 1860.

Voth, born in Brenkenhofswalde and educated in Leipzig and Berlin, had been converted through the writings of the widely known Pietist, Johann Heinrich Jung-Stilling.[28] Heinrich Huebert, first elder of the Mennonite Brethren Church, as well as other students, received their first indelible Christian impressions from him. In the 1820s Voth and his associates were in correspondence with the Moravian Brethren. This group of revitalized believers provided the leadership for the founding of the Mennonite Brethren Church in 1860.[29] The influence of Heinrich Heese (1787-1868), who came to the Ohrloff *Vereinsschule* in 1829, as well as Heinrich Franz (1812-1889), who joined the faculty in 1832, provided further impetus towards reform.[30]

Education was thus a major influence in the reform of a people in cultural and religious stagnation resulting from centuries of isolation. James Urry has furnished important evidence of the expansion of education, especially among families of successful farmers and estate owners. Beginning in 1820, children who showed ability but whose families lacked financial resources were selected for further education and supported by community funds.[31]

Of special significance in the march towards religious renewal was the immigration of a group from Brenkenhofswalde, Prussia, to Russia in 1835 under the leadership of Elder Wilhelm Lange. Lange, who established Gnadenfeld, came with a background of Lutheran Pietism strongly influenced by pietistic group meetings in Prussia.[32] According to P.M. Friesen, "Gnadenfeld became the center for a religious movement of greater warmth, the magnetic center for those who called themselves 'brethren' long before the Mennonite Brethren Church was organized. Many members of other Mennonite congregations formally joined Gnadenfeld because they sympathized with its position."[33] During this time there also sprang up private study groups interested in outreach. These included mission sewing circles, Bible studies and periodic mission festivals, all of which generated considerable opposition.

In 1845, Eduard Wüst, a Lutheran Pietist from Würtemberg, Germany, came on the scene.[34] A frequent preacher at the mission festivals in Gnadenfeld, his powerful messages fanned the flame of revival. Wüst's ministry, though brief (he died in 1858), made a significant contribution to the renewal movement. Peter M. Friesen's statement–"Next to God's Word and his spirit, Menno and Wüst have actually made the Mennonite Brethren Church what it is and will be in the church of Christ"[35]–overstated Wüst's historic significance. To be sure, his emphasis on a personal salvation experience and mission was important for the renewal movement. His ministry did not, however, provide a biblical theology of the church and the pathway of discipleship. The absence of these foundations in the renewal movements prior to 1860 was a major factor in the struggles during the initial years of the Mennonite Brethren movement.³⁶ According to John A. Toews, Wüst was a "'Moses' who led many people out of the bondage of a lifeless tradition and dead orthodoxy to a joyous assurance of a personal faith. But by training and experience he was not equipped to be the 'Joshua' to lead these redeemed people into the promised land of a believers church."³⁷

Reports of the renewal movement in Neu Kronsweide, Chortitza, in 1853 illustrated the distortion that can result when personal salvation is stressed without corresponding emphasis on the biblical implications for a life of faith. The church there, under the jurisdiction of Elder Jakob Hildebrand (1795-1867), experienced a spiritual revival. Kornelius Hildebrand, son of Elder Hildebrand, recounted the events and expression of the movement. He reported that his father "rejoiced with the newly converted, who openly declared the assurance of forgiveness of sin in the blood of Jesus and hoped that these people would become the salt of the church."³⁸ The younger Hildebrand expressed his father's satisfaction that the adherents of this group were the most ardent churchgoers. "Apparently they sought to translate their Christianity into practice and to prove with a new pure life that they were serious about a godly walk."³⁹ The joy of their newfound faith, however, soon found expression in emotional excesses. Their ethical lapses were inconsistent with their profession of faith. Leaders of the new group denounced the faith and practice of the mother church. The gift of tongues was emphasized. Improprieties occurred between men and women. Moderating efforts on the part of Elder Hildebrand failed. John B. Toews notes that "radical leadership encouraged the sister kiss, loud hallelujahs, lively rhythms beat on pots and pans during worship and the destruction of everything associated with the old piety."⁴⁰ This was not unlike the imbalances that appeared in the early years of the Mennonite Brethren when emotional excesses also overcame the new group of believers who were searching for direction in their newfound faith amid the stress of persecution and harassment by their own Mennonite people.[41]

**THE SECESSION DOCUMENT**

Bible study groups continued to nourish the inner life of the people who had experienced personal salvation. Of these meetings Jacob Reimer, a leader in the early Mennonite Brethren Church who attended regularly, wrote:

> Our purpose was to strengthen one another in the faith, to take cognizance of or admonish one another to conduct ourselves as worthy members of the body of Christ, whose treasure is in heaven, not on earth. We also wanted to learn to know each other in our depravity and Christ in His boundless love.[42]

He went on to say that

> As our fellowship established itself more firmly upon the Word of God, there arose in us the desire to celebrate the Lord's Supper more often, and we asked our Elder Lenzmann to break bread more often, even if this had to be done here and there in the homes, as they did in the Acts of the Apostles 2:46-47.[43]

When the request was denied, the group proceeded independently. In November 1859 it met for its first communion service without an officiating elder.

This separate communion service added to the mounting tensions in the Gnadenfeld church. At a congregational meeting on December 19, 1859, Jacob Reimer and Johann Claassen were openly challenged to leave the church. They did so, along with ten others.[44] Community ostracism followed shortly.

For their future fellowship a formal organization was necessary. On January 6, 1860 a secession document prepared by Abraham Cornelsen of Elizabethtal was reviewed by the other dissenters. After a prayer meeting that lasted all afternoon and evening, eighteen heads of households signed the document, fully conscious of the grave consequences that such a step might bring. On January 18 nine others also signed the document.[45]

There were six immediate issues in the document: (1) A disassociation from the decadent church which they perceived to be under the judgment of God: "We fear the inevitable judgment of God, since the openly godless living and their wickedness cry to God in heaven." (2) "A baptism on faith, as a seal of faith; not on a memorized faith, as is the practice, but on a genuine living faith effected by the Spirit of God. For without faith, it is impossible to please God . . . Except a man be born again, he cannot see the kingdom of God. Baptism is not the new birth, as some of the unconverted maintain, but serves as a sign for the baptismal candidate that he is really born again." (3) "Regarding footwashing, we confess that the Lord Jesus instituted it, John 13, to be practiced among one another, for the blessing is in the deed, not in knowledge." (4) A consistent practice in selecting ministers, with qualifications as specified in Scripture. (5) A biblical practice of church discipline to bring sinners to repentance and thus guard the purity of the church, the household of God. (6) A commitment to the articles of faith as held by Menno in life and practice "according to our conviction from the Holy Spirit."[46]

The long-range concerns were for a restoration of a biblical and Anabaptist church. The founders of the new movement felt intimately related to the sixteenth century. Though Pietism had strongly influenced their spiritual renewal, they chose not to become identified with it, preferring instead to remain clearly committed to sixteenth-century Anabaptism, primarily the Dutch stream as interpreted by Menno Simons.[47]

The new movement did fall prey to the emotionalism of the broader renewal movement among nineteenth-century Russian Mennonites. In the struggle to survive under extreme hardships and to gain recognition in the Mennonite community, the new group lacked the leadership required to chart a balanced way. The excesses in the Neu Kronsweide congregation of 1853 were also present in the initial years of the Mennonite Brethren.[48]

The hardships inflicted on the early Mennonite Brethren as they sought to gain the right to exist within the larger community was a sad chapter in the history of Mennonitism.[49] Even unidentified writers in the *Odessaer Zeitung* (a regional newspaper) described the confusion of the initial years regarding the identity of the Mennonite Brethren. One such writer, in part, attributed the problems to the absence of a clear group of leaders.[50] Not until June 1865 was there a clearly defined leadership and polity.

The Mennonite Brethren had developed considerable maturity by the time they assembled on June 26-27, 1865 to resolve the issues that had troubled the new group since its emergence five years earlier. Peter M. Friesen described this meeting, which began at noon on Saturday and remained in session all night and throughout Sunday, as a day where the "church united for a day of prayer, repentance and fasting."[51]

Having survived the initial struggle for the right to exist, as well as the pain of internal aberrations, this "June Reform" became the beginning of the Mennonite Brethren Church as a functional body, with a defined leadership, authority and polity.

The subsequent letter from this body to the government representative can be seen as an official confirmation of the birth. The document reviewed the struggle to survive the persecutions and oppression from the civil and religious leadership of the Mennonite community. It recognized the providence of God who had assigned a place for the Mennonite

Brethren as a renewal movement. It expressed deep repentance and shame over the failures of those early years; it listed failures in reaction to those who oppressed them and resolved to order their future according to Scripture.[52]

It is here where we recognize the historic beginning of the Mennonite Brethren Church. Abraham H. Unruh summarized the lessons that the Mennonite Brethren movement learned from these early troubled years: (1) The need for systematic Bible teaching. An overemphasis on the personal experiential dimension of salvation–free grace and joy in redemption–breeds an emotional imbalance that is inconsistent with true discipleship. (2) The importance of mutual admonition to test the spirits whether they are of God (1 John 4:1). (3) The need for leadership with knowledge and commitment to Scripture. (4) The importance of a firm church polity to give direction in questions of faith and life. (5) The centrality of ethics in the expression of a scriptural faith. (6) A form of meaningful worship, consistent with the character of God.[53]

The birth of the Mennonite Brethren was significant not only for the emergence of the new group but also for the broader Mennonite church. Robert Kreider noted that the "struggle with basic spiritual issues gave new vitality to a dormant church."[54] In time the older congregations appropriated many ideas and practices of the new church that they considered to be right and scriptural. Cornelius Krahn spoke to the importance of the Mennonite Brethren birth as follows: "What it gave to the Russian Mennonites was a rebirth of personal piety, a living piety in which the individual believer receives assurance of the forgiveness of sins, and orders his life definitely according to the teachings of Christ, particularly the Sermon on the Mount."[55] After enlarging upon these influences he concluded: "So we see that the new religious life that came into Russian Mennonitism through the *Brüder Gemeinde* [Brethren] movement exerted a powerful influence both upon the religious life and the social attitude of the group."[56]

CHAPTER 2

# A People of Bibliocentric Faith

The early Mennonite Brethren, rooted in the larger Anabaptist-Mennonite family and firmly committed to the teachings of Menno, also shared their forebears' aversion to doctrinal formulations. The Anabaptist view that a practical theology of life cannot be pressed into a doctrinal system found strong affirmation among them, and perhaps explains the void of written material with a specific theological articulation from 1860 to the close of the nineteenth century.[1]

Abraham H. Unruh observed that the early Mennonite Brethren were acquainted with the confession of faith by Cornelius Ris, translated from the Dutch in 1849, but they did not refer to it in matters of faith and practice. Instead, they emphasized Scripture as their only point of reference.[2]

The writings of Jacob P. Bekker and Peter M. Friesen shed some light on the community process that led to specific decisions in understanding and practice, including such crucial issues as baptism, communion, footwashing and the character of the church as reflected in the record of the June Reform.[3] Another written source is the collection of some 330 sermons by Elder David Duerksen (1850-1910)[4] and a collection of early leaders' sermons published by Jacob and Abraham Kroeker at the turn of the century.[5]

These resources did not offer any organized system of theology nor propositional statements of doctrine. Rather, they represented biblical texts applied to the historical and personal relationship of God to humankind. The redemptive provision of God–preparatory in the Old Testament and realized in Jesus

Christ—constituted the core of their theology. They emphasized the ethical standards governing the character and walk of the redeemed community. Only in 1902 did they find it expedient to prepare a confession of faith. The slightly altered German Baptist confession that Elder Abram Unger submitted as a document to the Russian government, was never recognized as a Mennonite Brethren statement. The 1902 confession, to which Mennonite Brethren have since subscribed in principle, was more a descriptive statement of scriptural understanding than a definitive theological statement.

The process used in adopting this descriptive document of faith was significant. Individual churches studied the scriptural bases of the various sections before adopting them at the congregational level. The document's concluding statement emphasized that the understandings were to be subject to the continued scrutiny of biblical teaching under the guidance of the Holy Spirit.[6]

The criteria of faith rested in the evidences of a new life (John 3:3, 2 Cor. 5:17) based on repentance, an experience of personal conversion resulting in an assurance of sins forgiven and the witness of the Spirit that "we are the children of God" (Rom. 8:16). The early Mennonite Brethren tested the claim of faith against the evidences of "being" and "relationships" measured by the fruits of the Spirit (Gal. 5:22-25). Their faith commitment was one of obedience to Scripture after the example of Jesus and the apostolic teachings related both to individual character and human relationships. To claim to believe the Bible as the Word of God meant to study it individually and communally and apply it to life.[7]

**COMMITMENT TO SCRIPTURE**

The records of the early Russian Mennonite Brethren Conference and local churches (1876-1900) provided little evidence of creedal concern. The point of reference for them was not a codified statement but the study of Scripture in order to find answers to questions arising in the life of the church. "What does the Bible say?" was their major concern.⁸ Their understanding of salvation was rooted in a "Christocentric theology." Briefly stated, this meant a fervent belief in Jesus Christ as God incarnate, his vicarious death and victorious resurrection as the all-sufficient provision for the redemption of sinful humanity, and his coming again to receive his own and to judge the world. To believe in Jesus as Savior meant "to follow Jesus in life," as Hans Denk had said centuries earlier. The model for the redeemed community, the church, was that of the apostolic fellowship, the church as found in the book of Acts.

Biblical truth for Mennonite Brethren was existential and governed all aspects of faith and life. Their rejection of institutional forms of religion left them no other point of reference but the Bible itself. In the initial years, when under continuous attack and persecution from both ecclesiastical and civil authorities, this emphasis on the teachings of the Bible as they understood it was their only anchor. "Faithfulness to the Word" became the overarching motif that provided the courage and the endurance during the early years of the movement.

This bibliocentric orientation was also evident at the first Mennonite Brethren conference in North America convened on September 30, 1878. The minutes of that meeting record the following statement of purpose: "The Conference has been called for brethren of like faith from our scattered churches to see whether at the hand of the Bible it is not possible to bring into harmony different views gleaned from the study of the Word of God and then proceed as a church fellowship according to the same rule (Phil. 3:16) under the banner of the cross of Christ."⁹

The early Mennonite Brethren were "readers of the Word of God and spoke about it in conversation with others."¹⁰ They met in their homes for Bible study, prayer and singing.

They studied God's Word with conviction and faith.[11] Rarely did a neighborly visit conclude without the host reading a portion of Scripture.[12] The focus on Scripture had been central in the revival movement that led to the birth of the new movement. The watchword, "What does the Bible say?", remained a constant in its early years.[13]

Abraham E. Janzen, writing on the biblicism of the early brethren, noted their need to search Scripture continually. He attributed their hesitancy to formulate a creed to their fear that theological formulations would dilute their dependence on Scripture as the primary source through which the Holy Spirit would give them understanding of truth for the changing circumstances of life.[14]

The 1902 adoption of the first official Confession of Faith came forty years after the beginnings of the Mennonite Brethren. Even then they were concerned that the confession not be considered on an equal basis with Scripture. They wrote: "*Unser Glaubensbekenntniss stellt sich nicht neben sondern unter die Schrift*–"our Confession of Faith is not to be considered side by side with the Scripture, but rather to be subordinate to the Scripture."[15] The Confession of Faith served as an instrument expressing a basic commitment to Scripture, not as a norm for the exposition of truth.

The concern for continued biblical orientation found strong expression in the establishing of Bible schools. As early as 1898 the conference passed a resolution "that the mission committee look for teachers in order that the conference may begin its own Bible schools."[16]

The claim that biblicism was "a distinctive of the Mennonite Brethren"[17] must be qualified with the recognition that commitment to Scripture was a legacy of the early Anabaptists. In fact, the Mennonite Brethren commitment to Scripture sounds, at points, like an echo from the sixteenth century. Of the sixteenth-century reformers, Donovan Smucker, a Mennonite scholar, asked "What was the supreme triumph of the original Anabaptist Mennonite declaration? The answer is this: These great Christians rediscovered the theology of the Bible!"[18] Michael Sattler wrote, "Let no one cause to depart from the standard that is laid through the letter of the Scripture which is revealed by the blood of Christ and of many witnesses of Jesus."[19] Conrad Grebel was equally forceful: "We should regard neither the opinion of civil authorities nor of any man, but should do only what God requires of you; and what the mouth of God has spoken, that you should heed".[20]

The admonition of Menno Simons was the most familiar point of reference for Mennonite Brethren: "I confess that I would rather die than to believe and teach to my brethren a single word or letter concerning the Father, the Son and the Holy Ghost (before God I lie not) contrary to the plain testimony of the world of God's Word as it is so clearly given through the mouth of prophets, evangelists and apostles."[21]

Many other sixteenth-century references confirm that the Mennonite Brethren emphasis on the divine inspiration and authority of Scripture was not unique to them. Their repeated affirmation of agreement with Menno Simons' "Foundations of Christian Doctrine" placed them firmly in the spirit of the Radical Reformation.[22]

## A COMMUNITY HERMENEUTIC

The early Mennonite Brethren in both Russia and the United States viewed Scripture as a revelation from God in history. Continuous references in the *Friedensstimme* and *Zionsbote* reflect an understanding of Scripture as the testimony of history as God had revealed it.(24) A distinguishing feature of the 330 sermons of David Duerksen (1850-1910) was a hermeneutic that anchored the text in its historical setting with reference to the implications of the unchanging character of God.[23] Henry D. Wiebe (1889-1949), in a 1925 article on the teachings of Scripture, began with the statement, "The Bible is the history of divine revelation on this earth." As a guide for the interpretation of the Bible he offered the following steps: (1) The basis for all interpretation of Scripture was to be faithful to the text. (2) The etymology of the key words needed to be established. (3) The passage was to be read in its historical context. (4) Each passage was to be viewed in the context of the book of the Bible in which it appeared. (5) The passage was to be studied in relationship to other Scripture references that spoke to the same subject. Scripture was to be compared with Scripture. It was self-interpretive. (6) Also to be considered was the time of history and culture in which the text was written.[24]

Nickolas N. Hiebert (1874-1957) spoke emphatically to the Christocentricity of Scripture in pointing to the history of revelation recorded in the Bible. He saw the New Testament as the culmination of the revelation of God in Christ, thus recognizing the principle of progressive unfolding revelation. For Hiebert, as for other Mennonite Brethren, the Bible was not merely a collection of common events of history. Although he recognized its great variety, the content of the whole was an account of the acts of God leading to culmination in the New Testament–God manifested in the flesh, the sacrifice for the sins of the world, the resurrection from the dead and the ascension into glory. The recitation of these divine acts, which took place in the frame of time, inspired the faith of the early Mennonite Brethren in God's power as sufficient for the needs of the present.[25]

The understanding that Christ was the culmination of divine revelation had definite implications for how Mennonite Brethren interpreted Scripture. The New Testament stood above the Old Testament in the progress of revelation. By presenting the perfection of Christ it took precedence over the Old Testament in formulating principles of doctrine.[26] All of God's dealings with humanity in the Old Testament were seen as a preparation for redemption. The Old Testament prophets looked forward to the revelation of God in Christ, of which the Old Testament, the Mosaic economy, was but a shadow of things to come (Heb. 8:1-7; 10:1-6).

Jesus Christ established a new covenant that was not nationalistic and temporal in character, but was universal in provision and purpose. Myron Augsburger's description of Mennonite hermeneutics applies to the Mennonite Brethren: "Christ is for them both the subject and the fulfillment of Scripture. He is the key for the interpretation of biblical truth." Augsburger goes on to capture the essence of all Mennonite biblicism:

> For the Anabaptists the total Bible was inspired by the Spirit of God as an unfolding revelation with its fullness in the person of Christ. Revelation not being presented on a flat plane could only be correctly interpreted by viewing each part in its relation to the fullness of Christ . . . Christ is both the Subject and Culmination of Scripture. Hence He is the Key to the Interpretation of Both Covenants.[27]

Christocentric interpretation characterized the expositions in sermon collections and articles in the *Zionsbote* dealing with biblical teachings. The cross and resurrection were the watershed of recorded revelation and the church was the community of the redeemed.[28]

The relationship of biblical understanding and the life of obedience was also vital to the Mennonite Brethren. "If any man will do his will, he shall know of the doctrine, whether it be of God" (John 7:17), appears to have been foundational. In the words of Hans Denk, "No man can know Christ unless he follows after him in life." The Holy Spirit gave understanding to the fellowship of believers as they searched Scripture for guidance on issues of personal and corporate discipleship.

The principle of a community hermeneutic governed the early years of Mennonite Brethren history. Conference minutes over the years reflected dependence on the wider fellowship to discern how Scripture applied to life and practice. This understanding of biblical teaching was considered normative for the walk of the local congregation and the individual. This community hermeneutic also governed their understanding of New Testament ethics related to human relationships, the state and the peace position.[29]

## THE USE OF SCRIPTURE

Mennonite Brethren were known as diligent students of the Bible. They considered personal Bible reading and meditation an integral part of the believer's daily life. Daily family devotions were the rule for the home. The weekly Bible study hour (*Bibelstunden*) in fellowship with other believers was a general practice. Each worship service opened with the reading of Scriptures and prayer led by a member of the congregation.

The neglect of personal Bible study and family devotions was seen as a major cause of a declining Christian walk. Failure to study Scripture was considered a grievous lapse in basic Christian priorities. In church renewals the neglect of personal devotions frequently became a matter of repentance and confession.

Regular personal devotions received strong emphasis in the counseling of new converts. "Bible reading and prayer are avenues of the soul's communication with God" was a common statement. "Are you faithful in your daily devotions?" was a frequent inquiry in meetings with groups and individuals.[30] For some, this emphasis degenerated into a legalistic ritual that was not always edifying.

This theology can be summarized as follows: Read your Bible for it is the light upon your path and a protection against false teachings (Ps. 119:105). It is a mirror which reflects the condition of your life to make you aware of what your needs are (James 1:23-24). The Bible–the Word of God–is the precious seed sown into your heart which needs to be cared for that it may bring much fruit (Luke 8:11; 1 Peter 1:23). It is food for your soul which provides the needed strength and growth for your Christian life (Jer. 15:16). The Bible is your shield against the darts of the evil one to protect you in temptation in your thoughts and deeds (Eph. 6:16).

**Family Bible Reading.** The family devotional period, or family altar, included the reading of Scripture, sometimes preceded by a song, and prayer. It frequently included Bible memorization by the entire family. Deuteronomy 6:6-7 constituted the biblical basis for the practice: "And these words, which I recommend thee this day, shall be in thine heart: and thou shalt teach them diligently unto thy children, and shalt talk of them when thou sittest in thine house . . . and when thou risest up." Proverbs 22:6 was also frequently quoted as a basis for this responsibility: "Train up a child in the way he should go: and when he is old, he will not depart from it." At weddings the minister would not fail to charge the young couple to establish a family altar as the cornerstone of their household.

The family devotion was a strong influence in keeping the spiritual needs of family life foremost. Usually it preceded breakfast. In many families a second devotional period occurred after supper or shortly before bedtime. Depending on the level of instructional emphasis, these devotional times became the basis of Bible knowledge in the development of young and old. Abraham E. Janzen, who in the mid-twentieth century travelled widely among Mennonite Brethren churches, claimed that he had been the recipient of hospitality in hundreds, perhaps thousands of homes and never found a home where family devotions were not practiced.[31]

House visitations by ministers or deacons always included an inquiry concerning the character and punctuality of the family devotions. The effectiveness of these exercises was a concern to the church, and instruction on how to improve their benefit was frequently a part of such house calls.

**Bible Study Hour.** A major encouragement toward a

strong biblical orientation was the weekly Bible study hour–a fellowship meeting in a private home to read Scripture together and discuss its meaning and implications for personal life. The Bible study hour was not something new in Mennonite history. Hans DeRies, a sixteenth and seventeenth-century Dutch Mennonite leader, referred to it. A report on the life of the Mennonites in the Netherlands by M. Simeon Friedrich Rues (1743) mentioned Bible study hours among the Anabaptists of the seventeenth century. Peter M. Friesen asserted that the practice did not come to the Mennonite Brethren from the Pietists, as frequently assumed, but rather the latter adopted it from the Mennonites who had let it lapse during their spiritual decline. The Mennonite Brethren, through the influence of the Pietists and Moravian Brethren, restored it as a legacy from their Anabaptist forbears.[32]

Among the early Mennonite Brethren the Bible study hour took place in two forms: the midweek study hour in private homes, and the annual three or four-day Bible study conferences in local churches. The midweek Bible study hour was informal. The people congregated in a home, gathering around the table with each one having a Bible. If not everyone could sit at the table they formed a circle. One participant suggested a song that the group sang. A favorite was "*Herr dein Wort die edle Gabe, diesen Schatz erhalte mir*":

> Lord thy Word, this precious gift, preserve this treasury for our good. It means more than all possessions, its value supersedes all other riches. Where thy Word does not prevail there is no foundation for our faith. My desire is not the possession of a thousand worlds, but to thy Word alone I wish to cling.

This song expressed a deep commitment to the Word and a desire for obedience. Each participant at the study hour would read a verse or two from the Scripture portion to be studied. The host of the home served as the discussion leader. The leader or other assigned person would give an overview of the passage and put it into context. Then the men would seek to expound the Scripture verse by verse. The women were usually silent listeners. The meaning of the passage for individual faith and life received major emphasis. Prayer followed some forty minutes of Bible study, with a strong focus on relating the truth gleaned from Scripture to the believer's life. Usually many participated in such prayer sessions. Another song, from memory, brought the meeting to a close.[33]

The Bible study conferences (*Bibelbesprechungen*) were held in the assembly houses (*Versammlungshaus*).[34] The ministers–teachers of the Word–and brothers and sisters from the neighboring congregations would assemble for a study conference lasting from three days to a week. A leading minister led the discussions. They studied a longer portion of Scripture, possibly several chapters from a book in the New Testament or one of the Epistles. A minister provided a general introduction, placing the scriptural passage into its historical and exegetical context. The ministers, alternating between themselves, interpreted its meaning and particularly sought out the implications for the life of the believers. Participation from all present was constantly encouraged.

These study conferences were coordinated to occur at spaced intervals in various localities to enable members to attend a series of such events each year. Such participation in the study of the Word provided an effective training in biblical interpretation for the members of the fellowship and those chosen from their midst to be teachers of the Word.

The Bible study hour, so basic for the life of the movement in Russia and North America, remained at the heart of the Mennonite Brethren fellowship even beyond 1910. Among the congregations coming out of Russia to Western Europe in recent years, this practice continues to be a vital source of spiritual nurture and edification.

CHAPTER 3

# The Mennonite Brethren Understanding of Salvation and Baptism

A central concern in the Mennonite Brethren movement was the salvation of the individual in a personal experience of repentance, conversion and new birth. When the German sociologist Ernst Troeltsch articulated his concept of a sect he could well have been describing the theological character of the Mennonite Brethren: "The sect is a voluntary society, composed of strict and definite Christian believers bound to each other by the fact that all have experienced 'the new birth'."[1] Nineteenth-century historian Max Gobel characterized the Anabaptist movement in a way that also applied to the Mennonite Brethren: "The essential and distinguishing characteristic of this church is its great emphasis upon the actual personal conversion and regeneration of every Christian through the Holy Spirit."[2]

Historically the Mennonite Brethren have their roots in the Dutch-Russian stream of Anabaptism, among whom personal experiential conversion was prominent.[3] Cornelius J. Dyck observed that the conversion experience of Menno "is different from what we find in Swiss Anabaptism and tends to fit into the classical Protestant and later Pietist model."[4] Conversion changed the direction of life, and refocused commitment, all of which are central to the biblical meaning of conversion as described in Matthew 13:15 and 2 Corinthians 5:17-20. Dyck states that "clearly, the new creature is the *sine qua non* [essential characteristic] of the church of the restitution as

Menno envisioned it."[5]

But the desire to recapture the fundamental belief and experience of their forebears did not alone explain the view of salvation that overtook the Mennonite Brethren. Their statement in the 1860 secession document–"In the articles, we are in agreement with our dear Menno, according to our convictions from the Holy Scripture"[6]–provided only a partial explanation. Nor did the influence of Pietism, with its strong emphasis on repentance, conversion and the new birth[7], complete the explanation. The main source of their understanding of salvation was Scripture itself.

Their bibliocentric orientation enabled the Mennonite Brethren to retrieve a lapsed doctrine from their own Anabaptist history and affirm again their forebears' understanding of personal salvation. Terms reflecting this understanding spoke of becoming "renewed," "justified," "regenerated," "born anew" and "transplanted."[8] This new awareness of the meaning of salvation helped them restore the historic Anabaptist linkage of inward renewal with membership in the corporate body of believers. Myron Augsburger's mid-twentieth century statement that for the Anabaptists conversion and church membership were "cause and effect"[9] was understood among the early Mennonite Brethren.

## THE VIEW OF SALVATION REFLECTED IN THE CONFESSION OF FAITH

The Mennonite Brethren statement on salvation in the 1902 Confession of Faith, translated into English in 1917, began with the focus on humanity's lost condition under the "curse of eternal death, the wages of sin and the wrath of God" and an emphasis on the sufficiency of the atoning sacrifice of Jesus Christ.[10] The emphasis that "man is conceived and born in sin as a child of wrath incapable of and not inclined toward the divine good, but capable of and inclined toward evil,"[11] expressed the need for redemption.

An emphasis on the divine initiative followed the description of human depravity. Divine initiative meant that God allowed humanity to exercise free will "that all that obey His gospel and believe in Him should not perish but have everlasting life."[12] The linkage of "obey" and "believe" was important to the early Mennonite Brethren. To believe and to obey were interdependent; there was no true belief except on the basis of volitional obedience to the gospel.

Making the invitation from Scripture part of the Confession of Faith gave further emphasis to the responsibility for obedience. "And the Spirit and the bride say come. And let him that hear it say come. And let him that is athirst come. And whosoever will, let him take the water of life freely" (Rev. 22:17). "Strive to enter in at the straight gate" (Luke 12:24). The powerful Word of God awakened humanity from sin. Conversion, renewal or the new birth was then described as follows:

> If he now is obedient and does not close his heart against the working of divine grace, he receives repentance unto life, to see his sin, repent of it, confess and forsake it; and in recognition of the holy and just judgement of God through prayer seeks refuge in Christ as the only Savior from the guilt of sin and the lust thereof and receives through faith in him forgiveness of sins, justification, and the witness and sealing of the Holy Spirit that he is a child of God and heir of life eternal.[13]

Clearly, the Mennonite Brethren view of salvation drew heavily on Menno's view as expressed by the title of his 1537 writing on the new birth: *The New Creature: A Fair and Fundamental Instruction from the Word of the Lord, Urgently Admonishing All Men Who Call Themselves Christians to Seek the Heavenly Birth and the New Creature, Without Which No Man Who Has Come to Years of Understanding Is or Can Be a True*

*Christian*.[14] For Menno and the Mennonite Brethren repentance was essential for regeneration and a pious life, and could only originate in the Word of the Lord, rightly taught and rightly understood and received in the heart by faith through the Holy Ghost.[15] The following statement further illustrates the centrality of regeneration in Menno's understanding of salvation:

> My dearly beloved reader take heed to the Word of the Lord and learn to know the true God. I warned you faithfully to take it, if you please. He will not save you nor forgive you your sins nor show you His mercy and grace except according to His Word; namely if you repent and if you believe, if you are born of Him, if you do what He has commanded and walk as He walks.[16]

For Menno Simons, conversion could not be separated from a complete inward transformation expressed in discipleship. The life and character of the believer reflected the evidence of true regeneration.

> The regenerate, therefore, lead a penitent and new life, for they are renewed in Christ and have received a new heart and spirit. Once they were earthly minded, now heavenly; once they were carnal, now spiritual; once they were unrighteous, now righteous; once they were evil, now good, and they live no longer after the old corrupted nature. . . . Their minds are like the mind of Christ, they gladly walk as he walked; they crucify and tame their flesh with all its evil lusts.[17]

Peter M. Friesen observed that the central concern for the Mennonite Brethren, both before and after withdrawal from the old church, was "conversion to God through repentance and faith in the reconciling grace in Jesus Christ and a life of sanctification according to the rules of the gospel through the gift of grace of the Spirit of Christ."[18] This emphasis remained predominant. A mere crisis experience or verbal profession did not provide the proof of a genuine conversion. A new life was the proof required. They took passages like John 3:3 literally, "Except a man be born again (anew) he cannot understand the kingdom of God," and 2 Corinthians 5:17, "If any man be in Christ he is a new creature; old things are passed away; behold all things are become new." Only a visibly new life in character and relationship was proof of a supernatural transaction of God in the salvation of a lost sinner. Harold Bender's observation that "the Reformation emphasis on faith was good but inadequate, for without newness of life . . . faith is hypocritical," expressed well the understanding of the Mennonite Brethren.[19]

A deep sin consciousness and stark sense of a "lostness" characterized the many recorded conversion stories of the early Mennonite Brethren.[20] This remained the normative experience for Mennonite Brethren into the 1950s. They generally spoke of days, weeks and often months of searching for peace in a spirit of repentance over sin. When the answer of forgiveness came to them through the Scriptures there was great rejoicing.[21] Regeneration of a heart of sin took place through the indwelling of the Holy Spirit. A person receiving assurance of forgiven sins was now ready, in thankfulness and love, to offer soul and body as a living sacrifice to God.[22]

The ongoing life of the church reflected the central concern for a genuine conversion. Mennonite Brethren publications like *Friedensstimme* in Russia and *Zionsbote* in North America carried many articles on the subject of conversion.[23] The articles generally focused on the work of the Holy Spirit through the Word, bringing conviction of sin, repentance, and leading seekers to claim the mercies of God who in turn performs the miracle of regeneration in which the repentant sinner becomes a "new creature."

The need for conversion and spiritual renewal also received strong emphasis in Mennonite Brethren preaching. One third of the collection of 330 sermons of David Gerhard Duerksen (1850-1910), a prominent preacher in the second generation of the Mennonite Brethren Church, dealt with revival and conversion.[24] They stressed that regeneration was followed by a life of sanctification which served as the verification of the genuineness of the new creature.

These sermons spoke of overcoming the reign of sin in the life of a regenerated person through the indwelling power of the Holy Spirit. The new nature expressed itself, as the confessional statement said, in "all diligence to add to his faith virtue and love, to make his calling and election sure and to offer soul and body as a living sacrifice to God in thankfulness and love, mindful of the words: We love him because he first loved us."[25]

The Mennonite Brethren described the essence of sanctification as implicit love toward God and a sincere love toward fellow believers and neighbors. The purpose of sanctification was the glorification of God.[26] Sanctification was a lifelong process: "Even in a holy walk the believers need at all times the forgiving, chastening and cleansing grace of God through the blood of Christ."[27]

The means of grace through which the Holy Spirit accomplished his work in the redeemed community was the Word of God, obedience in baptism, the fellowship of communion, and prayer. The dependence on these means of grace accounted for their prominent role in the believer's relationship and practice.[28]

Scripture passages that appeared prominently in Mennonite Brethren writings with reference to salvation were John 3:3-7, 2 Corinthians 5:17, and 1 Peter 1:23, which spoke in terms of the "new birth," a "new creature," and "old things passing away," making all things new. Salvation was seen as the work of God who performed the miracle of the new birth in response to the willing repentance of a sinner in turning from sin "to serve the true and living God" (1 Thess. 1:9). True faith in contrast to mere profession (often referred to by the Mennonite Brethren as *Kopfglaube*–head belief), rested in the evidences of the new life in sanctification and holiness.[29]

## BAPTISM: MEANING AND MODE

The Confession of Faith confirmed the importance of water baptism for Mennonite Brethren: "We believe and confess, that Christian baptism is a holy, visible, evangelical, sacred act and ordinance (institution) of Christ, commanded by the Lord himself for a sacred sign of regeneration and embodiment in Him and His Church."[30] To qualify for baptism one must have repented of sin and trusted Jesus Christ as personal savior and lord. Romans 6:2-6, Colossians 2:12-13, 1 Thessalonians 5:23-24 and 1 Peter 3:21 provided the biblical basis for understanding baptism. Through baptism the believer entered the full fellowship and work of the church. The commitment to discipleship, according to Romans 6:2-6, meant to be buried with Christ by baptism into death: "that like as Christ was raised up from the dead by the glory of the Father, even so we also should walk in newness of life." First Peter 3:21 added to the dimension of covenant with the statement that baptism was the answer of a good conscience toward God by the resurrection of Jesus Christ. Mennonite Brethren baptized by immersion as an expression of the Romans 6 passage–to be buried and to rise with Christ unto a newness of life.

The issue of true believers baptism, so central in the secession document, remained a major concern for the movement.[31] From early on, baptismal candidates faced an official examination in the form of an oral testimony before the congregation followed by probing questions related to the evidences of a true conversion. My own experience in 1921 illustrates the process of such an inquiry.

My initial conversion experience occurred at the age of

fourteen. David Reimer, a youth worker in Alexanderthal, Molotschna, South Russia spoke to a group of boys, known as "the village gang," in a tone similar to Jonathan Edwards. With fear and trembling I prayed for mercy. My soul found peace. A year later I applied for baptism. First, two brethren of the church leadership (Gerhard Derksen and Adolf Reimer) examined me. The inquiry was thorough. My past was examined to determine whether I had asked forgiveness of the men upon whom I had played many pranks in my youth. "Had I asked for forgiveness of those whom I had offended? Had I made restitution where needed? Had my relationship in the family and school toward brothers, sisters and classmates changed? Had my priorities, values and aspirations changed?" Satisfied with my responses, they made further inquiries of people who knew me in school, in the village, among my unconverted former friends and members of the village gang. Their inquiries satisfied them that an actual change had taken place and I was invited to give my testimony before the church community. After my brief story of conversion, some of the questions of the preliminary examination were asked from the floor. "Is Hans Toews too young for baptism at the age of fifteen? Is he mature enough to grasp the implications of a life surrendered to the lordship of Christ?" The question of age and maturity became a subject of concern when the church evaluated my readiness for baptism in my absence. Some members of the "village gang," my friends before the conversion experience, were consulted as to whether they believed that a genuine change had taken place in the life and relationship of their former companion. The church voted to baptize me even though there was concern about age and maturity.

For many years a candidate's qualifications for baptism and church membership were established by similar means. In retrospect one recognizes elements of legalism, a possible reaction to the old church where such evidences were not a condition for church membership.

The dogmatic emphasis of the Mennonite Brethren on immersion as the only biblical mode must be seen in the light of tensions between adult baptism and believers baptism.[32] John F. Harms, an earlier Mennonite Brethren historian, provided valuable background when he pointed to the distinction between a *Volkskirche* (peoplehood church), which practiced baptism by sprinkling, and a believers church, which the Mennonite Brethren sought to be.[33] Some have suggested that relationships with the German Baptists in Hamburg led Mennonite Brethren to adopt immersion as the only biblical mode. The influence of the Baptists cannot be dismissed. But granting full credit to them ignores P.M. Friesen's account of the extensive research and prayerful study on the topic by Mennonite Brethren in the 1860s. The matter of immersion remained a subject of careful study for many years. We also cannot discount their possible reference to the 1773 Cornelius Ris Confession of Faith.[34]

A significant factor contributing to dogmatism on the baptism question was the *severe persecution* of the Mennonite Brethren as a minority group within the larger Mennonite community. In some cases opposition groups from the Mennonites interrupted baptismal services by "driving ministers and baptismal candidates with sticks out of the baptismal waters."[35] According to Jacob P. Bekker, "the Mennonite District Government whipped with rods until the welts bled; yet this did not halt the secession. The bloody floggings only led to greater steadfastness among the brethren. Baptisms and the Lord's Supper continued according to God's Word."[36] This opposition and suffering no doubt helped harden the young movement's persistence into dogmatism.

Another factor furthering the dogmatism was the experience of the people themselves. Most of the early Mennonite Brethren had been baptized as adults by sprinkling. Now that they experienced personal conversion they found it difficult to accept the validity of their previous baptism. The mode of sprinkling, administered widely without the prerequisite of personal conversion, came to be seen as unbiblical. The staunchest critics of sprinkling tended to be those who themselves had been rebaptized by immersion after personal experience of salvation. It was at the 1963 convention of the North American General Conference that a vote of 325 in favor, 120 opposed removed the requirement of immersion as a condition for membership.[37] Some members of the Committee of Reference and Counsel made a study on background of members in the opposition to this decision. The finding was that the majority were people who had been rebaptized by immersion. They found it difficult to accept another mode which in their experience was not a true believers baptism.

CHAPTER 4

# The Mennonite Brethren Understanding of a New Testament Church

For Mennonite Brethren, conversion, regeneration and church membership were directly connected, like cause and effect. This linkage, which they saw as a basic characteristic of a New Testament church, was a central issue in the 1860 secession document. Thus they completely rejected the inclusive *Volkskirche*, which included members on the basis of Mennonite identity regardless of personal spiritual conviction. As they saw it, incorporating members on the basis of ethnicity was not unlike the Reformed practice of incorporating infants: both caused the church to deteriorate from a fellowship of faith to an indifferent population that was Christian only in name.[1] Such a practice, in their view, wiped out the distinction between church and world. The natural outcome, they believed, was that the church would become a mere religious institution mediating salvation by clergy or administering it by an apparatus of theologians and bishops.[2]

**THE CHURCH: A FELLOWSHIP OF TRUE BELIEVERS**

For Mennonite Brethren identifiable evidences of true faith–rooted in the atonement of Christ, manifested in the transforming power of God in repentance, conversion and regeneration, and resulting in a new creature in Christ Jesus–was inseparable from ecclesiology. This emphasis on a church of committed believers received central emphasis in the secession document:

Regarding Holy Communion we confess that it serves to

strengthen the faith of true believers . . . yes, it is a sign that they stand in very intimate union with Jesus, their Saviour. (1 Cor. 10:6). Furthermore, it serves as a sign of a covenant and fellowship of believers (v.17), and not as a sign of the fellowship of believers and unbelievers.[3]

They then invoked Menno Simons' *Foundations of Christian Doctrine* which also stressed that the church should consist only of truly born again believers.[4] The Confession of Faith of 1902 defined this understanding further:

> The Church of Christ is composed of all that through true faith in Jesus Christ and through obedience to the Gospel have separated themselves from the world and have their fellowship in the Holy Spirit with God the Father and Jesus Christ their only mediator, and have come unto an innumerable company of angels and unto the spirits of just men made perfect, as fellow-citizens with the saints, and of the household of God; and are built upon the foundation of the apostles and prophets, Jesus Christ himself being the chief corner stone. Eph. 1:1; 1 Pet. 1:1-2; cf. "choosing," "conversion," "sanctification"; Rom. 6:17; 10:16-17; 2 Cor. 6:17; Acts 2:40-41; John 15:1-5; Eph. 2:19-22; 1 Cor. 3:11-15; Matt. 6:16-18; 1 Tim. 3:15.[5]

It is also significant to note the characterization of the church as it appeared in the Confession of Faith:

> The characteristics of the true Church are the fruits of conversion and of the right faith in Jesus Christ revealed in a life of sanctification according to the teaching of Christ and His apostles; the diligent searching of the Scriptures and the preaching of the pure Gospel in all the world; practice of the holy ordinances of Christ which are, baptism and the Lord's Supper, the free confession of God

and Jesus Christ before all men; fervent brotherly love, fellowship and submission among themselves and love of their neighbors; diligence to uphold the unity of the spirit through the bond of peace; taking up the cross in following Jesus; watching with prayer and supplication and thanksgiving for all men, and the prayerful and joyful waiting for the coming of the Lord and the establishment of His Kingdom. 1 John 4:1; Matt. 3:8-9; Matt. 6:10; Acts 1:6-7; Luke 21:31; Heb. 9:28; 2 Thess. 1:7 and 10. 2 Pet. 3:12-14; (cf. II, "Church" and IV. "Prayer" and V.).[6]

The implications of this statement of faith were obedience to the Word of God and submission to the lordship of Christ in faithful discipleship. As described by Jesus, disciples were those who held to his teaching (John 8:31), who loved as he had (John 13:34), who reflected the character described in the Beatitudes and the Sermon on the Mount, and who fulfilled the teachings and example which he gave.

The church–the redeemed community in Mennonite Brethren understanding–was to be an interdependent fellowship. In the church every member was to be concerned for the welfare of fellow-members.[7] This principle applied not only to the local congregation but also extended to the churches' association as a larger fellowship or conference. The implications of such interdependence surfaced visibly in the crisis known as the June Reform of 1865.[8] Following are some of the basic principles reflected in the records of that occasion:

1. They acknowledged the aberrations that had beset some of the early Mennonite Brethren (1860-1864), as well as irresponsible actions of individuals in leadership. The meeting of the entire body for a day of prayer, fasting and repentance identified the whole church with the aberrations.

2. Recognition of the church's final authority was foundational for a life of interdependence. The resolution recorded on June 26 and 27, 1865 was significant:

The church chooses the minister, a brother from her midst who is considered capable and has the confidence of the church, to watch over them, thus it is the duty of the minister to serve the church and carry out whatever decisions the church may make. In return, the church is obligated to obey her minister as the shepherd of her soul as long as he remains true to the pure teaching of Christ. If this should not be the case, the church shall call him to account and admonish him. If the minister does not accept this admonition, he is to be deposed from his office and the office is to be given to someone more worthy. Meanwhile the church must keep in mind that the minister who leads well is worthy of double honor.[9]

3. The corporate church body, not merely a few members, was responsible for the discipline of members of the church (and the nature of that discipline).[10]

Despite their scattering into small local fellowships, the Mennonite Brethren considered themselves as one church. Those in the Molotschna Colony, the Old Colony (Chortitza) and the Kuban, though far-flung geographically, identified themselves as one fellowship under the words of Paul: "Let us walk by the same rule, let us mind the same thing" (Phil. 3:16). The designation, "The Conference of the Mennonite Brethren Church," expresses the sense of being one united community of believers.[11]

The revived emphasis on faith, salvation and newness of life was a major point of reorientation for Mennonite Brethren as well as for the larger Mennonite community. Out of this grew a new awareness that the church was responsible for what happened in the life of believers following their profession of salvation. The practice of church discipline was a natural result of this heightened sense of responsibility.

The church felt keenly a need to guard its corporate testimony and to discipline those whose walk did not conform to its understanding of scriptural standards. The secession document clearly expressed this:

> Regarding the ban, we confess that all carnal and reprobate sinners must be banned from the fellowship of believers, as Paul states in II Thess. 3:14-15. In the event that someone falls into carnal sin (God save us from it), and the Spirit of Christ, who alone can work true repentance, convicts him of his sin, so that he confesses and repents; in that case, the church has no authority to ban such a repentant sinner, because the forgiveness of sin is not obtained in or through the ban, but by the merit of Jesus Christ. This was also Menno's conviction, as recorded in Vol. III, p. 334 and 335. However, an unrepentant sinner may not be accepted into the fellowship of believers until he be genuinely converted to Christ.[12]

People beyond the Mennonite Brethren fold noticed this view of church discipline. Johann Harder, elder of the Mennonite church in Ohrloff, in writing to the Molotschna Mennonite area administrative office to make the case for the right of the Mennonite Brethren to exist as a separate fellowship in the larger Mennonite community, also commended their commitment to responsibly disciplining their own members.[13]

A Lutheran pastor from Prischib named Dobbert, responded to the division among the Mennonites in a document dated July 1864. He affirmed the legitimacy of the Mennonite Brethren because their call for discipline was lacking in the mother church. Johann Claassen and his followers, Dobbert said, "did not enter the conflict with carnal weapons" but "had clearly articulated and denounced the breakdown of church discipline, the Achilles heel [the weakest point] of the church–and had insisted upon reform."[14]

Peter M. Friesen contended that the stress on a consistent lifestyle as the testimony of true salvation attracted more and more people from the congregations of the mother church. In fact, this emphasis could be seen as a major reason for the movement's effective evangelism and rapid growth during the first quarter century after 1860. Some saw a clear parallel with Acts 2:47 which describes the believers "praising God and having favor with all people," and to whom "the Lord added . . . daily such as should be saved."

The Mennonite Brethren view of interrelatedness and church discipline did not prevail without difficulty. It faced its share of testing. In the early years (1862-1864) it became the redeeming element during the great crisis known as the "Exuberant Movement" (*Die Fröhliche Richtung*), which was an overreaction to the formality and tradition of the institutionalized Russian Mennonite church.

In 1907-1909 the interdependence of the local congregation and larger church was also seriously strained in the disciplining of church elder David Schellenberg, accused of financial indiscretions. Nonetheless, the principle prevailed. The question of the relationship between the local church and the larger fellowship continued to resurface in subsequent years.[15]

Mennonite Brethren use of church discipline was not always loving and redemptive. On occasions it lapsed into strict legalism. The basic principle of mutual caring and nurture, however, remained a major dynamic in the life of the movement. In its better moments it matched Abraham H. Unruh's description when he wrote: "In the church every member is to be concerned for the welfare of fellow members and to intercede for them in prayer. Through teaching, encouragement and counseling the fellowship provides the care for its members."[16] The Confession of Faith further stated: "All questions related to doctrine and life in the congregation are decided according to the example of the apostolic church, as we read: Acts 15:1-28; 1 Cor. 14:40; 2 Cor. 3:17, etc. Rule and guide for the church for all times are the Holy Scriptures, especially the New Testament."[17]

The Mennonite Brethren understood the basic prayer of the true church to be "thy kingdom come" (Matt. 6:10). In the knowledge that Christ at his first coming carried human sin to the cross, the church was waiting for his appearance for their salvation in glory (Heb. 9:28).[18]

While in a waiting position the church was not to be idle. Its members earned their livelihood amidst a relationship of love with their neighbors. The true church continued "steadfastly in the apostles' doctrine and fellowship, and in breaking of bread, and in prayers" (Acts 2:42). The command of Jesus, "teaching them to observe all things whatsoever I have commanded you" (Matt. 28:20), was central for the early Mennonite Brethren. The ardent application of this assignment, as they understood it, to the various situations of life, gave rise to tension and intolerance in their relationship to the wider Mennonite community.[19]

Members who did not conform to the scriptural standards, as understood by the corporate body, were to be admonished in love. Where private counseling failed, the church sought to exercise redemptive discipline. The offender was formally excluded from the fellowship of the church for disregarding warnings and persisting in rebellion.[20] The church, however, was to continue to love the erring member and seek restoration. When there was repentance, the church was to forgive, receive the member back into the fellowship and resume Christian nurture.[21]

Covenant community expressed the interrelated character of the church. Members committed themselves to a covenant statement–later referred to as "church rules"–that spoke to the nurture of their spiritual life, to their relationship within the larger fellowship, to the world and to principles of lifestyle. There was the expectation that local church members would accept the Confession of Faith of the larger church community and be willing to accept the decisions and resolutions of the conference on questions of faith, practice and program.[22]

The confessional statement hoped for one body even though scattered in many places: "Although the members of this church belong to all nations and ranks, scattered here and there throughout the world and are divided in denominations, yet they all are one and among one another brethren and members and exist as one body in Christ their head, who is the Lord, Chief, Shepherd, Prophet, Priest and King of the church."[23] The basis for this oneness was not a common background, or culture, but a unity created by the Spirit of God.

## THE MEANS OF GRACE

Mennonite Brethren did not speak of sacraments, but of the "means of grace."[24] According to their understanding, the perceptible means of grace that God had ordained were the Word (preaching), conversion, holy baptism and the Lord's Supper. Prayer accompanied all of these divinely ordained acts of the spiritual life of every Christian and was not to cease in the entire congregation of God.[25]

The Mennonite Brethren did not attach any magical powers to these channels of divine communication. Their effectiveness rested in a personal faith relationship with Christ. The natural person was unable to come into fellowship with God through the power of reason alone. The Word, through the convicting power of the Holy Spirit, was the means whereby God called people to repentance and faith. Christ's commandment "to preach the gospel to every creature" was the provision of God for the salvation of the world. The strong emphasis on the "Word" as the communicating means of God accounted for the centrality they gave to preaching and Bible studies in the life of the church and the spiritual nurture of believers.

Baptism as defined by the confession was an act of both obedience and relationship. "The practice of baptism consists of this that all that hear the Gospel and in repentance of heart accept it, on this confession of a new life from God (Col. 2:12-13) are baptized (immersed) in water according to the commandment of Christ."[26] Relationally,

> The believers are bound together through baptism as having died to sin to walk in newness of life. The believers have in baptism put on Christ (Gal. 3:27). Therefore everyone must contribute according to his calling and gifts towards the support and betterment of the body of Christ in spiritual and temporal things with diligence . . . as true members of the household of God and children of the kingdom (Matt. 13:38) they shall carefully guard the holy privileges of divine citizenship and duties received of Christ their head and be subject to all the commandments of their King and obedient to them according to his Word: Teach them to observe all things whatsoever I have commanded you (Mat. 28:20).[27]

## THE LORD'S TABLE

The confession contained a threefold emphasis on the Lord's Table: (1) The sacrifice of Christ for the remission of sins; (2) Christ as the source of the life-giving resources for the human soul (bread, meat and drink); and (3) the union of Christ himself with all true believers for spiritual communion.

> In this holy supper we are brought to see that Christ's holy body was sacrificed on the cross and His precious blood shed for the remission of our sin, and that He now being glorified in His heavenly state, is life-giving bread, meat and drink for our souls and unites Himself with all true believing souls for spiritual communion according to His Word: Behold I stand at the door and knock: if any man hear my voice and open the door, I will come in to him, and will sup with him and he with Me. Gal. 3:1; Eph. 1:7; Mark 16:19; Eph. 2:6; Phil. 3:21; John 6:51,53-58,63; Rev. 3:20.[28]

This fellowship with Christ was also to express the relationship of the believers among themselves. The passages of 1 Corinthians 10:16-17; 1 Corinthians 5:11 and 2 Corinthians 6:15 received strong emphasis: "The bread which we break, is it not the communion of the body of Christ? For we, being many, are one bread, and one body, for we are all partakers of that one bread."[29]

They also placed strong emphasis on the prerequisites for the participant. "Only the gracious enlightenment and fellowship of the Holy Spirit can enable the believer to rightfully examine himself and prepare him to partake of this holy supper in a worthy manner. . . ."[30]

These statements reflected a major objection to the practice of communion in the church from which they had withdrawn. Absent, in the opinion of the Mennonite Brethren, had been the basic prerequisites of personal salvation and Christian lifestyle. Thus they placed particular emphasis on self-examination in preparation for the communion service. "Let a man examine himself . . . he that eateth and drinketh unworthily, eateth and drinketh damnation to himself, not discerning the Lord's body" (1 Cor. 11:27-34).[31]

Later writings by Mennonite Brethren continued to reflect this emphasis on self-examination, confession and purification as a prerequisite for communion.[32] The practice of giving opportunity for confession and reconciliation of tensions between brothers and sisters prior to communion prevailed. This often resulted in emotional confessional meetings. Young converts sought a person in whom they could confide, confess any sinful practices and receive prayer and personal encouragement to overcome these "sacred" sins.[33]

## THE RELATIONSHIP OF BAPTISM AND COMMUNION

The 1860 secession document spoke only to the question of true regeneration–conversion–as a prerequisite for communion with no reference to the mode of baptism. Before long, however, the mode of baptism became a major concern. Immersion came to be seen as the only biblical mode. Abraham H. Unruh attributed this strict emphasis to the narrowness of some leaders. In 1865 it became the rule that only immersed believers could partake of communion. The Lord's table became the table of the Mennonite Brethren fellowship, excluding all true believers from other groups.[34]

This position softened with time. In 1899, in Steinbach, South Russia, the first "open" communion took place.[35] At the 1903 conference in Waldheim there was an agreement to accept differences on this question. In 1910 a fuller understanding and mutuality resolved the remaining tensions between the two camps.[36] After 1903 and 1910, Mennonite Brethren churches accepted guests at communion from fellowships that did not practice immersion, based upon recommendations from recognized leaders who could vouch for their spiritual character. Where possible the guests shared their testimony of salvation and continuing Christian life. In North America, however, Mennonite Brethren churches changed more slowly. Only in the 1920s and 1930s did they begin to accept non-immersed people from other fellowships at the communion table.

Prayer as a means of grace in addition to the Word (Bible), baptism, and communion was prominent in Mennonite Brethren practice. Worship services typically began with hymn singing, Scripture reading and prayer. Members of the congregation shared in a time of public prayer, the length of which was governed only by the spirit of participation. The need for personal daily devotions in Scripture reading and prayer was part of the fellowship covenant. There was also an emphasis on daily family devotions and prayer in which all family members participated. Mid-week Bible studies also emphasized prayer, where experiences of answered prayer frequently became the subject of testimony.[37]

## AN EXPANDING FELLOWSHIP

The Mennonite Brethren understanding of the New Testament church is not complete without recognizing the widening of their fellowship with other believers. In 1905 those Mennonite Brethren who felt strongly about an open communion, accessible to all true born-again believers, formed a new fellowship called "The Evangelical Mennonite Brethren Church," also known as the "Alliance" movement. They retained the 1902 Confession of Faith and practiced immersion baptism themselves but were willing to receive other believers who, upon confession of faith, had been baptized by other modes. The Alliance polity of appointing a council of elders also signalled the beginning of a gradual change in the Mennonite Brethren Church from that of one elder to a plurality of elders.[38]

The greater theological openness of the Alliance movement gave rise to other issues. Removal of the requirement of immersion baptism opened the door to a freer movement of teachers from other faith fellowships. Newcomers with a more liberal interpretation of ethics challenged some Mennonite Brethren standards of lifestyle. The subsequent legalistic development in Mennonite Brethren ethics was to some degree a reaction to the greater ethical freedom advocated by members of the Alliance movement. Other conflicts emerged. Benjamin B. Janz described them in this way:

> In conclusion we cast an overview on the character of the position of faith of the M.B. Church in the latter years under the leading influence of the "Free Brethren" (*freien Brüder*) when the formerly much rebuked conservative narrowness (*Engherzigkeit*) had been stripped. Normally there should have been basic growth according to the word of 2 Thess. 1:3: "We ought always to give thanks to God for you brethren, as is only fitting, because your faith is greatly enlarged and the love of each one of you all towards one another grows ever greater." Through the deeper exposition of Scripture, literature for devotional nurture and theology, ministers from abroad, professors,

doctors, theologians from the Baltic provinces, Germany, England who served with sermons and frequently with Bible courses of a week duration to larger groups of teachers and ministers with free provisions of lodging and meals supplied by the wealthy brethren in Steinbach and Apanlee, there came much light from above. . . . The pulpit ministry had become more effective. The inner warmth, however, with the concern for the lost was waning. There was much criticism. Life and walk had weakened. The struggles within the Conference had affected the unity which hovered like a mildew over the brotherhood, especially the leading brethren. In doctrine there were uncertainties. Not considering the exposition concerning the participation at the Lord's Table, there was the teaching concerning the distinction between the Kingdom and the Church, where some parts of the New Testament found no application for us, they applied only to the future of Israel and that quite inclusive. To have an Elder, is not scriptural for the church, there must be several Elders. . . . For a time it weakened my conscience; whether you believe or do so or otherwise, does not matter so much because it can be interpreted both ways. How far can we go in a dual interpretation of the Word?[39]

If Janz saw the negative effects of the struggles brought by the influence of the more liberal Alliance movement, there were positive contributions as well.

## CHURCH POLITY

The polity of the early Mennonite Brethren emerged from their understanding of the church as an interdependent fellowship. The June Reform of 1865 was significant in shaping their understanding of basic principles governing the life of the church.[40] We note the following:

1. To discern the meaning of scriptural teaching did not

rest with the individual alone, but with the corporate body. They continually sought to implement the Anabaptist belief in community discernment.

2. They recognized that the church as a body shared responsibility for unscriptural practices and sins within the church. They prayed and fasted together in repentance, seeking forgiveness and purification.[41]

3. The structure of church government was a fellowshipping community, not a hierarchy of bishops. The final decision-making authority rested in the congregation, not in a group of elders and ministers.[42]

Deliberations concerning the understandings of Scripture in relation to faith, life and ethics took place in the assembly of the "*Bundeskonferenz*," the larger conference. It was this body that articulated positions on the form of baptism, church organization, church discipline, relationships to civil government and war and many other issues needing regulation.[43]

CHAPTER 5

# Leadership and the Teaching Ministry

The Mennonite Brethren rooted their understanding of leadership and the teaching ministry in their commitment to Scripture. Quite simply, they understood ministers and leaders to be a provision of God. Ephesians 4:11-12 was foundational: "And he gave some, apostles; and some, prophets; and some, evangelists; and some pastors and teachers."

The Confession of Faith outlined a process for appointment according to the method of the Apostolic church (Matt. 9:37-38; Acts 1:15-26; Acts 13:1-5). The church was to unite in fervent prayer and call upon God, fully trusting that Christ as the head of the church through his Holy Spirit would reveal those who had the gifts for service, thus fulfilling his divine promise: "And I will give you pastors according to mine heart, which shall feed you with knowledge and understanding" (Jer. 3:15).[1]

The writings of Henry W. Lohrenz in the 1920s and 1930s reflected the Mennonite Brethren scriptural understanding on the matter.[2] He introduced the subject with the text of John 10:1-2. Entering the fold through "the door" identified one as a true shepherd called by God. Entering "some other way" disqualified one from being a true shepherd.

> Men, churches, may be instrumental in some way or another; but fundamentally it is a call from God. Where this is missing, the most essential element of the call is missing even when churches or conferences express a call by a unanimous vote . . . The call of the Eternal must ring

through the rooms of the minister's soul as clearly as the morning bell rings through the valleys of Switzerland calling the peasants to early prayer and praise.[3]

The manner of this call from God was not uniform but reflected the candidate's personality and circumstances. The call was transmitted in diverse ways, as the examples of the Old Testament prophets and the call of the disciples and Paul in the New Testament demonstrate. However, the man who entered the ministry through the right door would recognize the glory of his calling. He would continuously walk with the consciousness "that he has been appointed a servant in the treasuries of grace, to make known the unsearchable riches of Christ."[4]

Basic to the calling was a sense of unworthiness for this sacred responsibility as expressed by Ephesians 3:8: "Unto me, who am less than the least of all saints, is this grace given, that I should preach among the Gentiles the unsearchable riches of Christ."[5] Observed Lohrenz, "I do not wonder that men shrink from the calling even when they feel the glory of it! I do not wonder at the holy fear of men as they approach the sacred office."[6]

For Lohrenz, as for others, the ecclesiology of the Mennonite Brethren was vital to selecting candidates for ministry. "Where a church is alive to its obligation and its opportunities, the normal course is that the call of God comes through the church." The affirmation of the church superseded any inner call a candidate might have. Lohrenz noted that "where a person makes claims to a special call in spite of the church there is reason to doubt the genuineness of the call. Even though there may exist exceptions, the normal course is through the church."[7]

## QUALIFICATIONS FOR THE MINISTRY

The call to the ministry was subject to certain essential

qualifications. One, of course, was the experiential reality of personal salvation. Only those who had been "called out of darkness into his marvelous light" (1 Pet. 2:9), who knew they had passed from death unto life (1 John 3:14), and who knew "the power of God unto salvation" (Rom. 1:16) would be in a position to minister to seeking souls.[8]

A second essential criterion was a model lifestyle. Lohrenz underlined Paul's statement to Timothy, "Be thou an example of the believers, in word, in conversation, in charity, in spirit, in faith, in purity" (1 Tim. 4:12). He also pointed to Peter's exhortation to be "examples to the flock" (1 Pet. 5:3). "Everything about the preacher must preach–heart, mouth, and walk; what the mouth speaks must come out of the heart and must be confirmed by the walk. In his teaching he must thunder and in his walk he must shine."[9]

The centrality of the Word was fundamental. There could be no question as to the messenger's commitment to sound doctrine in the proclamation of God's truth. The church needed to practice vigilance in the examination of the doctrines preached.[10]

Lohrenz's high regard for the role of the ministry underlined the attitude of the first century of the Mennonite Brethren Church. The story of the second century represents both continuity and change.

## SELECTION OF LEADERSHIP

Ministers and deacons had the responsibility, under the guidance of the Holy Spirit, to discern the gifts of brothers and sisters within the body. Church leadership held meetings where they prayed for guidance. Brothers and sisters recognized as having gifts were to be encouraged to develop these gifts through the opportunities available to them. Those who met the spiritual qualifications of 1 Timothy 3:1-7, 2 Timothy 4:2-5 and 1 Timothy 1:5-9 and 2:7 were encouraged to share their inner call with the church for broader affirmation and encouragement. A positive response to the testimony affirmed the brother or sister as a gift to the church, after which they became co-workers with the existing leadership (*Mitarbeiter*).

After the workers had proved themselves the church prayerfully considered ordination. In 1951 the General Conference reaffirmed the process by which that could be done. "The local church who wishes to ordain a brother, should make its wish known to the representatives of the sister churches for their consideration and endorsement. Having received such endorsement, the church will call some experienced brethren, who will have the confidence of our conference to officiate at the ordination."[11]

## RECOGNITION OF LEADERS AND MINISTERS

The view that ministers were a gift of God, affirmed by the wider church, strengthened the profile of those chosen to lead. The conference was careful to preserve the effective function of the ministry. It took seriously any accusations that could reflect negatively on the service of ministers. In 1888, and again in 1901, the conference outlined special procedures to deal with such instances.

The 1888 conference studied Scripture to determine how to proceed when an elder or minister in the church experienced criticism or accusations. They concluded that the minister, like any other brother or sister, must repent when justly accused of wrongdoing. In cases where the charge affected his qualifications for the public ministry, the church would call an elder or brother from another church fellowship to assist in evaluating any accusations and suggesting appropriate action to remove the hindrances. In cases where the accusations were invalid, these elders or brothers were to remain and correct the accusers according to 1 Timothy 5:19-20.[12]

These procedures, and the larger concern to guard the spiritual qualifications of the ministry, remained the responsibility of the congregation and the wider conference. In later years the General Conference Board of Reference and Counsel assumed this task.

The admonition of 1 Timothy 5:17-18 to recognize the elders who rule well, to count them of double honor, especially those who labor in the Word and doctrine, received strong emphasis among the early Mennonite Brethren.[13] They took seriously the scriptural injunction of Hebrews 13:17: "Obey them that have the rule over you, and submit yourselves; for they watch for your souls, as they that must give account, that they may do it with joy, and not with grief; for that is unprofitable for you."

### PREPARATION FOR THE MINISTRY

The practice of referring to early Anabaptist and Mennonite Brethren leaders as "lay ministers" must be qualified when we review the training for ministry. Any inference that these ministers were amateurs is incorrect. Both the sixteenth-century Anabaptists and the early Mennonite Brethren knew the Bible well.

The educational system in the Mennonite colonies in Russia provided one hour per day for the study of the Bible. A student completing elementary school was required to pass an exam on the historical content of the Old and New Testaments. Bible instruction was also part of the standard curriculum of high schools and colleges. This educational process, plus the extensive Bible study program in the community of believers, as outlined in an earlier chapter, provided men and women with extensive Bible knowledge. Their biblical knowledge was far above that of Mennonite Brethren today. In fact, it was generally far superior even to that of men and women entering seminary in the 1970s and 1980s.[14]

Moreover, most of the early ministers were elementary and secondary school teachers. They had training in history, sciences, literature, mathematics and pedagogy. The weekly

Bible studies (*Bibelstunden*), intensive one-week Bible conferences (*Bibelbesprechungen*), which they attended several times every year, provided a solid biblical understanding and equipped them to be part of the hermeneutical community. Additionally, teachers attended Bible institutes of several weeks duration in the summer. Competent Bible instructors with advanced training, as well as visiting Bible expositors from Germany or Britain, served as resources for these institutes. German Pietists like General Von Viebahn, Otto Stockmayer, Frederick B. Meyer and Ernst F. Stroeter, as well as Friedrich W. Baedekker from England and J.G. Kargel from Latvia, served at these institutes for teachers and ministers.

Peter M. Friesen reported that at the turn of the century one-third of all ministers in the Mennonite Brethren Church of Russia had secondary education. Many also had theological training. At least five received training at the German Baptist Seminary in Hamburg. In the late nineteenth and early twentieth century thirty-one Russian Mennonite students attended the Berlin Mission Institute (now located at Wiedenest).[15] The St. Chrishona Bible School recorded the names of fourteen Mennonite Brethren from Russia who studied there between 1879 and 1907.[16]

Many Mennonite Brethren preachers between 1880 and 1935 had good Bible knowledge, exegetical teaching and preaching skills. Unfortunately, the loss of most of the written sermons of the churches during the Russian revolution robbed us of valuable resources from those days. Some of their expositions of Scripture appeared in *Friedensstimme* and *Zionsbote*. In addition a few collections of sermons and sermon outlines have survived. The 330 sermons of David Duerksen (1850-1910), the 248 sermon outlines of Abraham H. Neufeld (1860-1931), the three volumes of hand-written sermon outlines from John A. Toews (1876-1953), and the early writings of Abraham H. Unruh (1878-1961) and Johann Wiens (1874-1951) document the teaching and preaching of that era of the

Mennonite Brethren Church in Russia.[17]

Ministers in North America well known for their powerful expository preaching included Heinrich Voth (1851-1918) of Mountain Lake, Minnesota; David Dyck (1846-1933) of Lehigh, Kansas and later Waldheim, Saskatchewan; J.J. Regier (1839-1902) of Henderson, Nebraska; John F. Harms (1855-1945) of Hillsboro, Kansas; John F. Duerksen (1863-1932), educator in Buhler and McPherson, Kansas, and Corn, Oklahoma; Peter P. Rempel (1865-1938), teacher at Tabor College and later a minister in California; Henry W. Lohrenz (1878-1945); Peter C. Hiebert (1878-1963); William Bestvater (1879-1969); Peter E. Penner (1870-1944); and missionaries Daniel F. Bergthold (1876-1948); Johann Pankratz (1867-1952) and Nickolas N. Hiebert (1874-1947). These men of stature, some of them with advanced theological training, some self-taught, cannot be classified as "lay" preachers if by that we imply an uninformed ministry. In a number of instances the conference supported young men to receive advanced theological training, though at the same time it worried that their training might threaten the stability of the conference.[18] Abraham Schellenberg was one who feared that those who had training but no experience would step into influential leadership too early, without developing sensitivity to traditional relationships between ministers and congregations.

A document prepared for the Russian government describing the character and policy of the Mennonite churches spoke to the issue of preparation for ministry:

> With reference to the degree of educational preparation of our church leaders, the majority acquire their religious knowledge within the church fellowship, as already stated, others in theological schools of various levels in a foreign country. Especially many individuals are chosen from the ranks of gifted and God-fearing teachers (all these teachers also serve as teachers of religion). The lack

of a definite educational standard for our ministers does not adversely affect our church life, since every congregation does not only have one, but several leaders, and their ministry is a collective one. "Now there are varieties of gifts, but the same Spirit; and there are varieties of service, but the same Lord."[19]

The educational diversity was consistent with the Mennonite Brethren understanding of a multiple ministry in which not one but several had been endowed with the gifts of leadership and teaching. The strength of the ministry lay in the collective household of God.

**FINANCIAL SUPPORT FOR MINISTERS**

The early Mennonite Brethren Church was not averse to financially supporting its elders, leaders and ministers, and furnished support according to needs. From the outset it arranged assistance for elders who gave much time to administration and supervision and those assigned to an itinerant ministry.[20] Until recent decades the prevailing Mennonite Brethren view was similar to that of the sixteenth-century Anabaptists, who said: "To the question whether a congregation should support the ministers in a Christian way, we say yes. But we do not know whether they should have a fixed income."[21] They understood 1 Corinthians 9:14–"they which preach the gospel should live of the gospel"–to refer to one's livelihood.

The ministry was not, however, to be a means of accumulating wealth. To make the ministry financially profitable would place it on the level of a profession and undermine the motivation for the preaching of the gospel as a sacrifice unto God.

This concern also governed the missionary assignment. Those sent to India, Africa and other lands and those who ministered at home received a minimal salary. The cost of living in the respective area determined the amount. Workers who retired or were disabled through illness were granted continued maintenance. Itinerant ministers and elders and leaders responsible for extensive administrative duties also received modest support.[22]

The ministry at home and abroad thus required the sacrifice of profitable income. This continued past the middle of the twentieth century. The shift to equal financial remuneration between ministers, missionaries and other professionals is a recent one.

Peter M. Friesen expressed concern over the meager support given some ministers in comparison with the wealth of many other church members. "The virtue of sacrificial ministers will not be able to stop the damage which churches are heaping upon themselves by their unjust exploitation of poorer ministers, in comparison to the average wealth of the whole church."[23] Notice that he specified the "poorer" ministers of the church; he was not advocating that those of independent means be remunerated for preaching. He continued: "Each church should have a minister, adequately provided for, in charge of the regular services, alongside the largest possible number of ministers of equal stature, but who preach for the love of preaching'."[24] This position was commonly linked with that of the early Anabaptists, whose elders and preachers did not receive a fixed salary. Cornelius Krahn described them as being "strongly opposed" to the practice that prevailed in the state churches. He further noted that "the prevailing corruption and lack of integrity, religious convictions, and sincerity [was] linked to the practice of hiring and paying the ministry for its services. A voluntary church membership and a voluntary ministry with personal convictions and high moral integrity was the [Anabaptist] aim."[25]

## THE MULTIPLE MINISTRY

A statement by Elder Heinrich Huebert addressed to the government authorities in June 1868 expressed the Mennonite

Brethren understanding of the ministry in the church:

> In our assemblies and inspirational meetings we have tried to follow the rule and order given in 1 Cor. 14, i.e., that one or two or a maximum of three persons present their lectures–messages–and that in succession. We recognize herein the loving purpose of the apostle: that the church be edified, the gifts stirred up, and the saints prepared for the work of the ministry, in order that the body of Christ may be built up, 'til we all come to the unity of the faith and of the knowledge of the Son of God, unto a perfect man, unto the measure of the stature of the fullness of Christ, that we henceforth be no more children, tossed to and fro, and carried about with every wind of doctrine, by the sleight of men, and the cunning craftiness, whereby they lay and wait to deceive (Eph. 4:12-14).[26]

For the Mennonite Brethren, a multiple ministry was basic to building up the body of Christ. The gifts God gave the church were for the equipping of the saints and the stability of the body so "that we henceforth be no more children, tossed to and fro, and carried about with every wind of doctrine," (Eph. 4:14). The corporate multiple ministry provided strength through a community hermeneutic and a consultative body of leaders. In the same document Huebert defined the functional principles of the elders, ministers and deacons who shared the official duties of baptism, communion and leadership.[27] The emphasis was on the council of elders to lead the church and share the responsibility for the flock. The Old Testament references to the elders of Israel (Num. 11:16,17,24ff) provided the basis for this belief. In the ministry of Jesus they recognized the inner circle of the three disciples as symbolic of the council principle. Acts 11:30, 14:23, 15:4, 15:6, 15:23 and the continued reference in the epistles to "the elders of the church" (Phil. 1:1, Titus 1:5, James 5:14, 1 Pet. 5:1) suggested a model of leadership shared by a plurality of equals.[28] The people chosen for these leadership roles were to be those who had the Spirit of God (Num. 11) and the New Testament qualifications as defined in 1 Timothy 3.

The Confession of Faith further addressed the function of leadership: "In the household of the M. B. Church the order obtains, that one elder or a substitute for the elder acts as moderator of local churches and leader. The other ministers are his co-workers."[29] Until recently, leadership always came from among the ministers of the congregation. The 1951 General Conference decision underlined this longstanding principle:

> The appointment of brethren to the leadership of the church, who are not ministers, shall only be considered in such cases where a church has no minister, or where there is no one of them qualified for such a position . . . . As soon as the church again has a minister brother qualified for the leadership, the church should transfer such responsibility to him.[30]

This manner of selecting leadership remained a practice for the first eighty-five years of Mennonite Brethren history. The strength of this unsalaried, multiple ministry can be seen in the following areas:

1. The ministers engaged in gainful occupation could identify with members' daily experiences as farmers, teachers, businessmen, craftsmen and in some cases even as household servants. The theological framework of their preaching was not academic and propositional. They interpreted the Word from the platform of mutual experience. Their illustrations emerged from the life of the community, just as the teachings of Jesus contained illustrations drawn from the culture of his time. The strength of that communal identification of minis-

ters and people can hardly be overestimated.

2. They knew the people in their daily lives, including their individual and corporate strengths and failings. Most of the ministers lived with and served their churches over a period of decades. They addressed the needs and weaknesses of the congregation openly and directly. Their identity as servants of God added authority to their message. The fact that they were unpaid precluded the tension that can arise when a salaried pastor speaks words of exhortation and rebuke.

3. The diversity of gifts provided a broad exposition of biblical truth. Ministers prayed earnestly for spiritual guidance in the selection of texts. They would frequently introduce their message with the preface, "The Lord has laid the following word upon my heart as his message to us." The variation in the style of communication was an additional benefit. Usually there were two messages in a worship service preceded or followed by a period of prayer led by a third minister. In most cases a minister who was not preaching led the service. Younger men in whom the church had recognized the gift for preaching would usually bring the first of the two messages, thus gradually drawing them into the responsibility of the teaching/preaching ministry. Broad participation from the congregation was encouraged in the time of prayer and in the selection of songs. All this contributed to an informal worship service of the people, not a service conducted for the people.

4. Ministers did not limit their responsibilities to the pulpit. A vital personal caring ministry of house visitation undergirded their teaching and preaching. Each family received a visit once or twice a year (more frequently in the case of known spiritual needs). Two ministers or one minister with a deacon would make these visits, which consisted of personal sharing, study of the Word and prayer. The intimate personal acquaintance of ministers and members added much to the effectiveness of the church's caring, teaching and preaching ministry.

The multiple ministry also had its weaknesses, however. Where a minister lacked the proper educational preparation (and some did), the biblical exposition could be meager. The itinerant ministry provided periodic teaching and inspiration for such congregations by ministers of greater depth. In spite of some weaknesses, the multiple ministry provided stable leadership in contrast to the usually short tenure of the paid pastoral system.

**OFFICE OF THE ELDERS**

The office of elder, which required an ordination of its own beyond the ordination for ministry, has been a puzzle in Mennonite Brethren history. John A. Toews called it "somewhat of an enigma."[31] The records of the earliest years of Mennonite Brethren history provided no rationale for the creation of this office. Peter M. Friesen documented the first ordination of elders in the Mennonite colonies but gave no background to explain the phenomenon.

Second generation Mennonite Brethren leaders–Abraham H. Unruh, Bemjamin B. Janz, Johann A. Toews, H.H. Flaming and G.P. Regier (the latter two of whom were themselves ordained elders)–interpreted the creation of elders as a need arising from the storm and stress of the early years. As much as possible the new movement needed to replicate the church government model of the mother church if it was to receive the Russian government's stamp of approval. The office of an elder in the social and ecclesiastical Mennonite community was a symbol of authority and responsible leadership that appeared to be lacking in the first years of the Mennonite Brethren movement.[32]

The 1902 Confession of Faith defined the elder as a leader in a fellowship with other co-workers as equals.[33] As such, the function of the elder still conformed to the model of multiple leadership. But some were uneasy about this special office which could lodge much power in the hands of a few.

There was the example of David Schellenberg, ordained elder in the Rueckenau Church, who exercised very strong authority in the local church as well as in the larger conference. Others, influenced by western Pietism, insisted that according to the New Testament all ministers were elders with no provision for the office of one elder. Jacob W. Reimer asserted that "the leader of the church is a man who has the gift of leadership-administration. He is the leader in the fellowship of equals."[34]

Elsewhere in Russia and later in North America there continued to be considerable diversity of opinion about the position and function of elders. In the United States, the question of elders as distinct from other ministers became an issue in the late 1920s and 1930s. Some believed strongly that the specific designation of elders was scriptural and needed to be continued.[35] In 1921 H.W. Lohrenz declined to officiate at an ordination, stating that "the practice in the Mennonite Brethren Church is that an elder officiates in such a confirmation."[36] During 1924 there was extensive discussion over financial support of elders in the local church and the conference.[37] In 1933, H.H. Flaming, an ordained minister in Corn, Oklahoma, emphasized the biblical basis for the office as separate from teachers, preachers, and evangelists and thought it necessary to provide stable leadership. He warned that the absence of elders would weaken the church for lack of authority.[38]

Other interpreters, meanwhile, took the opposite view. They insisted that Scripture did not call for specifically designated elders but rather intended the words "elder" or "bishop" to apply to all ministers and teachers in the church. Those holding this view did not recognize elders who had been specially ordained for the office.

The most exhaustive biblical study on the subject was that of H.W. Lohrenz.[39] His conclusion corresponded with the findings of a group of leaders who met in Dalmeny, Saskatchewan, in 1934 for Bible study on the issue. They concluded that the words "bishop," "teacher" and "shepherd" were used interchangeably. Their resolution said: "Every brother who has been called by God to the ministry of the Word according to the Scriptures is also an elder." They based their position on the following references: Acts 11:30, 4:23, 15:2,4,6,22,23, 16:4, 20:17, 21:18; Titus 1:5; 1 Peter 5:11, 5:5; 2 John 1:1; 3 John 1:1.[40]

John F. Harms, one of the most trusted leaders in the Mennonite Brethren Church of his day, contributed the following statement to the question of the eldership as a special office: "The leadership in the church should not be dependent on an official ordained elder. The local church under the guidance of the Spirit of God selects its leaders according to the gifts and assigns the responsibility of officiating at the communion services and on occasions of ordination."[41]

The issue of specially ordained elders faded from view after 1935. The prevailing position was that the ordained elder was not a doctrinal but a functional position, and from then on the term elder would be applied to all who were called to the ministry.

## THE ITINERANT MINISTRY

The itinerant ministry played a vital role in spiritual renewal, both among the early Anabaptists and their later descendants, providing nurture for local churches and serving as an arm of evangelism. The itinerant ministry arose from the fundamental notion that the New Testament church encompassed both local congregations and the broader fellowship of believers. This notion, which began with the Anabaptists and carried over into Prussia and Germany, and later Russia, held one of the secrets to the movement's rapid expansion.[42] The spiritual renewal that led to the formation of the Mennonite Brethren can partially be traced to the influence of the itinerant ministry.[43]

Thus it was natural that the Mennonite Brethren would early adopt the itinerant ministry as a way to nurture local congregations and evangelize the unconverted. Following the June Reform of 1865, Christian Schmidt and Jacob Jantz were appointed for an itinerant ministry. Peter M. Friesen described them as "the ideal messengers of love and peace."[44]

Itinerant ministers strengthened God's people through house visitation and preaching in public gatherings. They were instrumental in kindling revival fires in the life of the community of believers and bringing unbelievers to salvation.[45] This ministry provided a spiritual pollenization and nurtured a spirit of love and unity. The 1872 conference, in Russia, provided limited stipends to set ministers free for such service. The congregational reading of their reports in the form of diaries generated unity and stimulated intercessory prayer.[46]

Conference reports from 1872-1906 recorded the concern for an effective itinerant ministry as the major mission of the larger church. *Friedensstimme* in Russia and *Zionsbote* in America give central place to reports of itinerant ministers. Under the category of home missions, this ministry continued, into the 1940s, as a significant force for spiritual renewal and revitalization.

CHAPTER 6

# In The World But Not Of The World

A fervent belief in two kingdoms–that the people of God are to be separate from "the world" in belief and lifestyle–lay at the heart of the formation of the Mennonite Brethren Church. While citing worldliness in the parent church as the underlying reason for the withdrawal, the secession document nonetheless emphasized the breakaway group's agreement "with our dear Menno, according to our convictions from the Holy Scriptures."[1] A particular point of agreement was Menno's articulation of a visible, separate identity for the community of the redeemed: "The entire evangelical Scriptures teach us that the church of Christ was and is in doctrine, life and worship, a people separated from the world."[2] This, they believed, was an identity the parent church had lost. The June Reform of 1865, the earliest record of a corporate action by the new movement, did not address issues of doctrine and beliefs but dealt extensively with biblical relationships and the lifestyle of a people living separately in the world.[3]

The words of Jesus are the basis for the Mennonite Brethren two-world concept: "They are not of the world, even as I am not of the world" (John 17:16). This did not mean separation from people but from the patterns of thought and behavior that dominate the people of the world.

> Love not the world, neither the things that are in the world. If any man love the world, the love of the Father is not in him. For all that is in the world, the lust of the flesh, and the lust of the eyes, and the pride of life, is not

of the Father, but is of the world. And the world passeth away, and the lust thereof: But he that doeth the will of God abideth forever" (1 John 2:15-17).4

The Kingdom of God within the believer was important for the Mennonite Brethren. Jesus' answer to the Pharisaic inquiry concerning the kingdom was pivotal: "The kingdom of God cometh not with observation: neither shall they say, lo here! or, lo there! for, behold, the kingdom of God is within you" (Luke 17:20-21). Jesus had chosen them "out of the world" (John 15:19) to become "the new man which after God is created in righteousness and true holiness" (Eph. 4:24). The indwelling of Christ in the believer, the new nature resulting from the new birth, produced a radical standard of behavior that was to be lived out in relationships with others. The Sermon on the Mount (Matt. 5-7) spelled out the extent of this new behavior: limitless love (even for persecutors), forgiveness, self-surrender. These values stood in stark, paradoxical contrast to the unregenerate mindset of "the world." To be "not of this world" meant to integrate the gospel of Jesus Christ with daily life and ethics fully and radically.

True faith in Jesus Christ was not mere verbal profession of "accepting Jesus into my heart." Transformed behavior and relationships measured by the teachings and life of Jesus were foundational to being "in the world but not of the world."[5] To be the people of God meant a distinct lifestyle with different priorities, values and conduct.[6]

The second aspect in the theology of two worlds was the ongoing conflict between the Kingdom of God and the kingdom of this world–the kingdom of light and the kingdom of darkness. Passages like 1 John 5:19, 2 Timothy 3:13 and 2 Thessalonians 2:11-12 reflected early Mennonite Brethren understanding of a wicked world in which evil people sought to seduce and deceive.[7]

The Schleitheim Confession of the early Anabaptists expressed well the Mennonite Brethren theology of two worlds:

> We have been united concerning the separation that shall take place from the evil and the wickedness which the devil has planted in the world, simply in this: that we have no fellowship with them, and do not run with them in the confusion of their abominations. So it is; since all who have not entered into the obedience of faith and have not united themselves with God so that they will to do His will, are a great abomination before God, therefore nothing else can or really will grow or spring from them than abominable things. Now there is nothing else in the world and all creation than good or evil, believing and unbelieving, darkness and light, the world and those who are [come] out of the world, God's temple and idols, Christ and Belial, and none will have part with the other.[8]

The people of the Kingdom of God have been delivered from the power of darkness and translated into the Kingdom of Christ (Col. 1:13). They "wrestle not against flesh and blood, but against principalities, against powers, against the rulers of the darkness of this world, against spiritual wickedness in high places" (Eph. 6:12).[9] The conflict between the two kingdoms provides the key to understanding history. The struggle recorded in the Old Testament, world history in general and the future consummation of history reflect the ongoing conflict between the two kingdoms, with the certainty of ultimate victory for the Kingdom of God (Phil. 2:9-11; 1 Cor. 15:28; Rev. 20:7-10; Rev. 22:12).

The most comprehensive treatment on this subject appeared in the writings of Henry W. Lohrenz under the subject "The People of God in the World."[10] Lohrenz went to great effort to distinguish between a universal relationship of God to humanity as the creator and provider, and the specific relationship of God to the members of the redeemed community.

He answered the question, "Who are the children of God?," by drawing careful distinctions between a mere profession to be a child of God–the claim of nominal Christianity–and the true members of the people of God. The latter are a people in whom God has performed the radical transaction of a new birth through which they have become partakers of a new nature in character, disposition and relationship (2 Pet. 1:4). The true children of God are followers of Jesus, a people who are under the leadership of the Holy Spirit (Rom. 8:14-15) and who seek perfection in character since their father in heaven is perfect.[11] He defined the concept of world according to John 17:6: those who were chosen from "out of the world."

In a second manuscript, "*Siegreicher Kampf gegen Teufel und Sunde*,"[12] he described the conflict of the people of God against Satan. The admonition "to stand against the wiles of the devil" (Eph. 6:11) was central in his exposition of conflict in the world. The holy life of the people of God stood in contrast to the struggle with the forces of evil in the world. Sanctification, according to Lohrenz, was the unfolding of the new life imparted to the true believer through regeneration.

In yet another document he summarized his theology on the calling of God's people in the world by invoking Edgar Y. Mullins:

> "Sanctification is the attainment of moral character by the people of God through struggle. In regeneration a new moral disposition is imparted to us by the action of God's Spirit. In sanctification we work out what God has wrought within us. By repeated acts of our own wills, by repeated acts of holy choice, by successive victories we are enabled by God's grace to achieve the ideal. Thus salvation for the children of God is both, a gift and a task."[13]

The church was a called out body of interrelated believers as summarized in Acts 4:32– "And the multitude of them that believed were of one heart and of one soul."[14] This body was not to adopt the world's democratic or hierarchical styles but was to remain an interdependent organism, purified from sin. Each member shared the responsibilities of corporate worship, intercessory prayer, faithful material stewardship and mutual exhortation.[15]

Lohrenz viewed the character and relationship of the church as rooted in a personal encounter with God, resulting in a volitional commitment.[16] An individual's character expressed a personal commitment to Jesus Christ. He viewed Romans 12:1-2 as the true expression of a redeemed life. The mercies of God, the basis for redemption, called for voluntary commitment of life as a living sacrifice. "Having accepted Christ, it is the logical conclusion that we *consecrate* our whole being to God." A life so redeemed could not conform to the values and lifestyle of this world. It was transformed– changed in inner character and in all the relationships of life. The people of God, in the theology of H.W. Lohrenz, were in the world but radically different from the world.[17]

One way this radical difference was to be expressed was in the church's response to war. The teaching of Jesus in the Gospels formed the basis for his notable lecture, "What the Bible Teaches about War and Peace."[18] Old Testament views on war could not be applied to a New Testament church; the teachings and life of Jesus superseded Old Testament ethics. For Lohrenz, other professing believers–and even Bible scholars–who held a pro-war position were simply inconsistent with the teachings and life of Jesus.

The Mennonite Brethren understanding of two kingdoms did not require a rigid sociological isolation from the rest of the world. It did not mean separation from people or groups of people of other cultures or religious persuasions. Being part of the Kingdom of God meant to live in the world and relate to its people. The prayer of Jesus in John 17:15-18 was an assignment to relate to the people of the world with a deep sense of mission: "I pray not that thou shouldest take them out of the world, but that thou shouldest keep them from the evil one . . . as thou hast sent me into the world, even so I also send them into the world." They were in the world for a purpose. This understanding had two key effects on the Mennonite Brethren. First, its high sense of purpose fired them with enthusiasm for winning the unredeemed and made them a missionary movement. Second, it heightened their fear of carnal influences and, like the early Anabaptists whom they sought to emulate, resulted in the strict discipline of erring members.

**A MATTER OF LIFESTYLE**

Recent generations of Mennonite Brethren have frequently referred to the lifestyle restrictions of early conference decisions and church covenants as harsh legalism. They recall tight boundaries that regimented individual behavior and forced conformity to a narrow ethnic lifestyle. Legalism was not what the early Mennonite Brethren intended. Their concern was the kind of righteousness suggested in 1 Peter 2:9-10:

> But ye are a chosen generation, a royal priesthood, an holy nation, a peculiar people; that we should show forth the praises of him who hath called you out of darkness into his marvelous light; which in time passed were not a people but are now the people of God: which had not obtained mercy, but now have obtained mercy.

To follow Jesus meant to subdue the desires of the flesh. Believers were in a constant struggle between the two worlds–the spirit and the flesh–as suggested in Romans 7 and 1 Corinthians 3.[19] Mennonite Brethren placed strong emphasis on Paul's statement to the Galatians: "they that are Christ's have crucified the flesh with the affections and lusts. If we live in the Spirit let us also walk in the Spirit" (Gal. 5:24-25).[20] Life in the Spirit demanded self-crucifixion in response to Christ's sacrifice (Gal. 2:20). Pride, complacency and carnal self-satisfaction had no place in true biblical discipleship.[21] Typical were the repeated urgings of Peter E. Penner to take seriously the admonition of Hebrews 13:13–"Let us go forth therefore unto him without the camp, bearing his reproach."[22] Christ was the model for all areas of lifestyle.[23]

Accommodation to the temptations of the prevailing village culture, so strongly censured in the secession document of 1860, received much attention in early Mennonite Brethren writings. Moderate behavior was an over-arching concern. Several articles stressed the importance of moderation in all human pursuits and activities. Farmers, for example, were warned about making unreasonable demands on workers in the quest for prosperity. Greed was clearly a sin. Moderation and discipline were also to extend to matters of eating, drinking, recreation and pleasure.[24] Pleasure and recreation, though necessary for a healthy body and mind, should not be overdone. Pleasure simply for the sake of pleasure represented selfishness and was contrary to a life of self-denial.[25] Pleasure for the sake of positive motivation was one thing; carnal self-gratification was quite another. Appropriate pleasures were those that contributed to the building of character and virtue, and were morally exemplary to the world.[26]

There were frequent practical applications of Romans 12:2–"Be not conformed to this world: but be ye transformed by the renewing of your mind." The tendency to identify with contemporary culture and fashions was "an expression of worldliness."[27] Such tendencies were dangerous for the people of God in the world.[28]

## SPECIFIC GUIDELINES

### Warning Against Materialism

Like Anabaptists generally, Mennonite Brethren saw virtue

in hard work and thrift. Integrity and honesty were to govern all relationships and transactions. Employers were to treat employees with respect and pay fairly. They warned against the aggressive pursuit of wealth lest possessions become a priority and dilute values.[29]

A conference resolution of 1893 stated: "Resolved, that a minister choose as simple a vocation as possible in order not to have his own spiritual life as well as that of others suffer on that account." Economic pursuits were not to interfere with the spiritual ministry.[30] Possessions themselves were not condemned, but strong warnings against materialism were numerous.[31] The following two stories demonstrate the danger of materialism.

A wealthy owner of a large estate was covetous and unwilling to share his possessions with the poor. The church leaders called him to account. They organized a prayer circle to pray that he would repent. After some months their prayers were answered. The wealthy brother publicly confessed his greed and asked God and the church for forgiveness. He acknowledged that at the time of his conversion he had responded to the benefit of Christ's provision for salvation but had failed to accept the responsibility of discipleship and faithful stewardship. He asked to be rebaptized. My father, Johann A. Toews of Alexanderthal, baptized the brother for the second time. In the public prayer preceding the baptism the brother prayed for victory over the sin of covetousness. Before entering the water he placed his wallet into his shirt pocket, stating this was to symbolize the surrender of all his riches to the Lord and his service.[32]

A second example concerned a prosperous farmer and leading minister in a Mennonite Brethren congregation in a village in the Molotschna. The Russian maids and servants reported that he paid the lowest wages in the village and was unwilling to help the poor. Those serving with him in leadership had spoken to him repeatedly about the sin of covetousness, but he showed no evidence of change and his riches accumulated. Finally the leadership recommended that the church place him under discipline and release him from all ministerial functions. The church pledged to pray for the man's repentance. After a few months it was the joy of the congregation to see him return to the fellowship in deep repentance. He was forgiven. Henceforth the poor in the village found him to be a warm and concerned helper in times of need. He later resumed his ministerial responsibilities.[33]

**Life Insurance**

Closely related to the sin of covetousness was the question of life insurance.[34] Care for the financial needs arising from the death of a family member was the corporate responsibility of the congregation. Life insurance represented a transfer of this obligation to a worldly economic institution. In matters of mutual aid the Mennonite Brethren at the turn of the century held views similar to those of the Amish Mennonites today.

**Amusements**

Behavioral boundaries were set by the Mennonite Brethren, using 1 John 2:15-16, which defines fleshly lusts and the pride of life as being "of the world." Theater attendance was prohibited since it nurtured the lust of the eye.[35] At issue was not the play but rather the larger institution. A person going to the theater would not be judged by the play presented as much as by the institution itself. The reasoning was that the better plays would not lift up the institution, but rather, the unsavory institution would drag the plays down to its level. The whole was stronger than any part and in fact gave quality to every part.[36]

The wearing of jewelry, cosmetic makeup, and sometimes even the wearing of rings was also prohibited. In the 1930s the cutting of women's hair became an issue of much concern and discipline. In 1927 the General Conference declared: "The cutting of hair by our sisters is in direct contradiction with the word of God as found in 1 Corinthians 11:6."[37] This resolution remained in force for some years, and prompted discipline when violated.

## Alcoholic Beverages and Tobacco

The use of tobacco and alcoholic beverages was also strongly prohibited.[38] At issue was the adverse effects on health and the possible enslavement resulting from their use.[39]

## Relation of Church and Government

Though governments were an institution from God (Rom. 13), the active participation in government by a people "in the world but not of the world" was questioned. The 1878 North American General Conference acted as follows: "Resolved, that our members are not permitted to hold government office or take any part at the polls. However, we appreciate the protection we enjoy under our government."[40] Ten years later the following modification appeared: "In regard to being delegates to National Political Conventions it is strongly advised that, while we desire to have a good government, members should be careful so as not to defile their conscience. However, the conference does not want to form a definite resolution in this matter."[41] This position remained the standard in America, as well as in Russia, until the crisis of the First World War. A notable exception was a Mennonite Brethren who served in the Duma, the highest institution in the Russian government, as a representative of the Mennonite people. However, his position was primarily one of recognition, in which the Russian government expressed its high regard for the cultural and industrial/agricultural contribution of the Mennonite colonies.

Mennonite Brethren had a long tradition of uneasiness with government. The interrelationship of ecclesiastical and civil power had been a major force opposing the initial renewal movement of the Mennonite Brethren, and the 1860 secession became the occasion that broke this alliance. Later, the threat of increasing government intrusion into the lives of the Mennonite colonies spurred the 1874 migration to North America. Broader church-government statements, dealing specifically with the question of military non-participation, emerged only during the First World War, the Russian Revolution and the Second World War.

**Awaiting God's Judgment**

The issue of divorce and remarriage arose surprisingly early for the Mennonite Brethren. In 1883 the North American conference passed the following resolution:

> In answer to the question relative to accepting into membership a man or a woman which has been divorced, married again and now after conversion seeks membership in our church, the conference decided without dissenting votes that even the seemingly innocent party be barred from membership until God has revealed the innocency by the death of the guilty party.[42]

By barring both parties from membership, the Mennonite Brethren thought they were leaving judgment in the hands of God. The guilty partner was the one who died first. This harsh position led to some tragic situations around the turn of the century. Though undocumented in written form, there were several cases of congregations that prayed for God's intervention in a divorce case. When one of the parties died suddenly, it was accepted as a manifestation of guilt–and of answered prayer.

**CONCLUSION**

The early Mennonite Brethren took seriously the tension

of living in two worlds. Their response was not an effort to develop coherent theological formulations but rather a practical concern to be a godly people in an evil world. The conclusions they reached, while perhaps lacking specific biblical reference, were an attempt to forge a life of self-denial and obedience to Scripture as they understood it. Some of their rules may appear narrow in our day.

The early Mennonite Brethren provided a prophetic critique to the culture of their day. They sought to live by an eschatological ethic; they did not expect the powers of darkness to be overcome in their lifetime. Nor were they concerned whether their "narrow" social ethics would find favor with the world and attract large numbers of people into their fellowship. They carried the resolute conviction that the people of God–the true church–could not conform to the values and lifestyle of the world in which they lived.

The hymns of their worship services expressed their self-understanding as pilgrims, strangers and aliens. Songs like "*Hier auf Erden bin ich ein Pilger*" (Here on earth I am but a pilgrim)[43] and "*O mein Jesu Du bist's wert*" with the chorus, "*von der Erde reiss mich los*" (From this earth O Lord detach me)[44] were favorites sung repeatedly in churches and in homes.

Our early Mennonite Brethren may not always have been correct in defining their relationship to society, but one cannot deny their deep, sincere effort to live as a people in the world but not of the world.

CHAPTER 7

# A Missionary Movement

While the Mennonite Brethren were conscious of being a missionary movement, they did not claim to have a unique theology of mission. The Anabaptist movement of the sixteenth century and the belief in the "believers church" nourished their missionary vision.[1]

## ANABAPTIST ROOTS

The Anabaptists were among the first Christian groups following the apostolic era to see the Great Commission as binding upon all church members.[2] Their missionary energy was legendary. But by the nineteenth century this vitality had largely vanished. With regard to evangelism, the Mennonites of Russia seemed to share the view held by many other Protestants—that the Great Commission had been a specific assignment to the apostles and had expired with them.

This casual view would have horrified sixteenth-century Anabaptists for whom personal salvation was crucial. For them "the world was populated with two kinds of people—those who witness and those who are witnessed to. For them there was no third category."[3] As the redeemed community, the church, their task was to witness to the world concerning God's redemption. To be the church, and to evangelize, were interdependent tasks. Mennonite theologian John Howard Yoder said that the Anabaptists "considered evangelism as belonging to the essential being of the church."[4]

The sixteenth century Anabaptists rejected the broadly inclusive *Corpus Christianum* of the state church. A church of born-again believers was not part of the kingdom of this world. The Kingdom of God and the kingdom of the world

81

were diametrically opposed to each other, as opposite as light and darkness.[5] According to George H. Williams, the proponents of the Radical Reformation viewed the whole territorial Christianity–Protestant scarcely less than Catholic–as anti-Christian or sub-Christian. Nominal Christianity was part of the world, thus in need of the message of redemption.[6]

Matthew 28:18-20 and Mark 16-15, which appear more frequently in the confessions of faith and in the testimonies of the Anabaptists than any other portions of Scripture, were a call to obedience to the Great Commission.[7] To receive personal salvation meant *Nachfolge*–to follow diligently in the footsteps of Christ without giving thought to method, strategy or consequence. Followers of Jesus understood their calling to be witnesses to the ends of the earth, according to the command of the risen Lord (Acts 1:8).

The witness of ordinary members was an important factor in the rapid expansion of Anabaptism. The "apostolate of the laity", as Wolfgang Schaeufele described Anabaptism, was the consequence of being knit together into a covenant relationship.[8] All believers, not just preachers or designated missionaries, had a *Sendungsbewustsein* (consciousness of being sent). The exclamation of Acts 4:20–"For we cannot but speak the things which we have seen and heard"–found new reality in the sixteenth-century movement. The passion of the movement can be sensed in the following statement by Menno Simons:

> Therefore, we preach, as much as is possible, both by day and by night, in houses and in fields, in forests and wastes, hither and yon, at home or abroad, in prisons and in dungeons, in water and in fire, on the scaffold and on the wheel, before lords and princes, through mouth and pen, with possessions and blood, with life and death. We have done this these many years, and we are not ashamed of the Gospel of the glory of Christ. Rom. 1:16. For we feel

his living fruit and moving power in our hearts, as may be seen in many places by the lovely patience and willing sacrifices of our faithful brethren and companions in Christ Jesus.[9]

The call in the 1860 secession document to restore this vitality of faith and life was a guiding force in the missionary spirit of the early Mennonite Brethren.

## PIETISTIC INFLUENCES

Exposure to Pietism led Mennonite Brethren to enlarge the scope of their missionary zeal to include all those around the world who were outside of the influence of Christianity. They shared the view of Philip Jakob Spener, the founder of Lutheran Pietism, who wrote more than a century earlier that "the Gospel shall be preached in the whole world and thus may continually be carried to other places whither it has not yet come, and that to this end no diligence, labor or cost be spared in such work on behalf of the poor heathen and unbelievers."[10] This mindset dominated Mennonite Brethren foreign missions from their beginning. The strongest missionary influence came from Count Zinzendorf, a disciple of Spener's, founder of the Danish Halle Mission and a key figure in the renewal of the Moravian Brethren, who later ignited revival in the Mennonite colonies in Russia. Zinzendorf's writings and reports of his mission efforts provided a major point of reference for Mennonite Brethren. Cornelius Krahn wrote that "no other single religious movement has had such an impact on the Mennonites in all countries with the exception of the Netherlands as Pietism."[11]

Wilhelm Lange, a Lutheran Pietist who became a leading minister of the Gnadenfeld Mennonite Church, initiated missionary festivals as early as the 1830s. These festivals were an important influence in the renewal movement that preceded the birth of the Mennonite Brethren in 1860. Tobias Voth and his wife were converted through the writings of Pietist Jung-Stilling while living in Germany. As a teacher in the Ohrloff *Zentralschule* Voth emphasized missions and encouraged missionary giving.[12] Heinrich Dirks, the first foreign missionary from the Russian Mennonites, went to Sumatra in 1870 under the Dutch Mennonite Mission Board, and received his training at the Missionshaus at Barmen, Germany, a school with Pietist roots.[13]

Eduard Wüst, the Pietist pastor from Germany, fanned the spiritual renewal in South Russia into a flame. "Either-Or" was the watchword of this man who knew only two categories of people–the converted and the unconverted. Wüst's joyous concept of justification by faith complemented the more earnest Reformation theology of Menno Simons to produce a heightened passion for the Great Commission.[14]

**A WITNESSING COMMUNITY**

These influences gave impetus and definition to the missions ferment that was already brewing in the Russian Mennonite colonies when the Mennonite Brethren emerged in 1860.[15] The new movement was born in an atmosphere of keen missionary spirit that would flourish for decades to come.

At first, mission efforts focused on other Mennonites who were not converted. They also reached out to native Russians, in spite of laws forbidding evangelism among them, and a goodly number responded. Imprisonment and threats of Siberian banishment did not deter them in this effort. The extension of their outreach to regions beyond–foreign missions–emerged as leaders of the young movement prayed and searched Scripture for further direction.[16]

The early Mennonite Brethren Church shared the zeal of the apostolic church as recorded in Acts 4:20, "We cannot but speak the things which we have seen and heard." Threats and interrogations took place in courtrooms; they suffered for the testimony of their faith in prisons. In all these places they spoke of Jesus as their Savior and called their suppressors to repentance. The story of Abram Unger and Heinrich Neufeld in the Tschernyschevo prison seems to echo the stories of Acts.[17] Heinrich Huebert's confinement in a dark, cold and damp prison cell reminds us of the story of Peter in Acts 12.[18] The persecutions endured by the early Mennonite Brethren, as reported by Jacob Bekker, bring to mind the words of Jesus in John 15:18-20: "If the world hate you, ye know that it hated me before it hated you . . . if they have persecuted me, they will also persecute you."[19] Some lost homes and positions as the result of their newfound faith.[20] But even this would not silence their witness. Many in the Mennonite community avoided them because at every contact they would inquire as to the individual's relation to Christ.[21] Cornelius Krahn characterized the early Mennonite Brethren as follows:

> The new emphasis upon a strong personal experience of the grace of God with its accompanying assurance of salvation produced a very sturdy and active type of Christian, and led to the development of an almost unbelievable zeal for witnessing for the Gospel in home and foreign missions.[22]

Early Mennonite Brethren diaries have a flavor of Acts 8:4, "They that were scattered abroad went everywhere preaching (telling) the word." Reports of their witness following the June Reform of 1865 depict a fervent, spontaneous witness. They went from village to village, visiting people in their homes and speaking of the grace they had experienced in their personal salvation. They read Scripture, prayed and invited people to accept Christ as Savior.[23] They witnessed out of their own personal experience of redemption and a love for those who were without Christ.

This zeal followed them to North America. Conference records of the early Mennonite Brethren churches in America contain only one major theme, that of "Home and Foreign Missions."[24] As in Russia, initially home missions focused on other Mennonites. Later outreach expanded to Lutherans and Congregational communities of German cultural background.[25]

It is significant to observe that the period 1860-1865, a time of internal turmoil and external persecution, recorded the most rapid increase in conversions and baptisms. By 1872 the Mennonite Brethren fellowship had 600 baptized members, and by 1914 the new church comprised one-fourth of the whole Russian Mennonite population.[26] Similar growth happened in America, which received its first Mennonite Brethren immigrants in 1874. Continued renewals in Mennonite churches provided the major increase in Mennonite Brethren fellowships. The Hillsboro (Kansas) Mennonite Brethren Church, for many years a key generator of leaders and resources, was born from a revival in the French Creek Mennonite settlement north of town. The church in Goessel, Kansas, which later joined Hillsboro, became a major factor in Mennonite Brethren growth through the ministry of Cornelius P. Wedel, who with a group of members from the Alexanderwohl Mennonite Church had founded that congregation.[27]

Two factors emerged as the major motivating dynamic in this movement. First was the experiential reality of their conversion. A favorite song in early Mennonite Brethren Church life went, "But I know whom I have believed, and am persuaded that He is able to keep that which I've committed unto Him against that day."[28] In contrast to the fear of eternal lostness that characterized many other Mennonites, their new certainty of forgiveness and eternal life produced an explosion of joy that the old wineskins could not contain.[29] They had to tell others.

The second factor was their world-view that assigned all people not genuinely saved to hell. To warn them against such destiny and plead with them not to reject the redeeming provision of God was the focus of their mission. They were acutely conscious of the "blood guilt" for failing to warn the wicked (Ezekiel 3:18). And the "either-or" theology of Eduard Wüst had impressed upon them that every person was "a child of God or a child of the Devil–on the way to heaven or on the way to hell."[30]

The effectiveness of their evangelism was due in no small way to its "lay" character. The conference selected itinerant ministers from the ranks of the pew. Their service was voluntary, since the stipend of $25 per month (to cover immediate expenses in 1878), could not influence their motives. Heinrich Voth, who received $400 for a full year of service in Canada, returned $100 to the conference with the explanation that his actual expenses had been less. For the Lord's work he did not wish to be paid.

Voth exemplified evangelistic fervor. His ministry in Manitoba, Canada, was one of walking from house to house, seeking the lost and spiritually hungry to bring them to Christ.[31] Many people hated him and persecuted him for the gospel's sake, but others responded to the message and were converted. In one village a local ordinance forbade him to remain overnight and he was chased into the fields. His only shelter in a cold night with the temperature below zero was a haystack into which he tunneled to survive.[32] Another winter night a Russian herdsman opened his humble cottage and permitted Voth to sleep on the floor with all his clothes on to keep warm.[33] On another occasion his persecutors escorted him to the United States border and forbade him to return to Canada. He was undaunted by the slander, beatings and rejection, and walked back in search of the lost. He would return again and again for several years until the Mennonite Brethren established their first church in Burwalde, near Winkler, Manitoba, in 1888.

His correspondence with David Dyck, a co-minister in the conference who later moved to Canada to lead the newly established Mennonite Brethren Church, reflected the spiritual stature of Heinrich Voth. This correspondence depicts Voth as a deeply spiritual man who invested all of his energies and abilities in his apostolic mission. Voth's method was typical of the itinerant ministry in Russia. Personal evangelism stood at the center. He and others went from house to house seeking the lost, speaking to them of forgiveness of sin and peace through faith in Jesus the Savior. Voth followed up these visits with day-long group meetings in private homes, a time of nurture and fellowship in the Word. Counseling was step three. The organization of fellowship groups in the localities provided ongoing opportunities for sharing, caring and worship.[34]

The spiritual dynamics of this style of ministry produced the kind of growth described by Luke: "And the Lord added to the church daily such as should be saved" (Acts 2:47).

## THE RUSSIAN NEIGHBOR MUST ALSO HEAR THE GOSPEL

Adolf Reimer, a Russian Mennonite Brethren minister, in a crucial moment of great danger when he knelt under the drawn sword of his persecutors, declared, "but I must, because even the murderers have a soul that needs salvation." This slogan symbolizes the story of some Mennonite Brethren outreach to their Russian neighbors. As early as 1862 the Russian authorities called the Mennonite Brethren into their courts because they were sharing the gospel with Russian servants working in the Mennonite villages. Conversions of Russian people in the years following led to the organization of the first Russian believers church with additional church groups emerging by 1879.[35] The Mennonite Brethren provided the financial sponsorship for these new Russian converts to carry out their own evangelistic ministry.[36] Johann Wieler and J.W. Kargel were instrumental in organizing the First Russian Conference of Baptized Christians in 1884.[37]

The first elder of the Mennonite Brethren Church, Heinrich Huebert, suffered prolonged imprisonment for baptizing a Russian servant upon the confession of her faith.[38] Abram

Unger and Heinrich Neufeld, in spite of mistreatment and imprisonment, could not be silenced from preaching salvation to their Russian neighbors. Johann Wieler, an early convert in the Mennonite Brethren Church, felt that God's purpose for the Mennonite Brethren movement was the evangelization of Russia. For years he was a preaching fugitive, moving from village to village. The intensity of the persecutions finally forced his escape to Romania, where he served in a Russian evangelical fellowship.[39]

Heinrich P. Sukkau sold all his possessions to become an apostle to the Russians. With no sponsoring body to provide his daily necessities, he followed Paul's example of working for his support, and seeking the lost amid much personal deprivation.[40] The imprisonment of Abraham H. Unruh and Gerhard P. Froese in the early 1900s, the work of Adolf Reimer and Heinrich Enns, and the Tent Mission under the leadership of Jakob Dyck, who prayed for his brutal executioners as he died under their sword, compares with the heroism of the gallery of faith recorded in Hebrews 11.[41]

In America the early Mennonite Brethren limited their evangelistic outreach to people of cultural affinity. Beyond other Mennonite groups, whom they considered their first mission field, they sought to evangelize people of Lutheran, Congregational and Catholic background who had immigrated to the middle west from the Russian German colonies and from Germany. They found it difficult to cross cultural boundaries to carry the gospel to English-speaking people. With the exception of the Minneapolis City Mission, established in 1907, it was not until the 1930s and 1940s that they launched programs to reach their English neighbors.

## THE "HEATHEN" MUST HEAR

As late as 1960 the Mennonite Brethren made a distinction between missionary outreach to people of Christian religious background and those of non-Christian religions. The latter were considered the "heathen," having never heard even the basics of the Christian message. (The term "heathen" as in *Heiden Mission* was in common use for many years. In recent decades it has been abandoned as imperialistic and pejorative.) The outreach to people with some Christian background was referred to as "home mission"; the outreach to non-Christians as "foreign mission."

Among the Russian Mennonites the concern for foreign missions predated the birth of the Mennonite Brethren Church. The strongly influential Moravian Brethren, besides fostering renewal tendencies, also imparted their missionary consciousness and vision to the larger Mennonite community in Russia.[42] Like a torch in a relay, the new Mennonite Brethren movement accepted this vision with eagerness and conviction. There is a detailed history of their foreign mission activity on record elsewhere.[43] The motivation and methods of that mission enterprise, however, merit review.

The Lord's words to Ananias in Acts 9:15–"He is a chosen vessel unto me, to bear my name before the Gentiles"–stirred the soul of the new Mennonite Brethren Church. They, too, felt born with an assignment from God to "bear my name" across cultural boundaries. From the start we can see a compelling sense of responsibility for the spiritual need of those beyond the usual spheres of Christianity.

Their isolation in Russia and North America may have sharpened this consciousness. With their outreach in home missions limited, at least at first by barriers of language and culture, they compensated with a strong emphasis on foreign missions. There is room to consider whether there was an overemphasis on foreign missions to the neglect of responsibility toward the spiritual needs of the people of their own immediate neighborhoods.

When in 1885, in Russia, the first young man, Abram J. Friesen volunteered for foreign service, one leader exclaimed: "We have been praying to God for a long time that He might make someone willing to go out as our missionary to the heathen."⁴⁴ He expressed the sentiment of the entire conference. The praying churches provided the basis for the early and rapidly expanding program of foreign missions.

In North America in 1879, only five years after the first Mennonite Brethren landed on the continent and while still in the midst of their struggle for social and economic survival, the conference spoke of its responsibility to bring the gospel to those who had not heard.⁴⁵ Two years later, 1881, the conference marked the official birth of Mennonite Brethren foreign missions in America when it designated half of its offering ($26.32) to this cause, applying the other half to home missions. This action formalized the two-prong missionary commitment of the early Mennonite Brethren.⁴⁶

The predominant interest in foreign mission in the decades that followed was reflected on several levels. As A. E. Janzen noted: "Expressions of deep compassion for the people of heathen nations, living in gross spiritual darkness and idolatry were a major part of the appeal in messages and lay testimonies."⁴⁷ The mission concern provided the major incentive for the birth of the conference periodical, the *Zionsbote*, in 1884 and the founding of a training school at McPherson College in 1898.⁴⁸

## MISSION METHODS

From the beginning, Mennonite Brethren pursued a holistic ministry. They did not separate the preaching of the gospel from needs such as education and health care. The Russian Mennonite Brethren missionaries to India–Abram and Maria Friesen, Abram and Katharina Huebert, Cornelius and Martha Unruh, Heinrich and Anna Unruh, Franz J. and Maria Wiens, Johan G. and Helena Wiens, John A. and Anna Penner, Anna Epp, Anna Peters, Katharina Reimer–did literacy training and medical work. The missionaries from North America–Nickolas N. and Susie Hiebert, John H. and Maria

Pankratz, and Daniel F. and Anna Bergthold–followed this pattern. Elizabeth Neufeld, a teacher, was part of the team of North American missionaries sent to India in 1898. The medical ministry in India of Dr. Katharina Schellenberg must be recognized as foundational for the extensive ministry to the physical needs of India.[49]

These progressive factors aside, however, the style of operation still bore the flavor of the colonial system of the eighteenth and nineteenth centuries. It was a ministry to a people, with most initiative and decisions lodged with the mission staff. The national Christians, helpers to the missionaries, followed assignments without the privilege of creative leadership.

A statement of policy recorded in 1936 reflected the independent orientation of the mission program:

> The missionaries that serve on any specific field (including both men and women) are considered to be a committee that participates in the management of the mission work by submitting its recommendations. Thus every field is represented.
>
> The organization of the work on the field is left to the respective missionaries. Likewise the arranging of all local affairs of their field rests in their hands. But they should always endeavor to obtain uniform procedures in all mission work.
>
> These committees of missionaries direct to the Board of Foreign Missions their recommendations for the work in their respective fields and give detailed information concerning the needs and the conditions. Provisions for the work are then made as far as possible on the basis of these recommendations and reports.[50]

The conference at home and the mission board were the supporting agencies of the work abroad. Questions of location as well as policies and program rested with the missionary council. In practice it developed into distinct missionary and mission station centered entities, each program developing as appeared best to the respective missionary. They embraced the colonial system of organization and relationships and adapted it to their spiritual objectives.

**NURTURE OF THE MISSIONARY SPIRIT**

The missionary festivals that developed in Gnadenfeld, Russia, in the mid-nineteenth century provided the seedbed for the nurture of missions and became a regular part of Mennonite Brethren life.[51] Among other things, the Gnadenfeld festival spawned the creation of women's missionary societies beginning in 1870. These societies met one afternoon a week to knit and sew for missions. Prayer and the singing of missionary hymns preceded work time. Missionary news reports were read while the women worked.[52]

Missionary societies appeared in North America as early as 1885. Their purpose was as follows: (1) For group Bible study and prayer to help cultivate the faith of its members; (2) To keep informed about missionary life and the needs of those who had gone out from their area; (3) To use their skills in sewing, which they enjoyed doing, to outfit missionaries with clothing and bedding; (4) To raise money to support their missionaries by way of offerings and the sale of articles made by the women; (5) Finally, to encourage others, especially their own group members, to become involved in foreign missions. This tended to be a natural outgrowth of their meeting together. Several early missionaries attributed their interest in foreign missions to these efforts.[53]

The societies' impact was phenomenal. The priority given them (many mothers devoted up to a day a week for this purpose), firmly established the importance of missions in family and church. Candidates volunteering for mission assignments often credited this work of their mothers with providing the earliest impressions of the church's obligation to those who didn't know the gospel of Christ.[54]

The cause of missions was a family concern, with all participating. Children were encouraged to glean grain during harvest time to help finance the missionary cause. Aaron A. Janzen, pioneer worker in Zaire, related that Wednesdays, the day of the mission society meeting, he and his siblings were not served a regular noon meal but received bread with syrup and milk. Mother did not have time to cook; she had to work at the sewing circle. Missions was more important than a full meal for the children at home.[55]

The mission sale, a special event in the church program, was instituted to translate the societies' work into money for missions. It was a special day. Often it was part of the quarterly festivals in which several church groups united for a full day of mission emphasis. In the Minnesota churches this practice continued until the 1960s. A service of singing, preaching and missionary reports filled the morning. A noon love-feast followed, with the mission sale held in the afternoon or evening. The income from these efforts provided a major part of the mission budget.[56]

**MISSIONARY REPORTS**

The relationship of the missionary to the home churches provided a further dimension for the nurture of mission responsibility. The *Zionsbote* in America and the *Friedensstimme* in Russia served as the echo of the mission needs abroad. The *Zionsbote*, in particular, had the character of a mission paper. Reports of God's moving came directly from the pen of the missionary and were widely known in the churches.

The deputation work of missionaries on furlough centered on personal relationships. They came into the church community for extended periods, visiting people during the day and holding meetings in the evenings. They became an extension of the local church and its families.

CHAPTER 8

# Early Mennonite Brethren Missionaries

The motivation of the early Mennonite Brethren missionaries is reflected in the words of the Apostle Paul: "But none of these things move me, neither count I my life dear unto myself, so that I might finish my course with joy, and the ministry, which I have received of the Lord Jesus, to testify the gospel of the grace of God" (Acts 20:24). The following sketches illustrate the dedication of foreign missions pioneers.[1]

**Abraham Friesen**, son of a wealthy industrialist and partner with his father in the operation of profitable factories and flour mills, could not find peace knowing that millions had never heard the gospel. He was arrested by the words of Jesus: "If any man come unto me, and hate not his father, and mother, and wife, and children, . . . and his own life also, he cannot be my disciple" (Luke 14:26). Leaving position, possessions and the security of a comfortable future, this gifted young man began preparing to evangelize the lost. With the backing of the Russian Mennonite Brethren Church, he and his wife Mary left for India under the American Baptist Missionary Union. The pioneering work of Abraham Friesen in establishing the mission in Nalgonda, India, in 1890 served as the base for the work of the American Mennonite Brethren in India beginning in 1899. Sixteen other Russian Mennonite Brethren missionaries followed during the years 1890 to 1914, when the First World War interrupted Russian support of the India work. Although precise demographics are difficult to establish, it is estimated that by 1910 the membership of the India church, served by missionaries from Russia, numbered three thousand.

**Peter Wedel** was a gifted young man who felt keenly the hand of God upon him. Sensing a call to ministry, he attended the Baptist seminary in Rochester, New York, and became an effective evangelist in Mennonite Brethren circles. At one time the question in Mennonite Brethren churches as to who had been converted through the preaching of Peter Wedel, brought scores of uplifted hands.

Wedel, after a career as a successful itinerant evangelist in North America, began feeling an inner burden for people in other lands who had never heard the gospel. Was it his responsibility to go to them? Was he being called to become a foreign missionary? This struggle tortured him until he finally came to the conclusion, "I must go to bring the gospel to those who have never heard."

At the 1884 conference in South Dakota he shared his concern with the assembled delegates. They were shocked. Not only would they lose their most effective evangelist, but he wanted to go to Cameroon, a country known as a graveyard for white foreigners because of its treacherous climate and raging black fever.

The conference pleaded with him to reconsider. Wedel said he would weigh the matter before God. Evening came. Unable to sleep, he went out into the South Dakota cornfields seeking an answer from God. In the early morning, wet from the dew of the night, he returned to his host's home and tried to sleep a little. When he appeared before the conference later that morning his decision was clear. "I have wrestled with God," he told the assembly. "Obedience supersedes all other opportunities. I cannot but go to the Cameroons."

And to Cameroon he went. Wedel lost no time in starting a Bible school to prepare others to become messengers of God to their own people. But his service lasted only eight months. The severe climate took its toll on his health, and he was advised to return home for medical help. Finally he agreed, and while aboard a ship to Hamburg, black fever overcame him. He died and his body was buried in the Atlantic Ocean. His term of service had been tragically short, but it launched a dramatic movement. Others felt compelled to bring the gospel to those who had not heard. His act of obedience became a cornerstone of Mennonite Brethren foreign missions.

**Heinrich Enns.** The message from Peter Wedel's ocean grave continued to reverberate among the Mennonite Brethren in North America. Heinrich Enns, a well-loved teacher, and his wife Maria suddenly became restless, burdened by the needs far beyond the shores of their chosen homeland. God had spoken to them. Sharing the vision of Peter Wedel they left in 1896 to go to Cameroon under the German Baptist Mission. A large crowd gathered at the railroad station in Mountain Lake, Minnesota, to bid them farewell. Heinrich Voth, elder and leader of the conference, offered a prayer of dedication and farewell. As the prayer concluded and the assembled well-wishers broke into the song, "God be with You Till We Meet Again," the train began to move. Heinrich Enns stood on the steps of the train and spoke one final time to his friends and neighbors. His words rang out above the sound of the train's gathering speed. "If we do not come back, if we must die, then from this group there will have to be others who will follow us in order that people who have not heard may hear."

Perhaps he had a premonition that he too would find his grave in African soil, for he was on the field only seven months when he succumbed to black fever. But his parting words continued to stir the heart of a youth, only fourteen and not yet a believer, who had been part of that crowd at the Mountain Lake station. Aaron A. Janzen was his name.

**Aaron Janzen** grew up in a godly pioneer family, the Aaron F. Janzens. At the age of twenty-three, in a revival meeting in Windom, Minnesota, he experienced personal salvation.  For some time he struggled with the question of his future.  The parting words of Heinrich Enns, which he had heard as a boy several years earlier at the Mountain Lake railroad station, would not leave him.  He surrendered to the wooing of the Spirit of God to become a missionary.

In preparation, he studied at Moody Bible Institute in Chicago and for a short time at the Baptist seminary in Rochester, New York.  He was deeply concerned to find a spouse who would share his ambitious vision.  This he found in Ernestina Strauss, a graduate nurse.  They married and continued their preparations, undaunted by the huge challenge they faced.  When reminded that two earlier missionaries had never returned home, they replied simply: "It is necessary for us to go.  It is not necessary for us to live."

The Mennonite Brethren Church had no missionary program in Africa at that time.  The Congo Inland Mission, an inter-Mennonite society, had just opened a field in 1911 in what was then known as the Belgian Congo (today's Zaire).  The Janzens applied to the mission and were accepted.  There was no guarantee of support or a salary, but friends and acquaintances from North America committed themselves to help as possible.  Such good intentions might be meager currency in the distant jungles of Africa, but it was enough for Aaron and Ernestina Janzen.

They arrived in the Congo in 1912 and were immediately sent on a dangerous pioneering mission to the hostile Balubas tribe.  The hardships were immense, and their lives frequently in jeopardy.  But the Janzens trusted God from day to day.  In time their patient kindness and friendliness broke through and gave entry to this tribe which today is a major force in the evangelization of Zaire.

Within a year on the field they suffered the loss of one of their sons to the fever and treacherous African climate.  Only a few years later their second son also fell victim to the harsh demands of missionary life.  But the Janzens did not waver.

Their declaration–"It is necessary for us to go, it is not necessary for us to live,"–apparently applied also to those dearest to them.

The First World War interrupted their connection with the homeland. Deprived of regular support from home, their subsistence was very difficult. Yet they continued to labor, unable to free themselves of the conviction that they were sent to establish a mission, not only under the Congo Inland Mission, but in the name of the Mennonite Brethren.

In 1920 their commitment to the Mennonite Brethren Church led them to request a release from the Congo Inland Mission. They spent months of travelling and searching, finally sensing a revelation from God that they should establish a mission station in the wildest area of the jungle, known as Kafumba, or "the nest of the elephants." Struggling against unbearable conditions, they finally established a base and in 1926 were able to see the initial fruits of their labor. The first baptism was conducted, and the beginning of a Mennonite Brethren church in Africa was underway.

The following year the Janzens returned home for their first furlough in fifteen years. Their purpose was to seek additional help for the overwhelming needs on the African field. A few years later, other missionaries joined them on a faith mission basis: Martha Hiebert, Katherine Willems, Anna Goertzen and Martha Manz.

The testings for Aaron Janzen were not over. In 1937 his wife, Ernestina, who had faithfully shared his vision and labors, was buried in the soil which earlier claimed their two sons. Now there were three gravestones, but Aaron Janzen pressed on.

Other missionaries also suffered under the continual onslaught of deprivation and fever. Martha Manz, who came out in 1938, soon became ill. When she was advised to return home to seek medical attention, her answer was, "I would rather die in Africa to show people that I love them than to go home." She died in 1941.

Over the years Aaron Janzen repeatedly appealed to the Mennonite Brethren Conference to assume responsibility for the growing success of evangelism in Africa. His concern was not for himself but rather for the future nurture and development of the emerging African church. He had to wait from 1920, when the work began for the Mennonite Brethren, until 1943 for the conference to take this step.

As a pioneer missionary, Aaron Janzen saw clearly that colonial methods would not build a permanent church. His ministry included a threefold program of assistance: He taught the native people how to build a solid agricultural base for their economic survival; he brought them education; and he developed a strong medical program to help the body as well as the soul.

The Africa story cannot omit some mention of Heinrich and Anna Bartsch, who went independently under the Afrika Missions Verein in Canada to assist Aaron Janzen, and later established their own missionary program elsewhere in Africa. The stirring spirit of the Bible schools inspired many to give themselves to this cause, including William and Margaret Baerg, Irwin and Lydia Friesen, John B. and Ruth Kliewer, John C. and Edna Ratzlaff and Anna Enns. These all followed the example and dedication of Aaron Janzen, who left a permanent impact on the missionary staff in Africa.

As General Secretary of the Mennonite Brethren Board of Missions and Services I had an unforgettable experience when visiting the Africa field shortly before Aaron Janzen came home because of failing health and advancing years. One night, while staying in a tent in the heart of the jungle, I awoke and noticed Janzen was gone. Listening quietly I suddenly heard a voice in the distance. Though fearful of the surroundings, I got up and proceeded in the direction of the sound. The veteran missionary, who by now had been on the African continent for more than thirty-five years, was on his knees in the middle of the night crying out: "Oh, God, awaken now the spirit of my brethren at home that the work here in Africa may never cease, that the great church would be built in thy name, and that those in darkness will finally see the gospel."

The year 1956 marked the completion of Aaron Janzen's African sojourn. Along with his second wife, Martha Hiebert, he returned to North America to give his final witness to the home churches. In 1957 God called his faithful servant home.

The church in the Congo of Africa, now called Zaire, has gone through many testings and trials. The turbulent 1960s brought enormous difficulties, and many wondered if the church could survive after the tremendous bloodshed of the revolution. But God nourished the seeds that Aaron Janzen had sown and other missionaries cultivated. Today, many decades after that remarkable beginning, the Mennonite Brethren Church in Zaire numbers 35,000 believers.

**Heinrich Voth.** In 1898, the burning issue at the conference in Winkler, Manitoba, was whether Mennonite Brethren should have their own foreign mission program. Young men and women who had gone out before had done so with the love and support of their own congregations, but were administratively independent of the wider church. Conference leader Heinrich Voth, feeling the burden of this vital issue, preached on the subject of John 10:16: "And other sheep I have, which are not of this fold: them also I must bring." Under the canopy of a huge tent, he spoke powerfully and persuasively. Surely God was urging them to take a step of faith and establish a missionary program in India. Money was scarce, yet the gathered assembly forged ahead under the conviction that "We must follow the assignment of God." They decided to send out Nickolas N. and Susie Hiebert.

On the way home from that historic meeting Heinrich Voth felt keenly the burden of responsibility for the decisions he had helped shape. Riding with his wife Sarah in a horse-drawn buggy, he announced, "Mother, we will need to sell one of our heifers." The Voths had only two heifers and needed both of them to support their large family. "But," his wife protested, "we have children who need milk." Heinrich Voth was quiet. Finally he said, "Mother, we have decided before God to begin the mission program in India and there is no money."

"Which of the two are you going to sell?" Sarah inquired. One was a very promising animal, the other one mediocre. Heinrich answered slowly, "If we give unto God, what do we give, the best or the second best?" The following week the Voths sold their best heifer in order to provide support for the new missionaries to India.

The Hieberts, along with Elizabeth Neufeld, were the first official missionaries to India from the North American church. In less than two years poor health forced the Hieberts to return home. But new recruits followed in quick succession. In 1902 John H. and Maria Pankratz went to India followed by Daniel F. and Tina Bergthold in 1904, Dr. Katharina Schellenberg, the first medical worker, in 1905, and John H. and Maria Voth in 1908.

The conditions they faced were extremely trying. A teeming population and a vastly different culture (some missionaries witnessed human sacrifices to alien gods), plus the usual missionary hazards of an unforgiving climate, insects and reptiles, tested their commitment at every turn. Yet they remained steadfast.

**Daniel Bergthold**, reared on the plains of Kansas, educated at McPherson College and Moody Bible Institute, was appointed conference evangelist in 1901. The next year he married Katharina (Tina) Mantler. Bergthold was one of the rising stars in the conference; his ministry in the churches was widely appreciated. When the question arose: "Where do we have recruits for India?," attention naturally focused on him. Even though he was needed by the conference at home,

Bergthold was approached about his availability for India. He received the inquiry as if it were a divine call: "The will of God, nothing less, nothing more, nothing else, and at all costs." For the Bergtholds, who had an infant child, the question was not a matter of choice or preference, but a matter of obedience. Said Bergthold: "Is God calling, then I answer, yes, without any consideration for self, for preferences, for conveniences, or for advantages that I may have as a servant of God."

Within a year of arriving in India, Katharina died, leaving Bergthold alone with a little child. He soon found another partner in Anna Epp, a missionary from the Russian Mennonite Brethren churches, who was also in India. God blessed this union with several more children. Ten years later, however, Anna was also taken from his side because of the absence of medical care in childbirth. The youngest child died six months later. Despite these personal tragedies and the continuous battle with hostile elements, even threats to his life, Bergthold pressed on heroically.

Bergthold founded the Nagarkurnool Mission Center which soon became known as a center for Bible instruction, and in 1920 became the site of the first India Mennonite Brethren Bible school.

His own bungalow had a unique "prophet's chamber" on the roof where he would slip away each day at dawn. A local boy would sit at the base of the narrow stairway, protecting him from interruptions during his three hours of prayer and study of the Bible. Despite the limited educational advantages before his departure to India, Bergthold became a scholar. He learned Greek and Hebrew, studied Scripture in the original languages, and became an outstanding expositor.

John H. Lohrenz, subsequent missionary to India, identified Bergthold as the first Mennonite Brethren missionary deeply concerned to establish the base for a healthful indigenous church. For this purpose he was interested in economic as well as spiritual development. He offered training in raising gardens and grain, and how to find the proper places for water and irrigation. He was known as one of the first missionaries to concentrate on developing reliable indigenous leadership to carry on the work of the church for the future.

Bergthold spent forty years establishing the church in India. He returned to North America in 1945. His dedication typified many subsequent Mennonite Brethren missionaries to India. Time and again they sacrificed personal goals and comforts in order to focus their entire life on the assignment that had come to them as a command of Jesus. Besides the difficulties of environment, climate and primitive conditions, they often suffered the pain of separated families. With a normal term being seven to eight years, their family life was often disrupted as children had to leave home to attend boarding school for eight months of the year. The sacrifice of a normal family life may have been the severest test of their commitment to the missionary cause.

An incident from the life of John Voth poignantly illustrates this part of the missionary sacrifice. Voth had been home on furlough and was ready to return to India, leaving from the railroad station in Newton, Kansas. One of his daughters, who was to remain behind while her parents resumed their work in a faraway land, was in her father's arms, clutching him tightly as the train pulled into the station. The moment of parting had come. The daughter cried, even screamed. People had to help release him from her clinging arms so he could board. Kissing his child goodbye, Voth entered the train, sat down and buried his face in his hands. His brother, Heinrich S. Voth, who was to accompany him as far as Kansas City, sat silent at his side. Suddenly, overcome by bursting emotion, John Voth sobbed, "Is this what Jesus meant when he said, 'He that loveth more father or mother, brother or sister, wife or children is not worthy of me'?"

The story of Mennonite Brethren missions in India includes ten missionary deaths. Some were victims of accidents, like Herman Warkentin and Eva Kasper and her children; others died from lack of medical attention. Frank Janzen died an excruciating death from deliberate poisoning. The sacrifices, though immense, were not in vain. In 1990 the Mennonite Brethren Church in India, by some estimates, numbered 60,000.

**Frank Wiens**, a farm boy from Henderson, Nebraska, was already an effective evangelist at home yet he sensed a growing vision for a far-off land. The Hakkas, a progressive people among the millions of China, weighed heavily on his heart. The conference was not ready for a mission program to China, but Wiens wondered: "Is not God able to do what the brotherhood cannot?" With enough money to purchase tickets halfway to China, he and his family went as far as Russia. He was sure God would do the rest. God used Wiens in Russia to bring about a renewal in the Mennonite Brethren churches there. His preaching resulted in the conversion of many people. God also provided the money needed to go to China to evangelize the Hakkas.

Wiens's motto was Psalm 18:29–"By Thee I have run through a troop; and by my God have I leaped over a wall." He did manage to leap over the China wall. He attempted the humanly impossible. Together with coworkers who followed, he founded the Mennonite Brethren Church in China. In 1919 the conference accepted China as a Mennonite Brethren mission field.

The Frank Wiens story in China can best be summarized in the words of Paul in 2 Corinthians 11:26-28:

> In journeyings often, in perils of waters, in perils of robbers, in perils of mine own countrymen, in perils by the heathen, in perils in the city, in perils in the wilderness, in perils in the sea, in perils among false brethren; In weariness and painfulness, in watchings often, in hunger and

thirst, in fastings often, in cold and nakedness. Beside those things that are without, that which cometh upon me daily, the care of all the churches.

Clearly, Mennonite Brethren missionaries can take their place in the missionary hall of fame with David Livingstone, Henry Stanley, William Carey and Hudson Taylor. God, through Mennonite Brethren missionaries, has done the humanly impossible. They did not count their lives dear. Could it be, as the twentieth century draws to a close, that God is again calling Mennonite Brethren to set aside their material comforts and give themselves anew to the task of world evangelism?

CHAPTER 9

# Eschatology: Not With One Voice

The Mennonite Brethren understanding of Scripture has historically governed its view of the end times. The Confession of Faith published in 1902 contained only Scripture passages on the matters of Christ's return, second coming and final judgment.[1] It included no interpretation as to the how and when of these events. The center of the confessional eschatology was Christ as supreme Lord who is leading history to its final consummation. The writers and adopting conference were not preoccupied with setting dates or speculating about specific events. They went no further than to echo the words of Jesus: "Watch therefore, for ye know neither the day nor the hour wherein the Son of man cometh" (Matt. 25:13).[2] Abraham H. Unruh was correct when he wrote: "The early brethren exhorted each other to watchfulness and a holy walk. The present views with regard to the rapture and the millennium were apparently foreign to them. However, they joined in the prayer: 'Amen, come Lord Jesus'."[3]

Nonetheless, speculation about the end times generated spirited debate in some circles and produced some awkward aberrations. The matter of an earthly millennium, for example, was pointedly dismissed in this comment by a Mennonite bishop named Isaak Peters:

> On earth Christ has no earthly kingdom, but a spiritual kingdom of grace consisting of His believers. But He possesses a heavenly kingdom of glory, into which He shall in the end lead all His believers. That is the biblical

> teaching of Christ's future [one and only one resurrection, that is a simultaneous resurrection of all men] and also the original Mennonite teaching; for the doctrine concerning a future kingdom of Christ was not accepted in the Mennonite churches until the previous century. Menno Simons never held to the doctrine of a millennium, and he who believes in it is no Mennonite.[4]

Meanwhile, the chiliastic vision of the Pietist Jung-Stilling[5] provided the impetus for the Claas Epp[6] movement resulting in the "Great Trek" of the Russian Mennonites to Central Asia in the 1880s.[7]

The early years of Mennonite Brethren history also record some inroads of the Temple movement (sometimes referred to as Friends of Israel), under the leadership of Johannes Lange. They believed the establishment of the Kingdom of God on earth would be centered in Jerusalem.[8]

Early in the twentieth century Peter M. Friesen expressed distress over the influence that invaded the Mennonite Brethren fellowship via the Blankenburg Alliance Bible Conference in Germany.[9] He worried that their dispensational interpretation of Scripture, with its undue focus on eschatology, obscured the central calling for believers to serve as salt and light in the world.[10] Friesen felt that ecumenical toleration of these views, aimed at preserving long-term unity of all believers, threatened clarity for the church in the present.

> What does God want of us as a group, a fellowship: that we, while calling ourselves Mennonite, become a conglomerate of Lutheran-ism, Baptist, and Plymouthism, etc. (we mean in the understanding and manner of expressing our Christianity)? What is the specific direction that God has assigned to us through our original doctrines, history and the present situation?"[11]

Friesen's concern was particularly notable, given that he normally placed strong emphasis on the unity of all believers and tolerated fellowship at the Lord's Table with those who had not been immersed and were not members of the Mennonite Brethren Church.[12]

## A STRONG ESCHATOLOGICAL CONSCIOUSNESS

A review of eschatological understanding in Mennonite Brethren history reflects a fascinating tension. Mennonite Brethren were passionately interested in the Lord's return and devoted much attention to it. They listened intently as leaders promoted various views imported from other fellowships, allowing some even to get carried away with calendarizing and predicting events. Yet they stopped short of adopting any official positions that went beyond awaiting the second coming with watchfulness and holy living.

An analysis of articles appearing in the *Zionsbote* indicated that no other topic related to the life of the believers church received as much emphasis as eschatology. Between 1884 and 1950 a total of 398 articles were published on the theme of the hope of the Lord's return and events related to it: forty-four before 1910; 176 between 1910 and 1935; and 172 from 1936 to 1950.

In the articles before the mid-1930s, the focus was on the hope of Christ's return as the motivation for holy living and service: "Are we ready for the Lord's coming? Are we a people waiting for the Lord's return?"

The 398 articles were written by a total of 120 authors, but four of the authors were responsible for 153 of the articles: William Bestvater, 62 articles; Peter E. Penner, 35; Nickolas N. Hiebert, 32; and J.J. Neufeld, 24. The writings of 116 authors carried as the central concern an admonition to purity and faithfulness. Likewise the writings of N.N. Hiebert were an admonition to God's people to be faithful and wait for the imminent return of Christ. To some extent the same applied to the writings of P.E. Penner, although he also frequently addressed the how and when of Christ's return. The writers who vigorously promoted a precise sequence of end time events, with details on the when and how, were William Bestvater and J.J. Neufeld.[13]

A common theme in many of these articles was the place of present-day Israel in God's plan for the consummation of history. Most of the writers in the *Zionsbote* understood eschatology in the framework known in Europe as Darbyistic millenarianism, and in North America as dispensationalism.

The Darbyistic hermeneutic came to the Russian Mennonite Brethren chiefly through the Blankenburg Conferences. Jacob W. Reimer, a prophetic voice in Russia and later in Canada, developed his system of interpretation through attendance at these conferences.[14] In the United States, the eschatological perception of a large segment of Mennonite Brethren came from the millenarian dispensational interpretation of fundamentalism, of which William Bestvater was a prominent exponent among the Mennonite Brethren. He had been a student of the legendary Cyrus I. Scofield, and had completely adopted his method of interpreting Scripture. Bestvater's series of thirty articles in the *Christian Leader* between April 1937 and May 1940 offered a comprehensive treatment of dispensational eschatology. A highly effective teacher, he had broad popular appeal to the people of his day. His large chart (twenty feet long and almost seven feet high) laid out the dispensational understanding, including details as to the how and when of future events.[15] Other Bestvater writings on eschatology, in addition to the sixty-two articles in the *Zionsbote* and the thirty in the *Christian Leader*, were his exposition of the Book of Revelation[16] and his text on biblical doctrine which he used while teaching at the Bible school in Herbert, Saskatchewan.[17]

## DIFFERENT LEADERS, DIFFERENT VIEWS

Mennonite Brethren leaders did not speak with one voice

on eschatological matters. While all agreed on the basic issue of the blessed hope, they had significant differences on the "how" and the "when."

**Henry F. Toews**, a graduate of the Baptist seminary in Kansas City, taught at Tabor College from 1910 to 1929. His book *Biblische Grundwahrheiten Heft I* gave a detailed outline of eschatological teachings with the following sequence of events: the rapture, the wedding of the lamb in heaven, the great tribulation on earth, the gathering and conversion of Israel, the conversion of many Gentiles, Christ's return and rule in the millennium, the binding of Satan for one thousand years, the release of Satan and his last rebellion against God, the final judgment of the nations, and the final triumph of Christ in the new heaven and the new earth.[18]

**Jacob W. Reimer**, a leading Mennonite Brethren evangelist and preacher in Russia and later North America, had been a frequent attender of the Blankenburg Conference where he imbibed Darbyistic views. In keeping with the dispensational understanding, he saw the church as a parenthesis and focused heavily on the national restoration of Israel.[19]

**Abraham H. Unruh**, prominent Mennonite Brethren Bible teacher in Winkler and Winnipeg, spoke to the various events of eschatology without following the schematic form of dispensationalism. His most extensive statement on the topic was an outline of the eschatology of the German theologian Adolf von Schlatter, of whom Unruh was an ardent student. Most significant in this analysis was the emphasis that one could not take the words of Jesus and Paul and add Old Testament prophetic utterances to build a conclusive theological scheme. According to Unruh, any scheme built on such a process was as much a matter of personal speculation as it was a reflection of Jesus or Paul.[20] For example, the passage in Romans 11:26–"And so all Israel shall be saved"–did not in Unruh's view suggest a national restoration. As in 2 Chronicles 12:1, "all Israel" referred to the individuals who made up the whole.  God wanted "to save all Israel," but this did not set aside the condition of individual decision (compare Zechariah 12:11-14).  So the place of Israel in God's future plans was not a matter of national restoration but rather depended on personal, individual response to God's provision of redemption.[21]

**Henry W. Lohrenz**, a contemporary of William Bestvater, P.E. Penner, and J.W. Reimer did not write specifically on eschatology except in his wider exegetical exposition of Scripture.  Some of his eschatological thinking, which balanced the more extreme views of some of his contemporaries, can be gleaned from his writings on 1 and 2 Thessalonians, 1 Corinthians 15, and Matthew 24 and 25.[22]

The Sermon on the Mount, which some dispensationalists saw as kingdom ethics applicable to the restoration of the Jewish nation, Lohrenz identified as appropriate for the church in all times.  He treated the eschatological references in Thessalonians in the context of the character and life of the people of God in the light of Christ's expected return.  Likewise, his extensive writings on the resurrection dwelt on Christian character rather than on any timetable of events.  For Lohrenz, the focal point of eschatological interest was clearly the importance of the blessed hope for the life of the church.[23]  On the matter of dispensational certainty he may have held the position of John A. Toews, one of his contemporaries, who stated: "It could be that the unfolding of the eschatological events will follow the timetable of the dispensational chart of William Bestvater and J.W. Reimer.  I would feel much more at ease, however, if these brethren would say 'it could be so' instead of their insistence, 'it will be so'."[24]

A 1907 article by Abram Kroeker, editor of the *Friedensstimme*, entitled "*Die darbystische Gefahr*" (the danger of Darbyistic eschatology) indicated uneasiness with this eschatology in the Mennonite Brethren Church at the turn of the century.  In his concern he pointed to prominent evangelicals of the day–Hudson Taylor, George Miller and A. Baedecker–who had disassociated themselves from the dogmatic eschatology of Darbyism. Kroeker's voice in the early days of this century was strongly representative of the wider Mennonite Brethren fellowship.[25]

## STRONG CENTRAL FOCUS

What does this eschatological ferment, this tolerance of widely divergent views, suggest about the Mennonite Brethren Church before 1950?

First, eschatology clearly occupied a central place in the Mennonite Brethren consciousness. None of the variations related to the central teachings of Scripture: the Lord's return, the rapture of the church, the resurrection of the dead, the judgment, and the consummation of the history of the ages. These truths were fundamental, shared by all, and reflected no variation. The Mennonite Brethren eschatological hope historically was a relational principle with emphasis on holy living and exhortation to be ready for the Lord's return.

Second, the Mennonite Brethren had room for different understandings of the how and when of the Lord's return. They spoke of these variations as "*Erkenntnissfragen*"–levels of understanding–which did not affect the relationship of trust and love within the fellowship. The shared focus on Christ as the center provided room for divergent opinions on the peripheral details of the blessed hope. One incident, widely referred to in conference lore, is telling: William Bestvater was presenting a series of prophetic messages using his large chart, outlining every detail of the events of eschatology. Abraham H. Unruh, who was present at these expositions, finally jested: "Brother William, do you think God will consider the outline on these canvasses in carrying out his plans?" Both men laughed together good naturedly. Their love and regard for each other overrode their differences of interpretation.

It is significant to observe that nearly all of the 398 articles in the *Zionsbote* and forty in the *Christian Leader* were written before 1950. Forty-four articles were written before 1910, 176 between 1910-1935 and 172 between 1936-1950, is important. The stress of world events (World War I and II, the Russian Revolution and severe persecution of the church in Russia) may account for the greater prominence of eschatology in the decades between 1912 and 1950. The absence of major emphasis on the blessed hope for the believer's life in the 1960s and 1970s suggests an important trend that interfaces with other more recent developments.

CHAPTER 10
# Mennonite Brethren at the Turn of the Century

The years 1890-1914, just prior to the First World War, were a period of rapid cultural and economic development for the Mennonite colonies in Russia. The fast growth of the Mennonite Brethren Church forced their integration into surrounding communities. Increasing involvement in education, alternative service and matters of social, civil and public welfare gradually broke down the walls that had kept them isolated.[1]

## MENNONITE BRETHREN IN RUSSIA

### Geographical Expansion

The first fifty years of Mennonite Brethren history was a time when the Chortitza and Molotschna colonies birthed many daughter settlements. Pressured by a burgeoning population, the colonies purchased large tracts of land and made them available to Mennonites who needed land. By 1910 there were thirty new settlements scattered from the Crimea in the south to areas in central Russia, to Samara, Orenburg and Siberia in the northeast and Turkestan in the southeast. Some 4,900 Mennonite families had moved out and established new communities.[2]

Meanwhile, the renewal movement born in the mid-nineteenth century continued. Many from the old church who came to a new life of faith had already sought fellowship in the Mennonite Brethren Church. Now the movement accelerated as pioneering Mennonites who migrated to the new areas broke with their old environment and sought new beginnings, both spiritually and geographically. Thus, geographical expansion contributed to the growth of the Mennonite Brethren Church. The movement toward larger land holdings, particularly in Chortitza and Molotschna, produced large estates with much wealth.³

**Educational Emphasis**

The spirit of progress reflected in the geographical expansion nourished a new appreciation for education. Peter M. Friesen graphically described the Mennonite attitude toward education before the expansion of the colonies:

> Two mortal enemies have constantly threatened our Mennonitism: dull "orthodox" (but not truly believing) obscurantism, hating education; and, superficial and pragmatic rationalism and deism, which ascribe to education the be-all and end-all. The former enemy is like a swamp, and we have wallowed long enough in this nauseating mess.⁴

Cultural and spiritual renewal dramatically altered the perceptions related to education, though it must be noted that a new regard for education had already begun to emerge from the early renewal movements in Ohrloff and Gnadenfeld. The implications of this change in the context of the renewal that gave birth to the Mennonite Brethren Church were again ably expressed by P. M. Friesen:

> We firmly believe that living faith and true knowledge are two forms of the same divine truth. Faith may be regarded as the soul; education as the body–or, as body and garment. Because our fathers in general despised education especially for their ministers, they sank gradually into the "swamp," and rescue came only through the believers of those churches and circles who valued both faith and education highly: through Moravian Brethren, Pietists, and so on. For us who battle for the faith there remains only

one alternative: to win "education" over to the Christian cause and place it into the service of Christ just as Moses and Daniel utilized the "wisdom of the Egyptians and Chaldeans" for the service of Jehovah. Let us inspire our youth in our area of influence for education and art, but let us teach them to know Jesus as "most glorious of all" and as the "fullness of all that is; in whom all fullness dwells."[5]

The concern for education in the context of Christian faith has remained a priority for Mennonite Brethren at home and in their mission abroad.[6]

At the beginning of the twentieth century the Mennonite communities in Russia maintained some four hundred schools, including a school of commerce, thirteen secondary schools, which met the academic standards of the Russian university, intermediate educational institutes for men and women, village schools and estate schools. Village and estate schools were co-educational, staffed by more than five hundred teachers required to be proficient in both Russian and German and qualified to give religious instruction as a central part of the curriculum.

An impressive roster of teachers provided the soul for educational progress. From the 1830s to the 1850s the most notable were Tobias Voth, Heinrich Heese and Heinrich Franz. By the turn of the century the educational giants were such men as Peter Holzricter, Franz Peter Isaak, Johann Braeul, Kornelius Unruh, Abram Goertz, David G. Duerksen and Heinrich P. Unruh.

The code for education prescribed by the legendary Johann Cornies in the mid-nineteenth century remained the standard for Mennonite schools until the Bolshevik Revolution in 1917. The central emphasis was on culture and morals based on intensive instruction in biblical history and catechism. This center, plus strong academic requirements in basic general education, art, memorization and languages, provided a unique character-building discipline. The influence of this system on the emerging Mennonite Brethren was considerable in that many of the leaders, especially the ministers, came from the ranks of Mennonite teachers.

**Publications**

By the turn of the century Mennonites in Russia were producing numerous publications, most of them related to faith, life and history. Collections of published sermons and poetry from this period were noteworthy, though much of this literature was lost in the turmoil of the revolution and the decades that followed.

Mennonite Brethren provided important leadership in the area of publications. The *Christlicher Familien-Kalender*, which appeared in 1897, was the vision of Abram Kroeker, father of the late Martin Kroeker who was prominent in U.S. Mennonite Brethren churches. The *Christliches Jahrbuch* (*Christian Almanac*) for the years 1900-1905 was also the child of Abram Kroeker. In 1903 Abram and Jakob Kroeker, as editors and publishers, launched *Friedensstimme*. They also published *Das Erntefeld*, launched by missionary A.J. Friesen in 1900. This paper, edited by Friesen until 1914, told the story of the Russian Mennonite Brethren mission in India. The voluminous work of P. M. Friesen, *Alt-Evangelische Mennonitische Brüderschaft in Russland (1789-1910)*, had its origin in the Mennonite Brethren Church.

**Economics and Industry**

Many Mennonites had become wealthy by the turn of the century. Their agricultural achievements were particularly notable. In pure-bred animal husbandry, for example, government officials, other non-Mennonite colonists and their Russian neighbors recognized the Mennonites as a model for agricultural development.

They were also known for their efficiency as tradesmen. Blacksmiths, joiners, wheelwrights, cobblers, saddlers, tailors, weavers, cloth workers and millers were an integral part of the communities. Early in their history the Russian Mennonites developed considerable self-sufficiency, and became an integrated economic unit with a strong system of exports and imports.

They developed industries to complement agricultural production. Seven factories produced agricultural tools and implements. Eighteen brick and roof-tile manufacturers provided building materials for the colonies' growing needs. Mennonites owned twenty-seven large motor and steam flour mills, many windmills and factories that produced wall clocks. Taxable property owned by the Mennonites in 1909 was valued at 246 million rubles–an enormous sum for that day and even for our day.

Many Mennonite Brethren were among these prosperous owners of large estates, factories, flour mills and farms. Others were prominent in the field of education and held leading positions in the affairs of all the Mennonite communities.

## Public Charitable Institutions

The material wealth of the Mennonite colonies financed the institutions needed for the care of their people. They had their own hospitals, a deaconess home, a school for the deaf and mute, senior citizen's homes, an orphanage and a psychiatric hospital. The maintenance of these institutions was the responsibility of the communities.

## An All-Mennonite General Conference

The *Kirchliche* Mennonites had over the years been open to Mennonite Brethren participation in various mutual events and institutions. The tensions rooted in the withdrawal of the Mennonite Brethren from the old church and the injuries resulting from it, gradually lessened. In 1910 the General Conference, renamed as "The General Conference of the Mennonite Ministry," marked the official participation of the Mennonite Brethren in deliberations related to concerns to all groups of Mennonites in Russia. One-third of the delegation was Mennonite Brethren. The two major groups of Mennonites in Russia recognized each other as equals and established a working relationship that previously had been much less than compatible. They formed a continuation committee for this ongoing inter-Mennonite relationship. According to the testimony of Mennonite Brethren in prominent leadership, even their more conservative members felt at ease. They had found true Christian fellowship with members of the old church.[7]

With the beginning of World War I in 1914, however, new tensions arose between the two groups. A group of influential leaders questioned the eligibility of Mennonite Brethren for military exemption and other privileges contained in the original charter given to the Mennonites by the Russian government. The Mennonite Brethren, they said, had violated the conditions of the charter by engaging in continuous religious propaganda–evangelizing Russian people. The intensity of this conflict was reflected in a document written by P.M. Friesen under the title *Konfession oder Sekte* (Confession or Sect).[8] A second obstacle in the relationship arose when members of the *Kirchliche* sought an official government decree forbidding baptism in the open, as practiced by Mennonite Brethren.

The Mennonite Brethren reacted strongly to these charges. To be called propagandists was to attack their commitment to be witnesses to the saving power of the gospel. A lengthy document submitted to the government brought clarity in the matter.

This incident notwithstanding, the conflict, accusations and counter accusations between the Mennonite Brethren and the *Kirchliche* greatly diminished during the half-century since

1860. The Mennonite Brethren, though sincere in their 1860 decision to withdraw, must nonetheless assume their share of responsibility for the tensions that existed between the two groups for so many years. Peter M. Friesen wrote with pain about the shortcomings of the Mennonite Brethren in their relationship to the *Kirchliche*. He particularly denounced their sin of artificial piety in refusing to recognize and fellowship with the many true believers in the Mennonite Church. Some in the Mennonite Church, Friesen says, displayed Christian meekness and humility in contrast to a holier-than-thou attitude of rejection on the part of the Mennonite Brethren.[9]

**MENNONITE BRETHREN SPIRITUAL LIFE**

By World War I the Mennonite Brethren in Russia had come of age. The sometimes persecuted minority had become a recognized entity in the larger Mennonite community. They had attained the status of equality and comprised one-third of the communities scattered over the various colonies born in the expansion. Strong and prominent leadership emerged in such men as Jacob Reimer, David Duerksen, David Schellenberg, Peter Bergmann, Isaak Koop, P. M. Friesen and Isaak Friesen. The itinerant ministry of David Duerksen, Jacob Reimer and David Schellenberg extended to the Mennonite Brethren churches in North America and Poland, and to other Russian Mennonite churches as well. Such ministry provided stability in faith and polity.[10]

This was a period of rich congregational life for the Mennonite Brethren as members, particularly those in ministry, sought diligently to practice the admonition of Ephesians 4:3, "Endeavoring to keep the unity of the spirit in the bond of peace." Those who strayed from biblical standards were admonished in a spirit that promoted reconciliation. Meetings of church councils and congregations reflected commitment and unity. The growing missionary movement generated a deep consciousness of purpose. This did not mean, however, that the church was without testings and trials.[11]

### Change in Leadership Style

A failure to heed the exhortation of 1 Peter 5:8–"Be sober and vigilant, because your adversary, the devil, as a roaring lion walketh about, seeking whom he may devour"–led to unhappy circumstances affecting some in leadership. David Schellenberg, the leading elder in Rückenau, was removed because his lifestyle did not meet the scriptural standards for the position. Similar circumstances developed in the church in Einlage.[12]

Questions also arose over the centralized authority vested in the eldership. In the early years of the twentieth century the style of leadership in the Molotschna changed from that of a presiding elder to a multiple leadership in which a group of leaders assumed the duties previously vested in one person.[13] The Chortitza churches followed suit soon after.

### Struggling with Intermarriage

Much agitation arose in the churches with regard to marriages where one party was not Mennonite Brethren. In the early years, prospective members promised, as a condition of membership, not to marry a non-Mennonite Brethren. Those who violated this pledge were excommunicated. Such restrictions in a socially integrated community created an extreme problem, and the resulting tensions were highly divisive. In 1895 the convention brought unity in this matter by agreeing to examine each case individually to distinguish between marriage with unbelievers or with believers who were members of the Mennonite Church.[14]

### The Influence of Pietism

While the birth of the Mennonite Brethren Church owed much to Pietism in the mid-1800s, another set of Pietist influences came at the turn of the century. This time the channel was a group of wealthy Mennonite Brethren estate owners in Russia who independently supported certain itinerant ministers not under the sponsorship of the church conference. One of these ministers was Dr. Fredrich W. Baedekker from the Plymouth Brethren Alliance Conference in England. He travelled extensively in Mennonite Brethren circles, spreading the dogmatic dispensationalism of John Nelson Darby, founder of the Plymouth Brethren movement.[15] These wealthy estate owners also organized and financed conferences for the benefit of ministers and church workers, with all expenses paid.

The points of commonality between Pietists and Anabaptists provided a favorable climate for this close relationship. Robert Friedmann described the similarities as follows:

> Both groups justified their policy on the basis of the leadership of the Holy Spirit, which taught them the correct understanding of the Scriptures. Both claimed to live strictly according to the Bible, that is, neither had confidence in a Christianity of the theologians and scholars. Both were seriously concerned with a Christian reality which lies beyond church and worship although they understand the ultimate nature of this Christian reality differently. After all how could it be determined who possessed the "right" Holy Spirit except through the evidences of the same in life.[16]

Pietistic writings became part of Mennonite Brethren libraries in Russia. The book *Wahres Christentum* by Johann Arndt was especially prominent.[17]

Pietistic influence on the Mennonite Brethren remained strong up to the First World War. Jacob Kroeker, one of the few theologically trained Mennonite Brethren at the time, affiliated closely with the Blankenburg Alliance Conference and provided a Mennonite linkage with the Alliance movement in

Western Europe. The Blankenburg Conference, of which F.W. Baedekker was the major architect, had been established in 1885 and became the center for the European movement of the Plymouth Brethren.

The Plymouth Brethren professed to have no creeds, for fear of honoring human opinions too highly (yet the writings of Darby and other leaders were themselves dogmatic). They placed strong emphasis on the inner spiritual life, sanctification, fellowship and prophecy. Baedekker typified the majority of the speakers at these conferences. He was not a theologian, nor did he see much value in serious theological inquiry. He was a charismatic personality and a gifted pastor. He gave unreservedly and spent much of his time in serving the prison population throughout Russia, even into the most remote Siberian labor camps. For Baedekker, the truth that "God loves you" took the place of any effort at theological dialogue.

Other teachers at the Blankenburg conferences who worked closely with Baedekker were General von Viebahn, Otto Stockmayer, Frederick B. Meyer, Ernst Gebhardt and Ernst F. Stroeter. Erich Beyreuther observed that the teaching at Blankenburg was one-sided and not always in accordance with healthy or generally recognized hermeneutical principles.[18]

Baedeker served frequently at the prolonged Bible conferences sponsored by wealthy land owners in the Molotschna at Steinbach, Apanlee and Vorwerk Juschanlee. Pietists considered him to be an authority in the exposition of Scripture. Among Mennonite Brethren, Stroeter was probably the second most influential person from the Blankenburg circle. He held repeated Bible studies of one or two weeks for teachers and ministers. But his influence did not last long because he became a universalist.

Mennonite Brethren ministers used the writings of other Blankenburg people such as Viebahn, Meyer and Stockmayer widely. According to the late Henry Cornelsen, Coaldale, Alberta, these publications were a primary resource for ministers of the tradition.[19]

Jacob Kroeker's position as a member of the Blankenburg board of directors permitted leaders of Mennonite Brethren fellowships to attend the Blankenburg conferences on a regular basis. Jacob W. Reimer, highly recognized as a Bible teacher in Mennonite Brethren circles, was a frequent attender.[20]

This close contact with the Pietistic movements in England and the continent were not without far-reaching effects upon the Mennonite Brethren. Most visibly, it bolstered the position in the 1902 Confession of Faith that recognized all true born again believers, irrespective of organizational and confessional affiliation, as brothers and sisters in Christ. This strong inter-confessional position was a source of serious tension, since many of the culturally isolated Mennonites in Russia felt threatened by the prospect of closer fellowship with believers from other confessions.

Jacob W. Reimer, called the pioneer of Alliance movements among the Mennonite Brethren, offered untiring leadership in relating to believers of other groups and vigorously taught the oneness of all true believers. The forming of the Alliance Mennonite Brethren fellowship in Lichtfelde, Molotschna (1905), later called the *Lichtfelder Gemeinde*, must be accepted as a direct result of the influence of Blankenburg. This influence, even though strongly resisted by the majority of Mennonite Brethren, paved the way for a more conciliatory relationship between fellow believers in the Mennonite world.

The periodical *Das Allianz Blatt* enlarged the growing sense of the oneness of all believers and openness to other fellowships. Published in Germany during the first quarter of the century, it circulated widely in Mennonite Brethren homes.

Blankenburg also affected the long and difficult struggle

over open and closed communion. Jacob W. Reimer met severe opposition for his effort to widen the fellowship of the Mennonite Brethren by accepting believers not baptized by immersion. In fact, a resolution to excommunicate him was introduced at a Ruekenau conference (just prior to the outbreak of the First World War). But the love and warmth of Reimer's testimony, and his insistence that even severance would not diminish his concern for his opponents, stayed the resolution.[21] Thus it can be said that the resolution passed at the Mennonite Brethren convention in Winnipeg in 1963 to allow non-immersed believers into the membership of the church has a long history dating back to the contact of the Mennonite Brethren with the Blankenburg Conference and the Pietistic movements of Western Europe between 1890 and 1914.[22]

While much good can be said for this positive Pietistic impact, other strains of influence were less beneficial. The Darbyistic system of scriptural interpretation with its tight eschatology also came to the Mennonite Brethren through Blankenburg. Jacob W. Reimer, the prophetic voice in eschatology both in Russia and Canada, developed his basic system of interpretation through his contacts with the Darbyistic movement.

Another unhappy consequence was felt in the Mennonite Brethren peace witness. Pietism, with its emphasis on personal salvation, the fellowship of all true believers, and eschatology, remained rooted in the state church in Germany and the confessional church in England. The Anabaptist concepts of discipleship with lifestyle implications and love for enemies remained peripheral for them, despite their emphasis on sanctification. National patriotism and unconditional obedience to the state were part of their basic theological orientation. The German Pietists were said to have followed the slogan, "When it comes to war, then we shoot." Their loyalty to Kaiser and country took precedence to the love ethic of Jesus.

Jacob Reimer and Jacob Friesen (who received his theological training in Germany) became important advocates of armed self-defense (the *Selbstschutz*) in 1918-1922. The crucial meeting at Ruekenau, in 1917, which led to the departure of the Russian Mennonites from their historic position of nonparticipation in war, must be recognized as one of the impacts of Pietism on basic Mennonite theology and ethics. It was the judgment of Benjamin B. Janz that the Mennonites in Russia would not have departed from their historic peace position had it not been for the leadership of Mennonite Brethren influenced by the Alliance movement of Europe.[23]

It must also be recognized, however, that strong support for military self-defense came from other quarters as well. Some of the wealthy landowners who in the pre-revolution era had sponsored the Blankenburg Bible conferences now also supported the *Selbstschutz*. The German culture and educational programs of the Russian Mennonites offered them a broad sphere of compatibility and influence with the German occupation army in the Ukraine, 1917-1920. It also encouraged military collaboration. The absence of any legal government following the Russian Revolution and the roaming hordes of lawless marauders who murdered, plundered and destroyed at will, offered circumstantial pressures for theological compromise.[24]

The theological openness of the Alliance movement laid a base for other tensions. The legalistic trend in the Mennonite Brethren fellowship was partially a reaction to the greater ethical liberty that the Pietistic Alliance movement left in its wake. According to B.B. Janz and A.H. Unruh, confusion also resulted from the Pietistic freedom for personal, individual interpretation of Scripture in contrast to the Anabaptist understanding of corporate discernment.

## The Influence of Baptists

The relationship of the Mennonite Brethren with the Baptists has been substantial. In the years following 1860 strong Baptist connections influenced church polity.[25] This contact may also have provided a point of reference for the early Mennonite Brethren when they faced questions regarding the form of baptism.

This fraternal relationship grew stronger as a result of an early cooperative program with the American Baptist Missionary Union. From 1889 to 1914 eighteen Mennonite Brethren missionaries from Russia served in India under this arrangement. The early foreign missions movement in North America also received directives through this relationship. Mennonite Brethren missions patterned their methods and policies after Baptist programs for the first sixty years.

Early Mennonite Brethren missionaries, with few exceptions, received their training in Baptist schools: the German Baptist Theological Seminary of Hamburg-Horn for those from Russia, Rochester Seminary for the North Americans. Consequently the theology, strategy and methods used by Mennonite Brethren missions were largely adopted from the Baptists without an independent study of Scripture or an attempt to formulate a theology of mission rooted in Anabaptist distinctives.

A positive result of the Baptist influence was their nurture of missionary vision and responsibility, as well as their contributions in evangelism and Christian education. For a number of years Mennonite Brethren resources and inspiration in these areas came largely from Baptist sources.

## MENNONITE BRETHREN IN NORTH AMERICA
### Expansion and Growth

Mennonite Brethren in North America at the turn of the century were expanding to new frontiers. The original settlements in the 1870s proved inadequate for the subsequent growth of these communities. Mennonite Brethren in Minnesota, South Dakota, Nebraska and Kansas moved south to

Oklahoma, west to Colorado, Oregon and California, and north to North Dakota, Montana, Manitoba and Saskatchewan. In all of these new settlements they established congregations. The number of churches increased. By 1909 there were sixty-five congregations with 4,725 members in North America.[26]

**Major Concerns**

General Conference minutes from 1890 to 1910 reflect four major concerns: missions, both home and foreign; the question of ethics; church polity; and education. Progress in missions was the central concern. The itinerant ministry, known as home missions, generated rapid growth as new churches were established. The new churches, frequently with inadequate leadership, struggled with consistency between spiritual profession and life; the code of ethics adopted by many churches emerged from the circumstances of their environment. The rulings of the conference–the corporate fellowship–became the standard of conduct. Philippians 3:15-16–"let us walk by the same rule, let us mind the same thing"–was seen as a hallmark of a true New Testament church. The many issues on church polity related to their view of the church as a mutually responsible fellowship of believers.

There were limited educational opportunities for Mennonite Brethren at that time. Those wanting advanced training in 1890 had no alternative but to attend schools outside the Mennonite Brethren fold. Responding to the urgent need, John F. Harms in 1892 established a small Bible school at Lehigh, Kansas. There was a second attempt to open a school in the Inman-Buhler area of Kansas under the leadership of John F. Duerksen. An affiliation with nearby McPherson College in 1899 was the first step toward a secondary education for Mennonite Brethren. Many of the leaders who emerged in the early 1900s got their training at McPherson College under the influence of J.F. Duerksen. In 1901 and

1902 the conference took steps towards a school that would meet the specific needs of Mennonite Brethren. In 1908, with the founding of Tabor College in Hillsboro, Kansas, this became a reality.[27]

### Change of Leadership

A turning point in the coherent articulation of Mennonite Brethren faith and practice was noticeable in the early years of the twentieth century. The leadership of Heinrich Voth, Abraham Schellenberg, Johann Voth and Johann Regehr was succeeded by younger leaders like Henry W. Lohrenz, Peter C. Hiebert, Nickolas N. Hiebert, Martin M. Just, Heinrich S. Voth, Johann Pankratz and Daniel Bergthold. The more advanced educational preparation of these leaders and the general maturing of the church in North America provided a new dynamic that was reflected in conference records and in the content of the *Zionsbote*, the conference periodical.

### Confession of Faith

In 1902 the Russian and North American Mennonite Brethren joined in adopting a new Confession of Faith, thus providing a written form of belief and practice heretofore not available. The first English edition was printed in 1917.[28]

Their understanding of being a separated people in the world, however, continued to express itself in isolationism. They maintained their prohibitions against marrying "outsiders" (including General Conference Mennonites).[29] The North American Mennonite Brethren also continued closed communion, making immersion baptism a condition of participation.

As late as 1897 the conference ruled unanimously that members should not take out life insurance. To do so meant a lack of trust in the provision of God and the church.[30] As late as 1915 they ruled against participation in the Mennonite Mutual Aid Union, thereby refusing a corporate relationship with other Mennonite groups[31] and reaffirming their characteristic isolationism. The American Mennonite Brethren, as a small group, felt threatened by any influence from the outside. They remained ultra-conservative and more legalistic than their Russian counterparts.

A major step of the North American conference at the close of the nineteenth century was to establish their own structure for administering foreign missions and thus end the need for their missionaries to serve under non-Mennonite Brethren societies.[32]

CHAPTER 11

# Summary Observations to Part One

The preceding ten chapters on the early Mennonite Brethren Church give occasion for some summary observations. The main source for a study of the early Russian Mennonite Brethren story is the voluminous work of Peter M. Friesen, a history based on the experiences and perceptions of people who were vitally involved in the actual struggle of the mid-nineteenth century. For them, objectivity was impossible. Friesen acknowledged this by saying, "What we have written . . . in a large part of the book is not 'history'; it is a statement of the subjective viewpoints of a contemporary; it is made up of 'chronicles' and 'memoirs' which will have to await the objective analysis of future historians."[1] The sympathies and antipathies of the contemporaries of that era encumbered objective analysis.

## ANSWERING THE "WHY" QUESTION

Friesen's major focus was on the "how" of the events with an under-emphasis on the "why." But the burden of time also requires us to focus on the "why."

The early Mennonite Brethren saw themselves as the bearers of the Anabaptist movement, an echo from the sixteenth century. The relationship of 1860 to 1525 has been well established. Cornelius J. Dyck referred to the 1860 event as "1525 Revisited."[2] John A. Toews, in *A History of the Mennonite Brethren Church*, provided further analysis of the linkage between the two movements.[3]

But the Mennonite Brethren were not alone in seeking new levels of spiritual experience. The 1860 event was only one link in a chain of calls for renewal. The emergence of the *Kleine Gemeinde* in 1812-1819, under the leadership of Klaas Reimer, was a forerunner to 1860.[4] It was a cry for new life which could not fully emerge for lack of qualified leadership. In 1853 and 1854 the hunger for new vitality sparked a religious awakening in Neu-Kronsweide.[5] Peter M. Friesen's chapter on "Unrest and Reform Efforts" in the Molotschna churches described a groundswell of yearning for new life.[6] The soul agony in the Mennonite Church at the time was poignantly articulated by an elder of the Ohrloff Mennonite Church: "There is no fear of God, no faithfulness or honesty in the land. . . . The keepers of Zion see it and remain silent.... Are all the keepers blind? . . . Do they hate discipline and order? 'Let them go their way for they are blind leaders'."[7]

This movement for reform in the old church continued into the twentieth century. The formation of the "Alliance" movement in 1905, which did not demand immersion baptism as a condition of membership, resulted in a new exodus from the old church. The statement of Franz Martens, elder of the Altona Mennonite Church at Sagradovka, who affiliated with the Alliance group in 1907, bears a tone similar to the 1860 secession document:

> Already for some years the majority of the ministers of the Nikolaifeld Mennonite Church of Sagradovka shared the understanding and conviction that our Mennonite churches had, in many points, departed from our Confession of Faith (and especially from God's Word), and that there was a need for a serious and thorough reform in respect to the administration of baptism, the Lord's Supper, and evangelical church discipline. Those ministers who longed for spiritual life in the church had for many years already pointed to the abuses and had pressed for reform in order that our church practices would conform with the

teaching and confession handed down to us by our forefathers. Everyone who loves truth must admit that this is presently not the case. This is also the reason why those dear ministers, who love to preach the Gospel with their whole heart, come into conflict with their consciences whenever it comes to the most solemn of church practices, such as baptism, communion, excommunication and acceptance into church membership. . . . Is this not the main reason why in the last forty years, most of those who have been awakened to a new life have left the Mennonite churches? Does not the Mennonite Brethren Church in its confession [1902] stress: "that their organization does not annul the Confession of Faith of other Anabaptist Mennonites in Russia, but that they protest against the church practices of these churches? All preaching and writing against "separation" will remain fruitless since the Bible under certain circumstances, commands separation (2 Cor. 6:14ff).[8]

The growth of the Mennonite Brethren came from the renewal movement within the old church in Russia as well as in North America. The beginning of the Mennonite Brethren churches in Hillsboro and Goessel, Kansas, in 1880 and 1882 followed the pattern of 1860. Groups of people who were converted in the French Creek and the Alexanderwohl Mennonite churches did not find nurture in existing congregations.[9]

Nineteenth-century Mennonitism, in both Russia and North America, hungered for a new vitality, an energizing piety, more intentional conversion and a renewed discipleship. In Russia P.M. Friesen thought that "the good house of Menno had become practically desolate and empty and was about to collapse."[10] The old church, however, resisted the new currents sweeping through the Russian Mennonite colonies. Secession rather than reform, schism rather than co-operation became necessary as the differing currents carried Mennonites towards differing kinds of faith understandings. For the Mennonite Brethren, being born again of the Spirit was a requirement for biblical faith. They hungered for a personal experience of salvation that stood in contrast to what they thought had become a *Volkskirche*.

## Human Failure and God's Mercy

The Mennonite Brethren were not without blemish in their departure from the institutional church. Their sweeping condemnation of the old church in the secession document reflected a judgmental spirit that came to typify them in the early days. This spirit of judgment was fed by the addition of other disgruntled defectors from the old church. No doubt this self-righteous "holier than thou" attitude has been a grievance to the Holy Spirit. Even so the Mennonite Brethren Church by the beginning of the twentieth century encompassed nearly twenty-five percent of all the Mennonites in Russia.[11] In North America they grew from a small nucleus of two hundred in 1875 to 4,700 by 1909.[12] Their commitment to nurturing the inner life in Bible studies, worship, fellowship and discipline attracted other Mennonites who found new life in personal conversion. In their fervor of evangelism and missions they were a burning flame used of God, despite their human frailties.

The wounded feelings between the two groups showed signs of healing by the beginning of the twentieth century. The pains of birth, the struggle for legitimacy and their search for theological identity moved towards resolution. The 1902 Confession of Faith gave coherence to their understanding of soteriology and ecclesiology, the two issues at the center of the renewal struggle.

## Shaped by Outside Influences

The theological openness of the early Mennonite Brethren

Church to outside influences left both negative and positive imprints. Pietism was a positive influence when it emphasized personal salvation and the fellowship of all true believers. The "benefit" of its rigid eschatology is open to question. More visibly negative was Pietism's casual approach to whole-life discipleship and the peace teachings of Jesus. Furthermore, Pietism was rooted in the state churches of Germany and England; national patriotism and unconditional obedience to the state were part of their basic theological orientation. This influence diluted the long-standing peace stance of the Mennonites. The subsequent impact on North American Mennonite Brethren became a major factor in their identity struggle during much of the mid-twentieth century.

What cannot be discounted, however, is the missionary vision and motivation that Pietism brought to the Russian Mennonites and which provided the heartbeat for the Mennonite Brethren movement. If growth had come only from within the Mennonite communities, the missionary outreach, which became a central purpose for their being, might not have occurred or possibly with less fervor.

**Amazing Grace**

What, then, is the answer to the question of "why" all these events and stirrings transpired in the nineteenth-century Russian Mennonite community? It certainly can be seen as a people returning to the missionary assignment that was so central to the Anabaptists of the sixteenth century and the New Testament church of the first century.

Paul's word of 2 Corinthians 4:7–"We have this treasure in earthen vessels, that the excellency of the power may be of God and not of ourselves"– can be claimed by many renewal movements. Though earthen vessels, fragile and inadequate, with many flaws and imperfections, the early Mennonite Brethren nonetheless became the catalyst to call people back to faithfulness in belief, walk and service.

CHAPTER 12

# In the Shadow of the Russian Revolution

The concluding chapter of Section II, "The Early Mennonite Brethren Church," addressed the "why" of faith and practice. Section III, "The Mennonite Brethren in a Time of Transition," does not fully chronicle the events emerging from the political and social panorama of the twentieth century. That story is well described in the book, *Czars, Soviets and Mennonites*.[1] Author John B. Toews introduces the era with the statement: "Discontinuity characterizes the Russian Mennonite experience during the first half of the twentieth century."[2] Mennonites during the first 140 years in Russia nurtured their homogeneity and perpetuated themselves as a self- contained community, only to be uprooted and nearly destroyed in the decades that followed.

The changes that engulfed the Mennonites were numerous. The previously cold relations between the Mennonite Brethren and the Mennonite Church became increasingly warmer. After fifty years of tension, that development played no small role in the survival of the Mennonite community in Russia during the years that followed.

The isolation of this ethnic people, guests in a foreign land, came to an end with the beginning of the First World War (1914-1918). Twelve thousand men from the colonies were inducted into civilian public service. Half served with the Red Cross to care for soldiers wounded on the battlefields; the other half served in the forest industry of the Russian Empire. This exposure to a world beyond the homogeneous confines of the colonies changed the course of Mennonite life in Russia.³

It was also the first time Mennonites faced the trauma of war so closely. The revolution of 1917 brought an abrupt stop to the peaceful life in the colonies of southern Russia. Floodwaters of horror drenched the Mennonite communities. Numerous publications have detailed the terror that befell them during this time.⁴ The German occupation from April to November of 1918 provided temporary relief.⁵ But the rampant anarchy prior to the occupation and the danger that lurked with the withdrawal of these forces, set the stage for a historic test of the Mennonites' commitment to their long-held profession of nonresistance. Life and property were at stake. More and more Mennonites took personal responsibility to protect life and possessions rather than cling to a peace position that seemed inadequate, given their deplorable treatment at the hands of plundering bandits. This would lead to one of the most unusual developments in four hundred years of Anabaptist history–the formation of a Mennonite self-defense army.

They did not reach the decision easily. The minutes of the Lichtenau all-Mennonite Conference of July 1-2, 1918 shed some light on the process.⁶ Extensive debate revealed a sharp division in the delegation. Those favoring the formation of a self-defense unit under German military leadership sought to differentiate between self-defense and military aggression. The other segment urged abiding by the teachings of Jesus and trusting divine providence for protection. Two days of debate produced two different resolutions.

> *Resolution One:* The All-Mennonite Conference abides with the confession of nonresistance as held heretofore. It recognizes the basis of this position exemplified in the life of Christ while in his earthly pilgrimage and commanded in his Word. It recommends, however, to the local churches not to bind the conscience of some members

in their fellowship who vary in their understanding on this position.⁷

*Resolution Two:* The Conference recognizes that the nonresistant position, held by our forbears, expresses the highest perfection of the character of the heavenly Kingdom taught and exemplified by Jesus and that this disposition provides the basis for our Confession of Faith which requires abstinence from all and any participation in armed conflict. In consideration that not all individuals have attained to this high standard of Christian character to accept the consequences which such a position implies, the Conference believes that our churches do not have the right to demand of all its members to decline the bearing of arms.⁸

A majority of the delegates voted to support resolution one, which upheld the principle of peace but left room for deviation. A careful reading of the debate preceding this vote shows that the historical Mennonite Brethren criterion–"What does the Bible say?"–was no longer central. In the face of serious stress and danger, the concern for the ethics of Jesus was set aside.

The occasion reflected a crisis in Mennonite Brethren biblical interpretation. Traditionally, they had viewed Scripture as a progressive unfolding of truth, with Christ as the culmination of divine revelation. The New Testament stood above the Old Testament. Church doctrine and ethics were bound by the New Testament. Yet Mennonite Brethren who participated in the Lichtenau debate testified that their own leaders spoke approvingly for armed self-defense, invoking the example of Abraham's rescue of Lot (Genesis 14). Benjamin B. Janz blamed this hermeneutical departure on the years of Mennonite Brethren participation in the Pietistic Blankenburg Alliance Bible Conferences.⁹ For whatever reasons, the result was that self-preservation with the weapons of war took precedence over faithfulness to the teachings of Jesus. The consequences were far-reaching. The Mennonites lost both their right of exemption from military service and their historic witness.[10]

**Anarchy and Starvation**

The occupying German forces withdrew in November, 1918. The Mennonite *Selbstschutz* (self-defense corps) proved inadequate. During the winter of 1919-1920 Mennonite colonies fell prey to the terrorizing anarchist bands of Nestor Makhno. A survivor from a village in the Sagradovka colony described the carnage:

> Nearly everybody in our village was struck down or murdered–old men of eighty as well as infants of a few weeks. This terror lasted from 7 to 8 o'clock, and during that time ninety-six persons were killed. After the bandits had robbed us of all our money and such personal belongings as they could carry with them they set fire to the buildings and departed for the other villages.[11]

According to John B. Toews, "the mutilations perpetrated by the bandits were particularly gruesome and mindless. It was violence for the sake of violence."[12] The movement of the White and Red armies–the Ukraine being the major theater of the civil war–spread typhus, venereal disease and cholera in epidemic proportions. The Chortitza Colony, with a pre-war population of 15,000, was most severely affected, recording a casualty list of seven thousand. Of the remaining eight thousand, 1,200 died of typhus.[13] Plundering by the warring armies and the communist government that followed, plus the natural disaster of extreme drought, caused the complete collapse of the economic structure. The result was widespread famine in Russia.[14]

Vast numbers of Mennonites were completely demoralized. The large relief operation mounted by the Mennonite churches from North America and Holland was the only ray of light in the dense darkness of despair.[15] Light and darkness were in intense conflict. The Spirit of God and the forces of wickedness struggled for the hearts of a people who professed to be heirs of the dynamic spiritual movement of the sixteenth-century Anabaptists. David M. Hofer, an American Krimmer Mennonite Brethren leader who visited the colonies in the early 1920s, noted that the "people became bitter, hard and cruel toward their own brothers. The spiritual and moral life of the people was in shambles."[16]

**Spiritual Renewal**

Material prosperity before the war no doubt also had impacted their spiritual vitality. Dietrich Doerksen and Peter Kornelsen, writing from Russia to America, noted that "while life in general was still like a colorful apple on the outside, it showed decay on the inside. Such virtues as humility, simplicity, compassion and selflessness were replaced by such vices as pride, extravagance, uncharitableness and selfishness."[17]

The persecutions and hardships of the civil war and its aftermath brought a revival of spiritual concern to the churches. Countless hearts turned to God, crying, "Lord help, lest we perish."[18] Renewal sprang forth in many Mennonite settlements. Jacob A. Loewen, a contemporary observer, described one such awakening:

> Suddenly, there was lightning and thunder in the spiritual sense. The Word of God struck mightily. Even many of the strong men and women were overwhelmed by the Word. . . . Thirty-six souls were saved. . . . At one point during the meeting nearly the entire congregation stood on its feet. Many were weeping and wailing; others were throwing their arms around one another, asking each oth-

er for pardon. Here and there people simply cried to God for forgiveness, while elsewhere they shouted praises to the Lord. Still others sang quietly among themselves, literally causing an audible sense of the movement.[19]

A letter from Gerhard Doerksen to minister Jakob Thiessen described the moving of God in the village of Alexanderthal, Molotschna:

> During these last days we are under the distinct impression that the Spirit of God is at work among us, that the field is white for harvest, and that the Lord has given us a wide, open door. There is a moving in our midst. The meetings are crowded, sometimes overcrowded. In deep humility we ask ourselves: "Lord, what is it that you would have us do?" This evening after prayer meeting several of us brothers stayed together for awhile and were clearly directed by the Holy Spirit to invite you, dear brother Thiessen, with these words, "Come over and help us." We anticipate special blessings from the Lord; but he still needs messengers to bring those blessings. Who will be that messenger of peace for us?[20]

The revivals brought cleansing for the Mennonite people in Russia. Friction between individuals and churches, including tension between the Kirchliche and the Mennonite Brethren, subsided. Ministers from both groups joined together to preach and provide guidance.

The renewal also touched the sad chapter of self-defense. Some of the Mennonites viewed the suffering they experienced as the judgment of God for their military experiment. The report of a conference in Halbstadt in 1925 expressed deep repentance for having taken up arms in self-defense, and declared anew their commitment to peace and nonresistance. The same conference also decided that church members who violated the peace principle by accepting military service could not remain part of the church fellowship.[21]

The political implications of the *Selbstschutz* continued to haunt the Mennonites. Their image as a defenseless religious body was shattered. Young Mennonites were now inducted into the military for service. Of 131 young men who applied for exemption from military service in 1925, I was one of only sixty-four who received exemption on the basis of their religious conviction. Forty-seven were sentenced to labor camps; twenty yielded to pressure and entered military service. From the Mennonite colonies in the Caucasus, twenty-two men were sentenced to prison; four of them died in prison and fourteen were executed. In the years that followed there were many cases of imprisonment, forced labor and execution for those who declined service in the Red Army.[22]

The functional oneness that the Mennonite Brethren and the Mennonite Church had achieved in 1910 was invaluable. Widespread renewal could not have come without healing in this relationship. The large Bible conferences between 1918 and 1925 provided devotional mutuality. Remaining unresolved, however, were issues of conversion as a condition of baptism, church membership and New Testament discipleship. At the 1924 Bible conference in the Ohrloff Mennonite Church there was open disagreement over John 3:3: "Except a man be born again, he cannot see the kingdom of God." Mennonite Church leaders insisted that it implied a process of becoming, which could also be an unconscious growth into faith, while Mennonite Brethren maintained it meant a conscious volitional decision and change of life as suggested by John 9:25, "One thing I know, that, whereas I was blind, now I see." Differences in interpreting salvation led to a wider separation during the 1925 Bible conference in the Mennonite church in Alexanderkrone.[23] The two bodies never reached official doctrinal agreement on this issue. However, they did maintain the common ground essential for their survival as a

Mennonite people in the difficult years that followed.

The spiritual renewal prompted Mennonite Brethren to pursue missionary opportunities (between 1917 and 1928) that had been illegal before the revolution. They began intensive evangelism among their Russian neighbors, and several colonies reported significant numbers of conversions of people surrounding the Mennonite settlements. One example of this resurgence of outreach was the tent mission led by Jakob Dyck and a staff of twenty-four. This moving spiritual phenomenon ended in a martyr's death for Dyck and several co-workers. Other leaders in evangelism to the Russian people were Adolf Reimer and Heinrich Enns, whose story was a heroic testimony of suffering unto death.[24] Unique also was the missionary extension to the northern regions of Siberia along the rivers Irtysch, Ob and Tomsk, some two thousand kilometers north, where the gospel was previously unknown.[25]

### The Test for Survival

The new communist regime tested the Russian Mennonites as never before. Vast numbers took the opportunity to leave. From 1923 to 1928, roughly 21,000 Mennonites emigrated to Canada.[26] In 1930, another four thousand fled via Germany and China, eventually finding their way to Paraguay and Brazil, with smaller numbers going to Canada.[27]

Of significance for the church during this time of increasing government pressure was the All-Mennonite Congress in Moscow, January 1925. The resulting petition to the government pleaded for religious liberty. It sought: (1) the right to hold religious meetings and discussions in church and private homes for adults and children; (2) permission to form religious societies and choirs, and to conduct religious instruction, especially to children and youth; (3) permission to establish Mennonite orphanages and provide Christian education; (4) permission to erect new church buildings, and exemption of churches and ministers from special taxes; (5) the right to acquire Bibles and other Christian literature, including periodicals for the congregations; (6) permission to conduct Bible courses to train ministers; (7) recognition of schools as neutral territory, free from anti-religious propaganda; (8) exemption from military service and basic military preparation, the granting of useful alternative service, and exemption from taking the oath.[28]

These requests were all denied. The conference immediately launched a second appeal, closing with the words: "Give us our children, give us freedom to train and educate them according to the commands of our conscience."[29] Again the requests fell on deaf ears. The Moscow meeting was one of the last organized efforts of the Mennonites of Russia to seek liberty to practice their religious beliefs. On October 5-9, 1926 one final all-Mennonite conference convened in Melitopol. The concern was again the perils facing them. As clouds darkened on the horizon, the Mennonite community braced itself for the approaching storm.

The papers read at these last all-Mennonite conferences appeared to be a direct response to the exhortation of Ephesians 6:10-11: "Finally, my brethren . . . put on the whole armor of God, that ye may be able to stand against the wiles of the devil." Subjects dealt with in these papers included: "Our Time in the Context of World History," "Why I believe in God and Cling to Religion," "Discipline in the Church," "How to Lift the Spiritual Life in the Churches," "Christian Marriage," and "The Church in Separation from the World."[30]

The 1925 and 1926 conferences represented the concluding chapters of corporate Mennonite church life in Russia. The government's Five-Year Plan, initiated on October 1, 1928, began the forced collectivization of farms and the systematic liquidation of the *Kulaks*, a name given the well-to-do farmers and property owners. Mennonites corporately were classified as *Kulaks* who opposed the new order. The anti-

Christian character of communism came to full expression. The period from 1930 to 1940 saw the dissolution of congregations and the cessation of all organized religious life. Ministers were systematically removed and exiled to labor camps in distant Siberia.

David Reimer and Johann Janz, leaders in Alexanderthal, my home village, were arrested and executed by a firing squad. Heinrich Enns, a third leader in this church, was forbidden to be resident of any community. Anyone providing shelter for him was subject to severe civil punishment. Enns finally became ill and died in a neighboring village. The church building in Alexanderthal was closed and later used as a clubhouse for Communist Party members.

Other churches and communities suffered similar fates. Among the Mennonite Brethren alone, 111 leaders died martyrs' deaths. Ministers from other Mennonite groups were also executed or died in labor camps.[31] The Second World War resulted in the dispersion of all Mennonites from the Ukraine. The curtain of history fell on the Mennonite colonies of Southern Russia.[32] The church in Russia had become legally nonexistent. The history of the church in the first four centuries was reenacted. The church "had trial of cruel mockings and scourgings, yea, moreover of bonds and imprisonment: They were stoned, they were sawn asunder, were tempted, were slain with the sword: they wandered about in sheepskins and goatskins; being destitute, afflicted, tormented" (Heb. 11:36-37). It became a church of martyrs, sharing with their spiritual ancestors the cost of suffering and death, thus providing another link in the march of the free church movement through history and testifying to the truth that "the gates of hell shall not prevail against it" (Matt. 16:18).

According to Heinrich and Gerhard Woelk's *A Wilderness Journey*, most able men were arrested and sent to labor camps, never to return. Women remained at home with their children and became part of the labor force on the collective farms. Public religious services were forbidden and Bibles confiscated. The only thing that could not be taken away was private prayer. Many stricken souls joined the psalmist's lament: "Therefore is my spirit overwhelmed within me; my heart within me is desolate. . . . I stretch forth my hands unto thee: my soul thirsteth after thee, as a thirsty land" (Ps. 143:4-6). Faith in God was to be replaced by atheistic naturalism. School became a place to impart atheistic propaganda. Children were interrogated and urged to confess any religious influences in their homes.

The spiritual heroes during this period of tribulation were the mothers, who now headed most Mennonite households. They preserved the seed of faith so it could be passed on. This was not without severe risk, as the communist leaders had threatened to remove children from any religious influence.[33]

The mothers were well-trained in spiritual matters. Daily Bible reading and family devotions had been not only an integral part of Mennonite Brethren home life but was even a condition of church membership. As children, they had learned the stories of the Bible; to graduate from high school they needed to pass an exam in Bible content. This background gave them a solid foundation to teach their children biblical truth and the way of salvation.

Scattered to isolated central Asian hamlets in 1942, the mothers continued to instruct their children in the Word of God. By day the children suffered a barrage of atheistic propaganda in the classroom; by night, in humble one-room dwellings amid the dim light of oil lamps, they learned the stories of the people of God and sang sacred songs from memory.[34]

The chronology of Mennonite Brethren persecution in Russia from 1929 to 1957 includes the following key events:

1929-1930: Ministers heavily taxed, many leaders banished; church buildings closed.

1935: All religious meetings forbidden, even in private

homes.

1941: The last men arrested; all families interned in Siberia and Kazakhstan, except those that managed to retreat with the German army.

1957: Founding of the first Mennonite Brethren Church in Kazakhstan, illegal and much persecuted. Only in 1967 was the Mennonite Brethren Church in the city of Karaganda given legal status to conduct public services.

In the decade from 1957 to 1967 many Mennonite Brethren ministers and leaders were arrested and exiled as they met in private homes and in forests to worship and nurture the spiritual life of the faithful.[35]

Meanwhile, in 1944, the Baptists received legal status, although they remained under stringent state regulations and suffered frequent interference from the communist authorities. The same authorities, however, considered the Mennonite Brethren a misguided sect and continued to persecute them for twenty more years.[36]

Theological affinity between the Baptists and the Mennonite Brethren in soteriology and ordinances (baptism and communion) provided the bridge for many Mennonite Brethren to relate to the Baptist movement for spiritual survival. When the Mennonite Brethren Church re-emerged organizationally on May 28, 1965, the relationship with the Baptists became an issue, resulting in the following statement:[37]

**Some Principles of the GMB Church of Karaganda**
(Confirmed by the brotherhood of the church on May 28, 1965)

According to the words of Jesus in John 17:21 "that they all may be one," we love all children of God and as members of Christ's body want to have fellowship with all true believers, including communion fellowship.

In spite of this brotherly love, which we want to hold high, children of God of various doctrinal kinds will go their separate ways in many questions until the coming of the Lord. So we, the MB Church of Karaganda, want to hold fast to the centuries-old teachings of our fathers in the faith, which teachings, on the basis of the Word of God, have become ours.

A. What are the differences between the GMB Church and the Baptists the AUCECB (apart from nonresistance and refusal of the oath)?

1. Complete separation of church and state, meaning no interference in our church matters. At the same time we wish to be obedient citizens of our land and recognize the rights of the authorities over us.

2. Independence of the individual congregation. Conferences only give advisory resolutions. Therefore no domination by a central church authority.

3. Free preaching of the whole gospel in our meetings according to the commission of our Lord Jesus.

4. Regular Bible studies and prayer meetings apart from the Sunday services.

5. A clearly Christian upbringing of children, independent of the opinion of the godless world.

6. Priesthood of all believers in the congregation, that is, a congregation of active lay members who are all involved in building the church and working for the Lord. That is why the examination of members, baptism and communion, questions of discipline, elections, consecrations and the like are all carried out in front of and with the whole congregation.[38]

While the Mennonite Brethren recognized some affinity with the Baptists, they held to several points of difference in doctrine and polity.

An indication of the impact of the renewed Mennonite Brethren Church was the fact that even communist writers took grudging note of it. In a publication titled *The Sects: Their*

*Faith and Their Affairs,* one writer noted a revival among Mennonites since 1957. He was referring to the sweeping revival of the 1950s, especially among Mennonite Brethren young people, which led to the rebirth of the Mennonite Brethren Church.[39] A later publication on the Mennonites by Viktor F. Krestyaninov in 1967 made special reference to the "New Mennonites" (Mennonite Brethren), expressing concern about the influence of their travelling preachers upon young people. "They have considerable experience as educators and are able to arouse the interest of youth in religious questions by organizing activities such as performance in choirs, orchestras, and Bible classes." Krestyaninov, though a communist, spoke highly of their behavior and quality of work:

> The Mennonites (new Mennonites) do not drink or smoke, and pay particular attention to bodily cleanliness as a symbol of spiritual purity. Their life tends to be concentrated upon the family, and their cultivation of reading, handicrafts, singing and other music serves as a protection against the distraction of political and antireligious club activities outside the home. The language spoken at home is usually Low German, and embroidered religious texts are a prominent feature in every Mennonite home. The Mennonites are noted for their industry and their conscientious attitude to the work entrusted to them at Soviet enterprises, collective and state farms.[40]

Significant was Krestyaninov's observation that the vibrant church of the Mennonite Brethren consisted mainly of members from middle and younger generations, people who had grown up in the era of communism. He also recognized that their central concern was salvation–the new birth so central for Mennonite Brethren.[41]

The church continued to grow following its legal recognition in 1967. By 1980 there were sixteen registered Mennonite Brethren churches in Asiatic Russia.[42] Mass emigration to Germany in recent years, following the relaxing of restrictions through *perestroika*, resulted, however, in a considerable decrease.

The influence of the Russian Mennonite Brethren Church stands out clearly in a statement by the General Secretary of the All-Union Council of Evangelical Christians-Baptists to a group of North American Mennonite Brethren visitors in Moscow in 1987:

> The Mennonite Brethren are an important influence in the development of the churches in Russia. They distinguish themselves from our native Russian believers in three areas:
> 1. They have a broad knowledge of the Scriptures (more so than our Russian people) rooted in their family life.
> 2. They are known for greater consistency in relation to faith and    life. They seek to live by what they profess.
> 3. They are a people with a missionary vision, evangelizing their neighbors and reaching out to people who do not know the gospel.[43]

Mennonite Brethren, as others, stood the test of seventy years under communist rule. Their restoration after forty years (1927-1967) of extinct congregational life stands as a testimony of divine mercy and grace.

CHAPTER 13

# Mennonite Immigration from Russia to Canada during the 1920s

**IMPLICATIONS FOR
THE MENNONITE BRETHREN CHURCH**

The Russian Revolution, with its political and economic upheaval and social instability following the First World War (1914-1918), provides the backdrop for the Mennonite exodus from Russia to Canada. Some twenty thousand Mennonites came to Canada in the years 1923-1930.[1] In the almost 150 years (1778-1920) preceding the Revolution, the Mennonites in Russia had become an ethno-religious people with their own culture, self-government and a strong capitalistic economic system. Their survival as a people was incompatible with many features of the new Soviet experiment, including Marxist philosophy.[2] Phillipp Cornies and Benjamin B. Janz, leaders of the Mennonite Association for Economic and Social Development, gave further reasons for the need to "leave" Russia:

> In addition to the motives already cited here there are chiefly the ethical, moral and religious motives for consideration. There are persons with deeper and clearer vision from all classes and all places of our society, especially in the original colonies, who are unable to make any compromise, or begin any rebuilding because they have recognized that not only the economic, but also the social and moral foundations for such building are missing,

which alone can be the determining factor for us. For the system of communistic influence, which is at present being carried out largely and with disregard for our principles of freedom of religion, goes contrary to our ideals and can therefore not be accepted by us. Therefore it is impossible for us to stay here.[3]

Exact data as to how many of the twenty thousand immigrants were Mennonite Brethren is not available. But considering that in 1925 they represented 22.5 percent of all Mennonites in Russia,[4] very likely some four thousand of the immigrants were Mennonite Brethren. The rapid growth of the Mennonite Brethren Conference in Canada during this time–1,770 members in 1924 to 5,200 members in 1934 and 7,600 members in 1945–supports this estimate.[5] The implications of this numerical growth were significant.

## KANADIER AND RUSSLÄNDER

The Mennonites who had come to North America fifty years earlier were a pioneer people who struggled to conquer the unsettled prairies of Western Canada and the plain states of Minnesota, South Dakota, Nebraska and Kansas. According to Cornelius Krahn, those who were culturally more progressive–approximately two-thirds of the total number of Mennonites–decided, in the 1870s, to remain in Russia. The other third, who chose to migrate to Canada and the United States, were somewhat conservative and had fewer economic resources.[6] John H. Lohrenz referred to the 1870s migration as the separation of the rich from the poor: "The wealthier families as a rule preferred to remain in Russia and to adjust themselves to the changing conditions. Of those leaving . . . many had very little means and some had none. The majority had to begin in dire poverty."[7]

Before the 1870s, Russian Mennonites were a basically homogeneous peasant society. After 1880 the isolation of these peasant communities broke down. Mennonites became more and more integrated into the complex structure of modern western culture.[8] They developed a sophisticated system of education. The secondary schools (*Zentralschulen*) elevated Mennonite culture and produced a class of intelligentsia. Many of their young people went to Russian universities for professional training; others went to Germany and Switzerland for advanced academic pursuits. The list of church leaders who studied in St. Crischona, Switzerland, and the Baptist seminary in Hamburg was substantial. After 1897, when the Russian language entered the village schools, the younger generation gradually absorbed Russian ideas and culture. By 1914, according to Emerick K. Francis, the Russian Mennonites

> had become an integral part of a highly differentiated, heterogeneous ... and to some extent, urbanized, industrialized, and capitalistic society with developed institutions of higher learning and a flourishing national literature, whose achievements in the sciences, fine arts, music, drama, ballet, and so on were considerable.[9]

The Mennonite Brethren who came to North America in the 1920s, therefore, were somewhat culturally removed from their kin already in Canada–known as "Kanadier"–who had come in the 1870s. These newcomers–called "Russländer"–were more sophisticated, better educated, had a broader world view, a progressive outlook and a more aggressive style. In the words of Francis:

> The two Mennonite groups were divided by cultural and class differences. In the eyes of the native Mennonites the newcomers appeared worldly, overbearing, and unwilling to do manual labor. The Russländer people, on the other hand, found their benefactors, on whose good will they were dependent, uncouth, backward, miserly and, above

all, ignorant and uneducated.¹⁰

Many of the Kanadier regarded the newcomers as proud and arrogant.¹¹ Yet the graciousness with which they extended hospitality to them was a model of humility and kindness.¹² Despite a common origin and a common faith, adjustment of the Russländer immigrants to the Kanadier group was in many ways as difficult as the adjustment to the society at large.¹³

The expansion of the Canadian Mennonite Brethren Conference from twenty congregations in 1923 with a membership of 1,778 to sixty-two congregations and 7,882 members in 1941 introduced new dynamics.¹⁴ The voices of Abraham H. Unruh, Benjamin B. Janz, Cornelius A. DeFehr, Franz C. Thiessen, Cornelius F. Klassen, Heinrich Regier, Johann Wiens, David D. Derksen, Heinrich Toews, Jakob Thiessen and other Russländer became prominent in conference deliberations during those years.

The leadership of the Canadian Conference, however, remained in the hands of the Kanadier until 1938 and 1939 when the conference chairman and assistant chairman first came from the ranks of the Russländer. From 1941 to 1943 the leadership was again with the Kanadier. Only from 1944, twenty years after the coming of the Russländer, was there a continuous pattern of mutuality in the conference leadership.¹⁵

General Conference Mennonite Brethren leadership followed a similar pattern. It took fourteen years (1924-1938) for the first Russländer candidate to be accepted for an assignment under the Board of Foreign Missions, and not until 1945 was a Russländer elected to this board.¹⁶ The Russländer generally assumed that marrying a woman from a Kanadier family would hasten a candidate's acceptance.¹⁷

In the spring of 1946 members of the Board of Foreign Missions interviewed a Kanadier student at the Mennonite Brethren College in Winnipeg. As the president of the college, I advised the board members against accepting the candidate because the college faculty felt she lacked the needed qualifications. The board's response was: "The time has not yet come that the Russländer will tell us whom we send to India as a missionary." They sent the candidate. In a few years she had to be recalled. The evaluation of the college faculty had proven to be correct. The incident illustrated the protectiveness felt by Canadian Conference leaders in the first decades following the 1924 arrival of the Russländer.

As the conference grew with the coming of the immigrants, the conference agenda expanded accordingly. The concern for preserving the German language, referred to in 1911 and 1922, became a major conference issue between 1926 and 1959.[18] During the same years the Canadian Conference minutes record vigorous discussions on church polity and practice and the dangers of false teaching in the church.

During these decades the conference also reviewed the structure of church organization and qualifications for conference membership. Membership in a local church was to be based on a candidate's personal conversion and consistent Christian lifestyle. Membership of a church in the conference required accepting the Mennonite Brethren Confession of Faith as well as adopted standards of Christian behavior. A committee would examine a local church with regard to its organization and polity and recommend acceptance of the church into the conference fellowship.[19]

A host of other issues also dominated conference discussions. After 1932 we find a continuous concern for Mennonite Brethren who left Russia and ended up in China, Paraguay and Brazil.[20] The subject of nonresistance became prominent during the 1930s and remained so into the 1950s.[21] In the 1930s the Canadian Conference also introduced the presentation of position papers to the delegates. The first such papers were read to the conference in 1936: "The church in its final perfection" (Johann Braun); "The threat of modernism for the believers church" (Heinrich Regehr); and "The sin of gossip and its effect on the life of the church" (John G. Wiens).[22]

By 1945, the Kanadier and Russländer had reached a level of integration within the Canadian Conference that mutually benefitted both groups. It could be argued that this process accounts for the increasing strength of the Canadian over the United States Conference in leadership, evangelism, church growth, urbanization and integration with the national environment in the decades that followed.

## MENNONITE BRETHREN AND THE GENERAL CONFERENCE: AN UNEASY RELATIONSHIP

Many Mennonite Brethren congregations in Canada, swollen with new members from numerous different colonies in several different regions of Russia, all bringing their own attitudes, habits and traditions, became like a mosaic. The close interrelationships demanded in the process of forming new communities and churches created many tensions. These tensions were not only among Mennonite Brethren, but with the General Conference (GC) Mennonites as well, who still conjured up memories of religious differences of the past. Historian Frank H. Epp placed major responsibilities for such tensions at the feet of the Mennonite Brethren.[23]

In Russia these MB-GC tensions had by now subsided considerably. The tempest of the First World War and the Russian Revolution had helped the Mennonite Brethren recognize the importance of better relationships with the wider Mennonite world. A visitation of God through a spiritual renewal in the larger Mennonite community in Russia brought about further healing. The Mennonite Brethren found fellowship in the company of their former opponents and began to establish common spiritual ground. The all-Mennonite conference in Lichtenau, June 30 to July 2, 1918, reflected growing spiritual warmth in the Mennonite peoplehood.

The outstretched arm of North American Mennonites in the relief work following the First World War and the Russian

Revolution also fostered unity. The Mennonite Brethren realized that there was room for diversity in spiritual understanding and practice within the Mennonite fellowship without disclaiming the common heritage of the sixteenth-century Anabaptist movement.[24]

But in North America the old tensions still simmered. Mennonite Brethren persisted in identifying the General Conference Mennonites with the *Kirchliche Gemeinde* in Russia. Though historically incorrect (the GC church began in North America in 1860, the same year as the founding of the MB), this was for them a circumstantial deduction. When renewals in General Conference circles brought members into new Mennonite Brethren congregations, the belief grew that the Russian experience was being repeated.

The French Creek renewal movement near Hillsboro, Kansas, created new stress. A group from this community, including some leaders of the Johannesthal General Conference congregation, became the founders of the Hillsboro Mennonite Brethren Church in 1880-1882.[25] Cornelius P. Wedel, a minister from the Alexanderwohl General Conference congregation in Goessel, along with a group of people from that fellowship, founded the Goessel Mennonite Brethren Church in 1881. One of his sons, Cornelius H. Wedel, became the president of Bethel, a General Conference college. The second son, Peter H. Wedel, was a very effective evangelist who preached renewal and the need for conversion among Mennonites and became the first Mennonite Brethren missionary to Cameroon in Africa.[26]

The birth of the Mennonite Brethren Church in Canada in 1886 was the fruit of the evangelistic ministry of Heinrich Voth, a Mennonite Brethren from Minnesota, who worked diligently among the Mennonite communities in southern Manitoba. He experienced much opposition there from Old Colony Mennonites. Events leading to the organization of the first Mennonite Brethren Church at Burwalde, near Winkler,

Manitoba, produced considerable tension. In many cases, the continued growth of Mennonite Brethren churches in Canada and the United States came from other Mennonites who experienced personal conversion, were rebaptized and joined the Mennonite Brethren.[27]

## RENEWAL IN THE BROADER MENNONITE COMMUNITY

It must be noted that renewal focusing on repentance and conversion was not unique to the Mennonite Brethren in North America. History records a broad stream of identical concern elsewhere. Martin Boehm (1725-1812), with his evangelistic fervor in Pennsylvania, brought to life the Brethren in Christ (River Brethren) in 1770. The Church of God in Christ Mennonite group was a renewal movement under the leadership of John Holdeman. John F. Funk (1835-1930), John S. Coffman (1848-1899), Daniel Brenneman (1834-1919) and Solomon Eby (1834-1931) are part of the gallery of evangelists in Mennonite history.[28]

Significant revivals in the 1940s and 1950s crossed Mennonite boundaries. The community revivals in British Columbia, southern Manitoba and Ontario, as well as in communities in the United States, enjoyed strong participation from varied Mennonite groups. The Mennonite Brethren understanding of faith and life found its General Conference parallel in men like Theodore Epp, for many years with the Back to the Bible Broadcast radio program in Nebraska; C.H. Suckau in the Berne, Indiana, congregation and founding president of Grace College of the Bible; and Henry J. Brown, a missionary to China. In the Mennonite Church (sometimes informally known as the "Old Mennonite Church") the parallel can be recognized in the Brunk Revival phenomenon and the evangelistic theology of Myron Augsburger.[29]

The level of inter-Mennonite involvement by the Mennonite Brethren has been conditioned by theological considerations and emphases. The recent assessment that "Mennonite

Brethren. . . found inter-Mennonite relations most difficult" and were known for a "traditional stance" of withdrawal[30] fails to recognize that they, like many other Mennonites in North America and Europe, have not understood Anabaptism as leaving room for a wide latitude of theological understandings, an openness held by some Mennonite groups.[31] Mennonite Brethren frequently have felt that some Mennonite groups have underemphasized essential aspects of New Testament truth as understood by the early Anabaptists.

The continued Mennonite Brethren relationship in North America with General Conference and other Mennonite groups does not rest on conference-to-conference relationships but on spiritual affinity at the local church level. An example of such mutuality is Columbia Bible College in Clearbrook, British Columbia, which the General Conference and Mennonite Brethren conferences of British Columbia own and operate jointly.[32]

Mennonite Brethren have not felt comfortable separating theology as represented in their Confession of Faith from their understanding of the church as a covenant community. Mennonite Brethren ministers are urged to subscribe to the Confession of Faith of the conference. For ordained ministers to have the latitude to question the preexistence of Christ, his virgin birth and his literal bodily resurrection, is unacceptable to Mennonite Brethren.[33] A quotation from a review of Katie Funk Wiebe's book *Who are the Mennonite Brethren?*[34] by a General Conference scholar, speaks further to the difference between General Conference and Mennonite Brethren:

> How can we be sure that the confessional issues at stake are gospel truth rather than incidents of language? . . . When General Conference Mennonites find themselves in disagreement on doctrine, they remind themselves that their conference has no official confession of faith and quickly move on to other matters on which they might agree such as the importance of overseas missions or, in a pinch, the

weather in California. We GCs tend to get nervous when others define us in doctrinal terms, as Howard Loewen does in his comparative study of Mennonite doctrine.[35]

Mennonite Brethren, meanwhile, get nervous when scholars like Gordon Kaufman take it for granted, without argument, that the Christian gospel cannot provide the center in the search for religious unity. He claims that "'modern historical consciousness' requires us to abandon the claim to Christ's uniqueness and to recognize that the biblical view of things, like all other views, is the product of a particular culture."[36]

Mennonite Brethren become very uneasy when Mennonite scholar Clyde Norman Kraus openly asks, "Is Christianity the only right religion? Must one belong to the Christian religion in order to be included under God's covenant?"[37]

Doctrinal differences, however, provide no justification for isolationism in local church relations as it existed between the early Mennonite Brethren and others over the mode of baptism and the understanding of Scripture.

The improved inter-Mennonite dialogue of recent years has enhanced mutual understanding in the larger Mennonite fellowship. Part of the Mennonite Brethren aloofness of the past decades must also be understood as part of the process of Mennonite immigrants finding their way in the North American context. The current trend toward Mennonite ecumenism, however, may generate new anxieties for Mennonite Brethren, especially in regard to the uniqueness of Christ in human redemption.

## FROM ISOLATION TO EXPOSURE

For four centuries Mennonites lived in closed communities. In Russia they settled in colonies isolated from the national population, maintaining their own local government and educational system. Their school curricula featured a strong religious component. Each school day in the Mennonite village opened with a devotional exercise, followed by a period devoted to the study of Bible stories. Memorization of Bible passages and selected hymns was an integral part of the educational process.

North American circumstances made no provision for this idyllic village pattern. Children generally attended public schools over which the parents had no final control. To remedy this loss they created schools for German and religion that met after regular class hours and on Saturdays. Educational concerns eventually gave birth to the introduction of the American Sunday school system, Bible schools, private high schools and colleges.[38]

A second factor accelerating the move out of isolation was the need for young people to go into the cities to work and supplement the income of the immigrant family. Hundreds of young women, for example, found themselves working as maids in affluent homes in Toronto, Winnipeg, Saskatoon and Vancouver. Their nurture and care became a special concern for the churches in the 1920s, 1930s and 1940s.[39] Reports from Winnipeg refer to special gatherings of these young women as sometimes exceeding one hundred. The earnings of these Mennonite "domestics" were a major factor in their families' financial survival during the initial years after the 1920s immigration and into the depression of the 1930s. This exposure to the wealthy and upper middle-class of society made inroads into Mennonite homes that heretofore had been locked into age-old traditions.

By the 1940s Mennonite Brethren in the United States were also beginning the move into urban areas. In California there were churches in San Jose, Los Angeles, Bakersfield and Fresno. Farmers left the farm and entered small business of various kinds. Entrance into local politics–school boards, city councils, village mayors–became commonplace. All of these movements pointed to a people less separated and increasingly moving into the networks and institutions of the larger culture.

CHAPTER 14

# Mennonite Brethren Education

The Mennonite Brethren were born in an era of educational ferment among a people who had been closed to outside influences for more than 250 years.[1] The Bible study groups that helped awaken the Russian Mennonite colonies continued to be a major avenue of spiritual fellowship for Mennonite Brethren. Furthermore the religious education in the colony schools provided a sufficient base upon which to build the spiritual nurture of the church.

Children and youth were integrated into the worship services. The preaching ministry was largely an interpretation of Scripture related to the experiences of life. Family devotions was a standard feature of home life. Faith was nurtured in a distinct cultural milieu.

The benefits of this unique "peoplehood" structure could not be replicated in North America, at least not to the same extent. Mennonite Brethren felt the need to provide their own religious education. As early as 1884 the North American Mennonite Brethren Conference addressed the need to educate the children and youth. The frequency of educational resolutions suggests the extensive concerns about education.[2] To this impressive list can be added the many deliberations and decisions at the national and regional conference levels. Clearly, the education of children and youth was central for Mennonite Brethren. The migration of the 1920s and 1930s added to the urgency of this concern.

The Mennonites of the 1870s came to the new world not as individuals but as cohesive groups. Immigration followed community patterns in the initial settlements and in daughter settlements: the Red River Valley of Manitoba; the Ebenfeld-Hillsboro community in Kansas; Henderson, Nebraska; Mountain Lake, Minnesota; and later the Hepburn-Waldheim-Dalmeny area of Saskatchewan; Coaldale, Alberta; and Yarrow, British Columbia.

Communal cohesiveness was doubtless an important feature of Mennonite history. Cultural and ethnic ties were carriers of faith and lifestyle values. While the interdependent community is a scriptural model of church life, it cannot remain locked in ethnic exclusivism. An interdependent community that finds its roots in Christ and in turn with each other demands exposure to the world in a sharing relationship.

Life in North America did not permit the economic and educational isolation Mennonites had known in Russia. Initially the cultural and religious barriers were sufficient to maintain a strong sense of separate identity. But more protection was needed. Strong legalism as a barrier against the intrusion of social practices from the outside was one measure employed. Another was a more deliberate emphasis on their separate cultural status. The establishment of schools for the preservation of the German language and biblical instruction was intended in part to shore up cultural and spiritual values that were thought to be endangered by exposure to the non-Mennonite environment.

## BIBLE SCHOOLS AND HIGH SCHOOLS

Corn (Oklahoma) Bible Academy which opened in 1902 listed its aim as preserving the German language, teaching Bible and preparing students for work of missions at home and abroad.[3] The Mountain Lake (Minnesota) Bible Academy, established in the same year, also stated its objectives as teaching German and giving Bible instruction.[4] The Gethsemane High School in Fairview, Oklahoma, established in 1905, sought to teach the Word of God, the German language and Mennonite customs.[5]

Clearly, language and cultural preservation was high on the educational agenda of early Mennonite Brethren in North America. Paul Toews in an article, "Henry W. Lohrenz and Tabor College," quoted from the *Tabor College Herald* that to forget the German language represented weakness of character:

> What nationality can boast of nobler ancestry? The Trustees were a strong and healthy race. They were pure and honest of heart and had the noblest aspirations. After they accepted the Christian religion, there were no other people more true to the faith.[6]

There are indications that the North American Mennonite Brethren linked the perpetuation of German culture with the retention of religious faith. As Toews wrote, "the point of the intersection between the two was not that German was the language of faith but that it was the language of a superior culture."[7]

In Canada the concerns were much the same. When thirteen Mennonite Brethren Bible schools emerged in Canada between 1924 and 1955, Bible instruction and German language got top billing. In terms of importance, cultural survival followed close on the heels of spiritual development.

A consultation about the need and purpose of Bible schools took place in Saskatoon, Saskatchewan, on August 8-10, 1941, with teachers from all Mennonite Brethren schools in Canada participating. This body agreed that "the necessity for Bible schools is: (1) to guard the souls of our youth from the danger of being lost; (2) to equip our youth to stand against the danger of our age; (3) to preserve our youth for the church to prevent the latter from gradual death." A subsequent paragraph added: "to meet the inner needs of the young people through Bible instruction" and "to prepare the youth for a defense against worldliness" (such as birth control).[8]

The Coaldale Bible School in 1944 stated its aim as: (1) to nurture the spiritual life of the family, church and society; (2)

to train workers to confront the dangers faced by the children of today; (3) to work towards unity among believers.[9] In 1954 the Mennonite Collegiate Institute (a high school) in Gretna, Manitoba, defined its task to "prepare youth for a Christian world view and strengthen their understanding of biblical truth."[10] But matching this concern for spiritual development were statements like the 1958 board-approved statement of Eden Christian College, also a high school, in Niagara-on-the-Lake, Ontario, that it was "to be a wall surrounding our youth and protecting them from the influence of the world."[11]

In 1975 John H. Redekop evaluated three Canadian Mennonite Brethren high schools (Eden Christian College, Niagara-on-the-Lake, Ontario; Mennonite Brethren Collegiate Institute, Winnipeg, Manitoba; Mennonite Educational Institute, Clearbrook, B.C.). He made three positive observations which in part also apply to the Bible schools: (1) All three stress high academic standards and seem to achieve these; (2) they have an excellent record of cultural and athletic achievement; (3) all three schools indicate a deep concern about the spiritual, physical and intellectual development of the student. But none, he added, "seem to have successfully eliminated the cleavage between the sacred and the secular. In this, of course, they reflect their sponsoring communities."[12]

Acknowledging that the high schools came into being following the Second World War, a time of cultural erosion and anti-German sentiment in some communities, Redekop concluded: "The original objectives of the high schools were at least partly defensive and negative; namely, to a significant extent the schools were established, dedicated leadership and sacrificial support notwithstanding, as holding operations."[13] Redekop noted that many of the original issues that led to the establishment of the schools had disappeared.

> What have we produced to replace the awareness of the spiritual richness of our Anabaptist heritage? . . . At best

we seem to have substituted a common denominator evangelical stance for the earlier ethnic-holding operation. Such a shift of objectives may be adequate in the short run, but in the long run will probably be insufficient . . . to perpetuate a distinctive Mennonite Brethren Church.[14]

Ironically, the pressing desire for cultural self-preservation as a motivation for establishing Bible schools and high schools was completely detached from any systematic effort to provide the educational resources needed to bolster a healthy self-identity. That inability was no doubt furthered by the absence of curriculum materials on Mennonite Brethren history, beliefs and missions.

In this, the Mennonite Brethren succumbed to a situation in which efforts to preserve spiritual and ethical values through isolation actually resulted in the loss of that which they intended to protect. They did not realize that these values could be preserved only as they became a dynamic expression of life in relationship to a broader society.

**HIGHER EDUCATION**

Interpreting the history of Mennonite Brethren higher education is a difficult task. The high schools and Bible schools began and drew resources from clusters of local churches. Higher education, however, addresses the needs of a broader constituency. In 1992 a relatively small conference of 17,000 members in the United States and 25,000 in Canada owned four colleges: Tabor College (Hillsboro, Kansas); Fresno Pacific College (California); Concord College (Winnipeg, Manitoba), formerly Mennonite Brethren Bible College; and Columbia Bible College (Clearbrook, British Columbia); plus the Mennonite Brethren Biblical Seminary in Fresno. The sheer scope of such a program of higher education for a small conference contains its own paradoxes.

Tabor College, founded in 1908, was the first Mennonite

Brethren institution of higher learning. Its founding goals were similar to those of the Bible schools and high schools. Henry W. Lohrenz called for a school "in which our youth may study and where it will not be alienated from our churches."[15] In 1912 Elder Abraham Schellenberg added: "If we want our youth to be brought up in the traditions of the churches we must have our own schools."[16] Two decades later, the articulated purpose of the college was to protect the spiritual unity of the conference in order to strengthen the objectives of its heritage.[17] In the mid-1940s H.W. Lohrenz offered a more complete description in a pamphlet entitled *Early Aims of Tabor College*:

> Tabor College was founded to provide trained leadership for the churches that would support the school. . . . Those who were entrusted with the administration of the school never thought of it merely as an institution for secular training. The preparation of young men and women for spiritual leadership was always uppermost in their minds. It is not enough to have trained leaders. The question is, what direction do they lead the people. Whither are we as a church and denomination going? Is there unity of aim? The greater the variety of schools to which our young people go, the greater will be the difference in our churches. If we do not achieve unity of spirit in our leadership, how can we have unity in our churches?[18]

The importance of Tabor College for the Mennonite Brethren Church has never been doubted. It provided leadership, prepared missionaries and nurtured a sense of community. The fact that it was not formally accepted as a conference-owned and operated school for more than twenty-five years, however, leaves unanswered questions. Not until Tabor fell on hard times and was in danger of closing, did the Mennonite Brethren General Conference in 1933 finally recommend that the school be adopted by the conference.[19] The report to the

1936 Mennonite Brethren General Conference, however, expressed deep concern that not all churches had participated in the voting on the referendum, and in those that did, only part of the congregation had voted.[20] Sections of the Pacific District and the Canadian District abstained from voting.

The strong traditional emphases on Bible school education raised the question–do we need a liberal arts college? Had the conference leadership in establishing Tabor as a conference school moved beyond the wishes of its constituency? Many constituents, still culturally isolated, did not sense the need for an institution to help them define and delineate their Anabaptist heritage. Their commitment to the Bible, in what Robert Friedmann called an "existential Christianity," made no demands on them for creedal formulation.[21] Finer questions of hermeneutics–"How do we *interpret* the Bible?"–were not being asked, and they saw little need for a school to help them do so.[22]

This constricted mentality was reinforced by the appearance of American fundamentalism. Mennonite Brethren caught in the cross-fire between fundamentalists and modernists knew that they were not modernists. While their alliance with fundamentalism should also have been an uneasy one, they apparently drifted into that orbit with little difficulty. The extent to which Tabor College became immersed in the milieu of fundamentalism could be seen in the annual Bible Normals (a week of spiritual emphasis) with speakers like Reuben A. Torrey, James Oliver Buswell, J.G. Drowell, William Evans, Paul Ruth, Gerald Winrod and others.

The degree of the college's captivity in an environment of isolation was illustrated by developments in the 1940s. Up to that time, trusted churchmen like Henry W. Lohrenz, Peter C. Hiebert and Abraham E. Janzen had been at the helm. But in 1942 Peter E. Schellenberg, a psychologist and one of the first Ph.Ds in the Mennonite Brethren Church, became president of Tabor. Schellenberg was perhaps the first Mennonite Brethren educator to seriously attempt to integrate faith and learning from an Anabaptist perspective. But his leadership raised immediate suspicion among churches with a fundamentalist orientation. Was a man with only a secular education and not a minister-churchman trustworthy? Could he give spiritual direction to the college? Students in the Bible department of the college were influenced by suspicious pastors at home. One zealous student felt called to demonstrate his crusading spirit in the library. Discovering the books *The Christ of the Indian Road* by Eli Stanley Jones and *How to Keep America Out of War* by Kirby Page on the shelves, he took them to the librarian and demanded that they be burned because they were "the vomit from hell."[23]

The Committee of Reference and Counsel of the General Conference was called in to investigate the school's biblical trustworthiness. The committee's chairman, Abraham H. Unruh, subsequently assured the churches that no issues of biblical faith were at stake. The attacks, however, did not stop. The storm spread a spirit of fear and became a "witch hunt" for modernism in the conference school. The struggle continued well into the 1950s, finally resulting in Schellenberg's resignation. To restore confidence in the college, John N. C. Hiebert, a missionary from India, was called as president to affirm and protect the "faith of our fathers."

Mennonite Brethren on the West Coast watched this "struggle for the faith" with apprehension. In 1944 they established a school of their own, Pacific Bible Institute, later to become Fresno Pacific College. Those who were close to the leaders of this new venture–George B. Huebert, Jacob D. Hofer, August A. Schroeter, Henry D. Wiebe and others–interpreted the move as a vote of no confidence in Tabor College.[24] The following statement spoke further to the motives for establishing the Bible institute.

> The reasons for this urge for a school here in the west are many. Three stand out predominantly. The first, of

course, was the realization for the great need of Christian workers in our churches who would be able to meet the intellectual progress of our time. Secondly, the horror on the part of parents and churches for the hazards that students confront today in some theological schools, and thirdly, the unmistakable but simple fact that a church body can not long continue in its true channel unless its doctrinal principles and church policy are definitely and squarely implanted in its coming generation. These are concerns to which God-fearing and Church-loving people cannot be indifferent without incurring harm.[25]

The belief that spiritual principles must be "implanted," as opposed to truth emerging from a careful reformulation of age-old truths in the light of a new and complex society, was consistent with Mennonite Brethren self-understanding in the 1940s. As a people in relative isolation, they felt no need for new theological precision.

The period following the Second World War changed that, however. The tension over conscientious objection, the surge in education in society generally in the post-war era, and increasing confrontations between faith and world, called for a new theological identity. The institutions of higher education were slow to provide the theological vigor to address this growing concern.

In the post-war years the calls for a more distinctive Mennonite philosophy of education appeared in various places. The most sustained effort began at Pacific College (later Fresno Pacific College) in the 1960s. Several faculty members attempted to focus the purpose of the newly-accredited senior college in the Pacific College Idea. Here was a specific call to be an "Anabaptist Mennonite college."[26]

Paul Toews, a long-time faculty member, examined the Fresno Pacific struggle for identity in a paper titled "From Pietism to Secularism via Anabaptism: An informal history of the changing ideals and relationships between Fresno Pacific College and the Mennonite Brethren Church, 1944-1984."[27] He observed that the early Pacific faculty of the 1960s and 1970s were children of the 1940s and 1950s who came of age at a time when their parents were busy acculturating to American society. "They were the first generation reared beyond the boundaries of the Mennonite village,"[28] Toews wrote, using imagery made prominent by fellow faculty member Delbert Wiens in his classic study, "From the Village to the City."[29] Toews referred to that era as the cultural and intellectual emancipation that came with breaking out of the boundaries of ethno-religious culture. Among other things it was a rethinking of the relationship between the past and the present. "The transitional nature of the 1940s to 1960s called for a reassessment of history. This was the generation that rediscovered the Anabaptist tradition."[30]

The Pacific College Idea was a codification of the Anabaptist faith as applied to higher education.

> It was a new charter for how Christians should function in the world. The Idea moved the definition of Mennonite Brethren education from its preoccupation with the purity of the soul and its witness of personal faith to the nature of the Christian's relationship to the dominant political and cultural realities. What distinguished the Idea was not its commitment to a liberal arts education within the Christian world view, but the linking of the two with communitarian and prophetic ideals.[31]

The theological implications of the Pacific College Idea were significant:

> Christian education was to educate for social transformation as much as for personal righteousness. Humanity suffered alienation from God, but also alienation from the

social world. The political and economic structures that divide people into rich and poor, liberated and oppressed, nourished and malnourished, were also in need of redemption.[32]

A document entitled, "Broadening the Base: My Vision for Fresno Pacific College," presented to the Pacific District Conference by president Edmund Janzen in 1983, called for enlarging the college's student potential as well its economic resources. The intent was not to surrender the theological distinctives of the institution as defined in the Pacific College Idea. The statement in part read:

I. We will establish a clear sense of our identity within the wider philosophical/theological framework of the current Christian College scene. F.P.C. is and will continue to be a Mennonite Brethren related school securely anchored in the Anabaptist/Evangelical tradition. Today (perhaps more than ever) both church and college need a vital "center"–a core of values that gives meaning to every program, and that provides the cohesive glue to our purpose. This means that the College will continue to stress the same key distinctives that are also the hallmark of our churches as noted in the M.B. Confession of Faith:
a. personal conversion to a new life of discipleship in Jesus Christ.
b. a high view of the Scriptures as the norm for daily living.
c. the importance of "the Believer's Church" as the vehicle of God's grace to the world.
d. the primacy of evangelism and mission in extending God's Kingdom.
e. the concepts of servanthood, voluntarism and mutual aid as a way of life.
f. the importance of "doing Kingdom ethics"–living so as

to conform to the lordship of Jesus Christ.

g. the application of limitless Christian love and active peacemaking to the hurts and injustices of the world.

These distinctives will allow us to position ourselves in the spectrum of Higher Education so that we may extend an invitation to the many who will profit from examining and accepting these life principles for themselves.[33]

The intent to "establish a clear sense of our identity" as given in the president's statement was not realized. The 1984 catalog changed the college's identification: No longer was it an Anabaptist Mennonite Brethren college, but rather: "Fresno Pacific College is a Christian College."[34]

How should this switch–from a "Mennonite Anabaptist College" to "Fresno Pacific College is a Christian College"–be interpreted? Paul Toews suggested it reflected a larger shift among local Mennonite Brethren.

> The problem with the Neo-Anabaptist ideal [referring to the Pacific College Idea] once it left the boundaries of the academic centers was that to many valley churchfolks it came not as recovery of a lost historical tradition but as a foreign import. Time and social movement had dimmed the Anabaptist part of the religious inheritance. Furthermore it was not only recovery, but also adaptation. This new ideal immediately ran into several barriers. While the revival of Mennonite history might bring nostalgic memories, the revival of Mennonite theology challenged the acculturation process with its embrace of the American order. To some parts of the church this Neo-Anabaptism seemed like the resurfacing of the older sectarian curbs.
>
> By refocusing the peace doctrines it restrained the growing patriotic identification with the American state; by revitalizing the communitarian ideal it challenged the growing individualism in a society built on a radical individualism;

by reviving the ethic of sharing it restrained self-indulgence in an indulgent age.[35]

Further complicating the identity problem of Mennonite Brethren higher education was a regional outlook that insisted on developing two colleges that were ambiguously "Christian" rather than concentrating on a single school with theological and denominational definition. This was despite counsel from two outside evaluating agencies in the 1950s and 1960s. A study commissioned by the Board of Education in 1955 concluded that the Mennonite Brethren constituency was too small to provide the resources for two colleges.[36] But the Mennonite Brethren evidently believed they could do the humanly impossible. Instead of consolidating to build one college, they expanded Pacific College, then a junior college, into a second four-year college.[37] A second evaluation of Mennonite Brethren higher education in 1968 by the Christian Service Fellowship counselled strongly against unrealistic attempts to maintain two colleges. It said the conference could not afford even one liberal arts program, let alone two. Persisting with two schools would mean they would be forced to become regional or interdenominational schools with Mennonite Brethren identification prevailing for some time into the future.[38] The summary of this report expressed a warning as to the possible consequences: "Historically the denomination (the United States MB Conference) has reached another plateau, where leadership is being exerted from churchmen and educators. The plateau is deceptively comfortable. Where are the prophets of the Brethren? Could not the Board of Education sound a call for a prophet?"[39]

The report urged the Mennonite Brethren Conference to address the issue of the purpose of a college for the nurture of the denomination's distinct faith and character. The prophetic word of the Christian Service Fellowship–that the colleges could not continue to be unique institutions expressing a particular Anabaptist ethic–was soon proven true. This failure, however, does not negate the dedication of those who sacrificed for a noble cause. The regret is that the colleges did not provide a theological frame of reference for their young people because of the provincialism in which the noble cause was attempted.

Both Tabor and Pacific, as "defender of the faith" institutions, were initially described as distinct from the culture around them and in tension with that culture. In their struggle for survival, both have become much like the hundreds of other generic Christian colleges which attract students by their dual emphasis on academic excellence and spiritual vitality. Like most Christian colleges, both are valuable, however they are not inclined to build the distinct theological identity essential for the growth of a church community with a New Testament/Anabaptist orientation.

## THEOLOGICAL EDUCATION

Preceding the changes that followed the Second World War the Mennonite Brethren lived by an intuitive theology emerging from an experiential emphasis rooted in a strong biblicism. The nurture of faith was provided from within the life of the church. Strong authoritative leadership provided the interpretive boundaries of faith and practice. An implicit faith can be sufficient for a church movement as long as it exists in the context of a homogeneous culture with a prescribed lifestyle that expresses the movement's understanding of faith and practice. Robert Friedmann's observation that implicit existential Christianity cannot be pressed into a theological system applies to the Mennonite Brethren. Such a system would contradict the very nature of their experiential understanding. "The Anabaptists were always willing to `give account of the hope that is in you' (1 Peter 3:15), but they were not willing, nor even able to construct a systematic theology, a rational edifice of thought. It would be foreign to them and inadequate to the subjectivity of the new birth."[40] Implicit theology became inadequate in the postwar era. Mennonite Brethren young people, scattered in academic and professional pursuits, demanded reasons for their faith and practice in relation to the pluralism of North American evangelical and mainline denominationalism. The widening relationship to the larger Mennonite communities, all claiming to be in the Anabaptist tradition, also called for a more explicit theological identity.

To more fully understand Mennonite Brethren theological education in its formative period it may be useful to relate a personal story. Among Mennonite Brethren in Canada I was the first to acquire an academic theological education, completing the requirements for a Bachelor of Divinity and a Master of Theology degree in 1940. Subsequently while pastoring the Mennonite Brethren Church at Buhler, Kansas, I continued studies toward a Doctor of Theology degree. My uncle, the well-known Benjamin B. Janz, together with a second leader from the Mennonite Brethren Conference in Canada, visited my wife and me in Buhler to share their concern about my graduate studies. They feared that people with scholastic training at the doctoral level were in great danger of losing the simplicity of faith and dependence on the enlightening of the Holy Spirit to understand and preach the Word. Colossians 2:8 was their scriptural warning: "Beware lest any man spoil you through philosophy and vain deceit, after the traditions of men." They even suggested that I might no longer be trusted with the responsibilities of leadership. My commitment to the Mennonite Brethren fellowship was such that I gave up my pursuit of a doctoral degree. A year and a half later B.B. Janz and A. H. Unruh came to Buhler requesting that I become president of the new Mennonite Brethren Bible College in Winnipeg. It had begun in 1944, with a student body of twelve and A.H. Unruh as president and the only full-time faculty member. In 1945, after a long inner struggle and encouragement from a larger circle of fellow believers, I finally accepted the invitation. But I could not miss the irony of the situation: In 1943 I had been asked to give up my theological studies. In 1945 the same conference leaders urged me to become president of "*eine hohere Bibelschule*" (a higher or advanced Bible school) because they had no other academically qualified for the position.

The new school was to be a Mennonite Brethren college, the first such school in Canada. Overtures from the General Conference Mennonites to establish a joint college were declined. There was no academic model to follow for this new type of school, and no resources in terms of a theological library or reference works. The only alternative was to expand existing Bible school curricula, with the emphasis on biblical and expository studies plus theology, with literary resources from evangelical seminaries as available. Augustus H. Strong's *Systematic Theology* and Edgar Y. Mullins's *The Christian Religion in its Doctrinal Expression* provided some of the intellectual framework for the initial years.[41] Interpretive lectures attempted to move from a mere implicit to an explicit theology in keeping with Mennonite Brethren understanding. In soteriology and eschatology, the works of Menno Simons were major resources.

The renaissance of Anabaptist interest led by "Old" Mennonite Church scholar Harold S. Bender was only emerging at this time. Mennonite Brethren were slow to benefit from this new interest, as they had not related strongly to the academics of other Mennonite groups. Furthermore, some available Mennonite literature did not offer a significant Anabaptist alternative. For example, Daniel Kauffman's *Doctrines of the Bible*[42] was largely based on Evans's *Great Doctrines of the Bible* and *What the Bible Teaches* by R.A. Torrey, both used in some Mennonite Brethren Bible schools.[43]

The historical journal, *Mennonite Quarterly Review*, which first appeared in 1927, offered some sources for outside thematic reading. Basic initial efforts at Mennonite theologizing like John C. Wenger's *Introduction to Theology* was not published until 1951[44] and Harold S. Bender's *These are my People: The Nature of the Church and its Discipleship According to the New Testament* did not appear until 1962.[45]

Helping compensate for the scarcity of published resources was the strength of faculty members at MBBC. Over decades teachers like A.H. Unruh, prince among Bible expositors, John A. Toews, historian and theologian with strong Anabaptist persuasion, Frank C. Peters and David Ewert, both strong in their respective fields, began the move from an implicit to more explicit (though still unwritten) Mennonite Brethren theological orientation.[46]

The second generation administration and faculty of the Bible college continued to struggle to retain constituency confidence. The population shift from the Prairies to the West, which produced a critical mass among the Mennonite Brethren churches in British Columbia, added to the distance between the college and major church constituencies. The quest for survival of the Bible institutes–Winkler, Bethany and Columbia, which in many areas are duplications of the original Bible college program–contributed to the tension. The change of Columbia Bible Institute to a Bible college placed it on equal academic level with the Mennonite Brethren Bible College.

To deal with the situation of four institutions at the post-high school level, the Canadian Conference appointed a task force to study the educational needs of the churches and chart a course toward coordination. Its report to the 1987 conference described the critical effects of such proliferation in the field of education. Under the heading "Compelling Issues," the report stated isolated eight compelling issues:

1. Theological and polity fragmentation. A major factor influencing denominational education is an increasing theological and polity fragmentation within our brotherhood. A weakening of denominational identity strikes deeply at the

heart of our education programs, and makes it difficult to enunciate a vision for Mennonite Brethren higher education.

2. Program articulation. For some years, three levels of higher education were offered among Mennonite Brethren–Bible institute, Bible college, and seminary. More recently, some of the distinctives among these institutional types have become blurred and costly duplication has developed.

3. Institutional planning. Institutional developments seem to be based upon expediency rather than a definitive master plan. Without systematic planning, programs have developed that overlap with those offered elsewhere and, consequently, institutions compete for the same students.

4. Attendance at non-M.B. schools. An increased number of students attending non-MB institutions has heightened the competition for students among our institutions and increased the theological and polity fragmentation within the denomination.

5. Declining demographics. Demographic data suggest a stabilization, if not an actual decline, in the potential student population. The enrollment in our schools follows closely the population trends in society, and unless we retain more M.B. students and/or attract more non-M.B. students our schools will not maintain quality programs.

6. Escalating costs. The escalating costs of higher education in a time of economic constraints present ever greater demands upon our resources. It is no longer economically feasible to maintain quality programs as student enrollment declines. We must realign our educational offerings to reflect the fiscal realities of our times, and to develop greater cost effectiveness in our programs.

7. Human resources. Our institutions also compete for scarce human resources. We cannot provide appropriate staffing for duplicate programs at our institutions.

8. Regional loyalties. In many respects, higher education

has become a national issue in Canada; none of our schools regards its boundaries in narrow regional terms. At the same time, however, regional loyalties to institutions provide a substantial part of the student and fiscal support base of an institution.[47]

The conclusions, while addressed to the Canadian conference educational program, also summarize problems of the U.S. Mennonite Brethren Conference schools. The Canadian Conference of Mennonite Brethren Churches stands at the threshold of a new era in higher education, particularly now that MBBC has changed its focus and adopted a new name (Concord College). Will Canada learn from the history of the U.S. Conference? The future of the program of higher education will to a large extent determine the future of the Mennonite Brethren Church in Canada and the U.S.

## MENNONITE BRETHREN BIBLICAL SEMINARY

The beginnings of the seminary in the U.S. parallels other Mennonite Brethren struggles to find a theological identity. The initial curriculum was modeled after existing seminary programs in which the founding faculty members had been trained.

The identity of the school for the initial years, 1956-1965, was described as follows:"Mennonite Brethren Biblical Seminary is a denominational school . . . and makes no apology for its evangelical position. It seeks to preserve and interpret the great truths of Christianity as revealed in the scriptures and understood by the sponsoring conference."[48]

The lack of a clear Mennonite Brethren identity for the first ten years may have been partly due to the fact that until 1964 the seminary was considered a provisional program awaiting endorsement as a graduate school under Mennonite Brethren General Conference sponsorship. Beginning in the 1964-1965 academic year, when the Mennonite Brethren Conference commitment solidified, the school also began a move toward a distinct Anabaptist/Mennonite Brethren identity.

The 1966-1967 catalog identified the seminary as a graduate school with a biblical theology emphasis. The 1967-1968 year expanded its identity as being a graduate school of biblical theology, with a Christian experiential focus, and an Anabaptist understanding of ecclesiology. The Anabaptist identification helped reopen conversations between the U.S. and Canadian conferences which led to the full integration of theological education at the General Conference level. The Canadians, who had observers on the administrative board for some years, officially became co-owners in 1975.

Being identified as Anabaptist, however, does not mean the process of "becoming" has been fully realized. To fashion a distinctly Anabaptist seminary that is distinct from the model of the mainline denominational and evangelical seminaries requires continuous innovative thinking. Most of the pressures on institutions are towards conformity rather than articulating a distinctive denominational position. A graduate school dependent on the broad literary resources of contemporary scholarship with limited sources of Anabaptist literature, faces a continuous task of biblical interpretation to focus the distinct understanding and application of Scripture in the light of present realities.

The Mennonite Brethren Church, with a world-wide constituency in an age of religious pluralism, cannot continue to sustain itself with an implicit, experiential theology. The challenge for Mennonite Brethren as the twenty-first century nears, is to renew the process of a community hermeneutics to interpret their faith and life in the context of modernity. The seminary, together with conference leadership, will need to accept major responsibility for this vital process.

## OBSERVATIONS AND IMPLICATIONS

Education has been central in the life of the Mennonite Brethren Church in North America. James DeForest Murch has identified the importance of education in his book *Teach or Perish: An Imperative for Christian Education at the Local Church Level*[49]. The process of education requires a continuous re-examination to remain faithful to the unchanging Word in a rapidly changing world. "The Church's paramount need is to become aware of the changed world situation in which it functions. It must then reorientate its educational function to the modern cultural situation in such a manner as to achieve more realistically and effectively its God-given purpose."

The era of the Bible school movement could be called the Golden Age of the Mennonite Brethren Church in North America. The centrality of Scripture as their main focus sparked a spiritual vitality that made the Mennonite Brethren fellowship one of the most exciting missionary movements of modern times. The life of the churches was fertilized by the exposure of Mennonite Brethren young people to Scripture.

The liberal arts colleges in the U.S. nurtured a Christian worldview, a training base for leadership, and a communal glue by providing a central focus for the spiritual, social and intellectual development of youth.

Nonetheless, Mennonite Brethren educational efforts have not succeeded in providing successive generations with a historical and theological frame of reference. Ignored have been the ravages of pluralism and individualism. Today's generation is still groping for spiritual and theological moorings. They do not have a sufficiently clear understanding of the capacity of either the Mennonite Brethren or the larger Anabaptist tradition to provide compelling answers to modern problems.

CHAPTER 15

# Identity amid Diversity

From their inception, the Mennonite Brethren never deviated from an unswerving commitment to Scripture. Throughout their history, however, they have been subject to the influence of others who shared this avowed commitment but responded to it in different ways. These influences have left their marks on the Mennonite Brethren struggle for theological identity.

Mennonites in Russia in the eighteenth and nineteenth centuries had become a socio-religious culture which no longer expressed the relationship of faith and life unique to their forebears of the sixteenth century. The early defection of the *Kleine Gemeinde* and the fellowship centers in Ohrloff and Gnadenfeld testified to a broad yearning for the vibrant Christian faith of the Menno Simons and the early Anabaptist variety.[1] The cry for a life of discipleship consistent with Scripture dominated the Mennonite Brethren founders and was reflected in their statement of secession and other confessional documents.[2]

This scriptocentric position directed the Mennonite Brethren pilgrimage in Russia and in North America. A statement in the *Mennonitische Blätter* of 1863 suggests the Mennonite Brethren fellowship's relation to Scripture: "They are better versed in the Holy Scripture, so much so that one is amazed and pleased at the understanding of the Scripture of the lowest and most humble among them."[3] Wesley Prieb noted that "the early members of our church were often recognized by the bulging coat pocket which contained a well-worn Bible. The *Bibelstunden* (Bible hours) became the basis of their fellowship and worship. Reading Scripture was part of their daily family pattern."[4] This centrality of the Bible may help explain why the small revivalistic movement within the larger Mennonite community remained connected to its Anabaptist roots, despite continual exposure to outside influences.

That other Mennonite groups were also shaped by the theological trends of their time has been borne out by other studies. Theron F. Schlabach, in his essay "Mennonites and Pietism in America, 1740-1880," showed that Pietistic influences also affected the wider Mennonite community.[5] A second document shedding light on these influences in the broader Mennonite family is Paul Toews's essay, "Fundamentalist Conflict in Mennonite Colleges: A Response to Cultural Transitions?"[6] To understand the Mennonite Brethren of today requires further probing of specific influences on the North American scene.

Tabor College and the regional Bible schools of the Mennonite Brethren churches were intended to maintain and nurture a strong ethnic character. Mennonite isolationism had produced a blend of culture and faith which the schools were charged with preserving.[7] This focus did not adequately equip students for the vital "lay ministry" upon which the movement had traditionally depended.[8] Deficiencies in their own educational program led many Mennonite Brethren to seek additional training in nationally known Bible institutes and seminaries.

## BIBLE INSTITUTES AND THE BIBLE SCHOOL MOVEMENT

The Bible Hour (*Biblestunde*) of the Mennonite Brethren in Russia had been basic to their spiritual nurture and development. The lifeline of the movement was their fellowship over an open Bible. The scattered farm life of North America, replacing the more intimate village settings in Russia, made these house meetings more difficult. The Bible school movement may have developed as the North American alternative to the *Bibelstunden*.[9] It was a new way to provide spiritual nurture to the youth of the churches and to spark the motivation for missionary service. The teachers of the Mennonite Brethren Bible schools traveled through the churches in the fashion of the former *Reiseprediger* (travelling preachers).

Prominent American Bible institutes like Biola in Los Angeles, Moody in Chicago and Northwestern in Minneapolis also had a major impact on the spiritual development of the Mennonite Brethren. Biola attracted many young Mennonite Brethren and contributed significantly to the development of church leadership. Cornelius N. Hiebert (Winnipeg, Man.), George B. Huebert (Reedley, Calif.), Jacob D. Hofer (Fresno, Calif.), Nick Janz (Herbert, Sask.), Abram A. Kroeker (Winkler, Man.), Henry K. Warkentin (Fresno), and others received much of their leadership training at Biola under the famous Reuben A. Torrey. Abram A. Kroeker became a pioneer in Christian education at the Winkler Bible Institute and in the Canadian Conference. For many years Nick Janz was an evangelist and Bible school teacher in Herbert and Hepburn, Saskatchewan. The missionary fervor which characterized the latter years of H.K. Warkentin's life was an expression of the inspiration received at Biola.

The writings of R.A. Torrey provided spiritual guidance for Mennonite Brethren. For several decades Torrey's book, *What the Bible Teaches*, was the primary guide for doctrinal studies. He conducted frequent Bible conferences in Mennonite Brethren churches and spoke several times at the Annual Tabor College Bible Conference.

Moody Bible Institute trained a number of early missionaries, such as Aron A. Janzen, pioneer of the African Mennonite Brethren church, and Daniel F. Bergthold, who went to India in 1904. The devotional books of Dwight L. Moody were mined for preaching material by lay ministers in many churches, and the Moody Colportage Library books met the devotional needs of the constituency. *Systematic Bible Studies* by James M. Gray, the successor to Moody as president of the institute, was a basic text in Mennonite Brethren Bible institutes during the 1940s.

Northwestern Bible Institute, led by the dynamic William B. Riley, also drew many students from Mennonite Brethren churches. Among its alumni were Jacob J. Wiebe, for many years pastor in Corn, Oklahoma and member of the Board of Foreign Missions; Tina Pauls, missionary worker in Minneapolis; Martha Janzen, veteran missionary in Africa; and pastors Rueben Baerg, David Wiens and Leo Wiens. The writings of Norman D. Harrison, a member of the Northwestern faculty, were part of many ministers' libraries between the 1930s and 1950s.[10]

The spiritual contributions of these schools were tributaries that enlarged the original stream of Mennonite Brethren faith and life. The emphasis on biblical content, missionary motivation and simple hermeneutics became a sustaining factor in Mennonite Brethren spirituality.

At the same time, however, this influence tended to submerge important Mennonite Brethren beliefs. Discipleship was supplanted by an overwhelming salvation emphasis in which conversion was seen most visibly as a personal experience assuring eternal life. For some the actual event of conversion assumed such primacy that knowing the precise time and date of accepting Christ became confirmation of salvation. Evangelism, instead of being a call to a disciple relationship with Christ in the context of a believing community, degenerated to a rescue operation to assure people the benefit of a final heavenly destiny. Salvation, so easily obtained, became detached from a life of love, self-denial and service within the believing community and to a needy world. For several decades in the mid-twentieth century Mennonite Brethren found themselves torn between an emphasis on individual salvation with its concern for devotionalism, and a focus on social service, social action and social justice.

Allied with the Bible institute movement was the World Fundamentals Association, organized in 1919 under the leadership of William B. Riley, Harry Rimmer, Arno Gaebelein and others. It brought to evangelical Protestantism a preoccupation with propositional truth, defending biblical inerrancy, a literal interpretation of creation, the virgin birth and physical resurrection of Jesus Christ, the substitutionary theory of atonement, and the imminent Second Coming. The public debates in the 1930s sponsored by the World Fundamentals Association gained a good hearing among Mennonite Brethren. Periodicals like *The Sword of the Lord*, edited by John R. Rice and the *Defender*, edited by Gerald Winrod, became household literature. Both promoted propositional truth and creedal doctrine so vigorously that the relational character of New Testament discipleship was overlooked. Previously foreign emphases on rigid creedal doctrine and apologetical systems to "prove" Scripture became increasingly dominant in Mennonite Brethren pulpits and classrooms. Their prominence came at the expense of Christ's central role in the life and character of the church.[11]

The influences of Biola, Moody and Northwestern were enlarged in the 1920s and 1930s by Prairie Bible Institute (Three Hills, Alberta) and Briercrest Bible Institute (Caronport, Saskatchewan). In later years Winnipeg Bible College (now Providence College and Seminary) moved into a position of prominence.

The emphasis on missions and evangelism in the Bible institutes had an awakening effect on Mennonite Brethren and accounted for much of the surge of missionary vision and commitment from 1930-1960. But the new evangelism also contained a strong emphasis on child evangelism. The subsequent trend toward "child baptism" (children aged 7-14) changed the character of a believers church built on principles of repentance and rigorous discipleship. Benjamin B. Janz addressed the problem:

The more it moved to child baptism, even though it was

immersion, the more there were people without a true conversion experience, and the new life and discipline in the church became more difficult. The character of the M.B. Church, in spite of all light of scriptural understanding and all Christian and spiritual education, changed from a deeply pious and pure church to a solemn confessional people's church where Christian ethics became private judgement and was impotent for a renewal of life and walk, the hallmark of our fathers in the period of their spiritual health.[12]

William Bestvater, who for many years offered dynamic leadership in the Bible schools, Bible conferences and evangelism, drew heavily from the dispensational resources of the Cyrus I. Scofield correspondence courses, Arno C. Gaebelein, William Evans, H.C. Dixon, William Riley and Harris Gregg.[13] In 1920 the Canadian Conference invited Bestvater to conduct a two-month Bible course for ministers, which extended his understanding of the Scripture to the grassroots.[14]

The theological influences of this era were well reflected in the two textbooks written by Bestvater: *Textbuechlein in Glaubenslehre*, an organization of material gathered from Scofield, Evans and Torrey; and *Textbuechlein in Bibelkunde*, a compilation of materials from James Gray, Gaebelein and Scofield.[15] A series of articles by Bestvater in the *Zionsbote* in the 1920s under the heading, *"Zeugniss der Schrift"* (witness of the Word), also effectively disseminated teachings gathered from the same sources.

The Bible school programs in the later 1920s and 1930s utilized texts with similar interpretations. Frequently used were Theodor Haarbeck's *Biblische Glaubenslehre, Der Dienst: am Evangelium in Predigt und Seelsorge* and *Das Christliche Leben nach der Schrift* for courses in Bible doctrine, pastoral theology and Christian ethics. Giesbert Stochmann's *Ringet Recht*, a text on Christian ethics, was adopted in the 1930s and later.¹⁶

Mennonite Brethren efforts to avoid rigid creedal formulations allowed them to draw benefits from the evangelical communities of North America and Europe without becoming locked into a dogmatic theological system. The absence of creedal systems among most Mennonite Brethren Bible school teachers gave them flexibility and an openness to see truth in new relationships. The earlier 1902 Confession of Faith illumined this receptivity:

> Every Confession of Faith, as every other teaching and exposition of Scripture is subject at all times to examination and estimation under the guidance of the Holy Spirit, according to the Holy Scriptures . . . the only infallible written preserved resource of the necessary and sufficient revelation of God to humanity for our salvation.¹⁷

While feeding at these outside sources, Mennonite Brethren schools (including institutes, colleges and even the seminary in its earlier years) made little or no effort to provide in their curriculum any systematic study of the historical and theological distinctives of the Mennonite Brethren. As late as 1971 a president of the Mennonite Brethren Bible College challenged the Canadian Conference to help establish a transdenominational theological graduate school with other evangelicals in Canada in preference to a Mennonite Brethren seminary.¹⁸ Commitment to the historic Anabaptist faith has been peripheral in many areas of the conference. The mission to proclaim a message to a needy world was dominated by an emphasis on obtaining numerical results, while other parts of the biblical emphasis suffered.

## OBSERVATIONS AND IMPLICATIONS

The transition from a church in a rigid cultural mold to a community influenced by broad theological and sociological exposure has enriched the Mennonite Brethren spiritually and culturally. In the larger Mennonite community and in the broader evangelical fellowship we have gained recognition as a believers community firm in biblical orientation and conservative in theological commitment. Within our own fellowship, however, there lingers uncertainty as to our specific theological identity in relation to these broader streams.

The rapid cultural change from a rural agricultural people to an educational and professional people has left us ill-equipped to answer a new set of questions: Who are we? What makes us different from the mainstream of North American evangelicalism? Are we justified in claiming a faith and mission different from those who are our brothers and sisters in Christ? Has our purpose as a "peculiar" people of God been fulfilled?

The questions strike at the essence of our faith and life. Has our lack of a clear New Testament (Anabaptist) ecclesiology clouded our self-understanding? Have Pietism and conservative evangelicalism left us with a gospel that doesn't impact our neighbors? Have we lost our passion for the call of Jesus: "Whosoever will come after me, let him deny himself, and take up his cross, and follow me. For whosoever will save his life shall lose it; but whosoever shall lose his life for my sake and the gospel's, the same shall save it" (Mark 8:34-35)?

Our theological pilgrimage has left us with three particularly troublesome issues. Over the years our congregations and schools have been preoccupied with questions about the nature of Scripture, the proper ecclesiology for the church, and the shape of the future.

## The Bible

The debate of recent years on the inerrancy of the Bible is historically foreign to our people. Our forebears saw no need to debate "how" God's revelation was inspired and transmitted. For them the major question was "who?" and "what?"–the person of Christ and the message of the Bible. The unfolding of God's relationship to humanity in history throughout the Old Testament, the special revelation through Jesus Christ, the character and purpose of a redeemed community, and the certainty of Christ's return–these were sufficient grounds for their faith.

In 1934 my father sat in on my classes in apologetics where I, as a young theologian, put forth great efforts to prove the inspiration of the Bible. The prooftext method of logical argument, borrowed from the World Fundamentalist Association, was the basis of my teaching method at the time. Father replied:

> Son, is it necessary to defend the Bible? Would you find it necessary to defend a lion? Would not a lion much better defend himself if he were turned loose? Is not the Bible itself proof enough to prove itself as the power of God to salvation? Is there any need to defend the Bible where the Bible is believed, lived, and taught? Is there any merit to prove the inerrancy of the Bible to people who do not believe it and do not know the witness of the spirit?

What was I to say? Were we wrong to let the Bible stand on its own merit, and through the witness of the Spirit confirm it as God's Word?

Abraham H. Unruh found my father's position common to an earlier generation.

> It is striking that our early brethren record no paragraph in their statement of faith in which they declare their position with respect to the Scriptures even though they were in possession of the Confession of Faith prepared by Cornelius Ris in 1747 . . . in which the Scriptures are declared as the only reliable infallible source of faith. Throughout their struggle for their convictions and answers to the at-

tacks upon the young Mennonite Brethren Church we find with fathers of the movement an unchanging faithfulness to the Holy Scriptures. The Bible was for them the unfailing Word of God from cover to cover. . . . In this commitment to the Word of God they reviewed every single truth and formed their concepts from the relationship to its content as they understood it.[19]

Has our separation of truth and life, salvation and responsibility driven us to prove and defend the propositional foundation of our faith? Is the evidence of the gospel so lacking in our lives that it must be reposited in a document? Is not newness of life a stronger proof for the truth of the Bible than some creed that can be challenged?

**The Church**
The church as understood by the Mennonite Brethren is a fellowship in a relationship of love with Christ and with one another. It is a community of inter-responsibility and discipline. The church of "ecclesiastical democracy" with room for individualistic independence in the local church and in the conference, well adapted from our North American culture, would appear strange to our forebears and possibly even more so to the community of faith in the first centuries. Viewing grace as a gift to be appropriated without the discipline of self-denial and death is not part of our understanding of the Christian life. The contemporary emphasis of many evangelicals–to offer free grace as the doorway to a life of ease and security in this world and in the world to come–was not known among the early Mennonite Brethren. Have external pressures led to a process of accommodation within? Have we become a comfortable church nurturing the hope of heaven without sharing the demands of the cross? Can we actually be the church without being in tension with the surrounding culture?

## The Future

The question of eschatology has a long history with the Mennonite Brethren. Abraham H. Unruh described the eschatological view of the early Mennonite Brethren as follows: "They exhorted (each other) to watchfulness and to a holy walk. The present views with reference to the rapture and the millennium were apparently foreign to them. However, they joined in the prayer: 'Amen, Come Lord Jesus'."[20] Fascination with end-times speculation was not part of our biblical foundation. It came to us from the outside (Darbyism in Russia and dispensationalism in North America), and was spread widely by leaders like William Bestvater. As the son of a minister and Bible school teacher, I received frequent admonitions from my father to view particular interpretations of eschatology as *possibilities* but not accept them as dogma. Fortunately, many in our fellowship, particularly the younger theologians, are shying away from the predictive certainties of dispensational eschatology.

There is no room to question the basic truths of Christian eschatology. The return of Christ, his ultimate triumph and the final judgment are beyond debate. Scripture is clear that God is sovereign and history will find its consummation and purpose in his plan. But preoccupation with the "how, when and where" of eschatology can deflect us from our God-given mission. Our task is not to fix the dates of the tribulation or the millennium or interpret the significance of every political event in the Middle East. Ours is to proclaim that the day of the Lord is coming.

The issues facing us in all three of these areas–hermeneutics, ecclesiology, eschatology–are vital, and our responses will shape the theological identity of the church. Our response can either renew us and revitalize our mission from the biblical perspective, or can erode the trust of history that God has given us as one part of his church.

The past and present pilgrimage of Mennonite Brethren

raises the question: Do we have a theological frame of reference, an ethos, which continues to float aimlessly among various streams of theology and polity, borrowing where it is most convenient? Or is it time to refocus the basic theological tenets of Mennonite Brethren faith? The 1976 revised Confession of Faith and the call for confessional integrity point to a recommitment that is fundamentally unchanged from that of the early Mennonite Brethren. It is best summarized under a five-fold declaration.

1. Commitment to the Holy Scriptures.
2. An emphasis on the new birth.
3. The church as an interdependent fellowship.
4. The church as a people in the world but not of the world.
5. The church as a missionary movement.

After 125 years we again ask the question: Do we live what we profess to believe? The exhortation of Paul to the Corinthian church–"examine yourselves, whether ye be in the faith; prove your own selves" (2 Cor. 13:5)–is a call to the Mennonite Brethren in the final decade of the century. Reinvigorating these five foundational areas could be a way to carry the ethos of the Mennonite Brethren Church into the future.

### Commitment to the Holy Scriptures

> We believe that all Scripture is inspired by God as men of God were moved by the Holy Spirit. We accept the Old and New Testaments as the infallible Word of God and the authoritative Guide for the faith and life of Christian discipleship. We believe that the Old Covenant was preparatory in nature, finding its fulfillment in the New Covenant. Christ is the key to understanding the Bible; the Old Testament bears witness to Him, and He is the One whom the New Testament proclaims. Ps. 19; 119:105;

Lk. 24:27,44; Rom. 1:18-23; 2 Tim. 3:15-17; 2 Pet. 1:16-21; Heb. 1:1-2; 8:5-13.[21]

This statement from the 1976 Confession of Faith is clear and consistent with the historic position of the Mennonite Brethren. The statement also expresses our Christocentric understanding of Scripture. The provision of redemption and the life of the redeemed are anchored in the incarnation of God in Christ who lived, died for our sins, rose from the dead, and ascended into Heaven.

Born-again believers under the guidance of the Holy Spirit seek daily nurture from Scripture. To understand biblical teaching in specific questions of life and practice, Mennonite Brethren seek to follow the example of Acts 15–a principle of community hermeneutics. A statement recorded in the 1878 Conference of Mennonite Brethren expressed this principle:

> The Conference has been called for brethren of like faith from our scattered churches to see whether at the hand of the Bible it is not possible to bring into harmony differed views gleaned from the study of the Word of God and then proceed as a church fellowship according to the same rule (Phil. 3:16) under the banner of the cross of Christ.[22]

The final application of scriptural truth for believers emerges from the fellowship of the redeemed community as they gather to study the Word together with prayer and dependence on the illumination of the Holy Spirit. "For it seemed good to the Holy Ghost, and to us" (Acts 15:28). "What does the Bible say" has been a continuous point of reference throughout Mennonite Brethren history.

**Emphasis on the New Birth**

The Mennonite Brethren movement emerged in an ethno-religious environment where being born of Mennonite parents was a condition for baptism and church membership. In the larger church, from which the Mennonite Brethren seceded, issues of faith and culture had become confused.[23]

Mennonite Brethren recognized that all people are sinful by nature, guilty before God and in need of forgiveness through Jesus Christ.[24] Scripture taught them that humanity is saved by grace through faith in Christ. Those who repent of their sin and trust in Jesus Christ as Savior and Lord receive forgiveness. By the power of the Holy Spirit they are born again and become the children of God. Saving faith in Mennonite Brethren understanding involves a surrender of the will to Christ, a complete trust in him and an obedience to his Word in faithful discipleship.

Born-again believers confirm their commitment to discipleship by baptism, "buried with him by baptism into death: that like as Christ was raised up from the dead by the glory of the Father, even so we also should walk in newness of life" (Rom. 6:4).

### An Interdependent Fellowship

For Mennonite Brethren, the issue of congregational structure, or ecclesiology, is inseparable from the new birth. New creatures form a new kind of body, a body composed only of those who share the same spiritual (not ethnic) birthright.

The church, the body of Christ, is not a mere organization or an association but an *interdependent* fellowship, a covenant community (1 Cor. 12). Every member is to be concerned with the welfare of fellow members. Through teaching, encouragement, counseling and, where necessary, rebuke, the church promotes constructive discipline. Members whose walk is contrary to the teachings of Scripture are subject to loving and redemptive discipline. Local congregations, meanwhile, are members of a larger fellowship, Mennonite Brethren Conference, in which the same principles apply.

The ministers and leaders of the church are recognized as a gift from God, emerging from within the body (Eph. 4:11-16). Their assignment is to equip fellow members for faithful life and ministry. Mennonite Brethren historically favored a plurality of leadership–in contrast to a hierarchy with a single pastor at the top of the pyramid. This traditional form of leadership has frequently been in tension with the trend toward individualism in North American culture.

**In the World but not of the World**

The words of Jesus in John 17:14-15–"They are not of the world even as I am not of the world. I pray not that thou shouldest take them out of the world, but that thou shouldest keep them from the evil"–is basic to the Mennonite Brethren understanding of the church. The cry of the founders was that we cannot claim to be the church of Christ and live in sin like the people of the world. This does not mean a separation from the people of the world, but from the lifestyle, ethics and values that dominate the lives of worldly people.

Mennonite Brethren accept the Sermon on the Mount (Matt. 5-7) as the biblical standard of ethics expressed in love, forgiveness, self-surrender and a love even for enemies. The early Mennonite Brethren seldom addressed issues of doctrine. Their concern was consistency of life–How do we live after the example of Jesus and the teachings of the apostles?

The Mennonite Brethren concern to harmonize what they believed with how they lived was linked closely with their understanding that "The kingdom of God is within you" (Luke 17:21). The indwelling of Christ in the believer (John 17:21-23) can only be recognized in a corresponding Christlike character.[25]

A second aspect in the theology of the kingdom for Mennonite Brethren is the ongoing conflict between the kingdom of light and the kingdom of darkness. 1 John 5:19, 2 Timothy 3:13 and 2 Thessalonians 2:11-12 describe the kingdom of this world: "the whole world lieth in wickedness . . . the evil man and the seducer (imposter) shall wax worse and worse, deceiving and being deceived."[26]

For Mennonite Brethren, being a people in the world but not of the world can be summarized as follows: The character and relationship of the church–the people of God–is rooted in a personal relationship with God, a response to his forgiving mercy on the basis of the atonement of the cross, and a volitional commitment to Jesus Christ. True conversion produces a new creature (2 Cor. 5:17). Those who are redeemed and transformed cannot conform to the values and lifestyle of this world.

**A Missionary Movement**

The emphasis on conversion naturally provided the basis for a world view which recognized only two kinds of people–"saved" and "unsaved." There was no third category. The redeemed community thus bears the responsibility to witness to the unsaved. To be the church and to evangelize were interdependent, if not identical. Like the early Anabaptists, the Mennonite Brethren considered evangelism and missions as mandates of the gospel.[27]

The Mennonite Brethren witness contributed to the general renewal that came to the Mennonite churches in Russia and North America in the second half of the nineteenth and early years of the twentieth century. Their outreach extended from Russia and North America to India, Africa, South America and Japan. Today, the combined Mennonite Brethren in those regions outnumber the members in Europe and North America. Missions has been and continues to be the heartbeat of the Mennonite Brethren.

These basic tenets of faith are the core of Mennonite Brethren belief. Our fundamental theology has not changed in more than 130 years of history. Yet the struggle continues to achieve a consistency between what we profess to believe and what we actually practice in life.

CHAPTER 16

# Wrestling with Modernity

Prior to the Second World War the Mennonite Brethren Church existed in a protected subculture where religious and social controls aided their efforts to be "people in the world, but not of the world." Life, theology and ethics were relatively fixed. Annual conferences helped them draw the boundaries between belief and unbelief, church and world.

The postwar era created a new context. The revolutionary changes that followed 1945 affected all areas of social as well as religious life. Members began to question long-held scriptural understandings and churchly practices. The moorings of the past grew slack.

## BUFFETED BY A SEA OF CHANGE

"Breakneck changes" was the way *Life* magazine described the period of its first fifty years (1936-1986). This era, it said, was "the most troubled, unsettling, costly, adventurous and surprising time ever. More has changed and faster, more has been destroyed, more accomplished than in any comparable interval in the five thousand years since recorded history began."[1]

The Second World War (1939-1945) was the most cataclysmic upheaval in the history of human warfare. Eighty million people were in uniform and an estimated fifty million people died, including ten million civilians. Germany lost four million men; and the estimates for Russian loss ranged up to twenty million. *Life* considered 1945 the watershed year of the twentieth century[2] as atomic bombs dropped on Hiroshima and Nagasaki changed the face of history. America, in the words of Churchill, was recognized as standing "at the summit of the world."[3]

The decades that followed were earthshaking. The world map was redrawn. Decolonialization set in. The world became smaller.[4] In the coming years the rocket became the symbol of scientific advance. In October 1957 the first satellite, albeit a Soviet one, orbited the globe and ushered in the space age. Moreover, *Life* said: "The deciphering of the genetic code in the 1960s may prove to be as important to the course of history as the splitting of the atom."[5] Communications exploded and shrank the world to a global village. Television revolutionized communication, perhaps more so even than the invention of print. World population passed the five billion mark. The cry of war did not cease.

Developments in the natural and social sciences altered the educational system forever. Liberal philosophers asserted that the only danger confronting society was narrowness that would hinder progress. Fundamental moral virtues went out of fashion. Allan Bloom in his attack on much of modernity noted that "this liberalism is what prepared us for the culture of relativism and the fact-value distinction which seemed to carry that viewpoint further and give it a greater intellectual weight."[6]

Relativism, which removes standards of absolutes, left society without norms to distinguish between right and wrong. People now decide morality on their own terms. Individualism dominates North American culture. Alasdair C. MacIntyre noted:

> For liberal individualism a community is simply an arena in which individuals each pursue their own self-chosen conception of the good life and political institutions exist to provide that degree of order which makes such self-determined activity possible. Government and law are, or

ought to be, neutral between rival conceptions of the good life for man, and hence, although it is the task of government to promote law-abidingness, it is on the liberal view no part of the legitimate function of government to inculcate any one moral outlook.[7]

Richard Reeves, in his book *American Journey*, quotes Robert Schrank, a labor union official, as saying:

The worst thing that's happening in America is that abhorrent behavior can always be explained now. It's dangerous to somehow apply Freudian thinking to justify people acting out their hostilities by stealing. But now it's explained, "I am not responsible because my mother and father didn't like me and I was brought up in a wrong way. . . ." In a democracy, if the individual isn't responsible then we're finished as a free people.[8]

Allan Bloom, in his book *The Closing of the American Mind*, describes American education as providing "no destined visage to the young person." He views the democracy of the disciplines at the universities as "an anarchy, because there are no recognized rules for citizenship and no legitimate titles to rule . . . there is no vision, nor is there a set of competing visions of what an educated human being is."[9] A culture which removes all moral and ethical standards destroys the structure of society and endangers the most basic social institution, the family. The pursuit of comfort and pleasure is but an expression of individualism and self-fulfillment.[10] This influence results in an increasingly fragmented society in which ties to kin and community erode. Binding relationships such as marriage, which once were seen as sacraments, became covenants, then contracts and finally irrelevant.[11]

A further factor which the church must recognize as it confronts modernity is the population explosion and the rapid urbanization of the twentieth century. World population reached its first billion in 1850, but it took only another seventy-five years to double to two billion and only fifty years to double again to four billion in 1975. In 1987 it reached the five billion mark. Missiologist Henry Schmidt reports that in the year 1800, 3.4 percent of the world population lived in cities (population 2,500 or more). In 1900, the number was 13.6 percent; in 1950, 28.2 percent; in 1975, 41.1 percent. By the year 2,000, fifty-five percent of the population will be urbanized.[12] The data for the United States are even more drastic. In 1789, by comparison, only five percent of the U.S. population lived in communities of 2,500 or more. Today more than ninety percent of Americans live within the orbit of 200 metropolitan areas that contain over 4,000 cities.

At the heart of urbanization is the shift from an agricultural to an industrial economy and specialized professionalism. Three characteristics emerge from this rapid urbanization: secularization, pluralization and privatization. All three are vitally important to understanding the role of religion in modern culture.

Secularization is defined as the process by which religion and its institutions lose their significance. The Oxford Conference of 1937 described this process as follows:

> Since the Renaissance the secular order has gradually established its independence of ecclesiastical control. The church is no longer authoritative and dominant, it is only one among the many influences and movements of the modern world. Today convinced Christians are everywhere in a minority in a predominately un-Christian world.[13]

Henry Schmidt comments:

> In the modern world Christian ideals become less meaningful. Church institutions become more marginal. The

premodern world, although not Christian, was conscious of a supernatural world which existed beyond the natural world. Family, sex, farming, and morality were interpreted in a supernatural framework. Today this is less the case. Secularization is the only reality. People worship the present. Peter Berger suggests that they live in a world with no windows; the "here and now" has become all. For secular men and women the supernatural is less real. This is true for a number of reasons. In part it is due to refusal to acknowledge God, but it is also because the image of humankind as "the creator" makes God more distant. Human planning, progress, technological advance, and achievement give people a sense of power and of being in control. Secularism removes the supernatural dimension from life in general and from Christianity in particular.[14]

Pluralization emerges from an environment of many options and choices. Diverse lifestyles, cultural values, fashions and occupations in the urban setting call for continuous choices of all kinds. In an industrial and relativistic environment with an untold variety of jobs, rapid transportation and mass communication, there is decreasingly a common sense of values and a common world view. Former bonds of shared experience are lost. Each individual forms his or her own world.

The impact of pluralism on religion is evident. Relativism has undermined, or destroyed entirely, any regard for absolutes. The Christian faith becomes one of many options in the marketplace of religions–Islam, Scientology, Mormonism, Hinduism, Buddhism. The choices of religious response become personal and utilitarian.

Secularization in the context of pluralism results in the privatization of the individual. People live in multiple worlds–business, civic, home, church, school and neighborhood. The difficulty of relating to so many spheres destroys the personal ethos, and privatization becomes an escape mechanism for survival. People lose focus and cease to integrate the various spheres of influence. The private sphere becomes a world of diversions aimed at personal fulfillment. People cease to be responsible to a community, selecting instead from a multiplicity of involvements on the basis of utilitarian benefit. Religion and the church become just another option, and a completely private one, at that.

Secularization, pluralization and privatization speed the process of paganizing culture. Modernity strips humanity of certainty and it miniaturizes faith. It shifts the focus from the absolutes and the content of faith to the subjective and experiential dimension of faith. "Marketing the gospel" trivializes the message as glitz supplants impelling power of truth. The gospel is truncated as the demand for repentance, newness of life and self-denying discipleship is omitted. The supernatural authority of religion is eroded and the gospel degenerates to neo-paganism. "Urban culture today has more affinity with the pluralism and paganism of Athens than with the homogeneous religious heritage of Jerusalem."[15]

## A PEOPLE WITHOUT A THEOLOGY OF CHANGE

Mennonite Brethren, bred in a rigid culture of traditionalism, have not developed a biblical theology of change. Their birth was a protest against what they saw as the corruption of Anabaptism.[16] Faith in the Mennonite colonies had become domesticated and integrated with a particular ethnic culture in which Mennonite identity was based not on a personal relationship with Christ, but along bloodlines. "This marriage of faith to a particular culture had a disastrous consequence for the life and ministry of the church," said John A. Toews, adding that the Russian Mennonites were not the only ones to succumb to this temptation.[17] Throughout their history, Mennonites have, for various reasons, clung to the status quo and resisted cultural change with great determination. Earlier, in Prussia, they retained their Dutch language and culture for two hundred years before fully adopting the German of their "new" homeland. In Russia their economic, civil, educational and religious autonomy gave them a static environment in which change did not seem necessary or desirable. In North America they managed to remain relatively isolated in locations such as Mountain Lake and Bingham Lake in Minnesota; Winkler and Steinbach in Manitoba; and Herbert, Hepburn and Waldheim in Saskatchewan. With considerable control over their outside influences, they gained little experience in coping with change. Other Mennonite groups experienced the same cultural patterns as the Mennonite Brethren. Yet it appears that the changes of the mid-twentieth century have affected Mennonite Brethren identity more than others.

Sociologist Calvin Redekop has addressed the phenomenon that renewal movements tend to assume that the true essence of faith or relationship with God is detached from a historical context and is abstractly personal and experiential. His case study on the Evangelical Mennonite Brethren Church offers persuasive evidence for this position.[18]

In a later study of "Religious Renewal Movements in Search of a Past," Redekop observes that identity loss in renewal movement (as an example he refers to the Mennonite Brethren and the Evangelical Mennonite Brethren) stems from an inability to deal with the rejection of one ideological tradition (ethos) and the subsequent replacing of it with another. He points out that both the Evangelical Mennonite Brethren and the Mennonite Brethren were born as a protest against, as they saw it, an unbiblical belief and practice with the purpose to return to the "pure faith," the preservation of the essential truth.

The emphasis on the biblical teaching and righteous living needed, however, to be based in a supporting social and cultural milieu. But since the old sub-culture had been rejected a new sub-culture had to be substituted. But sub-cultures are not created overnight, so the E.M.B. and the M.B. have been searching for a sub-culture on which to base their "reformed" beliefs and world view, and have found it in the fundamentalist and evangelical "ethnicity" in American Christianity.[19]

Redekop's analysis, if correct, goes far in explaining the ambiguous nature of Mennonite Brethren theological identity. In his theory, the Mennonite Brethren relinquished one identity and sought to replace it with another. That this shift took place precisely in the midst of a period of radical social change made their disorientation all the more pronounced.

Comparing Mennonite Brethren conference records from before the Second World War with those of the post-war era produces some startling contrasts that bear out the social observations of Bloom, MacIntyre and others. Before the war, conference attention was heavily weighted toward concerns of lifestyle, ethics and mission. In the period following, it began paying more heed to matters of function and belief, reflecting the shifting sands of the wider culture.

The General Conference of 1948 concluded with an exhortation from the Committee of Reference and Counsel under the heading: "Watchfulness Over the Spiritual Welfare of the Churches of the Mennonite Brethren Conferences of North America." Specific areas of concern included: (1) Polity and practice related to the call of ministers and their affirmation in ordination needed to remain within the framework of the scriptural guidelines as articulated in the Confession of Faith. (2) The need to retain community hermeneutics and not give in to the tendency of individualism in adopting policies and practices in church life, other than those as understood by the larger Mennonite Brethren community of faith. (3) That the relationship of the church to the leadership and teachers of the church remain biblical. (4) That Mennonite Brethren remain faithful to Scripture in walk, practice and unity.[20]

In 1986, thirty-eight years later, the Mennonite Brethren Conference leadership enlarged on these concerns. The nearly four decades of increasing modernity led them to highlight the following dangers:

1. Fragmentation/Autonomy

    1.1 An increased fragmentation and autonomy due to growing individualism, localism, nationalism, regionalism and theological pluralism.

    These socio-religious forces are fragmenting the Mennonite Brethren Church along Canadian/United States lines, mid-west/west coast regions in Canada and the United States. Internal re-alignments will occur by 2000, especially in Canada. The educational institutions will be the first agencies caught in these fragmenting forces.

    1.2 The increase of theological pluralism. It will follow Anabaptist-Mennonite Brethren/ evangelical, Anabaptist-evangelical/evangelism-church growth and non-charismatic/ charismatic lines. Lack of leadership consensus regarding the Confession of Faith and the theological orientation of the church will result in the further erosion of confessional consensus, especially on the peace position and related issues.

    1.3 Erosion of conference loyalty. Local churches and institutions will become more independent of the Conference. There will be increased competition for people and money between local church and the institutions of the church. The institutions will loosen Mennonite Brethren identity as they seek to broaden their people and financial base to survive.

    1.4 Post-secondary education will become increasingly divisive. It will serve to further divide the Conference regionally at the undergraduate level as in the U.S., so also

in Canada.
2. Theology
    2.1  Theological and ideological re-alignments will occur across Mennonite denominational bodies that will force the Mennonite Brethren to make some critical decisions about Mennonite identity and affiliations.
    2.2  Faith/theological questions will be determined by expediency and pragmatism.
    2.3  There will be increased biblical and theological illiteracy in our churches.
3. Church/Character/Polity
    3.1  The General Conference may become a loose federation of churches that will gather periodically for fellowship. Primacy will be placed on the local church with decreasing support for larger Conference and global concerns. The General Conference will carry responsibility for few programs. Foreign missions and the Seminary may remain a General Conference concern. All other programs may be nationalized.
    3.2  The character of the church will be determined more and more by evangelism and activism. The doing of church planting/evangelism will be the glue. There will be increased erosion of church as covenant community and of church discipline. Involvement in mission that demands sacrifice will decrease because of growing affluence and enjoyment of the good life. Many churches that are not growing will be closed.
    3.3  There will be numerical church growth in some regions. This growth may result in increased cultural and ethnic diversity in the churches. The growth will be missional and will move churches in the direction of community churches. These churches will tend to be more mainstream evangelical rather than Anabaptist-Mennonite Brethren.
    3.4  Church/Conference polity may move toward more

authoritarian/presbyterian models on the local church level and more radical congregationalism at the conference level. The clergy/laity distinction will accelerate. There will be more emphasis on authority roles and less on servant roles.

3.5 The gulf between institutional leadership and the local church may widen. The latter will be concerned primarily with local agenda, while the former will promote larger conference concerns.

3.6 The church population will continue to age. The church will need to think more and more of ministries to aging persons.

3.7 There will be an intensification of personal piety in the churches.[21]

These statements point to outside influences that threaten the Mennonite Brethren Church. But not all of the blame for increasing fragmentation and loss of consensual identity can be laid at the feet of external pressures. A looming question is why these influences so radically affected the basic biblical understanding and application to which Mennonite Brethren had been so deeply committed.

Issues of modernity pose urgent questions to Mennonite Brethren as they approach the twenty-first century. Is Calvin Redekop correct that a cultural milieu is needed to house the values of faith? Is it sociologically correct that membership in any group depends upon the ideological cohesiveness of the group, the commitment of the individuals to the core values and purposes (theology) of the group?[22] Was John A. Toews correct when he wrote, "Our present identity crisis is largely the result of our exposure to 'every wind of doctrine' from various theological schools of thought. Our problem is perhaps not so much one of exposure to various theological views, as our indiscriminate acceptance of them."[23] Does Redekop adequately explain the crusade to change the Mennonite Brethren name when he writes: "The reform of a degenerate Christian tradition (ethnicity), however valid and just in its own right, does not exempt the succeeding group from facing the very same problem in the second and third generation as the new ethnicity is formed."[24]

Clearly, the Mennonite Brethren have been seriously affected by dramatic changes in their surrounding environment. While they remain fervently committed to God's unchanging revelation in Jesus Christ, the environment of a changing culture may require new forms of expression. The more radical such changes, the more difficult it becomes for a believing community to order their life as true followers of Jesus. The task ahead for Mennonite Brethren will not be an easy one.

CHAPTER 17

# How shall we then be led?

An important strength of the early Mennonite Brethren movement was its distinctive form of church governance, or polity. Societal trends and imported religious influences have put this polity under increasing assault. Today it is at risk of disappearing entirely.

Christians have never agreed on which form of governance they should use. In the post-Reformation era, three major types emerged, all claiming to be drawn from biblical patterns: Episcopal, Presbyterian and Congregational.[1]

**Episcopal Polity–Governance by Bishops**

In this form, the primary unit of the church is the diocese, a district or province of churches. Each diocese is governed by a bishop. Every church belongs to the diocese, and is accountable to the bishop of the diocese.

Episcopal polity emphasizes the offices to which leaders are appointed or elected. It makes a sharp distinction between clergy and laity. Clergy often have the sole authority to govern the local church.

The biblical basis for this polity is the Jerusalem model: the leadership of the Apostles, especially Peter, John and James. It is practiced in the Roman Catholic, Eastern Orthodox and Anglican/Episcopal churches.

**Presbyterian Polity–Governance by Elders**

Here the primary unit of the church is the presbytery. Every church belongs to a presbytery and is accountable to it.

The presbytery is governed by a body of ruling and teaching elders. The ruling elders are laypersons; the teaching elders are ministers. The local church is also governed by a body of elders composed of lay elders and the ministers of the church.

The Presbyterian model, based on the letters of Paul, places emphasis on the gifts of the Spirit rather than on fixed offices. Lutherans and Methodists also follow this model of governance.

### Congregational–Local Church Governance

The Congregational model, used by Baptist and independent churches, emerged in England out of the struggle with the monarchial episcopacy of the Anglican state church. This model puts all power in the hands of the local church. Each congregation is self-governing, and claims local autonomy in all matters of faith, doctrine and administration. By definition, a local church recognizes no authority outside of itself, and each congregation is free to order itself as it chooses. The Congregational model stresses the gifts and the priesthood of all believers. In theory there is no clergy/laity distinction.

### Anabaptist-Mennonite Polity

The early Anabaptists accepted the teaching and examples of the New Testament church as normative. While considerable freedom and flexibility was given to the working out of these new teachings, the focus of their polity was always the mutual interdependence and accountability of believers and churches. Seeing the church as the body of Christ (1 Cor. 12) was central.

A modified presbyterian form of governance emerged as the polity of this movement. The primary church unit was the conference of churches. The conference served as the authority for all churches on matters of theology, common mission, ordination of ministers and inter-church relations. The local church was autonomous on local church matters only.

Bishops or Elders provided leadership within the conference and in local churches. These roles were not rooted in the Catholic or Anglican tradition of succession, but in the pastoral letters (such as Titus 1:5). Senior ministers and leaders were chosen from within congregations.

The priority of the conference led by bishops reflected a presbyterian polity. The local church was part of an organism larger than and prior to the local church. Anabaptist-Mennonite polity modified the presbyterian element with strong congregational and lay involvement in both conference and local church decisions. The congregational process was employed for the selection, affirmation and function of the leadership.

Mennonite governance structures have shifted somewhat in recent decades. Some Mennonite groups have moved from the bishop or elder system to a conference minister structure. Others have strengthened the bishop system. But all continue to practice a modified form of presbyterian polity: strong conference and centralized leadership together with congregational involvement in church governance.[2]

## Mennonite Brethren Polity

Mennonite Brethren church polity has historically reflected the modified presbyterian polity of the larger Anabaptist-Mennonite movement. The constitution of the General Conference of Mennonite Brethren Churches in North America clearly states that the conference is the primary unit of the church: "The Conference includes all churches founded on the Confession of Faith . . .and . . . the Conference shall have the right to make the final decision in all matters that relate to the united activities and the common welfare of the churches."[3]

Each local church belongs to the conference at three levels: the General Conference (North American); the national conferences (Canada and United States); and the regional conferences (district in the United States, provincial in Canada). The conference in session (at each level) has the authority to make final decisions on matters of faith, common church welfare and mission. Local churches are to accept these decisions as binding.[4] The biblical basis for this structure is found in Acts 11 (the report of the establishment of the Antioch churches to Jerusalem), Acts 15 (the Jerusalem conference and the report of the churches of the decision), and 1 Corinthians 11 and 14 (the common practice in all the churches).

The conferences at each level are led by the Mennonite Brethren equivalent of a council of elders. These boards have the authority to hold local churches accountable and intervene in local churches and agencies in special cases.[5]

Mennonite Brethren governance has always followed a modified presbyterian polity (though the term itself is rarely used). It has never been entirely congregational. Local churches belong to and are accountable to the conferences; they are autonomous only in the governance of local affairs.

Until the 1950s local Mennonite Brethren churches were led by a body of elders. The leadership and ministry was always multiple, chosen from among the membership on the basis of giftedness and service within the congregation. People gifted in teaching, administration, evangelism and the deaconate were recognized by the church and given opportunity to exercise these gifts. After a time of testing the gifts and the consistency of life according to the scriptural standards for leadership ministries, the candidates were formally acknowledged as a gift of God to the church. Ordination, a way of confirming them as servants of the church, was recommended to the conference. The local church, together with the conference, then performed the ordination.

The Board of Elders (usually called *Altestenrat* or *Vorberat*), provided the leadership of the local church. The governance structure was somewhat hierarchical, but the power of the hierarchy was always tempered by two factors: (1) authority was shared, and (2) the congregation had significant involvement in deliberations and decision-making. Furthermore, because the leaders had emerged from within the church, they had earned the confidence and trust of the membership. Time-tested service and earned trust provided the basis for authority.

In some congregations people who were not ordained as ministers or deacons, but had gained the confidence of the membership as models of faith and life, were added to the leadership team. The leading elder was always viewed as an equal in the leadership group.[6] In larger churches, where the deaconate required more deacons, boards of elders often functioned as an executive committee.[7]

The elders were the guardians of Scripture in nurture, fellowship and watchcare for the life and needs of the flock. The exercise of authority was implicit, guided by the motto, "Thus says the Scripture."

Until the 1930s in the United States and the 1950s in Canada, local ministers and elders were bivocational people. With the transition from an agrarian to an industrial, professional and commercial culture, the need emerged for full-time paid pastors (but still within the context of a multiple ministry). This transition to paid leadership caused repeated testing of the biblical teachings on leadership. Officially, the conference remained firmly committed to a multiple leadership model, with a clear preference that it emerge from within the congregation. The importance of the spirit of servanthood and mutuality was stressed even more than before.

Local church governance began to change with the introduction of paid pastors. The dislocations of immigration and the depression, as well as the professionalization of the ministry, disrupted the organic spiritual process of leadership development within local churches. People in growing urban communities no longer knew each other as well, and pastors preferred more centralized forms of church leadership. Church councils began to emerge as an alternative form of church governance.

Church council polity offered a representative form of leadership. Instead of leaders being discerned on the basis of spiritual giftedness, as before, they arose out of the various programs of the church, such as Christian education, youth, music, deaconate and board of trustees. The model was functional in character. The tenure of membership was limited to specific terms—one, two or three years.[8] By virtue of its composition, functional character and brevity of tenure, the church council form of governance had less authority than the Board of Elders form. The process of church leadership became more democratic, and authority shifted to the pastor. Collective responsibility for the spiritual nurture, watchcare and leadership gradually declined. The pastor became the center of all of these responsibilities. This was a pragmatic concession to the dominant cultural milieu during the second half of the twentieth century.

Growing numbers of churches have begun to sense that something important has been lost in the way leadership is selected. In their search to recapture responsible, authoritative leadership, some have returned to the board of elders model. In the absence of established organic processes to draw leaders from within the churchly community, various approaches have been used to reestablish the eldership pattern. It is becoming increasingly clear that there is an urgent need to change from church council (democratic) leadership to a more biblical model.

The switch from the bivocational ministry to paid pastors and ministers did not imply a retreat from traditional principles of polity and ministry. But it did raise new issues. At the 1951 General Conference sessions the Board of Reference and Counsel addressed a series of these polity issues in a document titled "A Frank Analysis of our Spiritual Status." It focused on four issues: (1) A lack of clear guidelines to help ministers, local churches and the conference deal uniformly with scriptural interpretation related to life and polity. (2) Increasing differences and uncertainty among ministers in relation to critical sections of the Confession of Faith. (3) An absence of unity in policies of local church administration and practice within the conference. (4) A hesitancy to accept conference decisions on social, ethical and spiritual matters.[9]

The first two points indicated a weakening of community hermeneutics as more leaders came into the churches from "outside", and as increasing numbers of aspiring ministers were trained in Bible schools and seminaries of varied theological persuasions. Moreover, the anti-German sentiment of the war years hastened the switch from German to English, and some senior leaders were handicapped by lack of fluency in the new language. Many younger pastors did not have the benefit of apprenticing under senior ministers as had been the case formerly. These changes produced departures from established policies that had been formulated by the conference through long years of biblical study and application.

Because congregations had become less willing to accept conference decisions on ethics and social and spiritual standards, the document called for a reaffirmation of the historic interdependence of Mennonite Brethren churches.[10] The 1951 conference agreed to a series of principles:

> 1. That each local church is independent in the administration of its internal affairs and functions as an independent unit.
> 2. That we as a conference are a brotherhood of churches. We are, as our official name implies, The Church of the Mennonite Brethren Conference of North America, not the Conference of Mennonite Brethren Churches of North America. As such we carry mutual responsibility for the spiritual conditions in the churches and for the preservation of the purity of faith and doctrine as expressed in our practice.
> 3. That we as churches of the conference recognize

resolutions and decisions of the conference as morally binding and obligate ourselves to observe and carry them out to the best of our ability as faithful and cooperating members of the brotherhood.[11]

The Board of Reference and Counsel–functioning as a board of elders–was charged to direct and oversee the expression of these policies.[12]

## THEOLOGICAL CONSIDERATIONS

The strong emphasis on individual spiritual gifts of the 1960s, 1970s and 1980s failed to sufficiently recognize the leadership priorities in the midst of plurality. While each gift of ministry is valuable, the New Testament singles out apostles, prophets and teachers. Three terms appear identifying these ministries as overseers, presbyters and shepherds (Acts 16:4; 20:28; Eph. 4:11; Titus 1:5). This body of leadership, always multiple in the church, is responsible for oversight, shepherding and teaching.[13] It has the assignment of equipping "all" members for the work of the ministry of the body of Christ. The "some" with leadership function (Eph. 4:11) are always multiple, never single. Their ministry is a function within the church, not an office.

The style of leadership, meanwhile, is one of servanthood, as Jesus so strongly asserted when he said, "He who is greatest among you shall be a servant." This emphasis appears seven times in the Gospels (Matt. 20:27-28; 23:11; Mk. 9:35; 10:43-44; Lk. 9:48; 22:26-27; John 13:14). Peter underlines this servanthood relationship: "Feed the flock of God which is among you, taking the oversight thereof, not by constraint, but willingly; not for filthy lucre, but of a ready mind; Neither as being lords over God's heritage, but being examples of the flock" (1 Pet. 5:2-3). The functional structure of leadership may vary according to gifts and cultural context, but the posture is always to be that of a servant.

## The Current Leadership Crisis

The traditional leadership style functioned well for the first eighty years of Mennonite Brethren history, though not without occasional tension. The authority for leadership was anchored in mutuality. Leaders were chosen not because they were trained specialists, but because they were recognized as gifted by God to offer leadership within the household of faith. They had demonstrated superior competence at the ordinary tasks of life and had displayed good judgment in matters concerning the welfare of the group as a whole. Their own ability and sanctity granted them a large measure of personal authority. They understood themselves as servants of God and of the church. The fact that some leaders received modest financial support did not imply greater rank or authority.

New patterns of leadership began to emerge in Mennonite Brethren churches in the 1940s in the United States and the 1960s in Canada. In the midst of convulsive social and cultural change, the church struggled to keep pace. A migrant generation in search of self-identity found itself incapable of following a process of thoughtful discernment in questions of spiritual formation. Instead it simply conformed to the models of mainline Protestantism.

The new "one man" style of pastoral leadership lacked a base of authority for directive leadership. In multiple leadership, which Mennonite Brethren had considered biblical, authority was authenticated by the trust of the community of believers. By adopting the single-pastor model the church dislocated the base of authority without which a New Testament ministry becomes extremely difficult, if not impossible.

Other Protestant churches tended to function as an institution, not as an interdependent organism which Mennonite Brethren perceived the local church and the larger conference to be. In an institution, leadership is delegated to those with special training, those who "know" (theologians), but these may lack the authority that is rooted in a mutual relationship of experiential commonality. Pastors in this scheme assume the assignment of managing the program of the congregation. They minister to the needs of the congregation and officiate over its rituals of worship and of passage (birth, baptism, marriage, death). They are held responsible for the spiritual health of the people while lacking the platform to shape the context that conditions spirituality.

The church becomes dependent on what the pastor can give to the congregation in terms of personal qualities and talents. But one person cannot provide all the resources to meet the needs of a large community. Thus the single-pastor ministry tends to become program-centered. The single pastor, no matter how faithful, gifted or sacrifical, cannot hope to achieve what God has not intended to be the assignment of one person. "He gave some (to be) apostles; and some, prophets; and some, evangelists; and some, pastors and teachers; for the perfecting of the saints, for the work of the ministry, for the edifying of the body of Christ" (Eph. 4:11-12).

**The Pastor as Chief Executive Officer**

The culture of modernity with a focus on individualism, pragmatism and production has given birth to church leadership models difficult to reconcile with the Mennonite Brethren understanding of biblical leadership. One such model was advocated by Matt Hannon in a lectureship at Mennonite Brethren Biblical Seminary on "Plateaued Churches and Their Renewal."[14] He recommended strong central leadership with the pastor serving as the chief executive officer. The major function of this "Chief Executive Officer" (CEO) pastor was to spend time with selected trainable people who can transmit the vision and motive for the pastor's program to the people of the congregation. In this model the primary concern of leadership is management, not relationship. "Leaders do not need to be relational, some may be."[15]

Questions about the single-pastor system have been raised

elsewhere. A letter to the editor of *Christianity Today* spoke to this concern:

> For centuries, mainline Christian groups have perpetuated the unbiblical practice of investing virtually sole spiritual authority in a single individual, to whom the faithful look up. Yet, in the new Testament prescription, the Holy Spirit appoints Elders in every local assembly–his wisdom is that there is power in the harmony and plurality of the spiritually mature. We witness how often a pastor falls from his pinnacle and how parish tension thrives when parishioners walk more spiritually than does their clerical head who, after all, sets the norm. Set against the Lord's design, such a pastor has been ecclesiastically entrusted with more power and influence than he could ever wield in a godly way. It is late, but not too late, to radically reform the 'Cleric Complex.'[16]

It is ironic–and alarming–that many churches have been drawn to the "pastor as CEO" model at precisely the time when the corporate world is recognizing the inadequacies of centralized autocratic leadership. In the early 1970s Robert Greenleaf's classic, *Servant Leadership*, advocated a management style that rings familiar to anyone acquainted with the teachings of Jesus. More recently Max DePree, chair of the Herman Miller furniture manufacturing firm with more than 6,000 employees, gained the ear of *Fortune* magazine and others with his company's modelling of "covenant relationships" between employers and employees. Said DePree: "The worker should participate in management. The chief executive's responsibility is to make that happen–to help each employee to reach his or her potential. . . . The roots of leadership are in whether what you say is what you do. You have to be open to people, you have to build quality relationships."[17] More and more business corporations are finding it profitable to nurture covenant relationships for effective leadership and workplace harmony. Must the church learn from the "world" to understand the importance of the shepherd-sheep paradigm as taught by Christ?

Congregations wishing to align their shepherd-sheep relationships with the biblical model would do well to consider the following contemporary expression of Mennonite Brethren polity, presented by Gerry Ediger at a study conference in 1986:

> Principles of Leading and Following
> for a Covenant Fellowship
>
> The past ten years have yielded extensive Mennonite Brethren literature related to the theology and practice of leadership. In this process of re-examining Scripture for principles of leadership, there has been a strong emphasis on certain central values. For example: We want to agree that leaders are servants. All members of the church are gifted for ministry. Leadership is a role and function rather than an office. Leadership is exercised by a plurality of persons called by the church or congregation for that purpose. These convictions suggest the following principles of leading and following.
>
> A. Leaders are qualified first of all through being spiritually mature, gifted and appointed through the congregation/church; they are not, in the first instance, qualified through their professional training or their designation of office.
>
> B. In the New Testament leadership is a shared function of a group of persons; it is not exercised independently by one individual apart. Leaders are accountable to their leader-colleagues and the members of the congregation/church.
>
> C. The first impression a congregation/church should have of its leader(s) is the image of a sacrificial servant–a servant engaged in teaching, enabling and shepherding; these activities undergird and support the other ministries

of the church, and in this sense have first place.

D. The congregation/church freely entrusts its leaders with the necessary authority and power to exercise their role (not office) of ministry.

E. Full-time, "professional" leaders are those individuals the church/congregation chooses to support financially so that it can more fully utilize their gifts for the common good, both within the context of the local congregation and the broader church.

F. The church is responsible to discern, call and appoint leaders under the lordship of Christ.

G. The church/congregation, under God, is responsible for the character, service and discipline of its leaders.

H. The church/congregation must follow the spiritually sound and biblically founded guidance of its leadership in a freely expressed attitude of submission, obedience and respect.

I. The church/congregation is responsible for the adequate support and maintenance of its leaders.

J. Leaders and followers are equally called to submit to the lordship of Christ as corporately discerned through the Holy Spirit and the examination of Scripture.

If we want our leading and following to be consistent with these principles, we must live in the spirit of covenant. This spirit is symbolized by the basin and the towel our Lord used as he introduced the New Testament. This new covenant was the covenant of the suffering servant, sacrificing himself for the redemption and healing of his fellows. Leaders in a fellowship of that covenant must minister in that same sacrificial spirit. Followers in such a fellowship must remember that the servant is not greater than the master, nor the pupil greater than the teacher.[18]

## LEADERSHIP RECRUITMENT

A significant casualty of the blinding cultural changes described earlier is the process churches use to call out new leaders from the church body. This is not surprising, given the loss of "social glue" and intimacy in most congregations. The wide variation of professions and occupations in which members find themselves through the week has decreased sociological cohesiveness. Families no longer work together; each has a separate workplace community. Young people leave for college and find new social spheres. Churches no longer enjoy experiential commonality. They may agree on spiritual principles and biblical teaching, but lack the functional capacity to help one another integrate them into their respective spheres. This cultural change, understandable as it may be, has had an impact on the Mennonite Brethren Church in general and the question of leadership in particular.

The 1951 General Conference called attention to the Mennonite Brethren understanding of Scripture with regard to the teaching ministry and leadership within the church, with instructions for application in the life of the church.[19] It recognized the prevailing cultural changes and their implications for ministry and leadership. The conference affirmed the directives as a biblical mandate to pray for God's call of leadership from within the church.

Twenty years later, the General Conference of 1972 renewed this concern over the shortage of ministers and pastors. Following is the admonition directed to the churches:

> There is today a shortage of ministers and pastors in our brotherhood. We now need more pastors for our churches than are becoming available. This shortage presses us to give this matter serious study and prayer.
> In addition to the shortage of ministers, a concern has arisen over the "one pastor" system in our churches. The roles both of the layman and also of the minister, are being reexamined and hopefully adjusted so as to follow more perfectly the New Testament pattern. More and

more, it is being recognized that lay people possess the gifts of the Spirit, and these thus become available to the ministry in the church.

Historically, our churches selected ministers and pastors from their own midst. Some thus called went out for further education and returned to minister in their home congregation. Churches usually had a multiple ministry.

Contrary to past practice, few churches today elect ministers from their own ranks. We depend upon our schools or look to other sources from which to secure pastors when these are needed. Because most local congregations no longer elect ministers, the churches have also shown decreasing interest and involvement in the recruitment of ministers. There is too little encouragement ("shoulder-tapping") and yet we recognize that (essentially), ministers must come from the local fellowships.

In view of the situations above described, we affirm the following:

1) That our churches heed our Lord's directive for worker recruitment as given in Matthew 9:38, "Pray ye therefore the Lord of the harvest that he will send forth laborers into his harvest."

2) That local churches seek earnestly the gifts of ministry in their own ranks, encourage persons possessing the gifts and offer support and assistance in their further training and development.

3) That our theological schools should be supported actively and be encouraged to recruit ministers, pastors and church workers, as the Spirit directs.[20]

A resolution from the 1981 General Conference directed another appeal to the churches:

We urge our congregations to work much more diligently at discerning potential pastors in their midst and at assisting them in the development of their gifts in preparation for ministry within the congregation.

We encourage congregations to undertake a study of pastoral leadership to help them understand the biblical model and function of the pastor.[21]

These concerns were not limited to official resolutions. Between 1960 and 1989, no fewer than 110 shorter and longer articles appeared in the conference periodicals, *The Christian Leader* and *Mennonite Brethren Herald*, on the question of leadership and the preaching ministry.[22] Among the authors were seasoned leaders like Waldo Hiebert, Orlando Harms, Henry Schmidt, Frank Peters, John Regehr, Henry Regehr, Henry Brucks and Elmer Martens. Three study conferences called by the General Conference Board of Reference and Counsel in 1970, 1980 and 1986 addressed the question of ministry and church polity.[23]

District and provincial conferences have also wrestled with questions of leadership. In 1983 Marvin Hein presented a study on "The Present State of Leadership in the Pacific District Conference." He found that during the 1970s the district imported twenty-eight percent of its pastors from outside the Mennonite Brethren Church. The report of Hein's study concluded:

> 1. Some interchange of leaders between districts and areas should be seen as normal and desirable.
> 
> 2. Importation of pastoral leadership from non-MB origins is not necessarily bad and has its benefits. One benefit is that new ideas, methods and practices that can enrich our church lives are brought to us. A potential problem exists in that non-MB-origin leaders may not understand our doctrine and practices well enough to prevent tension in the churches. A greater diversity of theology and practice may also result in the district.
> 
> 3. Our goal should be to produce adequate leadership

in our churches to meet our own needs (leadership in our present churches, new churches, mission fields and educational institutions). This is the burden of our emphasis at this convention. We propose several suggestions:

(a) We must provide an atmosphere in our congregations where there is a sense of expectation, encouragement and support for leadership selection and training.

(b) We must give attention to how leaders are called, selected, trained and supported in the congregation.

(c) We must develop in our congregations a model for church leadership selection and development.

(d) We must find methods of testing, evaluating and giving feedback for growth purposes to emerging leaders in the congregations.

(e) We must devise ways of sharing these leadership needs with the churches of our district. Discussion at a convention is not sufficient.

(f) We must recognize this burden for leadership as a long-range and ongoing process.[24]

It is ironic that amid the strong emphasis on evangelism and church growth throughout the Mennonite Brethren Conference, there is also an apparent sterility that prevents men and women from being called forward to the leadership ministries that are basic to healthy growth and maturing of the believers community.

## THE PASTOR'S ASSIGNMENT

How do local churches visualize the role of the pastor? A survey of the constitutions of forty-five representative Mennonite Brethren congregations showed the following "job description" as typical:

> The pastor shall be the spiritual leader of the church. He shall preach the gospel, administer the ordinances, watch

over membership of the church family, promote the spiritual interest of the church and develop the strength of the church for the best possible service to the glory of God and the conference. The pastor shall be the administrative officer of the church and ex-officio member of all the church committees.

Most constitutions included a paragraph spelling out procedures for termination, which indicates that the ministry is considered a term position. The content of these documents presupposes that the leadership will come from outside the local body, like a professional specialist.

This perception is corroborated by a study of pastoral "help wanted" advertisements in conference periodicals. In a recent five-year period, more than 190 public appeals appeared in the *Mennonite Brethren Herald* for pastoral applicants. Like other professional advertisements, these requested documentation describing academic training, experience and competence. Only one-fifth as many advertisements appeared in *The Christian Leader*, possibly because the United States has a longer tradition of employing district ministers who assumed the responsibility of finding pastoral candidates for the churches. When the pastoral ministry is so visibly regarded as a profession, it becomes a mere service that pastors render to congregations without necessarily identifying with the communities they serve.

Another study of Mennonite Brethren churches found further evidence pointing to the fragile nature of Mennonite Brethren leadership: the average pastoral tenure is less than four years; in the last fifteen years Mennonite Brethren churches have found it necessary to import 154 pastors from other denominations; in the same period 126 Mennonite Brethren pastors left the ministry and entered other professions or vocations. An inquiry of church members' perceptions as to "why their pastor left" turned up three basic observations: (1) The pastor came to the church not knowing the people or their specific needs. The pastoral assignment gave little opportunity, sometimes none, for the pastor to relate to people and enter into their lives. A typical comment was: "We know our pastor only from what he preaches and have shaken hands with him at the door." (2) The pastor came with a preconceived program (evangelism, small groups, missions) that became the major focus. The people, however, looked for a nurturing ministry to enable them to become more productive as an outflow from their inner life (John 7:17). (3) With a weakness in personal relationships and a focus on a program-oriented ministry, the pastor's preaching did not relate to the inner needs of the people. Within a few years a vacuum developed between pastor and flock.

In the single-pastor model, only an exceptionally gifted leader has the mental and spiritual resources to sustain the interest and productive response of a congregation over a period of years. The sharing of the preaching and teaching ministry with people from the congregation who are rooted in the community and have the appropriate gifts, appears to be essential for the continued effective service of both the pastor/leader and the congregation itself.

Members of Mennonite Brethren churches that have enjoyed lengthy pastoral tenures reported that the key to long service was special gifts of excellence either in the pastor's preaching ministry or in strong relational abilities. The final measurement of long tenure, however, does not rest only in number of years served but in the lasting impact of such ministry on the church's inner growth and outward witness.

**The Way Before Us**

It is unrealistic to expect Mennonite Brethren to go back and reinstitute the models of years ago. The point of praising earlier models of leadership is not to reach for the ashes of the past, but to the fire that raised a dynamic renewal through a small minority people. These were people who first and foremost wanted to lodge their identity in Christ and wanted to serve him faithfully. The assignment of the ministry, then, is not to do the work for the church, but to equip the church so that they can more genuinely be the people of God.

In today's complex culture, unlike earlier generations of Mennonite Brethren, we need various levels of trained–and paid–leadership. But what has not changed from earlier times is the urgent need for the church to cultivate and call out the gifts of its members. Sparking and directing this task falls on the pastor in particular. The pastor is responsible for encouraging the exercise of gifts within the congregation. The failure in recent decades to call and develop local leadership rests largely with paid (pastoral) leadership who neglected to guide the church in this important concern.

Programs of "discipling" are popular among many pastors today. Unfortunately, "discipling" sometimes means following the pastor, rather than following Jesus in costly obedience. Paul Hiebert describes the impact of such leaders as short-lived:

> They have great ministries, but when they pass from the scene there are no leaders to step into their shoes because they have trained followers not leaders.
>
> It is gratifying to train followers. They are an appreciative audience that makes us feel important. They imitate our ways. They do not challenge our thinking or go beyond our teaching.
>
> It is easy to train followers. We decide what they should learn and how they should learn it. We encourage them to raise questions and we give the answers. We teach them to follow our directives and to guess our mind.
>
> There is an immediate success in training followers. We can mobilize many to build our program. This approach

is also efficient. But its success is short-range. When we depart we leave sheep but not shepherds.[25]

## CONCLUSION

A crisis in leadership has beset Mennonite Brethren in a time of "breakneck changes" unprecedented in human history. An agricultural people with a rural mindset found themselves thrust midstream into modernity. In the urgency of the moment they turned to the leadership models of North American evangelicalism. The statements of the 1951 General Conference, outlining a scriptural understanding of leadership, passed as a mere echo in the whirlwind of change. Pragmatic solutions prevailed and supplanted earlier Mennonite Brethren commitments. The question of "being" was overshadowed by a preoccupation with "doing." Leadership models promising the most efficient programs were accepted as the answer for the hour.

Today we share with the larger Christian community a crisis of leadership that finds itself shorn of stature and authority. We find ourselves in a disturbing parallel to Ezekiel 34 where the Lord laments the failure of the shepherds and the scattering of the sheep. Efficient programs may attract spectators, but they do not necessarily nurture commitment. True commitment to God cannot be separated from a commitment to the church–the people of God, the community of the redeemed (1 John 1:6-7).

The first response to the leadership crisis is to rebuild the shepherding ministry as the primary assignment. What is urgently needed is leadership *identified* with the flock, *rooted* in fellowship of the flock, and *trusted* by the flock to guide them in the path consistent with biblical principles. This calls for a plurality of leadership in spiritual nurture and interdependent relationships.

CHAPTER 18

# Mennonite Brethren Evangelism

An English proverb says, "When the heart is afire, sparks will fly out of the mouth." So it was with the early Mennonite Brethren, whose hearts blazed with the love of God and the joy of redemption. Their evangelism was not a matter of programs or strategies; it was a simple, spontaneous witness. They told the story of their personal salvation experience and urged others to turn to Christ, be converted and know the joy of a soul set free. They quickly became known for their zealous efforts to win people to Christ.

The first corporate expression addressing the matter of evangelism appeared in the records of the conference in Andreasfeld in 1872. The major business of that first all-Mennonite Brethren assembly was to appoint five itinerant evangelists in order to broaden their one-on-one witness to the wider community of Mennonites, German colonists and native Russians.[1]

When the Mennonite Brethren migrated to North America they brought with them their zeal for winning others to Christ. Their steady growth in the first sixty years (1875-1935) in the United States and Canada was a direct result of a consistent individual witness and the itinerant ministry model they had adopted in 1872.[2] The increase came not only from within the immediate Mennonite community, but also from the larger population of the unchurched or members of mainline denominations–Lutherans, Congregationalists, Catholics–who had not yet experienced a personal living faith. Several Mennonite Brethren churches in North Dakota and Nebraska are examples of this outreach beyond the boundaries of immigrant Mennonite communities.³

The itinerant ministry remained central through the 1940s and 1950s. John A. Toews observed that farmer evangelists conducted services in the late fall and winter and teacher evangelists during the summer.⁴ Bible school and Bible college teachers were used extensively in this itinerant work. The district conferences in the United States and provincial conferences in Canada arranged for every church to have one or two weeks of special services. The 1947-48 records from the Pacific District Conference illustrated the extent of this effort:

Evangelists and Bible Conferences
Blaine–A.H. Ysker, 2 weeks, January 4-20; J.J. Wiebe, 2 wks, August 8-20.
Dallas–A.H. Ysker, 2 weeks, October 26 to November 6, Albert Regier, 1 week, February 1-8; Bible Conference speakers: Howard Belton and Oscar Zimmermann, 8 days, July 4 to 11.
Orland–A.H. Ysker, 2 weeks, October 17-31, David Hooge, 1 week, April 1-18.
San Jose–J.K. Warkentin, 2 weeks, February 29 to March. Bible Conference Speaker, G.W. Peters, 1 week, June 20-25.
Lodi–David Hooge, 2 weeks; H.G. Wiens, 1 week; Waldo Wiebe, 1 week.
Winton–David Hooge, 2 weeks, November 2-14; Bible Conference Speaker, H.G. Wiens, 1 week, February 29 to March 4.
Madera and Fresno–None.
Reedley–Waldo Wiebe, 2 weeks, May 2-14; Bible Conference Speaker, Wm. Evans, 1 week, February 1-18; Harry Vom (Union Meetings), 2 weeks, March 30 to April 11.
Dinuba–David Hooge, 2 1/2 weeks, January 4-20; Theo. H. Epp, one night, April.
Shafter–A.H. Ysker, 2 weeks, December 7-19.
Rosedale–Herb Tyler, 1 1/2 weeks, May 12-21; Conference

Speaker, H.G. Wiens, 1 week.
Bakersfield–Waldo Wiebe, 2 weeks, February 8-22; J.K. Warkentin, 2 weeks, September 20 to October 3.
Los Angeles–H.G. Wiens, 1 week, Fall of 1947; Waldo Wiebe, 1 week, Spring of 1948.
City Terrace–Joe W. Johnston, 1 week, May 9-16.
Salem–Conference Speaker, John Belton, 8 days.[5]

In 1959 the Manitoba Conference allocated twelve days to each of its twenty-seven congregations for special services. Sixteen leaders–local pastors, Bible school and Bible college teachers–were named as the evangelists and Bible conference speakers.[6]

Bible schools nourished the spirit of outreach. From the 1930s through the 1950s, courses in personal evangelism were a regular offering. The Pacific Bible Institute reported in 1953 that students in the previous school year counseled with 575 people, distributed forty thousand tracts, three thousand Gospels of John and twenty New Testaments, and through this activity 225 people made professions of faith. The Bible schools also promoted children's work in the form of vacation Bible schools and Bible club programs that continued into the regular school season.[7]

**The Task of the Local Church**

In the years before 1960, Mennonite Brethren evangelistic activity was solidly rooted in the local church and conference. In the homogeneous communities, with their close cultural, economic and occupational interdependence, the line separating "saved and unsaved," "believers and unbelievers," seemed clear even if sometimes experientially interpreted. If, during the frequent public revival meetings, the unsaved of the community failed to respond, the nagging question was less likely to be one of strategy but rather, "What hindrances in the church prevent the Holy Spirit from leading sinners to repentance?" The church understood, as George W. Webber would declare later, that "demonstration precedes proclamation."[8] The church could meaningfully invite others to faith only when it had authentically demonstrated the power of redemption itself.

The spiritual status of the church was seen as directly related to the response of the unsaved to the gospel. Revival campaigns lasting from seven to fourteen days were not only an invitation to the unsaved but also a challenge for the church to examine its own faithfulness. Frequently the entire first half of such campaigns would be a ringing call to self-examination, for repentance from worldliness (defined as ethical lapses, unfaithful stewardship and neglect of devotional life) and for shortfalls in personal and family relationships. In this, the Mennonite Brethren were reflecting a truth that has characterized all the great revivals in Christian history—repentance for sin and the subsequent change in relationship with a Holy God is foundational to effective evangelism.[9]

The Mennonite Brethren of times past grasped an important first century insight: the purpose and strategy of evangelism was inextricably interwoven with the mission and character of the local church.[10] The commitment to evangelism was at the center of the persecutions endured by the apostolic church. When Peter and John appeared before the Sanhedrin they were commanded "not to speak or teach at all in the name of Jesus," but this was an order they could not obey "for we cannot help speaking about what we have seen and heard" (Acts 4:18-20 *NIV*). Fears of physical abuse and even the threat of death were submerged by their zeal to proclaim salvation to an unsaved world. "Now, Lord, consider their threats and enable your servants to speak your word with great boldness" (Acts 4:29).

The commission of Christ—"You will be my witnesses in Jerusalem, and in all Judea and Samaria, and to the ends of the earth" (Acts 1:8)—outlines the church's basic assignment.

The church is expected to witness in the area of its location. That is the primary purpose of its existence. The most pressing obligation is the area at its door. However, if it is truly evangelistic, it will never stop there. The church must always remember the mandate is to reach the ends of the earth. It can do that only when it is strong at home. The loss of an effective witness in the immediate community will be reflected in impotence abroad. Missionary outreach to distant areas may temporarily compensate for failure at home, but in time, spiritual weakness and decline will set in.

Not only is the local church structurally vital to the task of evangelism, it is also a divine reservoir of spiritual power. Too often overlooked is the collective strength of those spirit-intoxicated men and women (Acts 2 and 4) who felt that each of them separately and all of them jointly shared in the common witness to the saviorhood and lordship of Jesus Christ. The universal body of Christ, which Paul calls the "whole family in heaven and on earth" (Eph. 3:15), is the habitation of God through the Spirit. The local church, through the endowment of the Spirit, is the communicating agency for evangelism. The church of today, in many instances wounded and defeated, will find renewal by rediscovering its divine assignment of evangelism.

**The Place of Perfection**

Mennonite Brethren have historically been known for their concern for spiritual perfection, striving toward spiritual maturity and moral excellence. When this concern has energized outreach, the results have been admirable; when it became uncoupled from the Great Commission, the results have been dismal.

Scripture places considerable emphasis on "perfection." Much of Christ's ministry was instruction related to social, ethical and moral matters. Major parts of Paul's writings address the doctrinal and social implications of divine revelation. But

Scripture does not separate the perfection of God's people from their basic mission. Israel was called to serve as a communicating agency of God's revelation (1 Chron. 16:23-31). In the New Testament the emphasis on perfection is not an end in itself, but a requirement for effective outreach (John 3:34-35; John 17:21; Acts 5:11). The glory of Christ is made known by a sanctified church that shows "forth the virtues of him who has called you out of darkness into his marvelous light" (1 Pet. 2:9). The church, as the embodiment of the Holy Spirit, must be concerned about perfection. However, this is not an end in itself, but rather a means to maintain the spiritual fitness to reflect Christ and bring others to the knowledge of salvation.

Perfection without communication results in spiritual sterility. As with Judaism during the time of Christ, separating the pursuit of perfection from the dynamic outward movement of the gospel mission produces only self-satisfied legalism. Perfection cannot be accomplished in the pursuit of moral standards alone, but is a natural result of the spiritual struggle for the lives and eternal destiny of others (Acts 11:26; 13:3-4; 11:29,30).

**When Churches Don't Grow**

The dynamic faith and life of the apostolic church produced enormous growth. "And the Lord added to their number daily those who were being saved" (Acts 2:47). Throughout the ages such continued growth through evangelistic outreach has served as basic evidence that the church was functioning as a healthy spiritual organism. When this ongoing demonstration of the power of the gospel is absent, something vital is lost. Individual members grow lax; the corporate body loses its sense of purpose. It lapses into maintenance and is governed by the status quo.

A pitfall for many churches (particularly those with an identifiable cultural tradition, like the Mennonite Brethren) is to become a secular subculture in which spirituality is submerged by social and cultural values. As Tom Allan has noted, many unbelievers reject the church because they see it as merely another secular culture, albeit with values different from their own. So when the church appears ineffective in penetrating the secularism of society it may be because the church has capitulated to a "secularism of another kind."[11]

A church can be scriptural in its dogma but completely impotent and unconcerned about proclaiming its soul-saving message to a lost world. Institutionalism, philanthropic endeavors and a preoccupation with cultural matters can become substitutes for true spiritual dynamics. Growth then becomes limited to additions from families in the church or through transfers from other similar groups. Neither of these sources, however, provides the inner rejuvenation that bursts forth when the body of Christ regularly hears the praises of the newly saved.

When churches don't grow, the problem is less likely to be a lack of strategy than a lack of intimate fellowship with the master soul winner. The simple words of Jesus–"Follow me, and I will make you fishers of men" (Matt. 4:19)–remain the key to effective evangelism. Careful planning and organization have their place in congregational witness, but they are only a means to an end. Most important is the relationship of church members to their Lord. Effective evangelism is not taught but born in the womb of a Spirit-filled church.

Throughout church history the rekindled embers of God's people fanned the flames of explosive growth. In fact, there is no record of phenomenal growth separate from a spiritual renewal within the church. In Great Britain, for example, the revival under John Knox (1515-1572) produced the Presbyterian Church, and the Wesleyan revival (John Wesley, 1703-1791) sparked the birth of the burgeoning Methodist movement. Likewise in America the Great Awakening under Jonathan Edwards (1703-1758) produced unprecedented church expansion, as did the renewals led by Charles G. Finney (1792-1875)[12] and Dwight L. Moody (1837-1899).[13] In all these cases the renewal of God's people expressed itself in a heightened consciousness of sin followed by repentance and radically changed behavior that dramatically impacted all of society.[14]

This identical pattern has manifested itself time and again among the Mennonite Brethren. Their birth in 1860 was the product of an awakening within the larger Mennonite church. Every subsequent episode of substantial growth–in Russia as well as later in North America–was directly related to spiritual renewal and confession of sin that deeply affected the moral character of the church and its relationship to the larger community.[15]

**SHIFTING SANDS**

The essential quality of effective evangelism was being pushed into the shadows by 1960, a victim of abrupt social change. In the years following the Second World War the Mennonite Brethren experienced in less than two decades a cultural transition that in earlier history took several generations.

The older ethnic and cultural glue lost its adhesive power as the Mennonite Brethren struggled with a new pluralism. Typical of such sudden shifts, they experienced a sense of trauma and disintegration. With one foot still in the narrow stream of past traditions, and the other in the mainstream of North American pluralism, they groped for ways to adjust their theological practices to the new reality. Old values seemed obsolete, and new but untested alternatives beckoned.

Particularly alluring were the methods gaining prominence among the many evangelical para-church organizations that burst on the scene in the years following the Second World War. Though not entirely consistent with their view of soteriology and ecclesiology, the Mennonite Brethren adopted strategies promoted by various fundamentalist/evangelical para-church organizations.

This looking to external agencies to provide new methods of evangelism was part of an honest effort to transcend cultural barriers, extend the gospel, and see sinners saved and added to the church. But in their search for new ways to proclaim the glories of God the Mennonite Brethren occasionally lost sight of the distinction between message and method.

## Mennonite Brethren Evangelism in the Context of Change

From the 1950s onward, the conference records are laden with attempts to enlarge the verbal proclamation of the gospel. In 1954 the conference created a Board of Evangelism for Canada and the United States with a two-fold assignment: to "set apart" ministers who would be available to the churches to help with outreach; and to initiate evangelistic ministries outside the regular organized church program to reach the unsaved with the gospel.

In May 1962 the U.S. Board of Evangelism adopted the following program to focus existing efforts and extend outreach:

1. Aid to churches and pastors in planning more vital crusades where intensive Biblical preaching awakens the consciences of the sinners.

2. Emphasis and training in visitation evangelism to reach the heretofore unreached.

3. The organization and establishment of churches in areas where the several District Conferences are not reaching in some of the great population areas. Plans for a decade should be laid with care and deliberation.

4. A careful re-thinking of conventional methods of evangelism with an updating of methodology to meet the need of 20th century society. Our archaic language "cliches" and illustrations are losing the minds of "atomic age" people.

5. A request to our higher Christian education institutions to place men on the staff who have fervent evangelistic zeal in training our youth how to witness and to lead them into the areas where they are encouraged to give their lives to soul winning and building the kingdom of Christ and His church.[16]

Conference evangelists were appointed to assume leadership for renewal and evangelism in the churches.[17] They reported holding up to twenty-two evangelistic series per year, plus providing assistance to local church efforts.[18]

In the latter half of the 1960s Mennonite Brethren evangelism found its focus in the "Decade of Enlargement," which was based on the following Scriptures: "Enlarge the place of thy tent, and let them stretch forth the curtains of thine habitations" (Is. 54:2), and "You must keep trying to excel for the upbuilding of the church" (1 Cor. 14:12).[19] These passages are well adapted to motivate people for evangelism, however they do not contain the spiritual laws prerequisite for effective soul winning. More appropriate may have been the prayer of Psalm 51:10-13:

> Create in me a clean heart, O God, and renew a steadfast spirit within me. Do not cast me away from Thy presence, and do not take Thy Holy Spirit from me. Restore to me the joy of Thy salvation, and sustain me with a willing spirit. Then I will teach transgressors Thy ways, and sinners will be converted to Thee.

In and around the Decade of Enlargement two slogans were frequently utilized: "Win 5 in 65" and "Double in a Decade." Subsequent programs and slogans that achieved varying degrees of prominence included "Friendship Evangelism" in the 1970s and later "I Found It" and "Win One in 91." While all were heartfelt expressions of enthusiasm, the anchor in biblical theology was often lacking.

In the 1970s special seminars were offered to groups of

churches in person-to-person evangelism.[20] The Canadian and U.S. Conferences appointed executive secretaries to assist and coordinate the work of evangelism in local churches, provinces and districts.[21]

A historic meeting in Denver on April 28, 1971 revealed several pressing concerns: (1) an erosion of a biblical theology on evangelism; (2) a feeling that the increasing interest in social responsibilities could diminish interest in evangelism; (3) the need to be a witnessing church at home in order to be a missionary sending church.[22]

Throughout the 1960s, 1970s and 1980s intense effort to generate a sense of responsibility for outreach is evident in the records of the various evangelism boards and the Evangelism Commission. The spiritual struggle for effective outreach was evident in periodic reviews undertaken by the Board of Evangelism. The summary of a gathering on August 15, 1971 reflected some of the agony of this struggle:

1. "Evangelism in real practice is failing in the Mennonite Brethren Conference. This indicates the leadership has failed. We must share the blame in our Board."
2. "We need a sound theology of evangelism. When simple biblicism characterized us we could arouse action more easily. It is still possible, but we cannot sustain a movement."
3. "We have not offered a workable and relevantly structured program for training nor a program of evangelism with a wide base."
4. "The cutting edge of our evangelism is dulled through provincialism and diluted with social concern."
5. "We need a theology of evangelism that is Bible-based rather than experience oriented."
6. "Is our name Mennonite Brethren a hindrance because it suggests ethnic characteristics?"[23]

Special attention was given in conference reports to the Crusades for Evangelism led by Rudy Boschman, a Canadian evangelist, with a team of singers and personal workers. Jacob J. Toews's institutes for personal visitation and evangelism and his lecture series on "A Happy Family with a Purpose" and "Group Dynamics" (Fellowship Evangelism) gained an enthusiastic reception in the churches. The revival crusades of Henry Schmidt received strong endorsement and parallel conference acceptance of the need for greater spiritual preparation in the churches in order to achieve greater and lasting results.[24]

On August 21, 1974 another Ad Hoc Evangelism Committee meeting was convened as a follow-up to Lausanne 74, the world evangelization congress. The decision was reached to host regional evangelism seminars to prepare the evangelism leaders from the churches and the pastors for greater effectiveness. The goals for the seminars were fourfold: (a) to discover an ongoing vision of evangelism; (b) to equip evangelism leaders to train others; (c) to acquaint the leadership with resources on evangelism; (d) to develop an evangelism with local churches. Henry Schmidt and J.J. Toews were assigned to assume major responsibility for the implementation of the seminars.[25]

The Evangelism Commission strongly endorsed the projected program and appealed to each church to pray out an evangelism chairperson and establish a congregational board of evangelism. The training of pastors and leaders for evangelism was to be provided in several sessions at a time when large participation was possible. Special concern was recorded to recognize that evangelism was born in the process of spiritual revitalization and to explore new methods of evangelism and guard that such methods be consistent with Scripture. Ten-hour marathons on lifestyle evangelism were scheduled in twelve different U.S. locations for 1976 and 1977 to provide biblical directives in three specific areas: (1) a visitation of God, of the gospel, of the church, of individuals and the meaning of evangelism. (2) Motivation, freedom and ability to share the good news "as you go, as He leads where to go." (3) Sharpen the edge on a personal and church lifestyle evangelism strategy.[26]

But by 1978-1979 new strategies for evangelism were in place. The Canadian Board of Evangelism appointed an executive secretary to assist congregations in church planting ministries and to assume responsibility for a Christian service program utilizing short-term ministries. The focus of the program was evangelism in Quebec and the Maritimes. A second projection was an emphasis on Church Growth Seminars.[27] The U.S. Conference underwent a parallel shift. The Christian service program for the region was assumed by the Evangelism Commission. Simultaneously the regional Home Mission Boards were encouraged to host seminars in church growth and church planting.[28]

"Discipleship Making '85" and its repeat program in 1988 in Canada provided special inspiration and instruction to promote evangelism in church growth. A quarterly publication, *Evangelism Canada*, focused the needs and opportunities for the Canadian churches. An Antioch plan, based on an exposition of Acts 8, was adopted as the church growth plan for the 1990s. Also in Canada a new youth ministry–"One Hundred Program"– sent youth groups to assist new churches in local outreach.[29] A close interrelationship with Evangelism Canada and Vision 2000–programs to evangelize the nation–provided a broad umbrella for increasing commitment to evangelism among the Canadian constituency.[30]

All of the activity did raise some questions and uncertainties. Reverses resulting from the over-emphasis on numerical growth came to light as instability was reported in various new churches. An important issue was the balance between a passion for growth and the matter of nurture, integration and assimilation of new members.[31]

These concerns would grow as Mennonite Brethren increasingly aligned themselves with the strategies of the

Church Growth movement, and as the prevailing North American culture continued to impact the popular understanding of evangelism and discipleship.

**Evangelism in Contemporary Perspective**

While Mennonite Brethren preoccupied themselves with numerical growth, the popular mindset around them was changing swiftly as a result of fifty years of startling "progress" in the natural and social sciences.

The impact of the liberal philosophy of John Stuart Mill and John Dewey, which suggested that the only hindrance for progress was a narrow world view, had been devastating. It undermined all fundamental moral principles that previously served as guides to virtuous behavior. Allan Bloom, a noted American social critic wrote:

> Liberalism without natural rights, the kind that we knew from John Stuart Mill and John Dewey, taught us that the only danger confronting us is being closed to the emergent, the new, the manifestations of progress. No attention had to be paid to the fundamental principles or the moral virtues that inclined men to live according to them. To use language now popular, civic culture was neglected. And this turn in liberalism is what prepared us for cultural relativism and the fact-value distinction, which seemed to carry that viewpoint further and give it greater intellectual weight.[32]

Relativism, which removes standards, leaves humanity without norms to distinguish between right and wrong. The Freudian psychology dominant in social sciences depersonalizes the concept of God and destroys the basis of virtues contained in Scripture. The resulting American sense of individualism is responsible for an increasing fragmentation which erodes traditional ties of kin, community and kind. Binding relationships such as marriage, once seen as sacred, become covenant, then contract, and finally irrelevant.[33] According to Daniel Yankelovich the basic character of American culture is the yearning for self-fulfillment.[34] It is a culture with a focus on intrinsic values, in which things are desired for their own sake without regard for anything else. In this ethic of self-fulfillment, values as a means to an end are not enough; they need to be worthwhile in and of themselves.[35]

Contemporary evangelism, in this mindset, replaces the emphasis on the divine sovereignty of God and the work of the Holy Spirit in convicting of sin and lostness, with an appeal to self-fulfillment–a "wonderful plan for your life."[36] Conversion becomes less a conviction of sin and a process of waiting on God to extend mercy and grace for salvation, than convincing God to give what is available. Salvation becomes a mere commodity for the benefit of humanity. Its theology is detached from the divine initiative of the Holy Spirit.[37] Potential converts are urged to pray a prayer–"invite Jesus into your heart"–and are assured that God responds the moment this petition is expressed. Sin is the hindrance for the experience of self-fulfillment, and confession is necessary to remove the hindrance. It is a condition to be filled with the Spirit.[38] Personal workers–one-to-one evangelism–prepare a review of their own experience of accepting Christ and its benefits as an introduction to motivate others to accept Christ.[39]

A classic example of evangelism focused on self-fulfillment is given in Tex Sample's strategy for reaching baby boomers:[40]

1. The program of the church needs to be intrinsically valuable, worthwhile in and of itself. This class of people will not go to church out of obligation. The programs need to be complex, high quality programs that provide instant gratification and are user friendly.

2. Worship services need to be emotionally expressive, offering plenty of movement, and using the language of the

world in which people live.

3. Programs need to "focus on building deep and lasting relationships." Baby boomers are relationally hungry. They desire a "rich community life with a lot of options: worship, study, recreation, social activities, social action, spiritual formation, community service and so on."

4. Effective evangelism to this class of people requires "strong community outreach opportunities and active groups concerned about issues such as liberation, social justice and ecology protection."

5. Today's generation "have not typically been willing to make long-term commitments." This means that programming should focus on shorter-term events, activities and actions.

The over-emphasis on the human dimension of salvation without due focus on God's holiness and the cross as judgment over sin is a theological accommodation to the culture of self-fulfillment. This is what Dietrich Bonhoeffer called the "gospel of cheap grace."[41]

This cheap grace gospel is highly popular in America, where three-fourths of the population say they believe there is a personal God, profess having had an experience with Him, claim He has a plan for their life, and believe in prayer. Nearly a third of Americans claim to be born again, yet display little evidence of changed lives.[42] When a prominent broadcasting vice-president, in charge of network variety and comedy specials, dedicated his life to Jesus Christ, he denied that his new outlook would lead to new moral standards in broadcasting. "All it does is give me peace of mind in my personal life . . . but whether it will affect my programming, it doesn't. It just makes me think clearer, but that just means that I will probably think more commercially than I did before."[43]

American pollster George Gallup notes that declining moral and spiritual values in a society that is so avowedly religious can be attributed to a gospel that "does not confront society, but is conformed to society."[44] A brand of evangelism based on self-fulfillment, with only marginal reference to the absolutes of God, results in a Christianity that is shorn of the central New Testament demand of discipleship: "let him deny himself, take up the cross and follow me" (Matt. 16:24; Luke 9:23).

## THE CHURCH GROWTH PHENOMENON

Church Growth theory has occupied center stage among North American evangelicals in recent decades and profoundly influenced Mennonite Brethren in their search for greater effectiveness in evangelism.

The Academy of Church Growth defines the theory as

> That science which investigates the planting, multiplication, function and health of the churches as they relate specifically to the effective implementation of God's commission to make disciples of all nations (Matt. 28:19-22).
> It strives to combine theological principles of God's Word concerning the expansion of the church with the best insights of contemporary social and behavioral sciences.[45]

Based heavily on the work of Donald McGavran and his missionary ministry in India, the movement pays much attention to social structures, and seeks to identify significant people groups in a given area. Various grids are used to determine a people's perceived openness to the gospel. Those appearing most receptive are then targeted.[46]

The theory also holds that numerical growth is a major criterion in determining the health of a church, and if a church isn't growing it is the fault of the members or their leaders. Growth-inhibiting church diseases are described, and cures prescribed.[47]

The effort to integrate this social science paradigm into a consistent biblical theology has proven difficult. Critics have pointed to a possible over-emphasis on sociology, anthropology and methodology. Delos Miles says "it poses questions of consistent scriptural interpretation, theological pollution, pragmatism and accommodation."[48] The strong reliance on human initiative as a basic condition for growth, with correspondingly less attention to spiritual factors such as ethical purity and self-denying discipleship as a condition of the Spirit's moving in evangelism, eclipses dependence on God for the ingathering of people who are saved through repentance and forgiveness of sin through the atoning provision of Christ. God's sovereignty is replaced by human sovereignty. Conversion is less a process of waiting upon God to extend salvation than of convincing the sinner to ask God for the grace which is immediately available. The theology of salvation is detached from the divine initiative of the Holy Spirit (John 16:7-14).

## Leadership in the Church Growth Model

The Church Growth Theory lodges primary responsibility for growth with a highly centralized and autocratic leadership. The pastoral role is defined in power terms, like the chief executive officer of a corporation or the commander of an army. According to Peter Wagner, the leading spokesman of the movement,

> This army has only one Commander-in-Chief, Jesus Christ. The local church is like a company with one company commander, the pastor, who gets his orders from the Commander-in-Chief. The company commander has lieutenants and sergeants under him for consultation and implementation, but the final responsibility for decisions is that of the commander, and he must answer to the Commander-in-Chief.[49]

The centralized model of leadership as expounded in

Church Growth literature places much emphasis on motivating and training lay leadership to reach people for Christ. In many cases this centralized leadership model has been highly successful in producing phenomenal numerical growth. But the examples of quantitative growth, as cited in Church Growth literature, do not provide corresponding data on the spiritual qualities resulting from such growth.[50] Nor does the literature contain any reference to known church crises resulting from the overemphasis on numerical increase. The frequent incidents of leadership reversals and subsequent radical declines in membership are not described, let alone assessed critically.[51]

The Mennonite Brethren experience with the Church Growth model of centralized leadership has been both positive and negative. Some churches, especially those located in geographic areas of rapid population growth, cultural diversity and industrial and economic expansion, have experienced significant growth. But the jury is still out on the overall impact. The record of numerous and devastating leadership casualties, as well as spiritual and numerical reverses in congregations, is cause for cautious assessment and critical review.

The Church Growth movement offers insight for mobilizing churches to more effective evangelism and missionary commitment. Its emphasis on numerical growth has provided a healthy corrective to many churches that previously paid little more than lip service to the Great Commission.

However, the potential for authoritarian, autocratic leadership, the temptation to neglect spiritual nurture in favor of numbers, and the inclination to rely too heavily on human effort at the expense of the divine, remind us that this movement must be continually tested by the discipleship demands of a more comprehensive biblical theology.

## OBSERVATIONS

The commitment to evangelism as an essential responsibility of the church continues to be important for Mennonite

Brethren. Over the years they have wrestled with how to carry out this task as they moved from a homogeneous social context to one of pluralistic individualism. The process of urbanization, which was more rapid with Mennonite Brethren than any other Mennonite group, contributed to a shift in the initiative for evangelism from the local church to the conference.[52] The conference boards of evangelism assumed a directive role. The decades of the 1960s, 1970s and 1980s record strong programs of evangelism. The appointed evangelists in the 1960s and the conference evangelism executives in the 1970s and 1980s generated powerful momentum and concern for effective evangelism extending beyond the local congregation. Church planting in new locations became a major concern for Mennonite Brethren.

The Canadian Conference grew from eighty-seven congregations and 14,185 members in 1960 to 125 churches and 17,025 members by 1970.[53] By the end of the 1970s the conference reported 140 churches with a membership of 21,579.[54] The growth continued in the 1980s to a record of 190 churches with a membership of 27,277.[55] Contributing to this growth, in addition to faithful evangelism, were population shifts from the prairies and eastern provinces to the West, immigration from the Orient and South America (including many Mennonites) and rapid industrial and economic developments. Evangelistic outreach to the French-Canadian province of Quebec was an additional spur to Mennonite Brethren growth in Canada.

With an equal degree of commitment to evangelism, the numerical growth of U.S. churches was somewhat less. In 1960 there were seventy-six Mennonite Brethren congregations in the U.S. with a membership of 11,709. In 1990, 30 years later, there were 119 churches with a membership of 16,794.[56]

Amid three decades of accelerated evangelistic activity Mennonite Brethren have not been spared from the trend of accommodating the message of the gospel to a culture that is open to the benefits of salvation but does not want to "take up the cross and follow me." Contemporary evangelicalism generally, has experienced a softening of those elements of traditional Protestant belief that today's society finds unpalatable. While the doctrinal core has remained unchanged, the message and methods of evangelism have accommodated to make it culturally more acceptable.

Social science describes this accommodation as acculturation under the pressure of modernity. Most Christian movements that have opened themselves to engage the world–and Mennonite Brethren are no exception–find themselves in the tension of compromising the message of the gospel to make it more acceptable. These observations bring to memory the words of William Booth, a powerful evangelist of his day and founder of the Salvation Army, who is said to have expressed the concern that a day may come when there will be a preaching of religion without the Holy Spirit, a Christianity without Christ, a forgiveness without repentance, a salvation without regeneration and a heaven without a hell.

These are sobering issues for Mennonite Brethren at the close of the twentieth century. How they grapple with crucial questions of the method and message of evangelism in the face of the continuing pressure of modernity will determine to what degree they will be a New Testament people–in the world, but not of the world–in the twenty-first century.

CHAPTER 19

# Missions in the Context of Change

The words of Emil Brunner, "The church exists by mission as fire exists by burning,"[1] apply well to Mennonite Brethren. The Mennonite Brethren Church was born in the fire of mission and for 130 years it has retained this focus. A loss of missionary zeal would spell gradual but certain extinction.

The call to mission is central to those who profess to follow Jesus. The mission mandate cannot be detached from the recognition of his lordship: "All power is given unto me in heaven and in earth. Go ye therefore, and teach all nations" (Matt. 28:18-19).

In a culture of rampant individualism and pragmatism, Mennonite Brethren along with other believers need to continually reevaluate their commitment to and practice of mission. The Lausanne Covenant, adopted in 1974 at an international gathering of evangelicals, suggested the basic principles for such an ongoing evaluation: (1) Is the mission characterized by a life of discipleship and self-denial? (2) Is the message one that transforms persons; does it imply judgment on every form of alienation, oppression and discrimination, denouncing evil and injustice wherever they exist? (3) Is the mission enterprise and its growing partnership of churches continuously seeking to reflect the true character of Christ's church?[2] Most Mennonite Brethren today would affirm these principles.

For the early Mennonite Brethren, missionary outreach was spontaneous; they had no explicit theology of mission. Their general motivation was simple: millions had never heard the gospel, and needed to hear. It was their task as followers of

Christ to make known the salvation of God. Some of the most gifted missionaries would not even wait on the readiness of the Mennonite Brethren Conference to officially send them. They were convinced God was sending them and would provide for their needs. During the first fifty years of Mennonite Brethren missions the administrative structure was limited to a church at home that recognized the various mission interests and assured those that went of the needed support.[3]

The target of missions from 1890 to the 1950s were the poor who had never heard–in North America the native Americans, in India the outcasts, in Africa the tribal people of the interior, in Colombia the people along the San Juan River, and in Paraguay the nomadic Indian tribes of the Chaco.

During the late nineteenth century and the first half of the twentieth reports from missionaries provided a major part of the content of the early denominational periodicals. Few Mennonite Brethren would have disagreed with David J. Hesselgrave's assertion that Christian mission is the greatest enterprise on earth: conceived in heaven, with its final outcome anchored in the redemptive purpose of God.[4]

### Mennonite Brethren Missions, 1950-1990

Rapid changes in the second half of the twentieth century profoundly affected the character, strategy, methods and relationships of Mennonite Brethren missions. Between 1945 and 1990 the tradition of Western colonialism was seriously challenged with the emergence of ninety-four new nations. Missionary operations in Africa, Asia and Latin America were forced to change accordingly.

The 1947 *Guiding Principles and Field Policies* for the Mennonite Brethren Board of Foreign Missions described the missionary's relationship to the national church as ongoing. Missionaries remained on the field even long after national churches were established. "The need for fathers in Christ among the national believers always remains and the missionary is seen in the role indefinitely."[5]

Ten years later, the 1957 conference adopted a document which called for strategic changes in this relationship.[6] This document modified the missionary-centered programs and called instead for a new kind of missionary who would help establish indigenous churches that could assume the responsibility for evangelizing their own constituencies. The document also called for structural changes in methods and relationships, projecting a larger role for the home board and administrative office in planning and evaluation.

The change was not easy. The churches had developed a very personal relation to specific missionaries and programs. The missionaries promoted their own specific assignments. They were autonomous with no direct accountability to the home constituencies. This sense of local church accountability weakened the overall common responsibility of the Mennonite Brethren Church at large. Mission needed a new focus to share the responsibility of the global assignment to "go into all the world." The conference responded with a strong affirmation for change. For the missionaries who had been in India and Africa for many years, these changes were not easy.

The implications of the 1957 document were sharpened in the 1960 and 1961 *Guiding Principles and Policies*: (1) The church is God's instrument of evangelism. (2) The planting and upbuilding of the national church is the primary assignment of mission. (3) The training of national leadership to assume responsibility is the central objective in national church development. (4) The mission program is subject to periodic evaluations on the basis of accepted standards established for a specific area to govern the development of the national church.

The new structure conceived of the missionary as only the initial agent in a church-planting program. The assignment was to evangelize, gather a group of believers, and plant a church.[7] This radically redefined the role of the missionary from the understanding that it was a lifetime assignment to a specific place and people. The purpose was not to diminish the missionary task but rather to harmonize it with new international realities. Missiologist Hans Kasdorf described the changes between 1947 and 1961 as "novel–if not radical–ideas of internationalization, ideas far ahead of their time in Mennonite Brethren mission thinking."[8]

The years 1961 to 1969 in Mennonite Brethren missions can well be classified as a period of reorientation followed by years of realignment.[9] The principles of "Partnership in Obedience," adopted at the 1960 and 1963 conferences, were to initiate relational mutuality between the sending churches (the Mennonite Brethren mission) and the receiving churches (national churches).[10]

A second major change occurred in 1966 with the merger of the Board of Foreign Missions and the Board of General Welfare and Public Relations. In principle this action was a theological corrective, interrelating the ministry of proclamation with the ministry of response to human needs.[11] The actions of 1960, 1963 and 1966 were appropriate in essence and honest in intent. The realization of these ideals, however, as Kasdorf pointed out, left much to be desired.

A decade later, the 1977 edition of *Principles and Policies* reaffirmed the directional decisions of the 1960s. The primary task of mission was defined as the building of Christlike, self-propagating churches in modern urbanized societies with the missionary serving as a planter to withdraw as soon as he or she could be replaced with national leadership.[12] This edition further committed the program to meeting human needs as part of the mission assignment.

> While our priority is to build churches, and through them to minister to the whole person, we recognize that this is not always possible in a world plagued by strong forces of nationalism. We realize, therefore, that in some situations we are called upon to minister to human needs in

areas where no public witness is allowed. We do so because we are called to be Christlike in all areas of life, and because we realize that even this is a witness to the love of God to those ministered to . . . .

We do invest in programs for ministering to human needs in areas where we are planting and nurturing churches. These programs should normally be carried out only where these needs (by priority: subsistence and family planning, medical and educational) are not met by local government programs, or where these programs do not meet the needs of the churches. However, these programs should be designed to operate on the local level, and with an emphasis on investing in people rather than in property. For the most part, these programs are seen as expendable and should be phased out as soon as the needs are met by other means.[13]

The 1975 North American conference described an international Mennonite Brethren Church with emphases on upholding the faith and promoting the fellowship and partnership in preaching, teaching and healing. The "Vision for the Future" called for a worldwide partnership in the assignment of mission.[14]

A century of Mennonite Brethren missions has resulted in an international fellowship. The 43,000 Mennonite Brethren in North America (26,000 Canada, 17,000 U.S.) constitute only one-third of the total number of Mennonite Brethren believers around the world. India, for example, numbers 50,000; Zaire 47,000. Mission literature reports Mennonite Brethren churches in fourteen countries of the world.[15]

## Missionary Vision for the Future

The continued commitment of Mennonite Brethren to missions found expression in the projections of the 1987 and 1990 conferences. The mandate for the 1990s was given in five affirmations: (1) We strongly affirm the centrality and urgency of Christian mission. (2) We must increase our efforts to reach the lost. (3) We must redeem the extending opportunities created through a new openness in the world. (4) A Mennonite Brethren worldwide partnership will provide more resources for our mission work. (5) Three priorities are to govern our ministry: evangelism and church planting; leadership training and nurture; social ministries to meet the human needs as part of the gospel.[16]

The missions budget for the 1990-1993 triennium projected an annual income of $5,320,000. Contributions from the churches in 1989 was $104 per member.[17] No other cause at any conference level reflects such broad and active participation. Throughout Mennonite Brethren history, missions has proven to be the strongest unifying factor. The nurture of this commitment is essential for the vitality of the Mennonite Brethren movement in years to come.

## AN INTERNATIONAL FELLOWSHIP

North American Mennonite Brethren speak with satisfaction of a worldwide church that significantly outnumbers the church at home. In the promotion of missions frequent reference is made to the 99,000 Mennonite Brethren abroad in contrast to only 43,000 in North America. A good deal of this satisfaction is justified. God has done great things through this small group of believers, a mere splinter from the larger Anabaptist movement.

Despite being isolated agrarian people of European stock, their message was carried to a multiplicity of countries and races simply because they could not contain the good news of redemption. Like Peter and John, they could not but speak of the things which they had seen and heard (Acts 4:20). The words of the Apostle Paul recorded in 1 Corinthians 1:27-28 may also apply to the history of Mennonite Brethren missions: "God hath chosen the foolish things of the world to confound the wise; and God hath chosen the weak things of the world to confound the things which are mighty."

The cultural and racial character of this worldwide church may well come under the description of Revelation 5:9, "For thou wast slain, and hast redeemed us to God by thy blood out of every kindred, and tongue, and people, and nation." The outcastes of India; the vendors from the streets of southern China; tribal people of the African jungle and along the San Juan River in Colombia; the urban dwellers of Cali, Bogota, Curitiba and São Paulo; the migrant Indian tribes of the Paraguayan Chaco; the fellowship groups of Mexico, Spain, Germany, Austria and Japan; all these, along with the original groups in Russia and North America constitute together a worldwide Mennonite Brethren Church. Indeed, "this is the Lord's doing, and it is marvelous in our eyes" (Matt. 21:42).

## MENNONITE BRETHREN MISSIONS IN CONTEMPORARY PERSPECTIVE

Numbers and scope aside, those involved in missions must not only do mission, but must also measure what they are doing by what God has said should be done.[18] Because mission is a sacred assignment there is often a tendency to leave the evaluation to God and the Holy Spirit. Jesus' parable in Mark 4:26-27–"So is the kingdom of God, as if a man should cast seed into the ground; and should sleep, and rise night and day, and the seed should spring and grow up, he knoweth not how"–affirms the hidden secret of the gospel. The outcome is with God. To the above parable, however, must be added the parable of the talents (Matt. 25:15-30) in which the master calls his servants to accountability for their stewardship.

Mennonite Brethren mission is based on a defined theological understanding: "The building of Christlike self-propagating churches."[19] Sowing the seed of the gospel is indeed necessary; it is the means of planting indigenous churches.

How does the mission measure up against this standard? To what degree have the partnerships been realized?

Hans Kasdorf reflects on the futuristic projections of the Mennonite Brethren Conference from the 1960s to the mid-1980s as, "The Unfinished Agenda of Partnership."[20] The visions and policies were in keeping with the broader framework of missionary objectives. They were genuine in their intent, but a gap remains between articulating and embodying the vision.

Calling for consistency between adopted principles and policies and actual performance does not negate the good which has resulted from the ministry of the gospel. The grace of God and the intercession of the Spirit apply even to that which is proclaimed with human imperfections and weakness (Rom. 8:26). However, the degree of effectiveness in Mennonite Brethren mission in the future will depend on openly evaluating and interpreting the past, examining the present and projecting the future in the context of rapid changes.

### "BANDWAGON" PUBLICITY

No small amount of mission publicity is based on what Hesselgrave describes as "the bandwagon effect: mission is where the action is; millions are waiting for us to come; thousands are responding to the message; the church is growing as never before."[21] Mennonite Brethren are no exception. Published reports speak of progress, open doors and the need for more missionaries. The appeals are justified. The needs are there; the harvest is ripe and the reapers are few.

Mission, however is also the battleground of light and darkness, with problems and reverses. Seldom does the public hear of the setbacks and failures. To illustrate the trend in mission reporting, Hesselgrave reports the following episode:

> Some years ago a major evangelical magazine ran a cartoon in which two missionaries sat side by side in the

front pew of a local church. As one prepared to ascend to the podium, he turned to the other and whispered, "Should we tell them the truth or should we keep them happy?"

The cartoon is funny until one thinks about it. Then it is not funny at all. And that, of course, is just the effect that the cartoonist was after. He wanted us to laugh; but more than that he wanted us to think.[22]

Mission appeals contain a great deal of truth, but not the whole truth. They are one-sided. Yes, missions are experiencing success and people are finding Christ. But there are also serious problems. Missionary prayer letters and head office press releases do not answer questions as to why, for example, we have been in some countries for decades without producing a viable indigenous church with national leadership.

A few years ago *Decision* magazine carried an article entitled "Bavarian Mennonite Brethren Conference Continues to Grow."[23] In reality, however, there was only one Mennonite Brethren church registered with a membership of forty-five; the other six churches referred to were small fellowships with memberships of twenty-six, seventeen, fifteen, thirteen, eight and five. The national leadership mentioned in the article had not emerged from the respective communities but had been recruited by the missionaries and subsidized from the North American office. Yet the article suggested seven viable churches organized into a viable conference. The projected public image did not entirely square with the reality of the situation.

Moreover, the leaders in Bavaria were themselves privately expressing misgivings about the absence of independent national churches. They noted that the situation in Bavaria following World War II was favorable to missionary activity. The population was growing. There were many refugees "open and searching for fellowship." People did join the young Mennonite Brethren churches but they "officially remained in their respective churches and have not remained true to our fellowship. The open church policy where members and non-members made decisions concerning the life of the church did not work out favorably." Also troubling was the apparent lack of agreement between the North American workers on various theological issues. "The missionaries offered no consistent position in relation to the teachings of Catholicism and the Lutheran Reformed Church. They also lacked a clear position with regard to sectarianism, the charismatic movement and the position of women in the church." The consequence of the lack of unity among the missionaries was that "the believers did not receive the needed instructions. The testimony of the church in the community was weakened."[24]

While "bandwagon" reporting may prove profitable for fundraising, the reality is distorted. The churches at home do not receive an accurate picture of what is actually happening in the mission they are asked to support.

**MISSION STRATEGY**

Strategy is fundamental if mission is to achieve its goals. Anthropologist Jacob A. Loewen distinguishes three basic strategies for cross-cultural mission: soul winning, self-replication and the catalyst.[25] The Mennonite Brethren mission has followed a strategy that incorporates the first two: Soul winning and self-replication (establishing Mennonite Brethren churches). In soul-winning, the missionary goes to the people, learns their language and something of their culture, develops friendships and seeks to lead them to Christ. But unless the converts have the potential to form a fellowship or a church, what is often created is a series of individual converts who remain an island: orphaned, detached from their own community, and targets of religious isms.[26] Short-term ministries of faith missions (this applies to Mennonite Brethren also) and mass meeting evangelism are especially prone to leave these regrettable results.

"Soul-saving," leading people to Christ, remains at the heart of mission, but it is only the first part of the assignment. The goal is to establish indigenous churches rooted in their own culture, and to train their own leaders to evangelize their own people. In other words, to be a catalyst.

This latter strategy has been difficult for Mennonite Brethren to achieve. In India and Zaire, for example, national Mennonite Brethren leaders emerged only as political changes removed Western missionaries (in India after sixty-seven years, in Africa only after 1962). Japan is an exception. The Mennonite Brethren Church there is strong and assumes responsibility for evangelism at home and beyond. The late Ruth Wiens Funk, returning from Japan after forty years as a missionary, said: "Our work in Japan is finished. God has raised up his own people in Japan."

Officially, Mennonite Brethren strategy in the post-colonial period has been to evangelize, establish the church, train national leadership and *leave the expansion to the native church and its leadership*.[27] But missiologist Hans Kasdorf suggests a slowness in the training of national leadership and transferring responsibility. There are countries where Mennonite Brethren missionaries have labored for decades and churches have been established, yet national leadership has not emerged. This phenomenon is difficult to reconcile with our mission theology. The gap between intention and accomplishment is probably best explained by a lack of basic understanding of what is required in authentic partnership. The rhetoric of "internationalization" and "globalization" is easy; but it requires cultural understandings that are difficult to achieve.

Part of the problem may lie with what Latin American Mission director Horace L. Fenton called–"the myth of the unqualified national":

> The myth of the unqualified national is not usually expressed so forthrightly; instead, it is implied by a host of things we say and do which indicate that we are not yet ready to trust the leadership God has raised up for his church in these countries.

He concluded:

> Most of us missionaries would pay glowing tribute to the maturing church in the lands where we have served and to the emergence of a true national leadership in it. Often, however, our actions belie our words. It is all too evident that we feel that for some time to come we shall have to hang on tightly to the reins of authority. Meanwhile, we grudgingly give in here and there by delegating some responsibility in less important areas, but seldom surrender major elements of the work into their hands unless we are forced to do it.[28]

## Test of Our Strategy

Roland Allen has described the spontaneous expansion of the church as an unexhorted and unorganized activity of individual members of the church explaining to others the gospel which they have found for themselves; an expansion which follows the irresistible attraction of the Christian church for people who see its meaningful life and are drawn to it by a desire to discover the secret of this life they inwardly desire.[29]

Allen questions the effectiveness of highly organized mission institutions. Missionaries, known to be well paid by an organization or denomination to propagate the faith and the expansion of their own denomination, may not always have the contagious dynamic of the Spirit that ignites fire in human hearts.

The modern era of missions reflects three typical stages of relationship with national churches: dependency, independency and interdependency. The dependency model, where the missionary was the initiator, overseer, policy maker, evangelist and doctor, theoretically ceased with the end of colonialism. National churches wanted an independent religious movement under their own direction and control.

The word indigenization–which meant the creation of national churches independent from the mission in organization and finances–became the slogan for a period of time. Leadership of institutions and programs was transferred to local people, with the missionary assuming the posture of servanthood. While the model was good, Western administrators and missionaries found it difficult not to develop a "helper-helpee" relationship in which the "helper" still defined the need and prescribed the solution.[30] Mennonite Brethren, while articulating the "Partnership in Obedience" commitment, in practice largely retained the "helper-helpee" stage with its prerogatives to define both needs and solutions.

The third stage of interdependence, where both sides equally share in planning and decision-making, has remained largely a theory. The central office in North America continues to be the service organization that consults with the churches abroad about the program in their respective geographical areas, but maintains a unilateral grip on decision-making.

Many national church leaders are skeptical of any rhetoric having to do with "Partnership in Obedience." They inquire, "partnership with whom?" National leaders continue to feel subordinate to the missionaries and the mission office. Said one national leader, "Yes, we were told the national conference was autonomous to make decisions, but since we were partners with the mission this partnership was understood to be only in one direction and not reciprocal. The Mission Office is the Vatican for us."[31]

Dr. Tite Tienou, a native African, for nine years professor at the Alliance Theological Seminary in Nyack, New York and the founding president of a seminary in Ivory Coast, recently defined an appropriate meaning for contextualization and globalization:

> Contextualization and globalization are two sides of the coin. I have been globalized for a long time [i.e. listening to westerners]. It is time that the West became globalized. Globalization means westerners now listen to the Third World. . . . We have been hearing you for a long time, do you hear us. . . . If we cannot listen, we cannot learn. Free-time is filled with noise. To listen, we need silence . . . creative ways of partnership are not now adequately dealt with. We need to treat brothers and sisters around the world as full gospel partners, not just as junior partners . . . partnership is to help us the Third World to do a better job.[32]

Actions speak louder than words. Have we failed to implement our partnership rhetoric in both our relationships and in sharing responsibilities with the nationals? How do we respond to national leaders in South America when they ask: "Obedience to whom? Partnership with whom?" National leaders continue to feel pressured to obey decisions made by the missionaries. In the end, North America always has the last word. National conferences are "autonomous" partners but the partnership was understood to be in only one direction and not reciprocal.[33]

A member of the Mennonite Brethren Church in Brazil and a graduate of the Mennonite Brethren Biblical Seminary in Fresno, Calif., has commented on the lopsided relationships that can develop in the missions setting. While deeply appreciating the missionaries who brought the gospel to her people, she is also aware of how the hardships her people endured have affected their functioning in the church. Most of them are poor and without educational opportunities. They have been oppressed by dictators and have little experience with showing initiative in many aspects of life, including the church. They have had little opportunity to assume responsibilities and respond to the challenge of leadership.

The missionaries, she recalls, came into this milieu with a mindset of power and control. They had money. They demanded a higher lifestyle than the local people. Nationals chosen to help were paid a small fraction of what missionaries received.

> When the missionaries start to open their eyes and perceive the underlying realities for what it means to live in an oppressed country, they will be able to understand and respect the suffering and revolt behind the passivity expressed by the national leadership. It's a silent suffering, hopeless cry and expectation for the "better." It's not an invitation for more invasion and control. It's a cry for help, for sharing knowledge, experience and faith.
>
> When Americans understand their roles as enablers and not as rulers, and step out of their comfortable thrones, they will be able to hear the cry, feel the feelings, and work together as brothers and sisters without the fear of being misunderstood in their purpose as missionaries.[34]

Similar sentiments are expressed by Hugo Zorrilla, for years a member of the Mennonite Brethren Church in Colombia. Educated at the Mennonite Brethren school there, he later earned a doctorate from the Pontifical University of Salamanca in Spain. For five years he served as a missionary in Spain under Mennonite Brethren Missions/Services. For several years he has taught at the Mennonite Brethren Biblical Seminary and Fresno Pacific College. He writes that few missionaries, despite their good motives, come with a humble attitude ready to learn the behavior and values of the culture that is adopting them. The "incarnation," the "being born again" into another culture after the model of Christ, is often lacking.

Nationals find it difficult to accept the lifestyle of missionaries, Zorrilla says. While the nationals work long hours for bare necessities, the missionaries live in relative ease. Their children go to special schools. They have cars. They live in modern houses. The nationals who struggle to survive economically are hesitant to assume leadership as long as there are missionaries who have the time to do the work. The missionaries' identification with the local culture is marginal. When they speak freely of furloughs and their need for rest, they give the impression that their ultimate loyalty is still at home.

Nationals often have the impression "that the mission of Christ is very ethnocentric, and very Americanized." Some missionaries seem to think God works only through them. In too many instances the missionary acts as a chief and not a facilitator.[35]

Paul, the apostolic missionary, addressed the basic prerequisite for an effective witness when he said, "I am made all things to all men, that I might by all means save some" (1 Cor. 9:22). In contemporary language, it is a call for identification and cultural sensitivity. Contextualization and incarnation are essentials for an effective transcultural witness.

This identification means to listen to and learn from the adopted culture. It is more than imitation. It means to learn a culture so well that one can feel with the adopted culture. The process of such identification takes time. Someone has said, "For God's sake do not do anything on the field for the first year" (some have even suggested waiting five years). By then the missionary would be approaching a position where meaningful identification is possible. Obviously, then, it becomes very difficult to accomplish anything when the missionary stays in an assignment for only two or three years.

We North Americans find it very difficult to identify with

another culture. Our affluence gets in the way of relational equality with the people to whom we are sent to minister. An emphasis on Western-style church organization is often premature and restricts the maturation of the spontaneous inner life of the believers.

Hugo Zorrilla has observed that despite their sincerity, only a minority of North American missionaries are really effective in reaching the people for Christ because it takes years to speak a language well and with confidence. "We are convinced that if more nationals would be called into the ministry without the controlling hand of North Americans we would see more responsibility, greater fruit and greater vision for the work of the kingdom."

He goes on to say,

> "For many of them [the missionaries] it is the first time they see or experience another culture and also the first time they leave their narrow social circle. Few are the missionaries who come with a humble attitude and are ready to learn the behavior and values of the culture that is adopting them. Is there a formula to use so that missionaries will stop showing arrogance and self-sufficiency when they present the gospel to persons in another culture?"[36]

## FINANCIAL PATERNALISM

Closely related to the issue of partnership with national churches is financial paternalism. Prolonged financial support, no matter how well-intentioned, can breed dependency and stifle initiative. William J. Kornfield, a veteran missionary from Ecuador, has raised serious concerns that ongoing financial subsidies from wealthy North American churches to less affluent churches in other lands can affect their programmatic independence and initiative. He believes this is one of the most important issues facing the church all over the world and, if not checked, will ultimately stagnate church growth.[37]

Kornfield quotes Charles Troutman, former director of Inter-Varsity Christian Fellowship in North America and a missionary with Latin American Mission for ten years, who calls financial paternalism the "worst curse" we could put upon the national church.[38] Continued economic support implies that the church of Jesus Christ cannot grow on its own native soil—or in some cases even exist—apart from Western funding.

Prolonged economic subsidies to individuals and churches in underdeveloped countries can become a tool of oppression rather than one that develops self-respect and initiative. More helpful is for missions to assist national churches in depressed economic areas to develop their own resources and gain self-reliance. Eventual economic independence for national churches is basic to a relationship of equality and mutual interdependence.

## WHERE IS THE ANSWER?

The testing of our strategy from the perspective of our churches abroad calls for a reassessment of how we best do missions at the end of the twentieth century and into the twenty-first. Voices from within the North American Mennonite Brethren Church corroborate what the national leaders from other countries are saying. Writings by Hans Kasdorf, Henry Schmidt, Paul Hiebert and Jacob A. Loewen all call for changes in how we are currently doing missions.[39]

The tension between the rhetoric of "Partnership in Obedience" and reality as expressed both by some national leaders and by various missiologists at home is not unique to the Mennonite Brethren. With few exceptions the same critique can be levelled at North American missions at large. Recognizing that we have company does not diminish the problem. Important voices speaking from home and abroad need to be heard. Are we not obligated, as we plead for more missionaries, to also insure that we change the image of the North

American missionary? Our task is not merely to send missionaries, but to build self-sustaining units of the kingdom of God.

## The Church in Panama

One example of Mennonite Brethren missionaries playing the role of catalyst within an existing culture is the work of Jacob Loewen and David Wirsche in Panama. In 1958 when they began employing that approach for evangelizing the Indians in Colombia and Panama, they met strong resistance. As a mission administrator, I too was resistant. The departure from the conventional pattern of "doing missions" was for me and others too radical. Could the gospel be communicated without a missionary in residence and without providing structure? It was a leap of faith. The missionaries would go to Panama only for several months at a time and then leave it the Holy Spirit to nurture the seed they had planted. They taught the Indians to read and produced literature for them, including translating parts of the New Testament. John and Janice Goertz and others who followed understood the approach. They served effectively as catalysts. The church in Panama today stands as a witness to the effectiveness of the catalyst approach.

## THE DAWN OF CHANGE

Other good steps have been taken towards fuller realization of "Partnership in Obedience." Partnership with our brothers and sisters in India and Zaire is gradually developing, encouraged by political circumstances. We need to give thanks for the church in Japan. There also have been growing conversations about new forms of partnership. The meetings with national leaders in Brazil in 1988, and during the Mennonite World Conference in Winnipeg in 1990 marked a good beginning. Of special significance was the meeting convened by Juan Veron in Asuncion, Paraguay in July 1992, when Mennonite Brethren leaders from North America met with national church representatives from Asia, Africa and

South America.  The meeting of the Board of Missions/Services in the fall of 1992 probed deeply into the status of Mennonite Brethren missions around the world and initiated a review.  Present were leaders of several national churches: Vedulla K. Rufus, India; Takao Nakamura, Japan; Alfred Foth, Uruguay and Emilio Zabala, Venezuela.

## REFLECTIONS ON OUR PAST AND A LOOK INTO THE FUTURE

The rapid changes of the past three to four decades have left Mennonite Brethren somewhat stunned.  Our preoccupation with the struggles at home may have blunted our sensitivity to the need for changed strategies and relationships abroad.  We failed in many cases to follow our own rheteoric of "Partnership in Obedience." Our missionaries, though sincere, reflected the lifestyle and relationships of the sending church.  Missions is seldom better than the church that nurtures and develops the missionaries that it sends.  Our response to our failures should not be retrenchment but rather repentance.  We should seek forgiveness from our brothers and sisters who failed to see in us and our missionaries the love and grace of Jesus expressed in partnership, identification and relationship.

Our Mennonite Brethren Board of Missions/Services has adopted the slogan of "Global Mission."  This suggests ending the division between missions abroad and missions at home. Mission abroad and evangelism at home are one in principle and must be our first passion. Our ability to act on this passion depends on the renewal of the Mennonite Brethren Church in North America.

CHAPTER 20

# Faith in Tension

The 1990 convention of the General Conference of Mennonite Brethren Churches adopted a vision statement for the 1990s. The central issues facing the church were articulated in a series of questions: "What does it mean to be a Mennonite Brethren people? What does it mean to be a Mennonite Brethren Church? What are the bonds that hold us together?"[1]

The Mennonite Brethren are not alone in asking "Who are we?" and "What does it mean to be the church?" In a time of cultural relativism and religious pluralism virtually all religious communities are asking the same question. The post-Second World War era appears to have removed all absolute standards. We find ourselves in a generation spiritually adrift. Pilate's question, "What is Truth?" (John 18:38), finds no definitive answer.

Our culture of relativity and individualism has eroded the fabric of social and spiritual interdependence. Churches in North America, be they Baptist, Presbyterian, Catholic, Methodist, Episcopalian or Pentecostal, are struggling like never before with questions of theology and ethics.[2]

Mennonite Brethren, heirs of the sixteenth-century Anabaptists and with a history tested in isolation and persecution, now find themselves buffeted on the open sea of American Protestantism. The vision statement presented to the Mennonite Brethren Conference in 1990 is a call for reexamination, reorientation, affirmation and recommitment. Perhaps this statement could be seen as a parallel of the words to the angel of the church of Ephesus (Rev. 2:1-7) which recognized the many good works of the church but nonetheless called for repentance because they had abandoned their first love.

"Repent, and do the first works" (v.5).

What does it mean, as we approach the threshold of the twenty-first century, to be the Mennonite Brethren people of God? To answer that question we must look at our crisis of identity from a threefold perspective:

1. Contending for the Faith (Jude 3);
2. Wrestling against principalities and powers (Eph. 6:12);
3. Examining whether we are in the faith (2 Cor. 13:5).

## CONTENDING FOR THE FAITH

Mennonite Brethren in North America are highly cognizant of the revolutionary cultural changes that followed the Second World War. The traditional way to address these changes has been to draw leaders together in a study conference to examine the church's scriptural understanding in the face of social and religious shifts. The study conference has been one of the ways by which Mennonite Brethren have contended for the faith. In the post-war era fourteen such conferences have been held by the General Conference and many more at other conference levels.[3]

Bland as they may sound, study conferences have provided an important mechanism to tap into the consciousness of the constituency and attempt to forge a biblical consensus on important issues. The process for these events has largely been the same. Pastors or teachers in the various denominational schools wrote the study papers on specific subjects under examination. The papers were then distributed for evaluation to the participants representing area conferences and churches. There the papers were examined for their consistency with Mennonite Brethren scriptural understanding. Later, the papers would be further studied, discussed and possibly revised at a public assembly of representative leaders. The results of these studies were frequently brought in the form of resolutions to conferences for possible adoption.

The fact that this thorough and sometimes tedious process has been followed with such frequency and regularity bears important testimony to the seriousness with which Mennonite Brethren took cultural change and its possible effects on basic principles of faith, polity and lifestyle. A listing of the topics reads like a roadmap of cultural and religious change.

The first study conference, held December 12-15, 1956, explored anew the Mennonite Brethren understanding of the work of the Holy Spirit. The context was the lingering pentecostalism and the rising charismatic movement which reached full crest in the late 1960s and early 1970s. Helping focus the study were presentations on "The Baptism and Infilling of the Holy Spirit" (George W. Peters), "The Gifts of the Holy Spirit to the Believer" (Jacob J. Toews), and "The Biblical Teaching on Sanctification" (Waldo Hiebert). A follow-up conference in July 1958 reviewed further the "Scriptural Definition of the Nature of the Church" (Waldo Hiebert) and "The Scriptural Teaching of Conversion and Regeneration in the Understanding of a Believers Church" (David Edmond Hiebert).

Study conferences of 1959 and 1967 addressed more specific doctrinal and social issues. One was the matter of biblical inspiration. The battle over the Bible was already simmering, though it would not reach full boil until the late 1970s. A paper on "Inspiration and the Scriptures" (Arthur Willems) served as a basis for the study. Other conferences of this period focused on "Christian Social Ethics from the Biblical Standpoint" (Abraham E. Janzen), "Marriage and Sex" (Waldo Hiebert), "The Christian and Race Relations" (Jake Loewen and Wesley Prieb), "The Church and State in the New Testament" (Frank C. Peters).

Beginning in 1967 some papers addressed more specifically personal issues as the conference wrestled with matters of individual liberty and ethics in the light of Scripture. There were additional studies on "Dealing Redemptively with the

Divorced and Remarried" (J.H. Quiring), "Christian Responsibility in Relation to Planned Parenthood" (A.B. Voth), and "Remarriage of the Divorced in the Light of Scripture" (G.W. Peters). The concern for personal ethics received further attention in the 1970s with study papers on "A Christian Perspective on Abortion" (Vern Ratzlaff) and "The Christian and His Material Possessions" (Len Siemens).

These conferences represent community hermeneutics in action–the church studying Scripture together and coming to consensual agreement on what it means for the issues of the day. The General Conference in 1966 gave special instructions on study conference procedures in an effort to maintain the principle of a community hermeneutics.

## CONCERNING THEOLOGICAL TRENDS

We recommend that three study conferences be held during the next conference interim. Careful planning should precede the meeting and the delegation should also include leading brethren who are not ordained.

Several steps might be observed in the planning of these meetings.

1. Reference and Counsel might decide on the issues to be discussed. Care should be taken to avoid overloading a program so that insignificant time is left for discussion. There should be discussion in depth.

2. Brethren should be invited to write introductory papers. Two papers on each subject.

3. Two brethren who have read these introductory papers in advance should write a short response as a basis for discussion.

4. Study group participants should break up into smaller units for preliminary discussions but final conclusions should come from the entire group.

5. One brother should summarize and from this should come a communique to the churches for study. Unless we

also initiate discussion at the local level we would again produce the effect of a handed down pronouncement.

6. At the next General Conference some of the statements could be accepted as speaking the mind of the brotherhood.

The strength and usefulness of this approach will depend largely on our openness to each other and to the leadership of the Spirit of God. We also feel that we have not deviated from one another to the extent that we could not find some common solution. What we need are love, humility, honesty and insight. We have in our brotherhood the potential for all four of these ingredients.[4]

## Revision of the Confession of Faith

In 1963 the General Conference felt it was time to revise the 1902 Confession of Faith. The process called for the participation of all ministers and local congregations in this first revision in Mennonite Brethren history. The directives issued to guide the revision process underline the relative role of a confession in the wider Mennonite Brethren effort of contending for the faith.

### REGARDING A REVISED CONFESSION OF FAITH

We recommend the following directives and guidelines for use in the review and revision of our Confession of Faith to be referred to the incoming Board of Reference and Counsel for implementation.

1. The Confession of Faith shall be prefaced by a statement describing the aims, purposes, and uses of such a document.

The following is a suggested preface:

The Mennonite Brethren Church has throughout its history emphasized biblical authority in all matters of faith and practice. This emphasis while exalting the centrality of Scripture also counsels caution in the use of any extra-biblical documents such as creedal statements and confessions. Such documents are to be regarded as descriptive more than normative. They are never to be given equal status with the Bible.

A confession such as this one is an echo of the brotherhood since it reflects the faith which such a fellowship believes and preaches. Its validity depends on its biblical character, its usefulness depends on its ability to communicate.

The Mennonite Brethren Church accepts God's revelation in its inscripturated form as final and considers the original documents to have been inerrant and reliable. It is not the task of the church to summarize the message of the Bible in a way which respects contemporaneity in speech while setting forth cardinal truth simply and clearly.

A confession of faith represents a brotherhood in conversation. Here we can see how a group of believers respecting the Word speaks concerning those vital subjects which are the content of a biblical faith. A confession, however, cannot tell us how such a fellowship practices what it says.[5]

By the time the revised Confession of Faith was finally adopted in 1975 it had gone through seven drafts in a study process led by the Board of Reference and Counsel with the participation of area conferences and local congregations. It was truly an exercise in community discernment. The widespread participation also deepened the covenant between agreeing churches.[6] This procedure, though sometimes arduous and perhaps frustrating to some who would prefer the speed and convenience of unilateral decisions, is the tuition a group pays in the school of community hermeneutics. Throughout its history, the Mennonite Brethren Church has felt the ultimate benefit was worth the price.

When the 1969 conference addressed the relationship of ethical integrity in the face of the changing environment, the comment was made that "the sum total of spiritual insight and understanding of any Christian group exceeds the sum total of such understanding of any one person of that group."[7] Consensus was also recognized as a way to encourage and strengthen individuals with the commitment to a larger community.

The conference recognized that in order to contend for the faith "the living church must grow in all essential aspects, one of which is understanding of the Word and will of God." Growth amidst a changing external environment "may also call for a change in relationship and conduct. Such changes must always be made in uncompromising obedience to the Word and Spirit of God."[8] As issues and situations change, the church and its individual members must be prepared to change the shape of their testimony of faith before the world.

The Word of God constitutes the abiding and unchanging authority for the Christian in all matters of faith and conduct.

While each individual Christian is to be involved in the process of interpretation and application to some extent, such action should occur within the context of the brotherhood and not in isolation from it.

Any change in ethical positions should be motivated by the desire to be more obedient, more loyal to the Will and Purpose of God as understood by His children. The result of the change will then be a more consistent expression of such Will and purpose.[9]

The process of change was not to be through legislation but through the group process of searching Scripture in a spirit of unity and love under guidance from the Holy Spirit. However, "once consensus has been arrived at concerning an issue, such a decision is accepted in the spirit of love and voluntary submission as a guideline by all persons belonging to the consensus group."[10]

## Pastoral Letters

In the 1980s occasional "pastoral letters" became a means for the General Conference to more visibly share the concerns of the various study conferences with congregations.

A key undercurrent of study conferences in 1986, 1988 and 1989 was the matter of being a "kingdom people" in the midst of rampant individualism. Specific issues included church polity concerns relating to baptism, church membership and the Lord's Supper, and the ministry of women.

The first pastoral letter, "A Call to Reason Together," was sent, in 1986, to all pastors and church moderators and published in *The Christian Leader* and *Mennonite Brethren Herald*. It was a clarion call to the churches to recognize the implications of rapid cultural change.[11]

No longer primarily a rural agricultural people, the Mennonite Brethren had become by the late twentieth century the most urbanized of the five major Mennonite groups in North America. In addition to being seventy-three percent urbanized by 1990 they were also the most highly educated, the most highly represented in the professions and business and had the highest average income.[12] One result of such rapid change, according to the pastoral letter, was a loss of peoplehood–a weakening of identity.

The letter also expressed concern about growing diversity of theological thinking and clarity in spiritual identity, a weakening of authority and commitment to the church and conference, and a loss of passion for evangelism.

A second pastoral letter in 1987, "Consensus, Change and Commitment," addressed the issues of ethics–lifestyle–in a swiftly changing culture.[13] It called the churches to accountability for leaving questions of behavior and lifestyle to individual members, and ended with a plea for corporate consensus decisions to be translated into individual behavior:

> Above all, the atmosphere for consensus-making ought to be prayerful, open, responsible and charitable.
>
> Reaching agreement on an ethical standard is only the beginning point. Once consensus is reached, the decision must be embraced as a guideline for daily living by each

participant in a spirit of love and voluntary submission.

The truth is, most of us operate at a level that is a far cry from unity and consensus. It is too easy, too "natural," to go our own way on matters of ethics and lifestyle. Society daily reinforces the heresy that the individual is king. But the Bible speaks of a different monarch: Jesus is king. When his people agree to submit to him and to each other, his kingdom marches forward.[14]

Attached to the letter were five questions to help congregations process the issue:

1. What are the advantages of working for consensus in the church? What are the disadvantages? How do you respond to the statement that working toward consensus is "far more effective and God-honoring than 'lone ranger' decision-making or even majority rule"?
2. As a believer, when should you submit to the consensus of the group and when should you stand up boldly for what you personally believe to be true?
3. Accountability to others is something most believers say they desire, but in reality most tend to avoid it. Why?
4. Practically speaking, how should one initiate a discussion of "change" in our understanding of Scripture regarding a particular lifestyle issue? What is the process?
5. How do we determine whether our motivation for change is "pure"? Is an individual capable of determining that without the help of his brothers and sisters?[15]

A third pastoral letter in 1990 echoed the diligent efforts toward a stronger bond of unity and the process of an emerging vision statement to express Mennonite Brethren commitment for the future.[16] Also in 1990 the vision statement was adopted. It offered three "calls" as a way of answering its own questions about the meaning of being Mennonite

Brethren people and giving guidance to the future.

1. A call to renewal and ethical faithfulness; to affirm that to be the people of God is more than "to accept Christ as Savior;" and to see the church as a sub-culture with a lifestyle distinct from the world.

2. A call to confessional integrity, to see the Confession of Faith as a key to understanding biblical revelation and as a covenant commitment to which all pastors and teachers serving in Mennonite Brethren churches and schools subscribe.

3. A call to missionary engagement and a renewed commitment to "the mandate of every Christian and every congregation to proclaim the message of Christ through example of life and message at home and around the world."[17]

The vision statement, the pastoral letters and the many study conference calls for the Mennonite Brethren to "contend for the faith" have also been echoed in the denominational periodicals–the *Mennonite Brethren Herald* and *The Christian Leader*. Many voices have spoken there. John Redekop has frequently provided important pointers related to the faith pilgrimage of the Mennonite Brethren.[18] Katie Funk Wiebe, with a deep love for the church, has written unceasingly on issues vital to Mennonite Brethren.[19] Other figures–Marvin Hein, Wado Hiebert, Elmer Martens, the late F.C. Peters–have also been prophetic voices in the pages of Mennonite Brethren periodicals. They are part of the biblical injunction for Mennonite Brethren to "contend for the faith."

## WRESTLING AGAINST PRINCIPALITIES AND POWERS

In 1975 while traveling from Vienna to Frankfurt I shared a train compartment with a U.S. army general. Out of curiosity I asked him about the purpose of his assignment in Europe, thirty years after the close of the war. With some irritation he responded, "You seem to be a man very ignorant of the Russian military danger." I asked: "What then is your assignment while waiting in the face of such danger?" With increasing irritation he responded: "The most difficult assignment I have is to keep the troops battle conscious while we are waiting." The general left the train in Munich while I continued on to Frankfurt. The general had given me the topic for my message that same evening, "The battle consciousness of the apostolic church, Acts 4:23-31."

The intense effort of contending for the faith has not made Mennonite Brethren immune to the pluralism that pervades North American life. Relativity, accommodation and pragmatism work together to dull the edge of spiritual discernment. As a consequence, vigilance in discerning the spirits of the age wanes and battle consciousness weakens.

The conference pastoral letters were sent to all pastors and congregational moderators with the request that they be presented to the local congregations for prayerful study. A subsequent inquiry as to the congregations' response revealed that most local churches had not even been informed of the issues, much less prayerfully considered them.[20]

In the early 1980s the Board of Reference and Counsel of the Pacific District Conference presented to its delegates a document titled, "Are We Being Squeezed into the World's Mold?" It addressed the deterring effects of individualism and other worldly influences on the inner life of the local church and conference.[21] Some delegates felt there was too much other urgent business to allow time to discuss the document. The clarion call of the spiritual guardians of the conference–the Board of Reference and Counsel–was then referred for discussion to the local churches. Again, later follow-up inquiries found no evidence that the document had ever been brought to the attention of local churches. It had essentially died on the conference floor. The referral simply became the means to prevent serious consideration of spiritual dangers facing the church.

These two examples of avoidance are symptomatic of grave dangers facing the Mennonite Brethren Church. Many churches are not prepared to deal with serious issues in open confrontation, and the Mennonite Brethren Church is no exception. Preoccupied by the need to show numerical growth, ministers and leaders are reluctant to "rock the boat." Questions of "Who are we?" and "What does it mean to be the church?"–questions of being–are overshadowed by the pragmatic need to gain acceptance from a generation intent on self-fulfillment. The prophetic voices of sociologists and theologians who speak to the implications of social/religious pragmatism seem to receive only a marginal hearing.[22]

When pragmatism reigns, religion is reduced to a spiritual supermarket. Everyone can find an evangelical organization to suit his or her tastes. Evangelicalism has lost the authority to shape cultures and institutions. Religious pluralism in a culture of relativity provides the liberty for people to satisfy their religious instincts on their own terms. According to *The Barna Report: What Americans Believe 1991*, sixty-two percent of Americans claim to have made a personal commitment to Christ, but sixty-four percent of them say the term "born again" does not apply to them, and only fifty percent agree that the Bible is the Word of God and is totally accurate in all its teaching.[23]

An article in *Mennonite Brethren Herald* described the variety of evangelical churches in a community, including Mennonite Brethren, as the latest venture in consumerism. People can inspect churches as they might inspect restaurants and never return to one that doesn't meet their particular taste or preference. To take advantage of this mentality, churches modify publicity, facilities, style of music, types of sermons and leadership so that people will attend. "Denominationalism, dogma, discussion of sin, discipleship, or challenging the world's perspectives are not priorities in these churches."[24]

Wrestling with the principalities and powers is difficult in an age when the forces of evil intrude with such stealth and subtlety. Satan's deception is less frequently the outright denial of truth than small, incremental distortions of truth. Thus, the systematic cultivation of the faculties of discernment is of utmost importance in wrestling with the principalities and powers.

Mennonite Brethren have not always exercised this gift of discernment, especially when they sought to resist change through various forms of legalism. The struggle against television in the 1950s and 1960s, for example, was less a struggle of discernment against the spirit of the age than it was an attempt to maintain protective barriers against the outside world.

The 1954 conference in Winnipeg issued a ruling against television as a danger of worldliness for the home and the Christian community.[25] In 1962 a second signal came from the conference decrying the influence of television,[26] with a further warning coming a year later. The "world," it was said, could be invited into the home with the "flip of a switch." Finally, however, the church capitulated by referring the responsibility for control of this intruding influence to the conscience of the individual, and especially Christian parents. The struggle with the problem as a corporate body–the church–concluded with the admonition, "Nevertheless, let us not close our eyes to the destructive effect of uncontrolled and indiscriminate viewing of television programs."[27] The battle against television, waged from a position of cultural isolation, was ineffective. Today it is a rare Mennonite Brethren home that does not have one or more television sets. Very likely the need for discernment on this matter is now greater than ever.

To be a people in the world but not of the world cannot be maintained by cultural isolation. Today more than ever before, Mennonite Brethren find themselves card-carrying citizens of the modern world. Critical in their struggle against principalities and powers is the ability to discern between good and evil. The coming Messiah in the prophetic vision of

Isaiah is described as one who would "know to refuse the evil, and choose the good" (Is. 7:15). The young King Solomon, overwhelmed by the magnitude of his assignment, prayed for the gift "that I may discern between good and bad" (1 Kings 3:9). The Old Testament concludes with a description of the people of God who discern between the righteous and the wicked, those who serve God and those who serve him not (Mal. 3:16-18). The Book of Hebrews exhorts the church towards maturity "who by reason of use have their senses exercised to discern both good and evil" (Heb. 5:14). Discerning the spirits, one of the gifts to the church (1 Cor. 12:10), becomes a special need in the context of change and religious pluralism.

The relativistic and pluralistic spirit of our day cannot be brushed off as a passing phenomenon. The church must recognize it as a force that endangers the very foundations of its calling. Identifying with a culture that removes the absolutes rooted in the character of God, expressed in the redemption through Jesus Christ and recorded in Scripture, presents a greater danger for the church than all the centuries of persecutions of the past.

## EXAMINING WHETHER WE ARE IN THE FAITH

An inter-Mennonite church membership survey in 1972[28] revealed trends among Mennonite Brethren that gave cause for concern. With the encouragement of the Mennonite Brethren Board of Spiritual and Social Concerns in Canada and the Board of Reference and Counsel of the General Conference, the Historical Commission of the General Conference conducted a second membership study of its own in 1982, with only Mennonite Brethren churches participating. The results were published in *Direction*.[29]

A follow-up study of the original five Mennonite denominations was conducted in 1989 to chart the changes that had occurred during the interval.[30] In general the 1989 profile affirmed the observations emerging from the 1982 Mennonite Brethren profile.

These studies show that seventy-three percent of Mennonite Brethren live in urban centers. The rapidity of change from the rural to the urban environment begs the question, to what degree have Mennonite Brethren retained a rural mindset in the midst of an urban culture? Instabilities in some city churches suggest a transitional adjustment.

In the move from the ethnic enclaves of the past into the larger society, Mennonite Brethren have become upwardly mobile and sophisticated. The rural-urban transition also brought an influx from the educational community which assisted in spiritual discernment and produced directional influence. The conference-wide study conferences emerged largely from the academic community. The broad educational program of Bible schools, high schools, colleges and seminary was guided by academics and was made possible by the capital of the Mennonite Brethren business community.[31]

Modernity has had only a minor negative effect on basic Mennonite Brethren doctrinal beliefs related to the existence of God, his revelation in Jesus Christ, and the inspiration of Scripture. There are evidences, however, of a slow decrease among Mennonite Brethren in Bible knowledge.[32]

Mennonite Brethren recognize a clear difference between the "Kingdom of God" and the "Kingdom of this World" (ninety-five percent). But then eighty-six percent do not recognize great tensions between the commandments of Christ and the laws of a worldly society. This indicates accommodation.[33] A major concern for Mennonite Brethren emerges from their response to questions on individualism. Forty-nine percent agreed with the statement, "Faith is a private matter for each to decide and practice oneself." More than twenty-five percent affirmed the statement, "One's own religion should be more a matter of personal choice than directed by the doctrine of the church and standards of behavior." Twenty percent endorsed the statement, "It is not the business of the church to be directly involved in my personal affairs" and nine percent disagreed with the statement, "For me to be a church member means to give and receive mutual admonition about how we live our lives."[34]

The strong individualism reflected in these data appeared in the context of strong Pietism. Ninety-four percent recognized that they were sinners and professed that they had experienced a conversion and the forgiveness of sins. Eighty-three percent prayed daily. Forty percent maintained daily personal devotions in Bible reading and prayer and thirty-three percent practiced daily family devotions. Forty-six percent believed in tithing, with twenty-eight percent contending that sacrificial giving went beyond the tithe. Fifty-five percent testified that they gave ten percent of their income to the church and charitable causes.[35] The data showed that evangelism was highly important to Mennonite Brethren. In relation to other Mennonite denominations, they ranked first in devotionalism, evangelism and educational achievements and second in stewardship,[36] but to the question of whether to be a Christian means to follow Jesus in life, only forty-seven percent gave an affirmative answer. Some seventy-eight percent affirmed that church discipline was important,[37] quite opposite from those who said being a church member did not mean accepting mutual admonition on how they lived.[38]

The issue facing Mennonite Brethren is to reconcile their strong individualism with their verbal affirmations of orthodoxy. The former stands in stark contrast to historical Mennonite Brethren beliefs in obedience to the Word of God, submission to the lordship of Christ in self-denial and discipleship, and an interdependent relationship to the wider fellowship. Is this contrast the fruit of modernity? Is this why the many study conferences, pastoral letters and conference resolutions have not brought a unifying response?

James Davison Hunter, in his book, *American Evangeli-*

*calism: Conservative Religion and the Quandary of Modernity*, outlines the process by which Pietism gradually accommodates modernity. Bible reading, prayer and a strong devotional life remain important, but take place without an emphasis on New Testament discipleship. Gradually the more hardline elements of orthodox Protestant faith, such as an inherent evil, sinful conduct and lifestyle, the righteous and jealous God and eternal agony and death in hell, are softened, polished and de-emphasized until they no longer offend.

> This deemphasis has been more quantitative than qualitative. The offensive elements are, in the main, neither substantively devalued nor glossed over as unimportant. They are simply not referred to as much as they have been in the past. These elements have not lost their doctrinal centrality but have lost a stylistic centrality.[39]

North American evangelicals, says Hunter, are soft and flabby: "The packaging of Evangelical spirituality has made it easy to adapt."[40] Things that previously caused them spiritual concern are now "entirely uncontroversial or else celebrated as part of the Christian experience."[41] There is a high degree of tolerance for a diversity of lifestyles.

> People should be free to live the way they want even if it is very different from the way I live. Finally self-fulfillment is no longer a natural by-product of a life committed to higher ideals, but rather is a goal, pursued rationally and with calculation as an end in itself. The quest for emotional, psychological and social maturity therefore becomes normative. Self-expression and self-realization compete with self-sacrifice as a guiding life-ethic.[42]

Hunter's observation parallels the supermarket-type church, cited earlier, which appeals to constituencies on the basis of personal taste. Lost in such churches is the sense of a covenant community demanding obedience, self-denial and sacrifice. They promote the benefits of salvation without its obligations. According to Tony Campolo,

> People need personal salvation. They need a personal mystic oneness with the resurrected Christ. They need the psychological wholeness and emotional wellbeing that accompanies becoming new persons in Christ. However the God of the Bible not only concerns Himself with establishing a personal saving relationship with His Son but also is committed to social justice for all the people of the world. The biblical Jesus not only is desperate to help lost sinners "find themselves" but also wills to express the righteousness of Heaven in the context of those social institutions wherein we must live our lives.[43]

The Bible exhorts us to "go forth therefore unto him without the camp, bearing his reproach" (Heb. 13:13) and to "run with patience the race that is set before us, looking unto Jesus the author and finisher of our faith who . . . endured the cross" (Heb. 12:1,2).

When forty-two percent of Mennonite Brethren say they do not believe Christianity means "to follow Jesus in life," then we must stop and take seriously the admonition, "examine yourselves, whether you are in the faith" (2 Cor. 13:5). Then we know that modernity has left its mark on the Mennonite Brethren Church.

CHAPTER 21

# A Call to Commitment

## STAND FAST IN THE FAITH (1 Cor. 16:13)

In his first letter to the Corinthian church nearly two thousand years ago (59 A.D.) Paul addressed a spiritual crisis not unlike the tensions in today's church near the end of the twentieth century. The Corinthian church struggled for survival in a pagan culture that while ancient, also contained elements of what we experience in modernity.

In the Corinthian church there was disunity because of the lack of a Christological center. They failed to recognize the relationship of faith as a commitment to be followers of Jesus. There was a need to recognize the divine order related to marriage and the limitations of individual liberty. Some were questioning the qualifications for participation in the Lord's Table. The church had disrupted the body life by focusing on the gifts of the Spirit as a benefit to the individual member. With the background of these serious disruptions in the life of the Corinthian church, the epistle concluded with the triumph of victory in the resurrection chapter. Within the purposes of God the ultimate outcome was not in question. "All things shall be subdued unto him . . . that God may be all in all" (I Cor. 15:28).

Parallels between the first century church and today's church make Paul's exhortation particularly relevant: "Watch ye, stand fast in the faith, quit you like men, be strong. Let all your things be done with charity" (16:13-14).

It is crucial for the current Mennonite Brethren Church to heed this apostolic exhortation. It is an urgent call for us not to drift on the waves of twentieth-century modernity. The church of Christ cannot tolerate relativism. It must rise to a new commitment of discipleship that has no room for a gospel of "self-fulfillment" without the cross.

In the history of the church no phenomenon is more apparent than the recurrence of renewal. In this the church is like its Savior and Lord. He died on Friday, but he rose again on the first day of the week. Periodically God visits his church in a special way. His Spirit brings conviction of sin and repentance. People who have been spiritually dead or indifferent are abruptly brought under conviction. James Burns, the scholar of revivalism observes that in these periodic renewal movements people "are arrested in the midst of their worldly occupations; they are suddenly seized by a terror of wrong doing, and fear as of an impending doom haunts their minds."[1]

Swedish historian Westin Gunnar provided a remarkable chronicle of such revivals in the history of the church.[2] Ernst Troeltsch, a German sociologist, described the renewal movements through history as periodic returns to new understandings of Scripture, movements that served as correctives to the life of the institutional church.[3] These renewals, followed as they were by radically new lifestyles, always created tension with the larger society of their time. The true church will always be a resident alien in the worldly cultural environment.[4] When it loses its alien status it also loses the ability to be salt and light in the world.

In the midst of the current evangelical resurgence in North America–sixty-four percent of Americans claim to have accepted Christ–an uneasy feeling persists that the church has been domesticated and become too comfortable.[5] Its distinct character of faith, virtue and commitment to absolutes has vanished as it sought to gain approval from the world. In the context of this tension comes the call to the Mennonite Brethren fellowship for a renewal of commitment.

The church cannot remain locked in a cultural cocoon. It must become adept at responding to change.[6] But a balance must be struck between past and contemporary relevance, a dynamic combination of both continuity and change.[7] We have a Christian heritage that should shape and mold our future. The biblical model is to look backward and recount the acts of God, so we can look forward with confidence. Forms, functions and expressions may change, but divine principles governing the redemption and character of the people of God cannot change. The apostolic message remains the criterion for New Testament faith: "Repent, and be baptized every one of you in the name of Jesus Christ for the remission of sins." The result is a community of the redeemed who continue "steadfastly in the apostles' doctrine and fellowship, and in breaking of bread, and in prayers" (Acts 2:38, 42).

## Commitment to Biblical Conversion

As repeatedly emphasized, conversion is central in the theological understanding of Mennonite Brethren. Confessionally we have not changed. Officially we still hold a high view of the need for conversion that expresses itself in new life. But like many evangelicals, some Mennonite Brethren, in the struggle to accommodate modernity, have softened and polished the more demanding aspects of the gospel.[8]

Another form of softening is an obsession with rational proofs and simplistic formulas. Edward R. Dayton notes that when evangelicals seek to prove that the Bible is scientifically correct, they are using science to judge the Bible and in so doing "place scientific understanding above the message of the revealed word." He calls this a pragmatic simplification of truth to make it more easily understood and accepted.[9] Formulas can simplify and promise final solutions but they do not completely represent reality. They provide simple, painless steps to the benefits of redemption, without spelling out the implications.

When a nationally known evangelist held meetings in the facilities of a Mennonite Brethren church, he made no reference to a specific message from Scripture. He merely told stories of how Jesus had provided deliverance from drugs, alcohol, immorality and debauchery. "Are you in trouble? Jesus is the answer. He can provide deliverance." The message presented Jesus as nothing more than yet another "product" to satisfy a personal consumer need.[10]

Roger Palms describes such a pragmatic appeal:

> For years, evangelism has too often been only a personal offer to "accept a plan, say `yes' to Christ." Jesus is My Savior, with emphasis on "my." Christ is "real" only if he is real to me. Christianity has no value except for what it gives to me . . . many books and magazine articles have catered to the me-centered belief. They are based on what Jesus can do for me.[11]

Dietrich Bonhoeffer described that as cheap grace: The "preaching of forgiveness without requiring repentance, baptism without church discipline, communion without confession, absolution without personal confession. Cheap grace is grace without discipleship, grace without the cross, grace without Jesus Christ, living and incarnate."[12]

Biblical conversion is more than a matter of finding the "right answer" or the "right formula." It demands a total change of direction and a new moral orientation. Repentance is the entrance, and faith is the new direction. The same Hebrew and Greek words may be translated as either repentance or conversion.[13] In the Old Testament, conversion is a call to turn from wickedness and sin (Ez. 18:21,27; 33:9,11; Jer. 26:3); from a life of disloyalty to God and his commandments, to a life of obedience (Jer. 34:5; Isa. 10:20,21; 44:2; Hos. 14:4).

John the Baptist began his ministry with a call to "repent and be baptized" (Mt. 3:2; Mk. 1:4; Lk 3:3). It was a call for people to radically change their minds and their lives, for the kingdom of God is at hand. Repentance is not just a call to change one's plans, intentions or beliefs, but rather a change of the whole personality, which the New Testament describes as the new birth (John 3:5-8). Such a change arises out of the proclamation of God's redemptive grace to a sinner and the correlative work of the Holy Spirit who, in the words of Jesus, "will reprove (convict) the world of sin, and of righteousness, and of judgment" (John 16:8). Such repentance accompanies saving faith in Christ (Acts 20:21). "It is inconsistent and unintelligible to suppose that any one might exercise faith in Christ as the divine Savior from sin who is not aware and repentant of his own sin."[14] Repentance and faith in Christ are in fact inseparable, though a convert may be aware of one aspect more than another. The need for repentance is not merely a condition for biblical conversion and faith. It is a continuous demand in the judgment of sin in the life of the believer (1 John 1:8-9). This view of repentance and conversion is firmly embedded in our history and our Confession of Faith. It must continue to be central in our message and embedded in our daily practice in this era of modernity.

An excellent biblical exposition of conversion in contemporary literature is the appropriately titled book, *Conversion: Doorway to Discipleship* edited by Henry J. Schmidt. The authors of the essays are all Mennonite Brethren.[15] They, like previous Mennonite Brethren, understand that salvation is not a "spiritual deal" by which God balances a moralistic ledger. It is not a mere provision of God to meet a human predicament. It is the gracious reconciliation of the individual to fellowship with God. Salvation is basically relational. Forgiveness is not a commodity, not a tonic for a psychological or emotional need. It is a new relationship in which God accepts us on the condition of repentance and faith. Conversion is always a surrender, a response of human sinners to the redemptive mercy of God in which the center of authority in one's life passes from self to Christ. This act of surrender is the supreme expression of human freedom to "be." Humankind does not do so in order to satisfy a moral drive and have a good conscience, but rather to acknowledge lostness as sinful creatures before a holy God.[16] It expresses humanity's volitional capitulation before God.

The actual experience of conversion may vary. For some it is a crisis experience, an immediate about-face; for others it is a long, slow process of understanding and response. In any case it will be a conscious decision of the will. The result will always be a new creature. "If any man be in Christ, he is a new creature; old things are passed away; behold, all things are become new" (2 Cor. 5:17).

**Biblical Discipleship**

Three passages from the Synoptic Gospels express the essential conditions of biblical discipleship as described by Jesus: "Then said Jesus to his disciples, If any man will come after me, let him deny himself, and take up his cross, and follow me. For whosoever will save his life shall lose it; and whosoever will lose his life for my sake shall find it" (Mt. 16:24-25; Mk. 8:34-35; Lk. 9:23-24).

The condition is two-fold–self-denial and crossbearing. The meaning of these conditions is given in Luke and Matthew: "If any man come to me, and hate not his father, and mother, and wife, and children, and brethren, and sisters, yea, and his own life also, he cannot be my disciple" (Lk 14:26-27). "So likewise, whosoever he be of you that forsaketh not all that he hath, he cannot be my disciple" (Mt. 10:33). "And he that taketh not his cross, and followeth after me, is not worthy of me" (Mt. 10:38).

Discipleship makes radical demands. Devotion to Christ supersedes attachment to family members, to possessions, and even to life itself. This is strange language indeed for a people in the culture of modernity. Discipleship is also an action plan. Two steps are needed to be identified as disciples. The first is baptism. "Therefore we are buried with him by baptism into death: that like as Christ was raised up from the dead by the glory of the Father, even so we also should walk in newness of life" (Rom. 6:4). This step of obedience by a new Christian signifies death to the old life and a commitment to walk in newness of life (Rom. 6:5-23). Peter speaks of baptism as "the answer of a good conscience toward God" (1 Pet. 3:21). The second step of the action plan is "teaching them to observe all things whatsoever I have commanded you" (Mt. 28:20).

The clearest teaching of Jesus to his followers is recorded in his Sermon on the Mount (Mt. 5-7). The qualities of character are given in the beatitudes:

> Blessed are the poor in spirit: for theirs is the kingdom of heaven. Blessed are they that mourn: for they shall be comforted. Blessed are the meek: for they shall inherit the earth. Blessed are they that do hunger and thirst after righteousness: for they shall be filled. Blessed are the merciful: for they shall obtain mercy. Blessed are the pure in heart: for they shall see God. Blessed are the peacemakers: for they shall be called the children of God. Blessed are they which are persecuted for righteousness' sake: . . . when men shall revile you, and persecute you, and shall say all manner of evil against you falsely, for my sake. Rejoice, and be exceeding glad; for great is your reward in heaven: for so persecuted they the prophets which were before you (Mt. 5:3-12).

From these qualities of personal character and relationships Christ moves on to identify the influence of discipleship on society. "Ye are the salt of the earth . . . Ye are the light of the world" (Mt. 5:13-14). The new standard of ethics addresses the sin of broken relationships with our brothers and sisters (Mt. 5:21-26), the sin of adultery and the new law on divorce (Mt. 5:27-32). He commands his followers to be truthful, not to swear an oath, to accept injustice and to love our enemies (Mt. 5:33-48).

Matthew chapter six speaks to our stewardship and prayer, the test of our basic values, material possessions versus spiritual treasures, the cure for anxieties and the exhortation to seek first the kingdom of God. The seventh chapter warns against judging others without recognizing our own imperfections.

The conclusion of the Sermon on the Mount sets forth a fourfold admonition and warning:

(1) The road leading to life is narrow, and "few there be that find it" (Mt. 7:13-14).

(2) Genuine Christlike character leaves no room for deception—"by their fruits ye shall know them" (Mt. 7:15-20).

(3) Mere piety and religiosity are not enough. "Not everyone that saith unto me, Lord, Lord, shall enter into the kingdom of heaven: but he that doeth the will of my Father which is in heaven" (Mt. 7:21).

(4) Profession without obedience is like building a house on sand. "Therefore whosoever heareth these sayings of mine, and doeth them, I will liken him unto a wise man, which built his house upon a rock" (Mt. 7:24).

The first century church understood the implications of discipleship. James, the apostle, was killed with the sword. Peter, according to tradition, was crucified. John spent his last years on the Island of Patmos. Stephen, the first deacon, was stoned. Paul's life ended in a Roman prison. Hebrews 11 summarizes the triumphs of faith and martyrdom in the Old Testament that were duplicated in the New Testament and which continue through the centuries of time.

Mennonite Brethren are no strangers to the demands of discipleship. Our own history, not to mention that of our Anabaptist forebears, has had its share of heroic martyrs for the faith. Today we are not called to face firing squads because of our acts of discipleship. Today we are more likely being called to take an unpopular stand against comfort, greed and self-fulfillment. In our culture of relativism, pragmatism and religious pluralism, that stand, if properly understood and followed, may also carry its costs.

**SELF-EXAMINATION**

The three church-wide surveys of the Mennonite Brethren–1972, 1985, 1989[17]–all point to two disturbing conclusions regarding the consistency of faith and practice.

1. "There is a continuing, strong affirmation of the basic tenets of the Christian faith among Mennonite Brethren. This is the case regardless of social influences.

2. "There is clear evidence of a disparity between faith and practice. This is noticeable particularly in the area of personal piety and social ethics."[18]

A number of persons in Mennonite Brethren leadership positions participated in evaluating the data from the 1985 survey. John Redekop, political science professor, reflecting on the "Influence of Rising Educational Levels," expressed the hope that

> Mennonite Brethren with higher levels of education may be able to help the brotherhood formulate and adhere to a set of ethical principles based essentially on Biblical imperatives. But in order to have credibility, they may need to take more seriously certain traditional Mennonite Brethren ethical norms which, according to the data, are now being increasingly set aside. The stretching of liberty weakens credibility.
>
> In order to overcome accusations of 'cheap grace'–right belief is easy–words must be sustained by action. This admonition applies to all members, regardless of educational level. In all ethical assessments, the brotherhood must determine what is essential and it must also address the problem of superficial compliance which may be

nothing more than lingering conformity.[19]

Roland Reimer, a veteran pastor and district minister of the Southern District, lamented the fact that "the trends perceived in our congregational life have brought about increasing tensions between our belief system and our patterns of behavior." It was his observation that the gap between faith and practice was growing wider. The data reflected "increasing diversity of faith and behavior in congregations and between countries (U.S. and Canada), some more and others less compatible with the historic faith and practices of the Mennonite Brethren Church and its current Confession of Faith."[20]

Abe Dueck, for many years professor at the Mennonite Brethren Bible College in Winnipeg, found "disturbing" the findings in the 1972 profile that while the Mennonite Brethren ranked highest of the various Mennonite groups on devotionalism, they ranked lowest in the area of social concern. In the area of stewardship there seemed to be "a general erosion of communal discipline. . . . Individualism is on the increase."[21]

Several important reflections were given by John E. Toews, professor of New Testament at the Mennonite Brethren Biblical Seminary.

> In summary the "feeling tone" of Mennonite Brethren piety was more positive, but the more objective criteria of authentic piety–conversion, Bible knowledge, evangelism, service–showed clear signs of erosion. Mennonite Brethren piety looks more like popular evangelical–"save me Lord and make me feel good, but ask little from me."[22]

He pointed to the finding that only forty-two percent of Mennonite Brethren believe that Jesus is normative for daily living. It was his observation that the profile raised profound questions about the Anabaptist-Mennonite identity of Mennonite Brethren. "The forces of religious group acculturation progressively pulled Mennonite Brethren into popular American evangelicalism." This acculturation has meant

> a shift from a discipleship centered understanding of the faith to a belief centered understanding of Christian faith. Consequently the profile revealed high orthodoxy/fundamentalism scores and eroding piety/Anabaptist-Mennonite Brethren scale scores. The profile suggests the Mennonite Brethren Church is at a critical moment in history. The trends identified in the profile point toward the loss of a particular theological identity in popular American cultural religion.[23]

Delbert Wiens, a professor at Fresno Pacific College, saw in the profiles a weakening of Mennonite Brethren congregational life.

> The congregation is more fragile and demands less of its members. It is a more "contractual" and a less "organic" form of association. Members join a congregation for fellowship and support. But, unlike more organic "tribal" or "ethnic" communities, it cannot insist on shaping all aspects of a member's life. There is a tacit "contract" regarding what the individual and the group owe to each other. Some aspects of our lives are not included in that contract and are not submitted to the group's direction. In general, political, economic (and some moral) disciplines are increasingly held to be outside the church's jurisdiction; they intrude into what is sensed to belong to the sphere of the individual.[24]

The three persons who administered the 1982 profile compiled their views of the implications emerging from this study of Mennonite Brethren faith and practice. Their findings, which were subsequently affirmed by the data in the 1989 profile, *The Mennonite Mosaic*, are reprinted here in their entirety.

## IMPLICATIONS OF THE MEMBERSHIP PROFILES

(J.B. Toews, Abram Konrad, Alvin Dueck)

We present a series of conclusions that have emerged from "examining ourselves." From these conclusions we draw some possible directions and specific implications. At best, the implications may serve as suggestions that will challenge us to greater faithfulness in our discipleship. Clearly, the process of church renewal depends upon the grace and guidance of our Lord and upon the obedience and commitment of God's people.

### Faith and Life

It was the fundamental understanding of Israel that when God spoke there was an effect. By God's Word the world was created. By the word of Yahweh a covenant was made with Israel. Word and deed were inseparable. Words without action were considered disobedience by the prophets and foolishness by the sages. Jesus condemned the Pharisees for their lack of consistency in knowing and doing.

Mere assent to truth without a response in lifestyle leads to a propositional faith which makes no personal demands. A Confession of Faith can become institutionalized when a considerable gap exists between the profession and the expression of faith. The Mennonite Brethren Church was not born out of commitment to new truths, but out of a concern that one's life should be a true expression of one's faith.

The results of the survey point to the following conclusions regarding the consistency of faith and practice (as stated above).

1. There is a continuing, strong affirmation of the basic tenets of the Christian faith among Mennonite Brethren. This is the case regardless of social influences.

2. There is clear evidence of a disparity between faith and practice. This is noticeable particularly in the area of personal piety and social ethics.

We submit the following implications from these conclusions:

1. The first and most appropriate responses to such evidence is a celebration of God's faithfulness and a repentance for the gap between faith and practice.

2. The Mennonite Brethren Church must develop an extensive program of preaching, teaching and writing regarding the integration of theology and ethics. Such a thrust must balance the emphasis on evangelism in the past decades.

3. Mennonite Brethren must go beyond conducting business at their conventions and provide a greater focus on faith and discipleship. Jesus called us to radical discipleship (Luke 9:23-24).

4. Christian education in both churches and postsecondary institutions must draw out the ethical implications of the gospel for life and vocation. Such themes as simplicity of lifestyle need higher visibility in our curricula. If we fail to do so, our ethics will be shaped more by popular culture or by the culture of academia, marketplace and work than the ethic of Jesus.

**Leadership**

The Scriptures place responsibility for the spiritual condition of God's people upon the leadership. In Israel, the prophets exercised leadership even when the message was unpopular. In the New Testament, Jesus held the priests, Pharisees and Sadducees accountable for the spiritual condition of Israel. The apostle Paul makes the qualifications for good leadership a central concern of the emerging church (Pastoral Epistles).

We suggest that our research warrants two conclusions regarding Mennonite Brethren leadership.

1. Our leaders affirm the fundamental beliefs of Christian faith and demonstrate a vital personal Christian life. They lead in matters related to life in the congregation (worship, fellowship, Sunday School, etc.) and in practical Christian living (stewardship, Bible study, prayer, evangelism and service). It is encouraging that our pastors support the idea of shared ministry and greater spiritual accountability.

2. In the areas where the larger denomination struggles with consistency in faith and practice, Mennonite Brethren pastors do not provide leadership. Our pastors appear to be biased more toward a subjective, pietistic view of Christianity than to a practical, discipleship view of Christianity. Mennonite Brethren pastors are not leading us in being reconcilers in a broken world.

The implications of these conclusions include the following:

1. We must develop consensus among Mennonite Brethren pastors regarding Mennonite Brethren identity–an identity that distinguishes us as followers of Jesus in covenantal community relationships.

2. Our congregations should emphasize the plurality of leadership, drawing upon all of the gifts bestowed upon God's people.

3. Mennonite Brethren should continue to invest heavily in college and seminary education to prepare leadership for church ministries.

4. A coordinated program of leadership formation and enrichment for pastors, lay leaders, faculty and staff of Mennonite Brethren educational institutions (e.g., retreats,

workshops, study-leave programs, etc.) will need to be developed.

5. Congregations should encourage young persons to enter into church ministries and they should also provide opportunities for them to participate in congregational activities.

6. Potential leaders studying in non-Mennonite Brethren institutions should be encouraged to maintain their identification with Mennonite Brethren and, if possible, attend one of our institutions before entering ministry within the Mennonite Brethren community.

**Peoplehood**

A central theme in the Scriptures is that God is in the business of creating a people. Without question Israel lives by the memory of the Exodus—the paradigmatic people-creating event. It is not only individuals or small groups of believers that make up the kingdom; God seeks the creation of "a chosen race, a royal priesthood, a holy nation, a people for God's own possession" (1 Peter 2:9). Such a people are first the people of God before they are Canadians or Americans.

Mennonite Brethren have always regarded themselves less a denomination and more a "brotherhood." To be sure the local congregation was primary in nurture and fellowship, but it was always regarded as a part of a larger network of churches that covenanted together in matters of faith and practice. It was also as a conference of churches that major programs in education, missions and service were undertaken.

The Church Membership Profile suggests the following conclusions regarding a sense of peoplehood.

1. Mennonite Brethren are becoming ethnically, geographically and economically more diverse. No longer are the Mennonite Brethren primarily an immigrant peo-

ple. They have become firmly established in society and have moved into middle-class status through higher education and occupational success.

2. There is an increasing focus on the local congregation to the exclusion of larger denominational concerns. Our members are more willing to support the local budget than they are the programs of the conference that address national or international needs.

3. Mennonite Brethren have weakened in their affirmation of denominational identity. We appear not to accept our distinctives in a pluralistic world as readily as we did in earlier times.

Some implications that might follow from these conclusions include:

1. The Mennonite Brethren Church must celebrate the ethnic diversity already present in its midst in a way similar to the Apostle Paul's affirmation of ethnic diversity (Greek and Jew) in the New Testament church.

2. A sense of peoplehood comes by common memories, common vision and common practices. If Mennonite Brethren seek such peoplehood, they will need to develop commonalities that include and go beyond memories of the Russian exodus, beyond a rural perspective and beyond ethnic foods and dialect.

3. The local congregation must develop a sense of ownership for conference decisions and activities. The conference is not a federation of loosely tied independent churches; we are a community of congregations in a covenantal relationship with each other.

4. Information about conference activities and programs should be regularly included in congregational worship and business sessions.

5. Conference structures and agencies must exist to serve the local churches through programs that can best be pursued jointly and independently.

6. We must be willing to change conference structures and programs when they have fulfilled their purposes; conference agencies should not be rigidly institutionalized.

7. The name of a local congregation reflects a large identification. When the connection with the Mennonite Brethren Church is not made explicit, we contribute further to denominational fragmentation.

**Theological Cohesion**

The Anabaptist movement followed the early Reformers in their acceptance of salvation by grace and of the Scriptures as the authority for matters of faith and life. It differed from them in their emphasis on radical discipleship and on the church as the context of discernment rather than relying upon purely individual interpretation. The will of god was to be found in the corporate searching of the Word of God in fellowship and prayer (Acts 2:42-47; 15; 17:11).

The 20th century Mennonite Brethren Church is no longer an isolated community. Its members listen to a diversity of voices about the Christian faith, and they are strongly influenced by social forces that promote the gospel of popular evangelicalism. Hence, the church is part of a pluralistic world with many "stories," including its own. How it listens to these voices and carves out a theological cohesiveness is of utmost importance. Can the Mennonite Brethren church develop a theology that is consistent with the Scriptures and true to its own unique history?

The data suggest two conclusions regarding theological diversity.

1. There is clearly a tension between pietistic and sectarian views of Christianity. As Mennonite Brethren have become more affluent, they have adopted a more subjec-

tive view of Christianity.

2. There is a lack of consensus on the historic peace position of the Mennonite Brethren Church.

The following implications are offered:

1. We again must commit ourselves to reading the Word of God together as we seek to do God's will. Individualism destroys the interdependence within a covenantal community of God's people.

2. We must learn to listen to all members of our community as we seek unity in matters of faith and practice. It was women who demonstrated the highest commitment to reconciliation in our survey and it was single individuals who showed the strongest commitment to a social/ethical agenda.

3. In our congregations and institutions we must avoid teaching propositional truth without at the same time teaching how to express it in personal communal life.

4. Pastors and conference teachers must demonstrate their full agreement with the Mennonite Brethren Confession of Faith.

5. Leaders who have studied at non-denominational institutions should be expected to affirm the teachings and practices of the brotherhood. New pastors from non-Mennonite backgrounds should be expected to complete additional study in Mennonite Brethren settings.

6. Ethnicity cannot be the primary glue which creates conference unity. Mennonite Brethren must expend considerable energy building a unity around a spiritual center that expresses itself in new traditions. If an older ethnicity is the bond, then the Mennonite Brethren posture will be one of defensiveness rather than mission.

**Individualism**

In Israel the faith of the individual was part of the corporate faith of the people of God. The New Testament church was seen as a covenantal community for the individual, one to which he or she was personally accountable. The kingdom of God comes to us less with a message of self-fulfillment than with a call to engagement and service.

In Mennonite Brethren history there is a strong emphasis upon individual faith as evidenced in a commitment to radical discipleship. However, it is understood that to be a Christian means to be incorporated into the community of believers. Believers' baptism signifies a voluntary identification with the people of God. Interdependence is a normal part of spiritual growth; body life concerns itself with corporate well-being.

The following conclusions are submitted:

1. There is a trend toward individualism in our churches and an increasing isolation of some from the corporate life of the congregation.

2. There are segments within the congregation which are isolated and alone, especially single individuals. Congregational ministries focus more on couples and often assume that individuals have all of the resources they need for Christian living.

3. Ethical decisions are viewed primarily as an individual's responsibility, whether they involve stewardship or morality.

The threat of individualism in our churches suggests several implications.

1. We must renew our commitment to covenantal community and be willing to sacrifice for the sake of the life of the church.

2. We must develop ways of being the church that take more seriously organic models which focus less on contract and more on radical covenantal relationships.

3. Local congregations should develop discernment groups which focus not only on fellowship and prayer but

also on faithful discipleship.

4. Pastoral and educational resources need to be developed to meet the needs of individuals and families torn apart by the impact of individualism.

5. Since affluence tends to reinforce individualism, we must continue to uphold the ideal of a simple lifestyle and address with greater clarity issues of economic inequality locally and in our larger world.

6. We must develop meaningful service programs that challenge our young people to serve in inner cities, northern communities and underdeveloped countries.

**POSTSCRIPT**

This research activity was undertaken upon the encouragement of a number of individuals and several conference boards. We have attempted to portray accurately the attitudes, beliefs and practices of Mennonite Brethren, and we have subjected our understanding of these findings to the scrutiny of faithful believers. It is our sincere prayer that the insights and concerns derived from this study will serve as an incentive to greater faithfulness to our high calling in Christ Jesus.[25]

The membership profiles provide a description of who the Mennonite Brethren currently are. The trends indicated may not apply to all individuals or all local groups. But in general they suggest that Mennonite Brethren have strayed from a consistency between faith and practice, profession and lifestyle. These findings are at odds with the character of New Testament discipleship and commitment.

It is not a conscious apostasy. It is something like what Paul describes as a "form of godliness but denying the power thereof" (2 Tim. 3:5). Loss of discernment sneaks up slowly in the form of worldly pleasures, self-indulgence, luxurious living, familial erosion and the desire to please. When we took our first steps into modernity we were not planning to be taken captive; we honestly wanted to evangelize those beyond our cultural boundaries, no matter what the cost. Pastors who withheld from their congregations the warning letters sent by the conference were not doing so out of malicious intent but out of an expression of individualism. They may have meant well, but they erred.

Mennonite Brethren were caught off guard by the rapidity of cultural change. We were wrenched out of our narrow ethnic enclave in one generation, a process that frequently takes several generations. We have been sincere in our efforts to evangelize with slogans and techniques, but we have lost sight of the quality of "being."

Christ's word to the seven churches in Revelation chapters two and three is very kind. He recognizes their work, their zeal for truth, their efforts and their suffering. His letter to the Mennonite Brethren Church at the end of the twentieth century would be no different. He would recognize their emphasis on evangelism and church growth, missions abroad and their many educational institutions. The results of their mission program abroad with a community of believers numerically larger than the Mennonite Brethren in North America, would not escape his recognition.

He would commend Mennonite Brethren for sharing in the worldwide outreach of Mennonite Central Committee in feeding the hungry, clothing the naked, bringing hope to the poor through economic development, and promoting peace and broader human understanding.

He would commend Mennonite Brethren for their place of leadership in the wider evangelical world, and in education, professional excellence, music and industrial efficiency. He would give recognition to many of these pursuits, and more, as he did to the seven churches of the first century.

In the light of the demands of New Testament discipleship, however, would he need to ask the question once posed to Peter: "Lovest thou me more than these?" (John 21:15). Or the word directed to the Ephesian church of the first century:

> I know thy works, and thy labour, and thy patience, and how thou canst not bear them which are evil . . . and hast borne, and hast patience, and for my name's sake hast laboured, and hast not fainted. Nevertheless I have somewhat against thee, because thou hast left thy first love" (Rev. 2:2-4).

Christ's word to the first century church was a call for correction–repentance where necessary–and renewed faithfulness. Christ's word to the Mennonite Brethren Church is the same. It is the word of 1 John 1:5-10.

> This then is the message which we have heard of him, and declare unto you, that God is light, and in him is no darkness at all. If we say that we have fellowship with him, and walk in darkness, we lie, and do not the truth: But if we walk in the light, as he is in the light, we have fellowship one with another, and the blood of Jesus Christ his Son cleanseth us from all sin. If we say that we have no sin, we deceive ourselves, and the truth is not in us. If we confess our sins, he is faithful and just to forgive us our sins, and to cleanse us from all unrighteousness. If we say that we have not sinned, we make him a liar, and his word is not in us.

The hope for the Mennonite Brethren Church in the future is expressed in the word: "I know thy works: behold, I have set before thee an open door, and no man can shut it: for thou hast a little strength, and hast kept my word, and hast not denied my name" (Rev. 3:8).

The qualification for the open door is the commendation

"you have kept my word and not denied my name." The future is conditioned with the call to keep his Word and give priority to a walk worthy of the name of Christ, based on the message of New Testament conversion, genuine discipleship and commitment to his church in the blessed hope of his return.

CHAPTER 22

# "The Race That Is Set Before Us"

**HEBREWS 12:1**

The Mennonite Brethren pilgrimage of faith is a small part of the much larger history of God's redemptive work in the world. The record of the Old Testament and the testimony of church history are a witness to human frailty on one hand, and the merciful grace of God on the other. The book of Hebrews is a reminder of how God's all-sufficiency in divine redemption triumphs over human imperfection. It recognizes Israel's failures, acknowledges the tragedy of human weakness, and points to the provision of the Word of God which is "sharper than any two-edged sword, piercing even to the dividing asunder of soul and spirit, and of joint and marrow, and is a discerner of the thoughts and intents of the heart" (Heb. 4:12). In contrast to the weaknesses and failures of humanity, the Holy Spirit calls attention to the great "high priest, that is passed into the heavens, Jesus the Son of God" and adds "let us hold fast our profession. For we have not an high priest which cannot be touched with the feeling of our infirmities; but was in all points tempted like as we are, yet without sin" (Heb. 4:15).

The record of the past, given in Hebrews 11, is not a display of human sin and unfaithfulness. In the gallery of faith Abel, Enoch, Noah, Abraham, Moses, Gideon, David and Samuel are people without a perfect record. But their imperfections were dealt with in divine judgment and forgiveness and they stand before us as heroes of faith, trophies of God's mercy and grace. They are recognized as a people who had trial of cruel mockings and scourgings, yea, moreover of bonds and imprisonment: They were stoned, they were sawn asunder, were tempted, were slain with the sword: they wandered about in sheepskins and goatskins; being destitute, afflicted, tormented (Heb. 11:36-37).

The Mennonite Brethren pilgrimage offers some parallels to the book of Hebrews. The movement began with a people searching for truth and assurance of salvation. Their vision was to restore the faith and life of the sixteenth-century Anabaptists, who in turn had sought to emulate the church of the first century.

Like the heroes of faith in Hebrews, the early Mennonite Brethren were not perfect, but God blessed them and they became an influence in evangelism and missions disproportionate to their numbers. They too learned to accept trials, mockings, scourgings, even bonds and imprisonment. With many other Christians in Russia, Mennonite Brethren were slain with the sword; they wandered about in "sheepskins and goatskins"; being destitute, afflicted and tormented in the Siberian wilderness.[1]

Throughout this book we have attempted to chronicle both the faithfulness and weaknesses of the Mennonite Brethren as they have sought to be a people in the world but not of the world. In their early years they were no strangers to persecution from without. Later, in North America, the major tensions would arise from within as this closely knit homogeneous group found itself thrust onto the open sea of a rapidly changing world.

The dramatic changes of the last half century logically pose the question "Who are the Mennonite Brethren today?" How are they different from their early forebears? In the process of adjusting to their exposure to modernity, what have they lost that they should have kept? Conversely, what have they kept that perhaps should have been given up?

The question of identity is not a new one for Mennonite Brethren. On numerous occasions this question has been answered by defining what they were not. From their inception, declared Frank C. Peters in 1959, Mennonite Brethren saw themselves as Anabaptists in distinction from the Baptists.[2] In time, however, they would be seen as having strayed from their Anabaptist moorings. In 1972 John A. Toews urged Mennonite Brethren to strengthen their Anabaptist ties and become more selective about their identification with other evangelicals. While recognizing that Mennonite Brethren had gained much from other evangelical groups, especially in the areas of evangelism and missions, he warned that "we must learn to borrow from them with much greater discernment and discrimination. Whatever we borrow from other theological traditions must be consciously integrated into our understanding of the New Testament Church and of Christian discipleship."[3]

In 1987 missiologist Peter Hamm maintained that "Canadian Mennonite Brethren are presently undergoing a crisis of identity,"[4] an assessment that applied equally well to the Mennonite Brethren Church in the United States. Sociologist Calvin Redekop, meanwhile, suggested that the identity problem could be traced back to the initial Mennonite Brethren withdrawal from the larger Mennonite church in Russia.[5] When the early Mennonite Brethren rejected their former theological tradition (ethos) they needed to replace it with another. Their new emphasis on biblical teaching and righteous living needed

> to be based in a supporting social and cultural milieu. But since the old sub-culture had been rejected a new sub-culture had to be substituted; but sub-cultures are not created overnight, so the . . . Mennonite Brethren have been searching for a sub-culture on which to base their 'reformed' beliefs and world view, and have found it in the fundamentalist and evangelical 'ethnicity' in American Christianity.[6]

Mennonite Brethren would perhaps consider Redekop's analysis too inclusive, however it may well be part of the answer to the questions posed by Mennonite Brethren Conference leadership in 1990: "What does it mean to be Mennonite Brethren people? What does it mean to be a Mennonite Brethren Church? What are the bonds that hold us together?"[7]

Does our identity in fact rest with North American evangelicalism? If so, what are the perils of such an alignment? A probing article in *Christianity Today*, evangelicalism's leading journal, recently suggested that this faith phenomenon may be in danger of being suffocated by its own success, a success due in no small measure to its absorption of versions of the gospel that do not give offence.[8]

"Evangelicals have abandoned...earlier definitions of worldliness that involve avoiding externals," say authors Nathan Hatch and Michael Hamilton. "Still, they have been less successful in defining how the spirit of Christ might differ from that of success-oriented, upwardly mobile American materialism."[9]

Hatch and Hamilton conclude with searching questions:

> To what extent have the idols of this age [pleasure, wealth, professional status and physical appearance] worked themselves into evangelical affection?
>
> To what extent has the goal of evangelical spirituality become self-fulfillment rather than self-denial, less a quest to know God and more a means to achieve the good life?
>
> In short, have evangelicals so tamed the gospel to accord with American habits that it has been shorn of its radical power to convict and convert?[10]

These questions demand an honest response from Mennonite Brethren as we review our spiritual pilgrimage.

Mennonite Brethren in 1993 hold great spiritual potential. The core of our profession is solid. Our quest to be in proper relationship to Christ and the gospel is sincere. Yet we continue to struggle with being a people in the world but not of the world. To be true to our calling in the context of a culture that rejects all moral and ethical absolutes may prove to be the most severe test of our history.

Carl Sandburg, the biographer of Abraham Lincoln, said: "When a society or a civilization perishes, one condition can always be found. They forget where they came from."[11] This is also true of spiritual movements. We cannot afford to forget where we came from. We must remember our past, our beginnings as a renewal movement seeking to rekindle the embers of faith that inflamed a people known as the Anabaptists of the sixteenth century. Our passion and resolve must be to follow Jesus in obedient discipleship, be a true church of faith, and spread the good news of salvation and the eternal hope of glory. We are the stewards of a great faith.

Remembering our past includes openly examining the various crises we face–ethics, evangelism and missions. Our biblical tradition equips us well to seek answers to the tensions reflected in the membership profiles of 1972, 1982 and 1989. Renewing our commitment to the basic tenets of our faith provides the only hope for correcting disparities between belief and behavior.

The example of Hebrews 11 applies also to the Mennonite Brethren, a people with whom God is not yet finished. We have painfully acknowledged our weaknesses. However, we look to the future with confidence, accepting the exhortation of Hebrews 12:

> Wherefore seeing we also are compassed with a great cloud of witnesses, let us lay aside every weight, and the sin which does so easily beset us, and let us run with patience the race that is set before us, looking unto Jesus the author and finisher of our faith; who for the joy that was set before him endured the cross, despising the shame,

and is set down at the right hand of the throne of God. For consider him that endured such contradiction of sinners against himself, lest ye be weary and faint in your minds (Heb. 12:1-3).

Fulfilling that resolve will empower Mennonite Brethren to continue their faithful pilgrimage–as a people in the world but not of the world–in the closing years of the 1990s, and into the century beyond.

# Endnotes

## CHAPTER 1
1. Note the frequency of the word "remember" as it relates to the past in exhortations of God to his people. Roswell T. Hitchcock, *Topical Bible and Cruden's Concordance* (Grand Rapids, Mich.: Baker Book House, 1955).

2. Jean Jaures, "What use is history?" *The Royal Bank of Canada Monthly Letter*, March 1977, 1.

3. *United Evangelical Action*, 1978.

4. Editorial, "Words of Admonition," *Mennonite Weekly Review*, 12 May 1977, 4.

5. Peter Regier, *Kurzgefasste Geschichte der Mennoniten Brüdergemeinde* (Berne, Ind.: Light and Hope Publication, 1901); Peter M. Friesen, *The Mennonite Brotherhood in Russia (1789-1910) [Alt-Evangelische Mennonitische Brüderschaft in Russland (1789-1910)]*, trans. J. B. Toews, Abraham Friesen, Peter J. Klassen and Harry Loewen (Fresno, Calif.: Board of Christian Literature, General Conference of Mennonite Brethren Churches, 1978); A. H. Unruh, *Die Geschichte der Mennoniten Brüdergemeinde* (Hillsboro, Kans.: General Conference of the Mennonite Brethren Church of North America, 1955); John A. Toews, *A History of the Mennonite Brethren Church: Pilgrims and Pioneers* (Fresno: Board of Christian Literature, General Conference of Mennonite Brethren Churches, 1975); Jacob P. Bekker, *Origin of the Mennonite Brethren Church*, trans. D.E. Pauls and A.E. Janzen (Hillsboro, Kans.: The Mennonite Brethren Historical Society of the Midwest, 1973).

6. The record of Israel in the Old Testament and the renewals of church history are the substantiating proof of this phenomenon. C. E. Autry, *Revivals of the Old Testament* (Grand Rapids, Mich.: Zondervan, 1960) is a good source on this subject.

7. 2 Corinthians 4:16; Ephesians 4:23; Colossians 3:10.

8. James Burns, *Revivals, Their Laws and Leaders* (Grand Rapids, Mich.: Baker Book House, 1960), addresses the renewals of recent centuries; A. Skevington Wood, *The Inextinguishable Blaze* (Grand Rapids, Mich.: Wm. B. Eerdmans Pub. Co., 1960).; J. Edwin Orr, *The Light of the Nations* (Grand Rapids, Mich.: Eerdmans, 1965); F. F. Bruce, *The Spreading Flame* (London: Paternoster Press, 1958).

9. Harold S. Bender and Robert Friedmann, "Anabaptist," in *The Mennonite Encyclopedia*, eds. Harold S. Bender and C. Henry Smith, (Scottdale, Pa.: Mennonite Publishing House, 1955), 113-15.

10. John A. Toews, *A History of the Mennonite Brethren Church*, 3.

11. Cornelius Krahn, "Russia," *Mennonite Encyclopedia*, 381-392; C. J. Dyck, ed., *An Introduction to Mennonite History* (Scottdale, Pa.: Herald Press, 1981), 164-87; Friesen, *The Mennonite Brotherhood In Russia*.

12. Friesen, *The Mennonite Brotherhood In Russia*, 91-92.

13. Robert Kreider, "The Anabaptist Conception of the Church in the Russian Mennonite Environment 1789-1870," *Mennonite Quarterly Review* 25 (1951): 22-24.

14. Gerhard Lohrenz, "The Mennonites of Russia and the Great Commission," in *A Legacy of Faith: The Heritage of Menno Simons*, ed. Cornelius J. Dyck (Newton, Kans.: Faith and Life Press, 1962), 173.

15. Quoted in John B. Toews, *Perilous Journey: The Mennonite Brethren in Russia, 1860-1910* (Winnipeg, Man.: Kindred Press, 1988), 5-7.

16. Bekker, *Origin of the Mennonite Brethren Church*, 18-19.

17. Friesen, *The Mennonite Brotherhood In Russia*, 234-35.

18. Ibid., 212.

19. John B. Toews, "Cultural and Intellectual Aspects of the Mennonite Experience in Russia," *Mennonite Quarterly Review* 53 (1979): 137.

20. Friesen, *The Mennonite Brotherhood In Russia*, 54.

21. John B. Toews, *Czars, Soviets and Mennonites* (Newton, Kans.: Faith and Life Press, 1982), 31. For broader analysis consult Kreider, "The Anabaptist Conception of the Church," 17-32; Burns, Revivals, Their Laws and Leaders, 21-76.

22. John A. Toews, *A History Of The Mennonite Brethren Church*, 19.

23. Cornelius Krahn, "Harder, Bernhard," *Mennonite Encyclopedia*, 659.

24. Friesen, *The Mennonite Brotherhood In Russia*, 252-53.

25. Cornelius Krahn, "Reimer, Klaas," *Mennonite Encyclopedia*, 278; See also Delbert F. Plett, *The Golden Years: The Mennonite Kleine Gemeinde in Russia (1812-1849)* (Steinbach, Man.: DFP Publications, 1985).

26. Friesen, *The Mennonite Brotherhood In Russia*, 94-95.

27. Ibid., 94-96.

28. Cornelius Krahn, "Voth, Tobias," *Mennonite Encyclopedia*, 859.

29. Friesen, *The Mennonite Brotherhood In Russia*, 96-97.

30. David H. Epp, "Heese, Heinrich," *Mennonite Encyclopedia*, 686; Friesen, *The Mennonite Brotherhood In Russia*, 698-712.

31. James Urry, *None But Saints: The Transformation of Mennonite Life in Russia, 1789-1889* (Winnipeg, Man.: Hyperion Press Ltd., 1989), 164.

32. Friesen, *The Mennonite Brotherhood In Russia*, 98-99.

33. Ibid., 99.

34. Ibid., 102.

35. Ibid., 212.

36. See inaugural sermon of Wüst in Friesen, *The Mennonite Brotherhood In Russia*, 213-23.

37. John A. Toews, *A History Of The Mennonite Brethren Church*, 31.

38. Quoted in John B. Toews, "Brethren and Old Church Relations in Pre-World War I Russia: Setting the Stage for Canada," *Journal of Mennonite Studies* 2 (1984): 43.

39. Ibid.

40. Ibid., 45.

41. For background on the aberrations in the early Mennonite Brethren Church see John A. Toews, *A History Of The Mennonite Brethren Church*, 58-64.

42. Quoted in Friesen, *The Mennonite Brotherhood In Russia*, 206.

43. Ibid., 228-229.

44. Ibid. For a more comprehensive report on the struggles which led to the withdrawal of the Brethren, consult Friesen, *The Mennonite Brotherhood In Russia*, 227-230, and John A. Toews, *A History Of The Mennonite Brethren Church*, 32-37.

45. Jakob P. Bekker, *Origin of the Mennonite Brethren Church*, 41-42.

46. Ibid., 43-46.

47. Sources to consult on the influence of pietism include Victor Adrian, "Born of Anabaptism and Pietism," *Mennonite Brethren Herald*, 26 March 1965, 2-3; Robert Friedmann, *Mennonite Piety through the Centuries* (Scottdale, Pa.: Mennonite Publishing House, 1949); Cornelius Krahn, "Pietism," *Mennonite Encyclopedia*, 176-179; A. J. Klassen, "Mennonite Brethren Confession of Faith: Historic Roots and Comparative Analysis" (S.T.M. dissertation, Union College of British Columbia, 1965).

48. Friesen, *The Mennonite Brotherhood In Russia*, 233-43, 262-82.

49. Ibid., 233-42; 244-62; 312-22; 327-38.

50. *Odessaer Zeitung*. Recall from memory, number and page not available at the time.

51. Friesen, *The Mennonite Brotherhood In Russia*, 436.

52. Ibid., 436-48.

53. A. H. Unruh, *Die Geschichte der Mennoniten Brüdergemeinde*, 130-34.

54. Kreider, "Anabaptist Conception of the Church," 31.

55. Cornelius Krahn, "Some Social Attitudes of the Mennonites in Russia," *Mennonite Quarterly Review* 9 (1935): 173.

56. Ibid., 174.

# CHAPTER 2

1. Robert Friedmann, *The Theology of Anabaptism: An Interpretation, Studies in Anabaptist and Mennonite History*, no. 15 (Scottdale, Pa.: Herald Press, 1973), 31.

2. A. H. Unruh, "Grundzuege der Theologie der Vaeter der M.B. Gemeinde," paper presented at a study conference of the Board of Reference and Counsel, 12-15 December 1956, General Conference of Mennonite Brethren Churches Board of Reference and Counsel records, Center for Mennonite Brethren Studies, Fresno, Calif.

3. Peter M. Friesen, *The Mennonite Brotherhood in Russia, (1789-1910)* [*Alt-Evangelische Mennonitische Brüderschaft in Russland (1789-1910)*], trans. J. B. Toews, Abraham Friesen, Peter J. Klassen and Harry Loewen (Fresno, Calif.: Board of Christian Literature, General Conference of Mennonite Brethren Churches, 1978), 230-32, 436-45. This first conference of Mennonite Brethren churches in June 1865 has subsequently come to be known as the "June Reform."

4. David Duerksen, *Sermons in their Original Form Preached by Elder David Duerksen* (Fresno, Calif.: Center for Mennonite Brethren Studies, n.d.).

5. Jacob and Abram Kroeker, eds., *Zeugnisse von Christo* (Elberfeld: F. W. Kohler, n.d.).

6. *Glaubensbekenntniss der Vereinigten Christlichen Taufgesinnten Mennonitischen Brüdergemeinde in Russland* (Halbstadt: P. Neufeld, 1902), 53.

7. *Bericht über unsere Conferenz abgehalten in Nebraska, Hamilton Co. am 12. November 1883.*

8. Peter M. Hamm, *Continuity and Change Among Canadian Mennonite Brethren* (Waterloo, Ont.: Wilfred Laurier University Press, 1987), 65-67.

9. Minutes of the General Conference of the Mennonite Brethren Churches 1878-1882, General Conference of Mennonite Brethren Churches Conference Records, Center for Mennonite Brethren Studies, Fresno, Calif., p. 2.

10. J. F. Harms, *Geschichte der Mennoniten Brüdergemeinde* (Hillsboro, Kans.: Mennonite Brethren Publishing House, 1925), 2.

11. P. C. Hiebert, *In Grateful Memory of 75 Years of God's Grace* (Hillsboro, Kans.: Mennonite Brethren Publishing House, 1956), 7-8.

12. A. E. Janzen, *Mennonite Brethren Distinctives* (Hillsboro, Kans.: Mennonite Brethren Publishing House, 1966), 2.

13. Jacob Peter Bekker, *Origin of the Mennonite Brethren Church*, trans. D. E. Pauls and A. E. Janzen (Hillsboro, Kans.: Mennonite Brethren Historical Society of the Midwest, 1973), 44-46.

14. A. E. Janzen, *Mennonite Brethren Distinctives*, 2-4.

15. *Glaubensbekenntniss*, 7.

16 *Verhandlungen der Zwanzigsten Bundes-Konferenz der Mennoniten Brüdergemeinde in Nord-Amerika, abgehalten in Manitoba am 31. Okt. und 1. Nov., 1898*, 20.

17. A. E. Janzen, *Mennonite Brethren Distinctives*, 2.

18. Donovan E. Smucker, "The Theological Triumph of the Early Anabaptist-Mennonites," *Mennonite Quarterly Review* 19 (1945): 6.

19. Quoted in John Horsch, *Mennonites in Europe* (Scottdale, Pa.: Mennonite Publishing House, 1942), 350-56.

20. Quoted in Ibid., 351.

21. Menno Simons, *The Complete Writings of Menno Simons, c. 1496-1561*, ed. John Christian Wenger, trans. Leonard Verduin (Scottdale, Pa.: Herald Press, 1956), 497.

22. Friesen, *The Mennonite Brotherhood in Russia*, 231-32.

23. David Duerksen, *Sermons*.

24. H. D. Wiebe, "Die Bibel," *Zionsbote*, 22 July 1925, l.

25. N. N. Hiebert, "Die Bibel, das Buch der Wunder," *Zionsbote*, 29 Feb. 1928, l.

26. See Myron S. Augsburger, *Principles of Biblical Interpretation in Mennonite Theology* (Scottdale, Pa.: Herald Press, 1967), 18.

27. Ibid., 20-21.

28. Duerksen, *Sermons*; Kroeker, eds., *Zeugnisse von Christo*.

29. For further examination of Mennonite Brethren hermeneutics consult: Abram John Klassen, "The Roots and Development of Mennonite Brethren Theology to 1914" (M.A. thesis, Wheaton College, 1966); George Warkentin, "The Dynamism in Biblical Authority: Its Biblical Basis and Influence in Mennonite Brethren History" (M.A. thesis, Mennonite Brethren Biblical Seminary, 1970); Kenneth Berg, "Mennonite

Brethren Hermeneutics in Anabaptist Perspective" (M.Div. thesis, Mennonite Brethren Biblical Seminary, 1975); Ben Ollenburger, "The Hermeneutics of Obedience: A Study of Anabaptist Hermenuetics," *Direction* 6 (April 1977): 19-29.

30. These observations are based on personal experience in many churches in Russia during my youth and early adulthood.

31. A. E. Janzen, *Mennonite Brethren Distinctives*, 8-9.

32. Friesen, *The Mennonite Brotherhood in Russia*, 72.

33. Observations based on personal experience and participation as a young adult.

34. The Mennonite Brethren chose to call their houses of worship *Versammlungshaus* (assembly house) rather than *Kirche* (church) as was the practice of the Mennonite Church in Russia. The name *Kirche* for them was symbolic of an ethnic institutional religion from which they had withdrawn.

# CHAPTER 3

1. Ernst Troeltsch, *The Social Teaching of the Christian Churches*, [*Die Soziallehren der Christlichen Kirchen und Gruppen*] trans. Olive Wyon, 2 vols. (Chicago: The University of Chicago Press, 1981), 2: 993.

2. *Geschichte des Christlichen Lebens in der Rheinisch-Westfälischen Kirche*, quoted in Harold S. Bender, "The Anabaptist Vision," *Mennonite Quarterly Review* 18 (1944): 74.

3. Cornelius J. Dyck, "The Life of the Spirit in Anabaptism," *Mennonite Quarterly Review* 47 (1973): 309-26.

4. Ibid., 319.

5. Ibid., 320.

6. Quoted in Peter M. Friesen, *The Mennonite Brotherhood in Russia, (1789-1910)* [*Alt-Evangelische Mennonitische Brüderschaft in Russland (1789-1910)*], trans. J. B. Toews, Abraham Friesen, Peter J. Klassen and Harry Loewen (Fresno, Calif.: Board of Christian Literature, Conference of Mennonite Brethren Churches, 1978), 231.

7. The character and influence of Pietism on Mennonite Brethren faith and life is considered in chapter one.

8. S. F. Pannabecker, "Conversion," in *The Mennonite Encyclopedia*, eds. Harold S. Bender and C. Henry Smith (Scottdale, Pa.: Mennonite Publishing House, 1955).

9. Myron S. Augsburger, "Conversion in Anabaptist Thought," *Mennonite Quarterly Review* 36 (1962): 243.

10. *Confession of Faith of the Mennonite Brethren Church of North America, American Edition* (Hillsboro, Kans.: Mennonite Brethren Publishing House, 1917), 12.

11. Ibid., 11.

12. Ibid., 12.

13. Ibid., 14.

14. Menno Simons, *The Complete Writings of Menno Simons, c.1496-1561*, ed. John Christian Wenger, trans. Leonard Verduin (Scottdale, Pa.: Herald Press, 1956),

87-102.

15. Ibid., 92.

16. Ibid.

17. Ibid., 93.

18. Friesen, *The Mennonite Brotherhood in Russia*, 261.

19. Harold S. Bender, "The Anabaptist Vision," in *The Recovery of the Anabaptist Vision*, ed. Guy F. Hershberger (Scottdale, Pa.: Herald Press, 1957), 40.

20. H. E. Reimer, *Wiedergeboren aus dem lebendigen Wort Gottes* (Hillsboro, Kans.: Mennonite Brethren Publishing House, n.d.).

21. Documents in the B. B. Janz Papers and John A. Toews Papers at the Center for Mennonite Brethren Studies, Fresno, Calif., reflect these kind of conversion stories.

22. *Confession of Faith*, 14.

23. See for example A. Wall, "False and True Conversion," *Friedensstimme*, 5 Aug. 1906, 1; P. Regier, "Conversion According to the Scripture," *Friedensstimme*, 9 July 1904, n.p.; Editorial, "What is Conversion," *Friedensstimme*, 28 Sept. 1904, 1; A. H. Unruh, "A Biblical Conversion," *Zionsbote*, 3 Oct. 1928, 1; Herman Neufeld, "Conversion According to the Reports from the Holy Scriptures," *Zionsbote*, 18 Sept. 1929, 1; P. Riediger, "The New Birth," *Zionsbote*, 14 July 1914, n.p.

24. David Gerhard Duerksen, S*ermons in their Original Form Preached by Elder David Duerksen* (Fresno, Calif.: Center for Mennonite Brethren Studies, n.d.).

25. *Confession of Faith* (1917), 15.

26. Ibid.

27. Ibid., 16.

28. Ibid., 17.

29. Ibid., 13.

30. Ibid., 28.

31. Friesen, *The Mennonite Brotherhood in Russia*, 231.

32. See Friesen, *The Mennonite Brotherhood in Russia*, 284-311; Unruh, *Die Geschichte der Mennoniten Brüdergemeinde* (Hillsboro, Kans.: General Conference of the Mennonite Brethren Church of North America, 1955), 73-81; J. A. Toews, *A History of the Mennonite Brethren Church* (Hillsboro, Kans.: Mennonite Brethren Publishing House, 1975), 55-57.

33. J. F. Harms, *Geschichte der Mennoniten Brüdergemeinde* (Hillsboro, Kans.: Mennonite Brethren Publishing House, 1925), 24-25.

34. Confession of Faith, 29; Friesen, *The Mennonite Brotherhood in Russia*, 291-300; Articles in *Friedensstimme*, 14 July 1901; *Zionsbote*, 22 June 1904; *Zionsbote*, 7 Feb. 1906; *Zionsbote*, 10 Aug. 1904.

35. Harms, *Geschichte der Mennoniten Brüdergemeinde*, 24-25; See also Friesen, *The Mennonite Brotherhood in Russia*, 290; J. P. Bekker, *Origin of the Mennonite Brethren Church*, trans. D. E. Pauls and A. E. Janzen (Hillsboro, Kans.: Mennonite Brethren Publishing House, 1973), 102, 111-12.

36. Bekker, *Origin of the Mennonite Brethren Church*, 102.

37. Yearbook of the 49th Session of the General Conference of the Mennonite Brethren Churches, August 3-7, 1963, 38-39.

# CHAPTER 4

1. Peter M. Friesen, *The Mennonite Brotherhood in Russia (1789-1910)* [*Alt-Evangelische Mennonitische Brüderschaft in Russland (1789-1910)*], trans. J. B. Toews, Abraham Friesen, Peter J. Klassen and Harry Loewen (Fresno, Calif.: Board of Christian Literature, General Conference of Mennonite Brethren Churches, 1978), 231.

2. Harold S. Bender, *These Are My People: The Nature of the Church and Its Discipleship According to the New Testament* (Scottdale, Pa.: Herald Press, 1962), 69-70.

3. Friesen, *The Mennonite Brotherhood in Russia*, 231.

4. Ibid.

5. *Confession of Faith of the Mennonite Brethren Church of North America, American Edition*, (Hillsboro, Kans.: Mennonite Brethren Publishing House, 1917), 19.

6. Ibid., 20.

7. Ibid.

8. Friesen, *The Mennonite Brotherhood in Russia*, 436-41. The first meeting of the Mennonite Brethren Churches in conference on June 26-27 is known as the June Reform. At these meetings the young church reached basic agreement on their understanding of Scripture, important for the governing of the life of the fellowship.

9. Ibid., 437.

10. Ibid.

11. A.H. Unruh, "Grundzuege der Theologie der Vaeter der M. B. Gemeinde," paper presented at the Board of Reference and Counsel Study Conference, 12-15 December 1956, General Conference of Mennonite Brethren Churches Board of Reference and Counsel Records, Center for Mennonite Brethren Studies, Fresno, Calif., 32.

12. Friesen, *The Mennonite Brotherhood in Russia*, 232.

13. Ibid., 241.

14. Quoted in Friesen, *The Mennonite Brotherhood in Russia*, 249.

15. See Unruh, *Die Geschichte der Mennoniten Brüdergemeinde* (Hillsboro, Kans.: General Conference of the Mennonite Brethren Church of North America, 1955).

16. Ibid.

17. *Confession of Faith*, 21-22.

18. Unruh, "Grundzuege der Theologie der Vaeter der M. B. Gemeinde," 32.

19. Ibid.

20. *Confession of Faith*, 25-27.

21. Ibid., 26-27.

22. See *My Church Covenant* (Winnipeg, Man.: Board of Reference and Counsel, Manitoba Mennonite Brethren Conference, 1968-69). The origins of this document

are unkown. It was already widely used in both Russian and North American Mennonite Brethren churches in the late nineteenth and early twentieth century.

23. Ibid., 19.

24. Unruh, *Die Geschichte der Mennoniten Brüdergemeinde*, 31.

25. *Confession of Faith*, 17-18.

26. Ibid., 28-29.

27. Ibid., 31-32.

28. Ibid., 33-34.

29. Ibid., 35.

30. Ibid., 34.

31. *Confession of Faith*, 33.

32. See P. Riediger, "Das Abendmahl," *Friedensstimme*, 15 July 1906, 296; Peter Schmidt, "Beteiligung am Abendmahl," *Friedensstimme*, 17 Nov. 1907, 605; R. A. Fehr, "Referat vom Abendmahl" *Zionsbote*, 31 July 1907, 1.

33. See Editorial, "Die Fehler unserer Brüder und Schwestern," *Friedensstimme*, 15 Sept. 1910, 1; Editorial, "Zum Artikel: Sündenbekenntnis," *Friedensstimme*, 29 Sept. 1910, 1.

34. Unruh, *Die Geschichte der Mennoniten Brüdergemeinde*, 227-33.

35. Ibid.

36. Unruh, *Die Geschichte der Mennoniten Brüdergemeinde*, 230-33.

37. Reflected in reports in *Friedensstimme* and *Zionsbote* as well as reported from parents and grandparents.

38. John A. Toews, *A History of the Mennonite Brethren Church: Pilgrims and Pioneers* (Fresno, Calif.: Board of Christian Literature, Mennonite Brethren Church, 1975), 103-05.

39. B.B. Janz, "Grundzuege im Charakter der Glaubensstellung unserer Vaeter," paper presented at the Board of Reference and Counsel Study Conference, 12-15 December 1956, General Conference of Mennonite Brethren Churches Board of Reference and Counsel Records, Center for Mennonite Brethren Studies, Fresno, Calif., 75.

40. Friesen, *The Mennonite Brotherhood in Russia*, 276-78, 436-53.

41. Ibid., 436-37.

42. Ibid., 439.

43. See P. H. Berg, comp., *Resolutions of the Conference of Mennonite Brethren Churches of North America* (Hillsboro, Kans.: Mennonite Brethren Publishing House, 1948).

# CHAPTER 5

1. *Confession of Faith of the Mennonite Brethren Church of North America, American Edition* (Hillsboro, Kans.: Mennonite Brethren Publishing House, 1917), 22-23.

2. H. W. Lohrenz, "The Minister's Life and Work," H. W. Lohrenz Papers, Center

for Mennonite Brethren Studies, Fresno, Calif.

3. Ibid., 4-5.

4. Ibid., 6.

5. Ibid., 7.

6. Ibid., 8.

7. Ibid., 11.

8. Ibid.

9. Ibid., 12.

10. Ibid., 13.

11. *Verhandlungen der 39. General Konferenz der Mennoniten Brüdergemeinden von Nord-Amerika abgehalten von 21. bis zum 25. Oktober 1933 in der Gemeinde zu Hillsboro, Kansas*, 65.

12. *Bericht über die zehnte Bundeskonferenz der Mennoniten Brüdergemeinde abgehalten in Reno County, Kansas, Nordamerika am 12. u. 13. Oktober, 1888*, 12.

13. B.B. Janz, "Grundzuege im Character der Glaubensstellung unserer Vaeter," paper presented at the Board of Reference and Counsel study conference, 12-15 December 1956, General Conference of Mennonite Brethren Churches Board of Reference and Counsel Records, Center for Mennonite Brethren Studies, Fresno, Calif.

14. The entrance exam in Bible content required at the Mennonite Brethren Biblical Seminary in Fresno records a sixty-eight percent failure at the first writing.

15. Data secured from Wiedenest Bible School, Wiedenest, Germany and St. Chrischona Bible School, Basel, Switzerland.

16. Abe J. Dueck, "The Changing Role of Biblical/Theological Education in the Mennonite Brethren Church," in *The Bible and the Church: Essays in Honour of Dr. David Ewert*, eds. A. J. Dueck, H. J. Giesbrecht and V. G. Shillington (Winnipeg, Man.: Kindred Press, 1988), 143-44.

17. All located in the Center for Mennonite Brethren Studies, Fresno, Calif. or Winnipeg, Man.

18. *Bericht über die XIV. Bundes Conferenz der Mennoniten Brüdergemeinde in Nord Amerika abgehalten am 31. Oktober und 1. November 1892*, 12-13.

19. Peter M. Friesen, *The Mennonite Brotherhood in Russia (1789-1910) [Alt-Evangelische Mennonitische Brüderschaft in Russland (1789-1910)]*, trans. J. B. Toews, Abraham Friesen, Peter J. Klassen and Harry Loewen (Fresno, Calif.: Board of Christian Literature, General Conference of Mennonite Brethren Churches, 1978), 634.

20. *Bericht über die sechste Bundes Conferenz der Mennoniten Brüdergemeinde, abgehalten bei Gnadenau, Hillsboro, Marion Co., Kansas, Nordamerika, am 27. Oktober 1884*, 10-11; *Bericht über die siebente Bundes Conferenz der Mennoniten Brüdergemeinde, abgehalten in Minnesota, Cottonwood County, Nordamerika, am 19. October 1885*, 10-11; *Bericht über die achte Bundes Conferenz der Mennoniten Brüdergemeinde, abgehalten in Dakota, Turner County, Nord Amerika, am 1. und 2. November 1886*, 8-9, and succeeding years.

21. Protocol, Dat is, allehandelinge des gespreck tot Emden (Emden 1579), 229b.

22. *Bericht*, 1888, 4.

23. Friesen, *The Mennonite Brotherhood in Russia*, 928.

24. Ibid.

25. Cornelius Krahn, "The Office of Elder in Anabaptist-Mennonite History," *Mennonite Quarterly Review* 30 (1956): 122.

26. Friesen, *The Mennonite Brotherhood in Russia*, 472.

27. Ibid., 472-73.

28. Gerhard Classen, "Der Vorberat," *Zionsbote*, 20 Feb. 1901, 1.

29. *Confession of Faith*, 27.

30. *Year Book of the 45th General Conference of the Mennonite Brethren Church of North America held at Winkler, Manitoba July 21 to 26 1951*, 137.

31. John A. Toews, *A History of the Mennonite Brethren Church: Pilgrims and Pioneers* (Fresno, Calif.: Board of Christian Literature, General Conference of Mennonite Brethren Churches, 1975), 3.

32. *Year Book of the 44th General Conference of the Mennonite Brethren Church of North America Held at Mountain Lake, Minnesota, August 28 to September 2, 1948*, 106; and *Year Book*, 1951, 130-33.

33. *Confession of Faith*, 27.

34. A. H. Unruh, *Die Geschichte der Mennoniten Brüdergemeinde* (Hillsboro, Kans.: General Conference of the Mennonite Brethren Church of North America, 1954), 235.

35. F. J. Wiens, "Zur Aeltestenfrage," *Zionsbote*, 1 Feb. 1933, 8; C. Grunau, "Zur Aeltestenfrage," *Zionsbote*, 28 Dec. 1932, 8.

36. H.W. Lohrenz Papers in possession of Mariana Remple, Lawrence, Kans.

37. See J.F. Harms, "Verschiedenes," *Zionsbote*, 12 Nov. 1924, 15-16.

38. H. H. Flaming, "Ein kurzes Wort über die Aeltestenfrage" *Zionsbote*, 4 Oct. 1933, 1-2.

39. H. W. Lohrenz, "Einige Fragen über Ältestendienste," *Zionsbote*, 23 Nov. 1932, 9-11.

40. Protocol einer Beratunger lehrenden Brueder und Diakonen...an 28. February 1934, Dalmeny, 1-2.

41. J.F. Harms, "Wie ich zu der Aeltestenfrage stehe," J. F. Harms Papers, Center for Mennonite Brethren Studies, Fresno, Calif.

42. Friesen, *The Mennonite Brotherhood in Russia*, 70-71.

43. Orlando H. Wiebe, "The Missionary Emphasis of Pietism," in *The Church in Mission: A Sixtieth Anniversary Tribute to J.B. Toews*, ed. A.J. Klassen (Fresno, Calif.: Board of Christian Literature, Mennonite Brethren Church, 1967), 126.

44. Ibid., 277.

45. Ibid., 416-424.

46. Ibid., 449-53, 515-22, 564-67.

## CHAPTER 6
1. Peter M. Friesen, *The Mennonite Brotherhood in Russia (1789-1910)* [*Alt-Evangelische Mennonitische Brüderschaft in Russland (1789-1910)*], trans. J. B. Toews, Abraham Friesen, Peter J. Klassen and Harry Loewen (Fresno, Calif.: Board of Christian Literature, General Conference of Mennonite Brethren Churches, 1978), 231.

2. Menno Simons, *The Complete Writings of Menno Simons, c. 1496-1561*, ed. John Christian Wenger, trans. Leonard Verduin (Scottdale, Pa.: Herald Press, 1956), 734-59.

3. Friesen, *The Mennonite Brotherhood in Russia*, 436-41.

4. At the time of my baptism and acceptance into church membership this was one of the passages given to me as a guide for Christian life.

5. A.H. Unruh, "Die Gleichstellung mit der Welt," *Konferenz-Jugendblatt*, May-August 1951, 3.

6. H. F. Toews, "Erlaubt und unerlaubt," *Zionsbote*, 9 Aug. 1922, 3.

7. P. E. Penner, "Wer ist ein Bibelchrist," *Zionsbote*, 11 Nov. 1925, 2.

8. John H. Yoder, trans. and ed., *The Schleitheim Confession* (Scottdale, Pa.: Herald Press, 1977), 11-12.

9. Heinrich Adrian, "Im Kampf gegen die Finsterniss," *Zionsbote*, 1 Feb. 1922, 2.

10. H. W. Lohrenz, "Das Leben der Kinder Gottes in dieser Welt," file "Bible School Addresses," H.W. Lohrenz Papers, Center for Mennonite Brethren Studies, Fresno, Calif., 1.

11. Ibid., 2-10.

12. H. W. Lohrenz, "Siegreicher Kampf gegen Teufel und Sunde," file "Bible School Addresses," H.W. Lohrenz Papers, 1-4.

13. H.W. Lohrenz, "The Life of Holiness in its New Testament Interpretation," file "Sermons preached 1919-1930," H.W. Lohrenz Papers, 1-2.

14. Ibid., 3-4.

15. H. W. Lohrenz, "Die Gemeinde Jesu Christe," file "Sermons preached 1919-1930", H.W. Lohrenz Papers, 1-4.

16. Ibid., 5-9.

17. H. W. Lohrenz, "Das Leben der Kinder Gottes in der Welt", file "Bible School Addresses," H.W. Lohrenz Papers, 16.

18. H. W. Lohrenz, "What the Bible Teaches about War and Peace," paper in the possession of Mariana Remple, Lawrence, Kansas.

19. P. Dolmann, "Geistlich oder Fleischlich," *Friedensstimme*, 7 July 1907, 339-41.

20. J. Penn Lewis, "Mit Christum gekreuzigt," *Friedensstimme*, 14 April 1907, 179-80.

21. Editorial, "Die Sünde der Selbstsucht," *Zionsbote*, 30 April 1913, 5.

22. P. E. Penner, "Mein Gott wo sind wir hingekommen," *Zionsbote*, 8 June 1927, 1.

23. H. P. Wieler, "Wie soll ein Christ sein," *Zionsbote*, 7 Oct. 1925, 1.

24. Editorial, "Seid mässig," *Friedensstimme*, 22 July 1907, 353-54; G. Ewert, "Mässigkeit oder Enthaltsamkeit," *Zionsbote*, 22 August 1906, 1.

25. Guth Georg, "Vergnügungssucht unserer Zeit," *Zionsbote*, 1 Sept. 1909, 1-2.

26. Ibid.

27. Editorial, "Weltgleichstellung," *Zionsbote*, 13 Jan. 1909, 6.

28. Johann Siemens, "Eine zeitgemässe Wahrnung Jesu," *Zionsbote*, 29 May 1929, 1-2.

29. F. W. Simoleit, "Wie erwirbst du dein irdisches Gut," *Friedensstimme*, 3 June 1906, 226-27.

30. P. H. Berg, comp., *Resolutions of the Conference of the Mennonite Brethren Churches of North America* (Hillsboro, Kans.: Mennonite Brethren Publishing House, 1948), 8-9.

31. N. N. Hiebert, "Materialismus," *Zionsbote*, 24 March 1909, 1.

32. Story told by my father, J. A. Toews.

33. Ibid.

34. Berg, *Resolutions*, 9.

35. Ibid., 6,9.

36. Editorial, "Ist das nicht Sünde," *Zionsbote*, 28 April 1909, 6.

37. Berg, *Resolutions*, 14.

38. J. G. Ewert, "Enthaltsamkeit," *Zionsbote*, 3 July 1907, 8.

39. Friedrich Betler, "Die Alkoholfrage," *Friedensstimme*, 22 Sept. 1910, 2-3; W. Goebel, "Die Alkoholfrage," *Friedensstimme*, 17 Nov. 1910, 2-4.

40. Berg, *Resolutions*, 3-4.

41. Ibid., 7.

42. *Bericht über unsere Conferenz abgehalten in Nebraska, Hamilton Co., am 12. November 1883*, 14-15.

43. *Gesangbuch der Mennoniten Brüdergemeinde*, (Winnipeg, Man.: The Christian Press, Ltd., 1952) 440.

44. Ibid., 36.

# CHAPTER 7

1. John A. Toews, "The Anabaptist Involvement in Missions," in *The Church in Mission: A Sixtieth Anniversary Tribute to J. B. Toews*, ed. A. J. Klassen (Fresno, Calif.: Board of Christian Literature, Mennonite Brethren Church, 1967), 85.

2. Franklin Hamlin Littel, *The Anabaptist View of the Church* (Boston: Starr King

Press, 1958), 112.

3. Leonard Verduin, *The Reformers and their Step Children* (Grand Rapids, Mich.: Wm. B. Eerdmans, 1964), 269.

4. John H. Yoder, "The Prophetic Dissent of the Anabaptists," in *The Recovery of the Anabaptist Vision*, ed. Guy F. Hershberger (Scottdale, Pa.: Herald Press, 1957), 98.

5. Toews, "The Anabaptist Involvement in Missions," 87.

6. George Hunston Williams, *The Radical Reformation* (Philadelphia: Westminster Press, 1962), 844-45.

7. Toews, "The Anabaptist Involvement in Missions," 89.

8. Quoted in Toews, "The Anabaptist Involvement in Missions," 91.

9. "Reply to Gellius Faber," in Menno Simons, *The Complete Writings of Menno Simons, c. 1496-1561*, ed. John Christian Wenger, trans. Leonard Verduin (Scottdale, Pa.: Herald Press, 1956), 633.

10. Quoted in Gustav Warneck, *Outline of a History of Protestant Mission* (Fleming H. Revell Co., 1906), 39-40.

11. Cornelius Krahn, "Pietism," in *The Mennonite Encyclopedia*, eds. Harold S. Bender and C. Henry Smith, (Scottdale, Pa.: Mennonite Publishing House, 1959), 176.

12. Orlando Wiebe, "The Missionary Emphasis of Pietism," in *The Church in Mission*, 126-27; Peter M. Friesen, *The Mennonite Brotherhood in Russia (1789-1910) [Alt-Evangelische Mennonitische Brüderschaft in Russland (1789-1910)]*, trans. J. B. Toews, Abraham Friesen, Peter J. Klassen and Harry Loewen (Fresno, Calif.: Board of Christian Literature, General Conference of Mennonite Brethren Churches, 1978), 127-28.

13. Wiebe, "The Missionary Emphasis of Pietism," 128-29. Also consult Hans Kasdorf, *Flammen unauslöschlich: Mission der Mennoniten unter Zaren und Sowjets, 1789-1989* (Bielefeld, Germany: Logos Verlag, 1991).

14. Ibid., 129-32.

15. A. H. Unruh, *Die Geschichte der Mennoniten Brüdergemeinde* (Hillsboro, Kans.: General Conference of the Mennonite Brethren Church of North America, 1955), 327.

16. For a broader background of factors contributing toward the awakening of mission interest in the early Mennonite Brethren Church consult the following: Gerhard William Peters, *The Growth of Foreign Missions in the Mennonite Brethren Church* (Hillsboro, Kans.: Mennonite Brethren Publishing House, 1947), 43-50; Jakob J. Toews, "The Missionary Spirit of the Mennonite Brethren Church in Russia," in *The Church in Mission*, 135-43.

17. Friesen, *The Mennonite Brotherhood in Russia*, 318.

18. Ibid., 447-54.

19. Jacob P. Bekker, *Origin of the Mennonite Brethren Church*, trans. D. E. Pauls and A. E. Janzen (Hillsboro, Kans.: Mennonite Brethren Historical Society of the Midwest, 1973), 97-105.

20. Friesen, *The Mennonite Brotherhood in Russia*, 375-76.

21. Jacob J. Toews, "The Missionary Spirit of the Mennonite Brethren Church in Russia," 139.

22. Cornelius Krahn, "Some Social Attitudes of the Mennonites of Russia," *Mennonite Quarterly Review* 9 (1935): 173.

23. Friesen, *The Mennonite Brotherhood in Russia*, 449-53, 514-22.

24. *Konferenzbeschlüsse nebst Konstitution der Mennoniten Brudergemeinde von Nord Amerika 1883-1919* (Hillsboro, Kans.: Mennonite Brethren Publishing House, 1920). The Mennonite Brethren made a distinction between mission efforts at home (Home Missions) and missions in other lands (Foreign Missions).

25. The churches in North Dakota (Harvey, McClusky, Sawyer, and John's Lake) were the fruit of evangelism in Lutheran and Congregational communities.

26. Jacob J. Toews, "The Missionary Spirit," 144-45.

27. J. F. Harms, *Geschichte der Mennoniten Brüdergemeinde* (Hillsboro, Kans.: Mennonite Brethren Publishing House, 1925), 78-80.

28. *Worship Hymnal* (Fresno: Board of Christian Literature of the Mennonite Brethren Churches, 1971), 318.

29. Friesen, *The Mennonite Brotherhood in Russia*, 442.

30. Ibid., 213-17.

31. J. A. Froese, *Witness Extraordinary: A Biography of Elder Heinrich Voth, 1851-1918*, (Winnipeg: Board of Christian Literature, General Conference of the Mennonite Brethren Churches of North America, 1975), 34.

32. Sara Voth, wife of Heinrich Voth, related this incident to me in 1932.

33. Froese, *Witness Extraordinary*, 34-35.

34. Arnie Neufeld, "The Origin and Early Growth of the Mennonite Brethren Church in Southern Manitoba," (M.A. Thesis, Mennonite Brethren Biblical Seminary, 1977), 127.

35. Adolf Ehrt, *Das Mennonitentum in Russland von seiner Einwanderung bis zur Gegenwart* (Berlin: Julius Beltz, 1932), 60.

36. Unruh, *Die Geschichte Der Mennoniten Brüdergemeinde*, 258.

37. Ehrt, *Das Mennonitentum in Russland*, 60.

38. Friesen, *The Mennonite Brotherhood in Russia*, 448.

39. Unruh, *Die Geschichte der Mennoniten Brüdergemeinde*, 265-66.

40. Ibid.

41. Ibid., 263-80.

42. Peters, The Growth of Foreign Missions, 43-45.

43. Friesen, *The Mennonite Brotherhood in Russia*, 674-87; the early chapters of George W. Peters, *The Growth of Foreign Missions in the Mennonite Brethren Church*.

44. Friesen, *The Mennonite Brotherhood in Russia*, 674.

45. P. H. Berg, comp., *Resolutions of the Conference of the Mennonite Brethren*

*Church of North America* (Hillsboro, Kans.: Mennonite Brethren Publishing House, 1948), 4.

46. Minutes of the General Conference of the Mennonite Brethren Churches 1887-1882, General Conference of Mennonite Brethren Churches Conference Records, Center for Mennonite Brethren Studies, Fresno, Calif., 49.

47. A. E. Janzen, "The Development of Missionary Dynamic Among American Mennonite Brethren," in *The Church in Mission*, 157.

48. *Konferenzbeschlüsse nebst Konstitution der Mennoniten Brüdergemeinde von Nord America 1883-1919*, 25, 35, 209. The German department at McPherson College, with Mennonite Brethren teachers, became the first Mennonite Brethren training school for Christian workers.

49. John H. Lohrenz, *The Mennonite Brethren Church* (Hillsboro, Kans.: Board of Foreign Missions, 1950), 230-36.

50. *Constitution of the Conference of the Mennonite Brethren Church of North America*, 1936, 26.

51. Bekker, *Origin of the Mennonite Brethren Church*, 25-26.

52. Ibid., 26.

53. Clint Seibel, "After 'Mission Sales?,'" 1984. Manuscript Collection, Center for Mennonite Brethren Studies, Fresno, Calif.

54. This is based on my observations of candidate applications during my term as Candidate Secretary for the Board of Missions and Services.

55. This was related to me by A. A. Janzen.

56. Report from Tina Dick, Mountain Lake, Minnesota.

# CHAPTER 8

1 The biographical data about missionaries given in this chapter has been drawn from mission records in the Center for Mennonite Brethren Studies (Fresno), interviews with members of their families and recollections of former missionaries who served with them. Much of this material was earlier prepared for the three part film series–"The Mennonite Brethren: A Missionary Movement" released by the Historical Commission of the Mennonite Brethren Church in 1988.

# CHAPTER 9

1. *Confession of Faith of the Mennonite Brethren Church of North America, American Edition* (Hillsboro, Kans.: Mennonite Brethren Publishing House, 1917), 44-46.

2. Ibid., 46.

3. A.H. Unruh, "Grundzuege der Theologie der Vaeter der M.B. Gemeinde," paper presented at the Board of Reference and Counsel Study Conference, 12-15 Dec. 1956, General Conference of Mennonite Brethren Churches Board of Reference and Counsel records, Center for Mennonite Brethren Studies, Fresno, Calif., 32.

4. Peter M. Friesen, *The Mennonite Brotherhood in Russia (1789-1910)* [Alt-Evan-

*gelische Mennonitische Brüderschaft in Russland (1789-1910)*], trans. J. B. Toews, Abraham Friesen, Peter J. Klassen and Harry Loewen (Fresno, Calif.: Board of Christian Literature, General Conference of Mennonite Brethren Churches, 1978), 309.

5. Mrs. H. S. Bender, "Jung-Stilling, Johann Heinrich," in T*he Mennonite Encyclopedia*, eds. Harold S. Bender and C. Henry Smith (Scottdale, Pa.: Mennonite Publishing House, 1957), 127.

6. Franz Bartsch, "Epp, Claasz, Jr.," in T*he Mennonite Encyclopedia*, 234.

7. Fred Richard Belk, *The Great Trek of the Russian Mennonites to Central Asia, 1880-1884* (Scottdale, Pa.: Herald Press, 1976).

8. Cornelius Krahn, "Temple Church," in *The Mennonite Encyclopedia*, 693-94.

9. J. B. Toews, "Mennonite Brethren Identity and Theological Diversity," in *Pilgrims and Strangers: Essays in Mennonite Brethren History*, ed. Paul Toews (Fresno, Calif.: Center for Mennonite Brethren Studies, 1977), 134-40.

10. Friesen, *The Mennonite Brotherhood in Russia*, 310.

11. Ibid.

12. Ibid., 499.

13. *Zionsbote Index Volume I 1884-1919* (Fresno, Calif.: Center for Mennonite Brethren Studies, 1984), 1-118; *Zionsbote Index Volume II 1920-1940* (Fresno, Calif.: Center for Mennonite Brethren Studies, 1983), 1-187; *Zionsbote Index Volume III 1941-1964* (Fresno, Calif.: Center for Mennonite Brethren Studies, 1983), 1-103.

14. J. B. Toews, "Mennonite Brethren Identity and Theological Diversity," 135, 138.

15. William Bestvater Papers, Center for Mennonite Brethren Studies, Fresno, Calif.

16. William Bestvater, *Betrachtungen über das letzte Buch der Bibel* (Hillsboro, Kans.: Mennonite Brethren Publishing House, 1919).

17. William Bestvater, *Textbüchlein in Glaubenslehre für die Herbert Bibelschule* (Regina, Sask.: Courier Press, n.d.).

18. H. F. Toews, *Biblische Grundwahrheiten Heft I* (Hillsboro, Kans.: Mennonite Brethren Publishing House, 1917), 27-30; H. F. Toews, *Jesus Kommt Wieder* (Hillsboro, Kans.: Mennonite Brethren Publishing House, 1919).

19. J. W. Reimer, *Der wundervolle Ratschluss Gottes mit der Menschheit: kurz dargestellt nach der heiligen Schrift* (Hillsboro, Kans.: Mennonite Brethren Publishing House, n.d.)

20. A. H. Unruh, "Der Grundriss der Christlichen Eschatologie," Centre for Mennonite Brethren Studies, Winnipeg, Man.

21. Ibid.

22. H.W. Lohrenz, "Exposition of I and II Thessalonians," Paper in possession of Mrs. Mariana Rempel, Lawrence, Kansas.

23. H. W. Lohrenz, "Studien in den Evangelien Lessons 15, 16, 17," Paper in the possession of Mariana Rempel, Lawrence, Kansas.

24. Statement frequently used by the late John A. Toews.

25. Abram Kroeker, "Die darbystische gefahr," *Friedensstimme*, 23 June 1907, 314-17.

## CHAPTER 10

1. Peter M. Friesen, *The Mennonite Brotherhood in Russia (1789-1910)* [*Alt-Evangelische Mennonitische Brüderschaft in Russland (1789-1910)*], trans. J. B. Toews, Abraham Friesen, Peter J. Klassen and Harry Loewen (Fresno, Calif.: Board of Christian Literature, General Conference of Mennonite Brethren Churches, 1978), 689-842.

2. Ibid., 843-65.

3. See Al Reimer, "Peasant Aristocracy: The Mennonite Gutsbesitzertum in Russia," *Journal of Mennonite Studies* 8 (1990): 76-88.

4. Friesen, *The Mennonite Brotherhood in Russia*, 786.

5. Ibid.

6. The following sections on education, publications, economics, industry and charitable institutions are based on Friesen, *The Mennonite Brotherhood in Russia*, 689-866.

7. Ibid., 645-50.

8. Peter M. Friesen, *Konfession oder Sekte* (Halbstadt: Raduga, 1914).

9. Friesen, *The Mennonite Brotherhood in Russia*, 645-46.

10. Ibid., 523-24.

11. Ibid., 551-72.

12. Ibid., 530-31.

13. John A. Toews, *A History of the Mennonite Brethren Church: Pilgrims and Pioneers* (Fresno, Calif.: Board of Christian Literature, General Conference of Mennonite Brethren Churches, 1975), 304-05.

14. Friesen, *The Mennonite Brotherhood in Russia*, 525.

15. Clarence B. Bass, *Backgrounds to Dispensationalism: Its Historical Genesis and Ecclesiastical Implications* (Grand Rapids: Wm. B. Eerdmans Pub. Co., 1960).

16. Robert Friedmann, *Mennonite Piety Through the Centuries* (Goshen, Ind.: Mennonite Historical Society, 1949), 12.

17. My father frequently referred to Arndt and read from this book during family devotions both in Russia and in our early years in North America.

18. Erich Beyreuther, *Der Weg der Evangelischen Alliance in Deutschland* (Wuppertal: Brockhaus, 1969), 61-64.

19. Personal interview with Heinrich Kornelsen, a minister of the Mennonite Brethren Church in Coaldale, Alberta, and author of *Der Schatz und die Perle*, a book on eschatology strongly reflecting the eschatology of Blankenburg.

20. A. H. Unruh, *Die Geschichte der Mennoniten Brüdergemeinde* (Hillsboro, Kan.: General Conference of the Mennonite Brethren Church of North America, 1955), 822-27.

21. Ibid.; Comments by A.H. Unruh at the 1956 General Conference Board of Ref-

erence and Counsel Study Conference.

22. *Glaubensbekenntniss der Vereinigten Christlichen Taufgesinnten Mennonitischen Brüdergemeinde in Russland* (Halbstadt: P. Neufeld, 1902), 3-6.

23. B. B. Janz, "Grundzüge im Character der Glaubensstellung unserer Väter," paper presented at the Board of Reference and Counsel Study Conference, 12-15 December 1956, General Conference of Mennonite Brethren Churches Board of Reference and Counsel Records, Center for Mennonite Brethren Studies, Fresno, Calif., 77.

24. Ibid.

25. John A. Toews, *A History of the Mennonite Brethren Church*, 53-57, 366-68.

26. John H. Lohrenz, *The Mennonite Brethren Church* (Hillsboro, Kans.: Board of Foreign Missions, 1950), 138, 154, 184.

27. J. F. Harms, *Geschichte der Mennoniten Brüdergemeinde* (Hillsboro, Kans.: Mennonite Brethren Publishing House, 1924), 329-38.

28. *Confession of Faith of the Mennonite Brethren Church of North America, American Edition* (Hillsboro, Kans.: Mennonite Brethren Publishing House, 1917).

29. P. H. Berg, ed., *Resolutions of the Conference of Mennonite Brethren Churches of North America* (Hillsboro, Kans.: Mennonite Brethren Publishing House, 1948), 12.

30. Ibid., 9.

31. Ibid., 12.

32. Gerhard William Peters, *The Growth of Foreign Missions in the Mennonite Brethren Church* (Hillsboro, Kans.: Mennonite Brethren Publishing House, 1947), 73-80.

# CHAPTER 11

1. Peter M. Friesen, *The Mennonite Brotherhood in Russia (1789-1910)* [*Alt-Evangelische Mennonitische Brüderschaft in Russland (1789-1910)*], trans. J. B. Toews, Abraham Friesen, Peter J. Klassen and Harry Loewen (Fresno, Calif.: Board of Christian Literature, General Conference of Mennonite Brethren Churches, 1978), 978.

2. Cornelius J. Dyck, "A Comparison of Anabaptist and Mennonite Brethren Origins," in *Pilgrims and Strangers: Essays in Mennonite Brethren History*, ed. Paul Toews (Fresno, Calif.: Center for Mennonite Brethren Studies, Mennonite Brethren Biblical Seminary, 1977), 56-73.

3. John A. Toews, *A History of the Mennonite Brethren Church: Pilgrims and Pioneers* (Fresno, Calif.: Board of Christian Literature, General Conference of Mennonite Brethren Churches, 1975), 362-66.

4. Friesen, *The Mennonite Brotherhood in Russia*, 93-95.

5. John B. Toews, "The Early Mennonite Brethren: Some Outside Views," *Mennonite Quarterly Review* 58 (1984): 83-124.

6. Friesen, *The Mennonite Brotherhood in Russia*, 92-109.

7. Ibid., 234.

8. Ibid., 921-22.

9. John B. Toews, "Mennonite Brethren in the Larger Mennonite World," *Menno-

nite Quarterly Review 57 (1983): 260-62.

10. Friesen, The Mennonite Brotherhood in Russia, 212.

11. Cornelius Krahn, "Russia," in *The Mennonite Encyclopedia*, eds. Harold S. Bender and C. Henry Smith (Scottdale, Pa.: Mennonite Publishing House, 1959), 390.

12. J.H. Lohrenz, *The Mennonite Brethren Church* (Hillsboro, Kans.: Board of Foreign Missions, 1950), 138, 154, 166, 184.

## CHAPTER 12

1. John B. Toews, *Czars, Soviets and Mennonites* (Newton, Kans.: Faith and Life Press, 1982), vii. The background given in the preface and chapters 1 and 2 provide an overview essential for the understanding of the setting in which the Mennonite Brethren Church found itself in the first decades of the twentieth century.

2. Ibid., vii.

3. Adolf Ehrt, *Das Mennonitentum in Russland: von seiner Einwanderung bis zur Gegenwart* (Berlin: Julius Beltz, 1932), 112 ff. See also Ernst Crous, "Nonresistance," *The Mennonite Encyclopedia*, eds. Harold S. Bender and C. Henry Smith (Scottdale, Pa.: Mennonite Publishing House, 1957), 901.

4. Toews, *Czars, Soviets and Mennonites*, 79-106; Abram Kroeker, *Meine Flucht* (Striegau: Theodor Urban, 1931); Abram Kroeker, *Bilder aus Soviet Russland* (Hillsboro, Kans.: Mennonite Brethren Publishing House, 1922); Peter Arshinov, *History of the Makhnovist Movement, 1918-1921*, trans. Lorraine and Fredy Perlman (Detroit: Black and Red, 1974); Ehrt, *Das Mennonitentum in Russland*, 106-163; Dietrich Neufeld, *A Russian Dance of Death* [*Ein Tagebuch aus dem Reiche des Totentanzes*], trans. A. Reimer (Winnipeg, Man.: Hyperion Press, 1977).

5. Toews, *Czars, Soviets and Mennonites*, 80-83.

6. John B. Toews, ed., *Mennonites in Russia from 1917-1930: Selected Documents* (Winnipeg, Man.: Christian Press, 1975), 404-27.

7. Ibid., 416.

8. Ibid.

9. B.B. Janz, "Grundzuege im Charakter der Glaubensstellung unserer Vaeter," paper presented at the Board of Reference and Counsel Study Conference, 12-15 December 1956, General Conference of Mennonite Brethren Churches Board of Reference and Counsel Records, Center for Mennonite Brethren Studies, Fresno, Calif., 75.

10. Toews, *Czars, Soviets and Mennonites*, 95-106.

11. Quoted in C. Henry Smith, *Smith's Story of the Mennonites*, ed. Cornelius Krahn, 5th ed. (Newton, Kans.: Faith and Life Press, 1981), 314.

12. Toews, *Czars, Soviets and Mennonites*, 110.

13. Smith, *Smith's Story of the Mennonites*, 315.

14. J.G. Rempel, "Machno, Nestor," *The Mennonite Encyclopedia*, 430-31; Frank H. Epp, *Mennonite Exodus: The Rescue and Resettlement of the Russian Mennonites Since the Communist Revolution* (Altona, Man.: D.W. Friesen and Sons, 1962), 28-38.

15. P.C. Hiebert and Orie O. Miller, *Feeding the Hungry: Russian Famine, 1919-*

*1925* (Scottdale, Pa.: Mennonite Central Committee, 1929); D. M. Hofer, *Die Hungersnot in Russland und unsere Reise um die Welt* (Chicago: K. M. B. Publishing House, 1924).

16. Hofer, *Die Hungersnot in Russland*, 69.

17. Dietrich Heinrich Doerksen and Peter John Kornelsen, "An unsere Mennoniten Geschwister in America!," *Der Wahrheitsfreund*, 6 June 1923, 9-12.

18. Ibid.

19. Jakob Abr. Loewen, "Nachklang von dem Erweckungsversammlungen im Dorfe Lindenau, Russland," *Der Wahrheitsfreund*, 11 July 1923, 9-12.

20. I.G. Neufeld and Hans Kasdorf, "Revival Among Mennonites in Russia: 1921-1925," photocopy, 1983, 12. Doerksen was our neighbor in my home village of Alexanderthal. The renewal he described affected my own life as a high school student. See also Gerhard Hein, "Russland," in *Mennonitisches Lexicon*, eds. Christian Hege, et al. (Karlsruhe: Heinrich Sneider, 1958), 578; Ehrt, *Das Mennonitentum in Russland*, 114.

21. J.W. Reimer, "Aus unserem Gemeindeleben," *Der Bote*, 21 Oct. 1925, 5.

22. Ehrt, *Das Mennonitentum in Russland*, 145.

23. B.B. Janz, "Grundzuege im Charakter der Glaubensstellung unserer Vaeter."

24. John A. Toews, *A History of the Mennonite Brethren Church: Pilgrims and Pioneers* (Fresno, Calif.: Board of Christian Literature, General Conference of Mennonite Brethren Churches, 1975), 115-18.

25. A. H. Unruh, *Die Geschichte der Mennoniten Brüdergemeinde* (Hillsboro, Kans.: General Conference of the Mennonite Brethren Church of North America, 1955), 349-74.

26. Epp, *Mennonite Exodus*, 3-182.

27. Heinrich J. Willems and C. C. Peters, *Vor den Toren Moskaus, oder Gottes Gnaedige Durchhilfe in einer schweren Zeit* (Yarrow, B. C.: Komitee der Flüchtlinge, 1960). See also Henry P. Isaak, *Our Life Story and Escape: From Russia to China to Japan and to America* (Fresno, Calif.: By the Author, 1976).

28. Cornelius Krahn, "Russia," *Mennonite Encyclopedia*, 390-91.

29. Ehrt, *Das Mennonitentum in Russland*, 141-46.

30. See Editorial, "Welche Stunde ist's jetzt auf der Weltenuhr?" *Unser Blatt*, Feb. 1926, 82-83; Peter Dück, "Warum ich an Gott glaube und an der Religion festhalte," *Unser Blatt*, Jan. 1926, 59-62; Johann Wiebe, "Referat über Disziplin in den Mennonitischen Gemeinden," *Unser Blatt*, Feb. 1926, 100-102; Gerhard Kopper, "Die Hebung des geistlichen Zustandes in der Gemeinde," *Unser Blatt*, Dec. 1925, 47-48; Heinrich Voth, "Die Christliche Ehe," *Unser Blatt*, Dec. 1925, 68-69; Ehrt, *Das Mennonitentum in Russland*, 146.

31. Aron A. Töws, *Mennonitische Märtyrer: der jüngsten Vergangenheit und der Gegenwart*, 2 vols. (Clearbrook, B. C.: A. A. Töws, 1949-1954).

32. Information on the events and circumstances that befell the Mennonites are recorded in the following: Toews, *Czars, Soviets and Mennonites*; Unruh, *Die Geschichte der Mennoniten Brüdergemeinde*.

33. Heinrich Woelk and Gerhard Woelk, *A Wilderness Journey: Glimpses of the Mennonite Brethren Church in Russia, 1925-1980* [*Die Mennoniten Brüdergemeinde im Russland 1925-1980*], trans. Victor Doerksen (Fresno, Calif.: Center for Mennonite Brethren Studies, 1982).

34. Gerhard Woelk, "Erhaltung des Geistliches Leben in der Zeit der aufgeloesten Gemeinden," manuscript in posession of author.

35. Heinrich Woelk and Gerhard Woelk, *A Wilderness Journey*, 71-72.

36. Ibid.

37. Ibid., 70-71.

38. Ibid., 101-02.

39. Toews, *A History of the Mennonite Brethren Church*, 125.

40. Quoted in Ibid., 125-26.

41. Ibid.

42. Heinrich Woelk and Gerhard Woelk, *A Wilderness Journey*, 133.

43. I was among the group of visitors to whom this statement by Secretary Bychkov was addressed.

# CHAPTER 13

1. Frank H. Epp, *Mennonites in Canada, 1920-1940: A People's Struggle for Survival* (Scottdale, Pa.: Herald Press, 1982).

2. Adolf Ehrt, *Das Mennonitentum in Russland von seiner Einwanderung bis zur Gegenwart* (Berlin: Julius Beltz, 1932). This book describes the struggles for survival of the Mennonites in Russia in the post-revolution era.

3. Quoted in John A. Toews, *A History of the Mennonite Brethren Church: Pilgrims and Pioneers* (Fresno, Calif.: Board of Christian Literature, General Conference of Mennonite Brethren Churches, 1975), 120. On the 1920s migration consult the following: Frank H. Epp, *Mennonite Exodus: The Rescue and Resettlement of the Russian Mennonites since the Communist Revolution* (Altona, Man.: D.W. Friesen and Sons, 1962); Frank H. Epp, *Mennonites in Canada, 1920-1940: A Peoples Struggle for Survival* (Scottdale, Pa.: Herald Press, 1982); E.K. Francis, *In Search of Utopia: The Mennonites in Manitoba* (Altona, Man.: D.W. Friesen and Sons, 1955); John B. Toews, *Lost Fatherland: The Story of the Mennonite Emigration from Soviet Russia, 1921-1927* (Scottdale, Pa.: Herald Press, 1967).

4. Toews, *A History of the Mennonite Brethren Church*, 116.

5. *Verhandlungen der fünfzehnten Nördlichen Distrikt Konferenz der Mennoniten Brüdergemeinde von Nord Amerika in der Gemeinde zu Winkler, Manitoba, vom 28. Juni bis zum 2. Juli, 1924*, 37; *Verhandlungen der 25. Nördlichen Distrikt Konferenz der Mennoniten Brüdergemeinde von Nord Amerika abgehalten von 30. Juni bis zum 4. Juli 1934, zu Winkler Manitoba*, 79-87; *Verhandlungen der 35. Nördlichen Distrikt Konferenz der Mennoniten Brüdergemeinde von Nord Amerika, abgehalten in Yarrow, B.C., von 16. bis zum 21. Juni 1945*, 147-58.

6. Cornelius Krahn, ed., *From the Steppes to the Prairies: 1874-1949* (Newton, Kans.: Mennonite Publication Office, 1949), 8.

7. John H. Lohrenz, *The Mennonite Brethren Church* (Hillsboro, Kans.: Board of Foreign Missions of the Conference of the Mennonite Brethren Church of North America, 1950), 62.

8. Francis, *In Search of Utopia*, 194-98.

9. Ibid.

10. Ibid., 212.

11. Epp, *Mennonites in Canada 1920-1940*, 245.

12. Ibid., 139-226.

13. Toews, *A History of the Mennonite Brethren Church*, 164.

14. *Verhandlungen der fünfzehnten Nördlichen Distrikt Konferenz, 1924, 38; Verhandlungen der 35. Nördlichen Distrikt Konferenz*, 1945, 147-58.

15. *Verhandlungen der 34. Nördlichen Distrikt Konferenz der Mennoniten Brüdergemeinden von Nord Amerika, abgehalten zu Coaldale, Alberta, vom 8. bis zum 12. Juli 1944*, 83.

16. *Year Book of the 43rd General Conference of the Mennonite Brethren Church of North America held at Dinuba, California, November 24-29 1945*, 125.

17. The first candidate from the Russländer was A. A. Unruh who married Annie Elias, from a prominent Kanadier family in Winkler, Manitoba.

18. Frank C. Peters, ed., *Beschlüsse und Empfehlungen der Kanadischen Konferenz der Mennoniten Brüdergemeinde: 1910-1960* (Winnipeg, Man.: Kanadischen Konferenz der Mennoniten Brüdergemeinde, 1961), 65-68.

19. Ibid., 92-97, 102, 106-07.

20. Ibid., 130, 135, 167, 209.

21. Ibid., 168, 227-30, 234-40.

22. J. P. Braun, "Die Gemeinde in der Vollendung," *Verhandlungen der 27. Nördlichen Distrikt Konferenz der Mennoniten Brüdergemeinde von Nord Amerika abgehalten vom 4. bis zum 8. Juli 1936, zu Waldheim, Saskatchewan*, 83-93; Heinrich Regehr, "Der Modernismus," *Verhandlungen*, 1936, 3-6; John G. Wiens, "Diedungensünden und ihre Einwirkung auf das Gemeindeleben," *Verhandlungen*, 1936, 27-32.

23. Epp, *Mennonites in Canada: 1920-1940*, 401-10.

24. J. B. Toews, "Mennonite Brethren in the Larger Mennonite World," *Mennonite Quarterly Review* 57 (1983): 257-64.

25. J. F. Harms, *Geschichte der Mennoniten Brüdergemeinde* (Hillsboro, Kans.: Mennonite Brethren Publishing House, 1925), 78-80.

26. Cornelius Krahn, "Wedel, Cornelius Heinrich," in *The Mennonite Encyclopedia*, eds. Harold S. Bender and C. Henry Smith (Scottdale, Pa.: Mennonite Publishing House, 1959), 907-08; J. H. Lohrenz, "Wedel, Peter H.," *Mennonite Encyclopedia*, 908.

27. Toews, A History of the Mennonite Brethren Church, 154-55.

28. Harold S. Bender, "Revival Meetings," Mennonite Encyclopedia, 312-13.

29. For revivals among Mennonites consult: A. J. Klassen, ed., *Revival Fires in British Columbia* (Denbigh, Va.: Brunk Revivals Inc., 1958); Frank H. Epp, ed., *Revival Fires in Manitoba* (Denbigh, Va.: Brunk Revivals, Inc., 1957); Katie Florence Shank, *Revival Fires* (Broadway, Va.: By the Author, 1952).

30. J. Howard Kauffman and Leland Harder, *Anabaptists Four Centuries Later: A Profile of Five Mennonite and Brethren in Christ Denominations* (Scottdale, Pa.: Herald Press, 1975), 247.

31. Samuel Floyd Pannabecker, *Open Doors: A History of the General Conference Mennonite Church* (Newton, Kans.: Faith and Life Press, 1975), 382-88.

32. *Minutes of the Annual Convention of the British Columbia Conference of the Mennonite Brethren Churches June 8-9, 1979,* 10-12.

33. Walter Unger, "Mennonite Brethren and General Conference Theology—A Common Center, A Single Foundation," paper presented at the symposium "Inter-Mennonite Relations: M. B.'s and G. C.'s in Canada, 4-5 Nov., 1983, Centre for Mennonite Brethren Studies (Winnipeg) Records, Center for Mennonite Brethren Studies, Fresno, Calif.

34. Katie Funk Wiebe, *Who Are the Mennonite Brethren?* (Winnipeg, Man.: Kindred Press, 1984).

35. James C. Juhnke, review of *Who Are the Mennonite Brethren?*, by Katie Funk Wiebe, in *Direction* 15, no. 2 (1986): 78.

36. Quoted in Lesslie Newbigin, "Religious Pluralism and the Uniqueness of Jesus Christ," *International Bulletin of Missionary Research* 13, no. 2 (1989): 50.

37. Quoted in John Redekop, "An Agenda for the '90s," *The Christian Leader*, 16 Jan. 1990, 9.

38. Toews, *A History of the Mennonite Brethren Church*, 216-38.

39. Anna J. Thiessen, *Die Stadtmission in Winnipeg* (Winnipeg, Man.: By the Author, 1955), 48-108.

# CHAPTER 14

1. Frank C. Peters, "Monuments of Early Mennonite Brethren Teaching," *The Voice* 9, no. 3 (1960): 14-17.

2. A. E. Janzen and Herbert Giesbrecht, comps., *We Recommend: Recommendations and Resolutions of the General Conference of the Mennonite Brethren Churches* (Fresno, Calif.: Board of Christian Literature of the General Conference of Mennonite Brethren Churches, 1978), 42-61; John A. Toews, *A History of the Mennonite Brethren Church: Pilgrims and Pioneers* (Fresno, Calif.: Board of Christian Literature, General Conference of Mennonite Brethren Churches, 1975), 216-38.

3. Vernon R. Wiebe, *A History of the Corn Bible Academy: 1902-1977* (Hillsboro, Kans.: By the Author, 1977).

4. "Bruderberatung abgehalten im Versammlungshaus in Carson den 16. Dezember der 1902," Carson Mennonite Brethren Church Records, Center for Mennonite Brethren Studies, Fresno, Calif.

5. Frank C. Peters, "The Coming of the Mennonite Brethren to the United States

and their Efforts in Education" (Th.D diss., Central Baptist Theological Seminary, 1957), 1966-70.

6. Quoted in Paul Toews, "Henry W. Lohrenz and Tabor College," *Mennonite Life* 38, no. 3 (1983): 14.

7. Ibid., 14-15.

8. Minutes of the Meeting of Bible School Teachers on August 8-10, 1941, Centre for Mennonite Brethren Studies, Winnipeg, Man.

9. Statuten des Schulvereins, Coaldale 1944, Centre for Mennonite Brethren Studies, Winnipeg, Man.

10. Prospectus of the Mennonite Collegiate Institute 1954-1956, Centre for Mennonite Brethren Studies, Winnipeg, Man.

11. Eden Christian College Prospectus 1965, Centre for Mennonite Brethren Studies, Winnipeg, Man.

12. John H. Redekop, "Mennonite Brethren Schools in Canada," October 1975, Centre for Mennonite Brethren Studies, Winnipeg, Man.

13. Ibid.

14. Ibid., 10.

15. *Konferenzbeschlüsse nebst Konstitution der Mennoniten Brüdergemeinde von Nord Amerika*, (Hillsboro, Kans.: Mennonite Brethren Publishing House, 1920), 439.

16. Ibid., 440.

17. *Verhandlungen der 23. Nördlichen Distrikt Konferenz der Mennoniten Brüdergemeinden von Nord Amerika vom 2. bis zum 5. Juli, 1932*, 48-49.

18. H. W. Lohrenz, "Early Aims of Tabor College," Tabor College Records, Center for Mennonite Brethren Studies, Hillsboro, Kans.

19. *Verhandlungen der 27. Nördlichen Distrikt Konferenz der Mennoniten Brüdergemeinden von Nord Amerika, abgehalten vom 4. bis zum 8. Juli 1936, zu Waldheim, Saskatchewan*, 45.

20. *Verhandlungen der 40. General Konferenz der Mennoniten Brüdergemeinde von Nord Amerika abgehalten vom 21. bis zum 26. November in der Mennoniten Brüdergemeinde zu Reedley, California*, 40.

21. Robert Friedmann, *The Theology of Anabaptism: An Interpretation* (Scottdale, Pa.: Herald Press, 1973), 27-29.

22. see William Vance Trollinger Jr., "The Rileys Empire: Northwest Bible School and Fundamentalism in the Upper Midwest," *Church History* 57 (1988): 197-212. This article particularly provides context for the discussions about higher education in the midwest where many MB people linked to Tabor were affected by fundamentalism.

23. Rachel Hiebert, interview with author, n.d. Mrs. Hiebert was librarian at Tabor College from 1942-1945.

24. I participated in the discussions with the founders of Pacific Bible Institute.

25. Pacific Bible Institute, *Catalog: 1945-46*, 1.

26. Fresno Pacific College, *Catalog: 1969-70*, 9.

27. Paul Toews, "From Pietism to Secularism via Anabaptism: An informal history of the changing ideals and relationships between Fresno Pacific College and the Mennonite Brethren Church," Center for Mennonite Brethren Studies, Fresno, Calif.

28. Ibid., 9.

29. Delbert Wiens, "From the Village to the City," *Direction* 2, no. 4 (Oct. 1973 and Jan. 1974): 98-149.

30. Paul Toews, "From Pietism to Secularism via Anabaptism," 9.

31. Ibid., 10.

32. Ibid.

33. Edmund Janzen, "Broadening the Base," Fresno Pacific College President's Records, Center for Mennonite Brethren Studies, Fresno, Calif., 1-12.

34. Fresno Pacific College, *Catalog: 1983-84*, 5.

35. Paul Toews, "From Pietism to Secularism via Anabaptism," 11-12.

36. M. G. Neale, "Report to the Board of Education of the General Conference of the Mennonite Brethren Church of North America on a program of higher education for the Mennonite Brethren Church of North America," Board of Education Minutes, 8 Feb., 1955, Mennonite Brethren Church of the United States Board of Education Records, Center for Mennonite Brethren Studies, Fresno, Calif., 22-27.

37. *Minutes and Reports of the Seventh Convention of the Mennonite Brethren Church of the United States Convening at Mountain Lake, Minnesota, July 31-August 1, 1963*, 36-37.

38. Christian Service Fellowship Report to the Mennonite Brethren Board of Education, 21-23 Aug., 1968, Minutes of the Board of Directors, Mennonite Brethren Church of the United States Board of Education Records, Center for Mennonite Brethren Studies, Fresno, Calif., 244.

39. Ibid., 254.

40. Friedmann, *The Theology of Anabaptism*, 30-31.

41. Augustus H. Strong, *Systematic Theology* 3 vols (Philadelphia: Judson Press, 1907-09); Edgar Y. Mullins, *The Christian Religion in its Doctrinal Expression* (Philadelphia: Judson Press, 1932).

42. Daniel Kauffman, ed., *Doctrines of the Bible* 2nd. ed. ( Scottdale, Pa.: Mennonite Publishing House, 1949).

43. William Evans, *Great Doctrines of the Bible* (Chicago: Moody Press, 1939); R. A. Torrey, *What the Bible Teaches: A Thorough and Comprehensive Study of All the Bible Has to Say Concerning the Great Doctrines of Which it Treats* (Chicago: Fleming H. Revell Company, 1898).

44. John C. Wenger, *Introduction to Theology* (Scottdale, Pa.: Herald Press, 1951).

45. Harold S. Bender, *These are My People: The Nature of the Church and its Discipleship according to the New Testament* (Scottdale, Pa.: Herald Press, 1962).

46. A. J. Dueck, "The Changing Role of Biblical/Theological Education in the Mennonite Brethren Church," in *The Bible and the Church: Essays in Honour of Dr.*

*David Ewert*, eds. A. J. Dueck, H. J. Giesbrecht and V. G. Shillington (Winnipeg, Man.: Kindred Press, 1988), 132-48.

47. *76th Convention, The Canadian Conference of Mennonite Brethren Churches, Three Hills, Alberta, July 3-6 1987*, 13-14.

48. Mennonite Brethren Biblical Seminary, *Catalog: 1957*, 4.

49. James DeFrost, *March, Teach or Perish: An Imperative for Christian Education at the Local Church Level* (Grand Rapids, Mich.: Eerdmans, 1961).

# CHAPTER 15

1. John A. Toews, *A History of the Mennonite Brethren Church: Pilgrims and Pioneers* (Fresno, Calif.: Board of Christian Literature, General Conference of Mennonite Brethren Churches, 1975), 26-29.

2. Peter M. Friesen, *The Mennonite Brotherhood in Russia (1789-1910)* [*Alt-Evangelische Mennonitische Brüderschaft in Russland (1789-1910)*], trans. J. B. Toews, Abraham Friesen, Peter J. Klassen and Harry Loewen (Fresno, Calif.: Board of Christian Literature, General Conference of Mennonite Brethren Churches, 1978), 189-92; Abram Klassen, "Mennonite Brethren Confessions of Faith: Historic Roots and Comparative Analysis" (S.T.M. diss., Union College of British Columbia, 1965), 133-35.

3. Cited in Jacob P. Bekker, *Origin of the Mennonite Brethren Church*, trans. D. E. Pauls and A E. Janzen (Hillsboro, Kans.: Mennonite Brethren Historical Society of the Midwest, 1973), 121.

4. Wesley Prieb, "The Prospect of the Future," in *A Century of Grace and Witness, 1860-1960*, ed. Walter Wiebe (Hillsboro, Kans.: Mennonite Brethren Publishing House, 1961), 78.

5. Theron F. Schlabach, "Mennonites and Pietism in America, 1740-1880," *Mennonite Quarterly Review* 57 (1983): 222-39.

6. Paul Toews, "Fundamentalist Conflict in Mennonite Colleges: A Response to Cultural Transitions?" *Mennonite Quarterly Review* 57 (1983): 241-56.

7. Chapter 10 provides the analysis of this phenomena. A doctoral dissertation under preparation by Gerry Ediger of Concord College in Winnipeg is a major study to interpret this chapter of history of the Mennonite Brethren movement.

8. The term "lay ministry" in this context is not to imply an untrained ministry. The competence of many of the leaders and ministers of Mennonite Brethren Churches were well trained as described in Chapter 5.

9. John A. Toews, *A History of the Mennonite Brethren Church*, 255-65.

10. I purchased the full series of Harrison's writings for my library.

11. John Waltner, "Gerald B. Winrod, Deluded Defender of Faith," *Mennonite Life* 24 (January 1969): 30-33. Waltner's analysis provides insight into the theological perception governing the content and influence of the *Defender Magazine*.

12. B. B. Janz, "Grundzuege im Charakter der Glaubensstellung unserer Vaeter," paper presented at the Board of Reference and Counsel Study Conference, 12-15 December 1956, General Conference of Mennonite Brethren Churches Board of Reference and Counsel Records, Center for Mennonite Brethren Studies, Fresno, Calif., 5.

13. Anna Redekop, "Life Story of William Bestvater," photocopy, n.d., 12-14.

14. *Verhandlungen der elften Nördlichen Distrikt Konferenz der Mennoniten Brüdergemeinden von Nord Amerika abgehalten in der Gemeinde Gnadenau, zu Morse, Sask. von 3. bis zum 7. Juli, 1920*, 20.

15. William J. Bestvater, *Textbüchlein in Glaubenslehre für die Herbert Bibelschule* (Regina, Sask.: Courier Press, n.d.); William J. Bestvater, *Textbüchlein in Bibelkunde fur Deutsche Bibelschulen* (Regina, Sask.: Courier Press, n.d.).

16. D. Theodor Haarbeck, *Kurzgefasste Biblische Glaubenslehre fur Nachdenkende Christen*, 8th ed. (Elberfeld, Germany: Evangelischen Gesellschaft für Deutschland, 1922); D. Theodor Haarbeck, *Der Dienst am Evangelism in Predigt und Seelsorge* (Elberfeld, Germany: Evangelischen Gesellschaft für Deutschland, n.d.); D. Theodor Haarbeck, *Das Christliche Leben nach der Schrift* (Giessen u. Basel: Brunnen Verlag, 1922); Giesbert Stochmann, *Ringet Recht* (Schwerin, Macklburg: Friedrich Bahn, 1926).

17. *Confession of Faith of the Mennonite Brethren Church of North America, American Edition*, (Hillsboro, Kans.: Mennonite Brethren Publishing House, 1917), 47.

18. *Minutes of the June Convention of the British Columbia Conference of the Mennonite Brethren Churches, June 11-12, 1971*, 6.

19. A.H. Unruh, "Grundzuege der Theologie der Vaeter der M. B. Gemeinde," paper presented at the Board of Reference and Counsel Study Conference, 12-15 December 1956, General Conference of Mennonite Brethren Churches Board of Reference and Counsel Records, Center for Mennonite Brethren Studies, Fresno, Calif., 22.

20. Ibid., 39.

21. *Confession of Faith of the General Conference of Mennonite Brethren Churches* (Hillsboro, Kans.: Board of Christian Literature, General Conference of Mennonite Brethren Churches, 1976), 11-12.

22. Minutes of the General Conference of the Mennonite Brethren Churches 1878-1882, General Conference of Mennonite Brethren Churches Conference Records, Center for Mennonite Brethren Studies, Fresno, Calif., 2.

23. Friesen, *The Mennonite Brotherhood in Russia*, 230-32.

24. *Confession of Faith* (1976), 12-13.

25. Ibid., 13-14.

26. H. F. Toews, "Erlaubt und Unerlaubt," *Zionsbote*, 9 Aug. 1922, 3; P. E. Penner, "Wer ist ein Bibelchrist," *Zionsbote*, 11 Nov. 1925, 2.

27. J.A. Toews, "The Anabaptist Involvement in Missions," in *The Church in Mission: A Sixtieth Anniversary Tribute to J.B. Toews*, ed. A.J. Klassen (Fresno, Calif.: Board of Christian Literature, Mennonite Brethren Church, 1967), 89.

# CHAPTER 16

1. David McCullough, "Extraordinary Times: Living in an Era of Breakneck Change," *Life* (Fall, 1986): 189.

2. Ibid., 192.

3. Ibid.

4. Ibid.

5. Ibid.

6. Allan Bloom, *The Closing of the American Mind* (New York: Simon and Schuster, 1987), 29-30.

7. Alasdair MacIntyre, *After Virtue: A Study in Moral Theory* (Notre Dame: Notre Dame University Press, 1981), 195.

8. Richard Reeves, *American Journey: Traveling with Tocqueville in Search of Democracy* (New York: Simon and Schuster, 1982), 203.

9. Bloom, *The Closing of the American Mind*, 337.

10. Robert Bellah, *Habits of the Heart: Individualism and Commitment in America* (Berkeley: University of California Press, 1985), 128-130.

11. Bloom, *The Closing of the American Mind*, 47-61, 82-137.

12. Henry J. Schmidt, "The Urban Ethos: Building Churches in a Pagan Environment," *Mission Focus* 8 (1980): 27.

13. Quoted in Ibid.

14. Ibid.

15. Ibid., 28.

16. Peter M. Friesen, *The Mennonite Brotherhood in Russia (1789-1910)* [*Alt-Evangelische Mennonitische Brüderschaft in Russland* (1789-1910)], trans. J. B. Toews, Abraham Friesen, Peter J. Klassen and Harry Loewen (Fresno, Calif.: Board of Christian Literature, General Conference of Mennonite Brethren Churches, 1978), 276, 325-26.

17. J. A. Toews, "Christian Encounter with Culture," *Mennonite Brethren Herald*, 22 Feb. 1974, 2-3.

18. Calvin Redekop, "The Embarrassment of a Religious Tradition," *Mennonite Life* 36 (1981): 17-21.

19. Calvin Redekop, "Religious Renewal Movements in Search of the Past," photocopy, n.d.

20. *Year Book of the 44th General Conference of the Mennonite Brethren Church of North America held at Mountain Lake, Minnesota August 28 to September 2, 1948*, 106-08.

21. "General Conference Vision Goals: Probable Future," Board of Reference and Counsel Minutes 15-17 October 1986, General Conference of Mennonite Brethren Churches Board of Reference and Counsel Records, Center for Mennonite Brethren Studies, Fresno, Calif.

22. Redekop, "Religious Renewal Movements in Search of the Past."

23. J. A. Toews, "In Search of Identity," *Mennonite Brethren Herald*, 3 March 1972, 3.

24. Redekop, "Religious Renewal Movements," 4.

ENDNOTES *pages 217-227*

# CHAPTER 17

1. The section on polity draws heavily on a presentation by John E. Toews to the New Pastor's Orientation sponsored by the General Conference Board of Faith and Life, Fresno, Calif., 20-23 January 1991.

2. Herman Enns, "Forms of Ministry," in *Call to Faithfulness: Essays in Canadian Mennonite Studies,* Henry Poettcker and Rudy A. Regehr, eds. (Winnipeg Man.: Canadian Mennonite Bible College, 1982), 93-102; Rodney J. Sawatsky, "Autonomy and Accountability: Church Polity within the Conference of Mennonites in Canada," *Mennonite Reporter,* 19 September 1983, 1-4.

3. *Constitution and By-laws of the Conference of the Mennonite Brethren Churches, officially adopted at the 55th Session of the Conference August 7-11, 1981, St. Catharines, Ontario,* 15.

4. Ibid.

5. Ibid., 23.

6. *Year Book of the 44th General Conference of the Mennonite Brethren Church of North America held at Mountain Lake, Minnesota August 28 to September 2, 1948,* 106-08; *Year Book of the 45th General Conference of the Mennonite Brethren Church of North America held at Winkler, Manitoba July 21 to 26, 1951,* 130-43; *Yearbook, 52nd Session, of the General Conference of Mennonite Brethren Churches Convening at Reedley, California November 11-14, 1972,* 14; Victor Adrian, "The Call and Ordination to the Ministry," John E. Toews, "Leadership Styles for Mennonite Brethren Churches," Herbert Brandt, "Church-Pastor Relations," all papers presented at the Conference, "Current Issues in Church Leadership," 8-10 May 1980, General Conference of Mennonite Brethren Churches Board of Reference and Counsel Records, Center for Mennonite Brethren Studies, Fresno, Calif.; *Yearbook of the 74th Pacific District Conference of Mennonite Brethren Churches, San Jose, California November 10-13, 1983,* 18-22.

7. In Russia, the larger churches such as Rückenau, Alexanderthal and Tiege and in North America, Reedley, Coaldale, Yarrow and Hillsboro, functioned with an executive of the Board of Elders.

8. A survey of leadership patterns in Mennonite Brethren churches for the last two decades records an average of three to four years for a complete turnover in church council membership, including the pastor. Questionnaires were sent to all the churches to determine pastoral and church council tenure. A second survey tested these findings with district and provincial conference records.

9. *Year Book, 1951,* 127.

10. *Year Book, 1951,* 127-30.

11. Ibid., 129-30.

12. Ibid., 130-31.

13. Ibid., 134-44.

14. Matt Hannan, "Hope for Plateaued Churches and their Renewal," lecture at Mennonite Brethren Biblical Seminary, 27 April 1990.

15. Ibid.

16. John Schwane, letter to the editor, *Christianity Today,* 9 April 1990, 7.

17. *Fresno Bee* 23 April 1991, A8-9.

18. Gerry Ediger, "The Mennonite Brethren Church as a Covenant Community," paper presented at the Conference, "The Mennonite Brethren Church as a Covenant Community," 15-17 October 1986, General Conference of Mennonite Brethren Churches Board of Reference and Counsel Records, Center for Mennonite Brethren Studies, Fresno, Calif., 46-47.

19. *Confession of Faith of the Mennonite Brethren Church of North America, American Edition*, (Hillsboro, Kans.: Mennonite Brethren Publishing House, 1917), 16-17.

20. *Year Book, 52nd Session of the General Conference of Mennonite Brethren Churches convening at Reedley, California November 11-14, 1972*, 13-14;

21. *Year Book, 55th Session of the General Conference of Mennonite Brethren Churches August 7-11, 1981, St. Catharines, Ontario*, 13.

22. This information is based on a survey of articles in *The Christian Leader* and *Mennonite Brethren Herald*. The subject cards used for the survey are in my possession.

23. Board of Reference and Counsel Study Conferences: "Study Conference on the Ministry," 5-6 March 1970, Buhler, Kans.; "Current Issues in Church Leadership," 8-10 May 1980, Clearbrook, B. C.; "The Mennonite Brethren Church as a Covenant Community," 15-17 October 1986, Fresno, Calif.

24. *Pacific District Conference Yearbook, 1983*, 21-22.

25. Paul G. Hiebert, "Banyan Trees and Banana Trees," *Mennonite Brethren Herald*, 9 March 1990, 9.

# CHAPTER 18

1. John A. Toews, *A History of the Mennonite Brethren Church: Pilgrims and Pioneers* (Fresno, Calif.: Board of Christian Literature, General Conference of Mennonite Brethren Churches, 1975), 76.

2. *Verhandlungen der dreissigsten Bundes-Konferenz der Mennoniten Brüdergemeinde von Nord Amerika abgehalten in der Gemeinde, Süd-hoffnungsfeld, bei Isabella, Oklahoma, am 9. 10. u. 11. November, 1908*, 47. See also other annual conference yearbooks, 1883-1912, under the headings "Reiseprediger."

3. *Verhandlungen, 1908*, 46; The churches in Eldorado, Sutton and Culbertson, Nebraska; V*erhandlungen der zweiunddreissigsten Bundes-Konferenz der Mennoniten Brüdergemeinde von Nord Amerika*, 68; The churches in Harvey, McClusky and Dogden, North Dakota.

4. Toews, *A History of the Mennonite Brethren Church*, 315.

5. *Year Book of the 39th Pacific District Conference of the Mennonite Brethren Church of North America Held at Bakersfield, California, October 23 to 27, 1948*, 11.

6. *Protocoll No. 25 der Provinzialen Konferenz der Mennoniten Brüdergemeinde von Manitoba abgehalten den 5. und 6. Juni 1959 in der Kirche der Süd End Mennoniten Brüdergemeinde, Winnipeg, Manitoba*, 12-13.

7. *Year Book of the 44th Pacific District Conference of the Mennonite Brethren Church of North America held at the Reedley, Calif., Mennonite Brethren Church No-*

vember 14-18, 1953, 54. The theological implications of this "child evangelism" emphasis awaits further analysis.

8. George W. Webber, *Today's Church: A Community of Exiles and Pilgrims* (Nashville: Abingdon Press, 1979), 33.

9. C. E. Autrey, *Revivals of the Old Testament* (Grand Rapids, Mich.: Zondervan Publishing House, 1960); James Burns, *Revivals, Their Laws and Leaders* (Grand Rapids, Mich.: Baker Book House, 1960); J. Edwin Orr, *The Light of the Nations: Evangelical Renewal and Advance in the Nineteenth Century* (Grand Rapids, Mich.: Wm. B. Eerdmans Publishing Company, 1965).

10. While Mennonite Brethren evangelism was centered locally, certain leaders were nonetheless endowed with special evangelistic gifts and ministered with distinction around the world. Among them: Heinrich S. Voth (1878-1953); Cornelius N. Hiebert (1881-1975); Henry D. Wiebe (1889-1955); George B. Huebert (1887-1970): David Hooge (1891-1950); John A. Toews (1912-1979); Jacob J. Toews (1914-). George B. Huebert was one of five evangelists to speak at the 1933 World's Fair in Chicago. Cornelius N. Hiebert's ministry in Europe and South America in the post-World War II-era produced good results. John A. Toews and J.J. Toews ministered widely in Europe and South America. Henry D. Wiebe is remembered by some as the John the Baptist of the North American Mennonite Brethren preaching repentance, confession of sin and renewal.

11. Tom Allen, *The Face of My Parish* (New York: Harper and Row, n.d.), 37.

12. C. A. Holbrook, "Finney, Charles Grandison," in *Encyclopedic Dictionary of Religion*, ed. Paul Kevin Meaghes, et al. (Washington D.C.: The Sisters of Saint Joseph of Philadelphia, 1979), 1352.

13. J. A. R. Mackenzie, "Knox, John," *Encyclopedic Dictionary of Religion*, 1997-1998; D. R. Chandler, "Methodism," Ibid., 2353-55; C. A. Holbrook, "Finney, Charles Grandison," Ibid., 1352.

14. C. E. Autrey, *Revivals of the Old Testament* (Grand Rapids, Mich.: Zondervan Publishing House, 1960); William G. McLoughlin, "Revivalism," in *The Rise of Adventism*, Edwin Scott Gaustad, ed. (New York: Harper and Row, 1974), 119-150.

15. This is documented in Mennonite Brethren Conference yearbooks under the headings "Innere Mission" or later "home missions" and evangelism. Numerous local congregations also report periods of rapid growth in direct relationship to periods of repentance and confession of sin.

16. Loyal Funk, "Long Range Objectives in Conference Evangelism," Board of Evangelism Minutes, 22 May 1962, United States Mennonite Brethren Conference Board of Evangelism Records, Center for Mennonite Brethren Studies, Fresno, Calif., 4-6.

17. Ministers who served as evangelists were: Waldo Wiebe (1957-1963), David Wiens (1962-1966) and Henry Schmidt (1971-1977) in the United States; Henry Epp (1960-1964), J. J. Toews (1966-1975) and Rudy Boschman (1971-1973) in Canada.

18. *1966 Year Book of the fifty-sixth Canadian Conference of the Mennonite Brethren Churches of North America, convened at Niagara-on-the-Lake, Ontario, July 2 to 6, 1966*, 93.

19. Report on the Decade of Enlargement, *Year Book, 55th Session, Pacific Dis-*

trict, *The Conference of the Mennonite Brethren Churches convening at Butler Avenue Mennonite Brethren Church, Fresno, California November 7-9, 1964*, 7.

20. *Year Book, 61st Convention, Canadian Conference of Mennonite Brethren Churches, St. Catharines, Ontario, July 1-4, 1971*, 14-25.

21. Serving as executive secretaries for evangelism were: Elmo Warkentin (1961-1969), Loyal Martin (1969-1974) and Dennis Becker (1975-1980) in the United States; J. J. Toews (1966-1975), Henry Brucks (1975-1981) and James Nikkel (1982-1991) in Canada.

22. Board of Evangelism Meeting, 28 April 1971, United States Mennonite Brethren Conference Board of Evangelism Records, Center for Mennonite Brethren Studies, Fresno, Calif.

23. Board of Evangelism Ad Hoc Meeting, 15 August 1971, United States Mennonite Brethren Conference Board of Evangelism Records, Center for Mennonite Brethren Studies, Fresno, Calif.

24. *Year Book, 62nd Convention, Canadian Conference Mennonite Brethren Churches, Three Hills, Alberta, July 7-10, 1973*, 46-49.

25. Board of Evangelism Ad Hoc Meeting, 21 August 1974, United States Mennonite Brethren Conference Board of Evangelism Records, Center for Mennonite Brethren Studies, Fresno, Calif.

26. Board of Evangelism and Christian Education Meeting, 13-14 January 1976, United States Mennonite Brethren Conference Board of Evangelism and Christian Education Records, Center for Mennonite Brethren Studies, Fresno, Calif., E1-E22. Take special note of E12-E22, the detail plans for Encounter with Christ and Bicentennial Seminar for Church Leaders focusing on evangelism.

27. *Year Book, 67th Convention, The Canadian Conference of Mennonite Brethren Churches, Three Hills, Alberta, July 1-4, 1978*, 127-132; *Year Book, 68th Convention, The Canadian Conference of Mennonite Brethren Churches, Richmond, B. C., July 6-10, 1979*, 19-20, 53.

28. Executive Secretary's Report to the Board of Evangelism and Christian Education Meeting, 26-27 January 1979, United States Mennonite Brethren Conference Board of Evangelism and Christian Education Records, Center for Mennonite Brethren Studies, Fresno, Calif.

29. *75th Convention, The Canadian Conference of Mennonite Brethren Churches, Waterloo, Ontario, July 4-7, 1986*, 69-73; *76th Convention, Canadian Conference of Mennonite Brethren Churches, Three Hills, Alberta, July 3-6, 1987*, 89-99; *77th Convention, Canadian Conference of Mennonite Brethren Churches, Winkler, Manitoba, July 8-11, 1988*, 81-97.

30. *78th Convention, Canadian Conference of Mennonite Brethren Churches, Richmond, British Columbia, July 6-9, 1989*, 111-12.

31. Report from the church leadership in Quebec, 1991. This video is in my personal files.

32. Allan Bloom, *The Closing of the American Mind* (New York: Simon and Schuster, 1987), 29-30.

33. Daniel Yankelovich, *New Rules: Searching for Self-fulfillment in a World*

*Turned Upside Down* (New York: Random House, 1981), 85-105.

34. Ibid., 3-15. For further analysis of this self-fullfilment theme as a way to analyze American culture see Alasdair MacIntyre, *After Virtue: A Study in Moral Theory* (Notre Dame, Ind.: Notre Dame Press, 1981); Bloom, *The Closing of the American Mind.*

35. Yankelovich, *New Rules*, 7.

36. *The Four Spiritual Laws* (San Bernadino, Calif.: Campus Crusade for Christ International, n.d.), 2-3.

37. Bill J. Leonard, "Evangelism and Contemporary American Life," *Review and Expositor* 77 (1980): 497.

38. Al and Lorraine Broom, *One-to-One Evangelism* (Vista, Calif.: By the Authors, n.d.), 1-10.

39. Ibid.

40. Tex Sample, *U. S. Lifestyle and Mainline Churches: A Key to Reaching People in the 90s* (Louisville, Kent.: Westminster/John Knox Press, 1990), 33-35.

41. Dietrich Bonhoeffer, *The Cost of Discipleship* (New York: MacMillan Publishing Co., 1961).

42. George Gallup Jr., "How do the Unchurched View the Church?" Princeton Religious Institute, paper released February 17, 1988, p. 1-3.

43. "Born Again Exec Draws the Line," *Sojourners*, January 1978, 9.

44. Gallup, "How do the Unchurched View the Church?", 3.

45. Quoted in C. Peter Wagner, "Recent Developments in Church Growth Understandings," *Review and Expositor* 77 (1980): 509.

46. Ibid., 510.

47. C. Peter Wagner, *Your Church Can Grow* (Ventura, Calif.: Regal Books, 1976); C. Peter Wagner, *Your Church Can Be Healthy* (Nashville: Abingdon Press, 1979).

48. Delos Miles, *Church Growth: A Mighty River* (Wheaton, Ill.: Tyndale House Publisher, Inc., 1981), 134-44.

49. Wagner, *Your Church Can Grow*, 65.

50. Orlando E. Costas, *The Church and its Mission: A Shattering Critique from the Third World* (Wheaton, Ill.: Tyndale House Publisher, Inc., 1974), 124-131.

51. The Lake Avenue Congregational Church of Pasadena, California offers one example of rapid growth followed by a crisis in leadership and membership decrease.

52. J. Howard Kauffman and Leo Driedger, *The Mennonite Mosaic: Identity and Modernization* (Scottdale, Pa.: Herald Press, 1991), 36.

53. See *Year Book of the Fiftieth Canadian Conference of the Mennonite Brethren Church of North America*, 260; *Year Book, 61st Convention, Canadian Conference of Mennonite Brethren Churches, St. Catharines, Ontario, July 1-4, 1971*, 97.

54. *70th Convention, The Canadian Conference of Mennonite Brethren Churches, Saskatoon, Saskatchewan, July 3-7, 1981*, 158.

55. *80th Annual Convention of the Canadian Conference of Mennonite Brethren Churches, July 4-7, 1991*, Forest Grove Community Church, Saskatoon, Sask., 37.

56. *1990 U.S. Mennonite Brethren Conference Yearbook*, 50.

# CHAPTER 19

1. Emil Heinrich Brunner, *The Word and the World* (Lexington, Ky.: American Theological Library Association, 1965), 108.

2. *International Congress on World Evangelization* (Lausanne: The Congress, 1974), 83.

3. *Year Book of the 47th General Conference of the Mennonite Brethren Church of North America Held at the Mennonite Brethren Church, Yarrow, B.C., October 20-23, 1957*, 40-43.

4. David J. Hesselgrave, *Today's Choices for Tomorrow's Mission* (Grand Rapids, Mich.: Zondervan Publishing House, 1988), 13.

5. *Foreign Missions Guiding Principles and Field Policies* (Hillsboro, Kans.: Board of Foreign Missions of the Conference of the Mennonite Brethren Church of North America, 1947), 22-23.

6. *Year Book, 1957*, 41-43.

7. *Guiding Principles and Policies of Mennonite Brethren Church Missions* (Hillsboro, Kans: Board of Missions of the Conference of the Mennonite Brethren Church, 1960), 6-7.

8. Hans Kasdorf, "A Century of Mennonite Brethren Mission Thinking, 1885-1984," (Ph.D. diss., University of South Africa, 1986), 559.

9. G. W. Peters, *Foundations of Mennonite Brethren Missions* (Winnipeg: Kindred Press, 1984), 125-47.

10. *Yearbook, 50th Session, General Conference of Mennonite Brethren Churches convening at Corn, Oklahoma Nov. 25-29, 1966*, 104-05.

11. Ibid., 22-23.

12. *Mission Principles and Policies of the Mennonite Brethren Board of Missions and Services* (Hillsboro, Kans.: Mennonite Brethren Board of Missions/Services, 1977), 10-11.

13. Ibid., 14-15.

14. *Year Book, 53rd Session, General Conference of Mennonite Brethren Churches Convening at Winnipeg, Manitoba August 8-12, 1975*, 60-95; *A Biblical Agenda for a Faithful Church, 58th Convention of the General Conference of Mennonite Brethren Churches Sept. 28-Oct. 2, 1990 convening at the Hillsboro (Kan.) Mennonite Brethren Church*, 57-58.

15. Statistical data from the office of Mennonite Brethren Missions/Services.

16. *A Biblical Agenda for a Faithful Church*, 57-58.

17. Ibid., 84.

18. Hesselgrave, *Today's Choices for Tomorrow's Mission*, 14.

19. *Mission Principles and Policies of the Mennonite Brethren Board of Missions and Services, 1977*, 10.

20. Kasdorf, "A Century of Mennonite Brethren Mission Thinking," 646.

21. Hesselgrave, *Today's Choices for Tommorrow's Mission*, 14.

22. Ibid.

23 "Bavarian Mennonite Brethren Conference Continues to Grow," *Decision*, Nov. 1989, 21.

24. Correspondence in possession of author.

25. Jacob A. Loewen, "Strategies for Cross-Cultural Mission: Past, Present, and Future," *Mission Focus* 16, no. 4 (1988): 84-90.

26. Ibid., 85.

27. *Missions Principles and Policies, 1977*, 10-12.

28. Horace L. Fenton, Jr., *Myths about Missions* (Downers Grove, Ill.: InterVarsity Press, 1973), 87-98.

29. Roland Allen, *The Spontaneous Expansion of the Church—and the Causes Which Hinder It* (Grand Rapids, Mich.: Eerdmans, 1978), 10.

30. Norman Kraus, "Authentic Witness- A Call for Reappraisal," in *Mission Focus: Current Issues*, ed. Wilbert R. Shenk (Scottdale, Pa.: Herald Press, 1980), 169-85.

31. Document in possession of author.

32. Minutes of Resource Lectures by Tite Tienou, Board of Missions/Services Minutes, 30 Sept.-2 Oct. 1992, pp. 3-5.

33. Documents in possession of author.

34. Documents in possession of author.

35. Documents in possession of author.

36. Ibid.

37. William J. Kornfield, "Financial Paternalism and Western Cultural Transplant: An Open Letter to Missionary Leaders," Center for Training in Mission/Evangelism Records, Mennonite Brethren Biblical Seminary, p. 2.

38. Ibid., 6.

39. see Henry Schmidt, "Church Growth in Latin America," photocopy, 1989; See also papers presented at the symposium "Missiological Issues Facing the Church in Century 21," 21-23 Jan. 1988, Mennonite Brethren Biblical Seminary Records, Subgroup "Center for Training in Mission/Evangelism," Center for Mennonite Brethren Studies, Fresno, Calif., Hans Kasdorf, "Mission Future: Issues We Face;" Paul G. Hiebert, "World Trends and their Implications for Mennonite Brethren Missions;" Jacob A. Loewen, "Strategies for Cross-Cultural Mission."

# CHAPTER 20

1. *A Biblical Agenda for a Faithful Church: 58th Convention of the General Conference of Mennonite Brethren Churches, Sept. 28-Oct. 2, 1990 convening at the Hillsboro (Kan.) Mennonite Brethren Church*, 21-25.

2. For examples on the question of doctrine and moral ethics see the following issues of *Christianity Today:* 29 April 1991, 37-38; 24 June 1991, 20-23; 19 Aug. 1991, 46-47; also *Christian Century:* 10 July 1991, 684-85, 688-90; 7 Aug. 1991, 740-41.

3. An index of study conferences with program content and participants is located in the Center for Mennonite Brethren Studies, Fresno, Calif.

4. *Yearbook, 50th Session, General Conference of Mennonite Brethren Churches convening at Corn, Oklahoma November 25-29, 1966,* 36.

5. Ibid., 27.

6. *Confession of Faith of the General Conference of Mennonite Brethren Churches, 1976 Edition* (Hillsboro, Kans.; Winnipeg, Man.: Board of Christian Literature, General Conference of Mennonite Brethren Churches, 1976), 5; The revision process can be seen by comparing *Yearbook, 51st Session, General Conference of Mennonite Brethren Churches Convening at Vancouver, British Columbia, August 23-26, 1969,* 38-45; *Yearbook, 52nd Session of the General Conference of Mennonite Brethren Churches convening at Reedley, California November 11-14, 1972,* 17-22; *Yearbook, 53rd Session, General Conference of Mennonite Brethren Churches convening at Winnipeg, Manitoba, August 9-12, 1975,* 7-17.

7. *Yearbook, 1969,* 11.

8. Ibid.

9. Ibid., 12.

10. Ibid.

11. General Conference Board of Reference and Counsel, "A Call to Reason Together," *The Christian Leader,* 18 March 1986, 18-19.

12. J. Howard Kauffman and Leo Driedger, *The Mennonite Mosaic: Identity and Modernization* (Scottdale, Pa.: Herald Press, 1991).

13. *The Christian Leader,* 18 August 1987, 14-16.

14. Ibid., 16.

15. Ibid.

16. "A Stronger Bond of Unity," *The Christian Leader,* 16 Jan. 1990, 16-17.

17. *A Biblical Agenda for a Faithful Church,* 20-25.

18. John H. Redekop has been a columnist for *Mennonite Brethren Herald* for the past thirty years. For a compendium see his *Two Sides: The Best of Personal Opinion, 1964-1984* (Winnipeg, Man.: Kindred Press, 1984).

19. Katie Funk Wiebe has been a regular columnist in *The Christian Leader* since 1962. Some recent examples of important articles addressing important issues include "The Growing Minisry Gap: Can the Church Survive the Professsionalization of its Leadership," *The Christian Leader* 23 May 1989, 8-10; "Can the Church Survive the Preaching of a 'Carbonated' Gospel?," *Mennonite Brethren Herald* 7 June 1989, 10-11; "The Price of Radical Faith," *The Christian Leader* 9 May 1989, 15.

20. This statement is based on responses from conference ministers of the districts and provinces and selected pastors whom I contacted either by phone or interviewed personally.

21. Marvin Hein, "Are We Being Squeezed into the World's Mold?," *Yearbook of the Pacific District Conference of the Mennonite Brethren Church, 73rd Session Convening at Visalia, California November 11-13, 1982,* 16-22.

22. Robert Wuthnow, *The Restructuring of American Religions: Society and Faith Since World War II* (Princeton, N.J.: Princeton University Press, 1988); Robert Neelly Bellah, et al., *Habits of the Heart: Individualism and Commitment in American Life* (Berkeley: University of California Press, 1985); Alasdair MacIntyre, *After Virtue: a Study in Moral Theory* (Notre Dame, Ind.: University of Notre Dame Press, 1981); Allan Bloom, *The Closing of the American Mind* (New York: Simon and Schuster, 1987); Daniel Yankelovich, *New Rules: Searching for Self-Fulfillment in a World Turned Upsidedown* (New York: Random House, 1981); Reginald W. Bibby, *Fragmented Gods: the Poverty and Potential of Religion in Canada* (Toronto: Irwin Publishing, 1987); Robert Webber, *Secular Humanism: Threat and Challenge* (Zondervan, 1982); James Davison Hunter, *American Evangelicalism: Conservative Religion and the Quandary of Modernity* (New Brunswick, N.J.: Rutgers University Press, 1983); Richard Quebedeaux, *By What Authority: The Rise of Personality Cults in American Christianity* (San Fransisco: Harper and Row, 1982); Michael Scott Horton, *Made in America: The Shaping of Modern American Evangelicalism* (Baker Book House, 1991); Walter Tony-Need, *The New Religion* (Inter-Varsity Press, 1985); Scott Sernau, *Please Don't Squeeze the Christian into the World's Mold* (Inter-Varsity Press, 1987); Tex Sample, *U.S. Lifestyles and Mainline Churches: A Key to Reaching People in the 90's* (Louisville, Ky.: Westminster/John Knox Press, 1990).

23. "What do Americans Believe?," *Christianity Today,* 16 Sept. 1991, 48;

24. Wally Sawatzky, "Northview Community Church, What Makes it Grow," *Mennonite Brethren Herald,* 28 June 1991, 18-19.

25. *Berichte und Beschluesse der vierundvierzigsten Kanadischen Konferenz der Mennoniten Brüdergemeinde von Nord Amerika abgehalten in Virgil, Ontario vom 3. bis 8. Juli, 1954,* 84-86.

26. *Berichte und Beschluesse der zweiundfünfzigsten Kanadischen Konferenz der Mennoniten Brüdergemeinde von Nord Amerika abgehalten in Clearbrook, British Columbia von 30. Juni bis zum 4. Juli, 1962,* 222-23.

27. *1963 Yearbook of the Fifty-third Canadian Conference of the Mennonite Brethren Churches of North America held at the Auditorium of the Mennonite Brethren Churches of South Saskatchewan, Herbert Saskatchewan, June 29-July 3, 1963,* 118.

28. J. Howard Kauffman and Leland Harder, *Anabaptists Four Centuries Later: A Profile of Five Mennonite and Brethren in Christ Denominations* (Scottdale, Pa.: Herald Press, 1975).

29. *Direction* 14, no.2 (1985).

30. Kauffman and Driedger, *Mennonite Mosaic.*

31. John H. Redekop "The Influence of Rising Educational Level," *Direction* 14, no.2 (1985): 54-59.

32. Kauffman and Driedger, *Mennonite Mosaic,* 69.

33. Ibid., 91.

34. Ibid., 97.

35. Ibid., 72-75.

36. Ibid., 145, 217-19.

37. Ibid., 71.

38. Ibid., 97.

39. Hunter, *American Evangelicalism*, 73-100.

40. Ibid., 87.

41. James Davidson Hunter, *Evangelicalism: The Coming Generation* (Chicago, Il.: The Chicago University Press, 1987), 75.

42. Ibid.

43. Tony Campolo, *Wake Up America* (Grand Rapids, Mich.: Zondervan Publishing House, 1991), 117.

# CHAPTER 21

1. James Burns, *Revivals: Their Laws and Leaders* (Grand Rapids, Mich.: Baker Book House, 1960), 21.

2. Westin Gunnar, *The Free Church Through the Ages* [*Den Kristna fri församlingen genom tiderna*], trans. Virgil A. Olsen (Nashville: Broadman Press, 1958).

3. Ernst Troeltsch, *The Social Teaching of the Christian Churches* [*Die Sociallehren der Christlichen Kirchen und Gruppen*], vol. 1, trans. Olive Wyon (Chicago: University of Chicago Press, 1981), 328-33.

4. Stanley Hauerwas and William H. Willimon, *Resident Aliens: Life in the Christian Colony* (Nashville: Abingdon Press, 1989).

5. Editorial, "What do Americans Believe?," *Christianity Today*, 16 Sept. 1991, 48.

6. Alvin C. Porteous, *The Search for Christian Credibility: Explorations in Contemporary Belief* (Nashville: Abingdon Press, 1971), 21.

7. Ibid.

8. James Davison Hunter, *American Evangelicalism: Conservative Religion and the Quandary of Modernity* (New Brunswick, N.J.: Rutgers University Press, 1983), 73.

9. Edward R. Dayton, *What Ever Happened to Commitment?* (Grand Rapids, Mich.: Zondervan Publishing House, 1984), 38.

10. Nicky Cruz crusade, Fresno, 21 September 1991.

11. Roger Palms, "The State of Evangelism in America Today," *Action*, 50, no. 6 (1991): 4-5.

12. Dietrich Bonhoeffer, *The Cost of Discipleship* (New York: The Macmillan Company, 1960), 36.

13. "Conversion," in *Baker Encyclopedia of the Bible*, ed. Walter A. Elwell, vol. 1 (Grand Rapids, Mich.: Baker Book House, 1988), 512.

14. Paul Helm, "Repentance," *Baker Encyclopedia of the Bible*, 1837.

15. Henry Schmidt, ed., *Conversion: Doorway to Discipleship* (Hillsboro, Kans.: Board of Christian Literature of the General Conference of Mennonite Brethren

Churches, 1980).

16. Myron Augsburger, Introduction to Ibid., v-vii.

17. J. Howard Kauffman and Leland Harder, *Anabaptists Four Centuries Later: A Profile of Five Mennonite and Brethren in Christ Denominations* (Scottdale, Pa.: Herald Press, 1975); John B. Toews, Abram Konrad and Al Dueck, "Mennonite Brethren Church Membership Profile, 1972-1982," *Direction* 14, no. 2 (1985); J. Howard Kauffman and Leo Driedger, *The Mennonite Mosaic: Identity and Modernization* (Scottdale, Pa.: Herald Press, 1991).

18. "Conclusions and Implications," *Direction* 14, no. 2 (1985): 82.

19. John Redekop, "The Influence of Rising Educational Levels," *Direction* 14, no. 2 (1985): 58-59.

20. Roland Reimer, "Faith and Practice in Congregational Life," *Direction* 14, no.2 (1985): 69-70.

21. Abe Dueck, "Economics, Faith and Practice," *Direction* 14, no. 2 (1985): 53.

22. John E. Toews, "Theological Reflections," *Direction* 14, no. 2 (1985): 61.

23. Ibid., 67-68.

24. Delbert Wiens, "Cultural Change," *Direction* 14, no. 2 (1985): 47.

25. "Conclusions and Implications," *Direction* 14, no. 2 (1985): 82-85.

# CHAPTER 22

1. Aron A. Töws, *Mennonitische Märtyrer der jüngsten Vergangenheit und der Gegenwart*, 2 vols. (Clearbrook, B.C.: By the Author, 1949).

2. Frank C. Peters, "The Early Mennonite Brethren: Baptist or Anabaptist?" *Mennonite Life* 14 (1959): 176-178.

3. J. A. Toews, "In Search of Identity," *Mennonite Brethren Herald*, 10 March 1972, 25.

4. Peter M. Hamm, *Continuity and Change Among Canadian Mennonite Brethren* (Waterloo, Ont.: Wilfrid Laurier University Press, 1987), 226.

5. Calvin Redekop, "Religious Renewal Movements in Search of the Past," photocopy, n.d., 3.

6. Ibid.

7. *A Biblical Agenda for a Faithful Church: 58th Convention of the General Conference of Mennonite Brethren Churches, Sept. 28- Oct. 2, 1990, convening at the Hillsboro (Kan.) Mennonite Brethren Church*, 21-22.

8. Nathan O. Hatch and Michael S. Hamilton, "Can Evangelicalism Survive Its Success?" *Christianity Today* 5 Oct. 1992, 20-31.

9. Ibid., 31.

10. Ibid.

11. Quoted in Tim Croter, "America's Forgotten Heritage of Faith," *United Evangelical Action* 51, no. 4 (1992): 4-6.

# Index

## A

Acculturation, 259
Alexanderthal, 36, 144
Alexanderwohl, 86, 161
All Mennonite Conference, 119-121, 139-142, 167-147
Allen, Roland, 272
Alliance Movement, 123-127, 134
Alliance Theological Seminary, 273
Anabaptists, 2-3, 13-17, 29, 81-83, 170-177
Augsburger, Myron, 23, 30, 162

## B

Baedekker, Fredrich W., 58, 123, 124
Baerg, Margaret, 100
Baerg, Rueben, 192
Baerg, William, 100
Baptism, 35-38, 48-49
Baptist Influence, 189-190
Baptists, 37, 18, 58, 97, 128, 157
Bartsch, Anna, 100
Bartsch, Heinrich, 100
Bekker, Jacob P., 5, 17, 37, 85
Bender, Harold S., 33
Bergmann, Peter, 121
Bergthold, Anna, 92
Bergthold, Daniel F., 59, 92, 102-104, 130, 191
Bergthold, Tina, 102
Berlin Mission Institute, 58
Bestvater, William, 59, 109, 110, 111, 113, 194, 199
Bibelstunden, 24, 189-190
Bible Institue of Los Angeles, 191, 193
Bible Institutes, 190-195
Bible Schools, 20-21, 168-171
Biblicism, 20-21
Blankenburg Alliance Bible Conference, 123-127, 141
Bloom, Allan, 206, 207, 212, 252
Boehm, Martin, 162
Bonhoeffer, Dietrich, 254, 302
Boschman, Rudy, 249
Braeul, Johann, 117
Braun, Johann, 159
Brenneman, Daniel, 162
Briercrest Bible Institute, 193
Brown, Henry J., 162
Brucks, Henry, 232
Brunner, Emil, 261
Burns, James, 300
Burwalde, Man., 87, 161
Buswell, James Oliver, 173

## C

Campolo, Tony, 298
Canadian Conference of M.B. Churches, 173, 183, 185, 186, 191, 194, 195, 249, 258
Chortitza, 5, 11, 115, 116, 122, 142
Church and Government, 78-79
Church Growth, 255-257
Church Leadership, 53-60, 122-130, 217-237
Church Membership Profile, 307-321
Church Polity, 202-203, 217-224,
Claassen, Johann, 12, 43
Coaldale Bible School, 169
Coffman, John S., 162

369

Columbia Bible College, 163, 171
Community, 84-88
Concord College, 171, 185
Confession of Faith, 130-131, 195, 285-287
Conversion, 29-35, 152, 201-202, 302, 304
Corn Bible Academy, 168
Cornelsen, Abraham, 13
Cornelsen, Henry, 125
Cornies, Johann, 7, 117
Cornies, Phillipp, 155

## D

Darby, John Nelson, 123, 124
DeFehr, Cornelius A., 158
Denk, Hans, 19, 23
DePree, Max, 227
Derksen, David D., 158
Derksen, Gerhard, 36
Dewey, John, 252
Dixon, H.C., 194
Doerksen, Dietrich, 143
Doerksen, Gerhard, 144
Drowell, J.G., 173
Dueck, Abe, 308
Dueck, Alvin, 310
Duerksen, David, 17, 21, 34, 58, 117, 121
Duerksen, John F., 59, 129
Dyck, Cornelius J., 29, 133
Dyck, David, 59, 87
Dyck, Jakob, 89, 146

## E

Eby, Solomon, 162
Economics, 118-119
Eden Christian College, 170
Ediger, Gerry, 228
Education Task Force, 183-185
Elders, 65-67, 220, 221
Elizabethtal, 13
Enns, Anna, 100
Enns, Heinrich, 89, 97, 98, 146, 148
Epp, Anna, 91, 103
Epp, Claas, 108
Epp, David, 5
Epp, Frank H., 160
Epp, Theodore, H., 162, 240
Eschatology, 107-114, 199-200
Ethics, 75-79
Evangelistic work, 84-88, 239-259
Evans, William, 173, 182, 194
Ewert, David, 183
Exuberant Movement, 44

## F

Fast, Bernhard, 9
Fenton, Howard L., 271
Flaming, H.H., 65, 66
Foth, Alfred, 280
Fragmentation, 213-216
Francis, Emerick K., 157
Franz, Heinrich, 9, 117
French Creek, Kans., 86, 135, 161
Fresno Pacific College, 171, 174-180, 241, 275, 309
Friedensstimme, 21, 33, 58, 68, 118
Friedmann, Robert, 123, 173, 180
Friesen, Abraham, 95
Friesen, Abram J., 90, 118
Friesen, Isaak, 121

Friesen, Jacob, 127
Friesen, Lydia, 100
Friesen, Maria, 91
Friesen, Peter M., 5, 6, 10, 14, 17, 26, 32, 37, 43, 58, 61, 65, 68, 108, 109, 116, 118, 120, 121, 133-135
Froese, Gerhard P., 89
Fundamentalism, 173-174, 192-198
Funk, John F., 162
Funk, Ruth Wiens, 271

# G

Gaebelein, Arno, 193, 194
Gallup, George, 254
Gebhardt, Ernst, 124
General Conference Mennonite Church, 160-161
General Conference of M.B. Churches, 38, 52, 56, 57, 63, 78, 119, 120, 129, 130, 158, 160, 161, 162, 163, 172, 173, 174, 182, 185, 186, 212, 219, 222, 230, 231, 232, 237, 281, 282, 284, 285, 287, 293-294
Geographical Expansion, 115-119
German Language, 168-171
Gethsemane H.S. (Fairview, Okla.), 168
Gnadenfeld, 10, 12, 83, 93, 116, 189
Gobel, Max, 29
Goertz, Abram, 117
Goertz, Janice, 279
Goertz, John, 279
Goertzen, Anna, 99
Goessel MB Church, 161
Grace, 46-49
Grace College of the Bible, 162
Gray, James M., 191, 194

Grebel, Conrad, 21
Gregg, Harris, 194
Gunnar, Westin, 300

# H

Haarbeck, Theodor, 194
Hamilton, Michael, 326
Hamm, Peter, , 325
Hannon, Matt, 226
Harder, Bernhard, 7
Harder, Johann, 43
Harms, John F., 37, 59, 67, 129
Harms, Orlando, 232
Harrison, Norman D., 192
Hatch, Nathan, 326
Heese, Heinrich, 9, 117
Hein, Marvin, 232, 290
Hesselgrave, David J., 262, 268
Hiebert David Edmond, 283
Hiebert, Cornelius, 191
Hiebert, John N.C., 174
Hiebert, Martha, 99, 101
Hiebert, Nickolas, 22, 59, 102, 109, 130
Hiebert, Paul, 236, 278
Hiebert, Peter C., 59, 130, 173
Hiebert, Susie, 91, 101
Hiebert, Waldo, 232, 283, 290
Hildebrand, Jacob, 11
Hildebrand, Kornelius, 11
Hofer, David M., 143
Hofer, Jacob D., 174, 191
Holdeman, John, 162
Holzrichter, Peter, 117
Huebert, George B., 174, 191
Huebert, Heinrich, 9, 61, 62, 85, 88

# INDEX

Huebert, Katharina, 91
Hunter, James Davison, 296, 297

## I

Immigration, 155-160
Individualism, 206-208, 295-297
Inman, Kans., 129
Isaak, Franz Peter, 117
Itinerant Ministry, 67-68, 191
Ivory Coast, 274

## J

Jantz, Jacob, 68
Janz, Benjamin B., 50, 51, 65, 127, 141, 155, 158, 181, 193
Janz, Johann, 148
Janzen, Aaron A., 94, 97, 99-101, 191
Janzen, Abraham E., 20, 25, 91, 173, 283
Janzen, Edmund, 177
Janzen, Ernestina, 98
Janzen, Frank, 105
Janzen, Martha, 192
Jones, Eli Stanley, 174
Jung-Stilling, Johann Heinrich, 9, 84, 108
Just, Martin M., 130

## K

Kanadier, 156-160
Kargel, J.W., 58, 88
Kasdorf, Hans, 264, 268, 271, 278
Kasper, Eva, 105
Kauffman, Daniel, 182
Kaufman, Gordon, 164
Kingdom of God, 71-74
Kirchliche Mennonites (Russia), 119-121, 144, 161
Klassen, Cornelius F., 158
Kleine Gemeinde, 8-9, 134, 189
Kliewer, John B., 100
Kliewer, Ruth, 100
Konrad, Abram, 310
Koop, Isaak, 121
Kornelsen, Peter, 143,
Kornfield, William, 277, 278
Krahn, Cornelius, 7, 15, 61, 83, 85, 156
Kraus, Norman, 164
Kreider, Robert, 5, 15
Krestyaninov, Vitor F., 152
Kroeker, Abraham, 17
Kroeker, Abram, 112-113, 118
Kroeker, Abram A., 191
Kroeker, Jacob, 17, 123, 125
Kroeker, Jacob, 118
Kroeker, Martin, 118
Kuban, 42

## L

Lange, Johannes, 108
Lange, Wilhelm, 10, 83
Lenzmann (Elder), 12
Life Insurance, 77
Life Style, 74-79
Loewen, Howard, 164
Loewen, Jacob A., 270, 278, 279
Lohrenz, Gerhard, 5
Lohrenz, Henry W., 53, 54, 55, 59, 66, 71, 72, 73, 112, 130, 169, 172, 173
Lohrenz, John H., 103, 156
Lord's Supper, 47-49

# M

M.B. Secession, 12-15
MacIntyre, Alasdair, 206, 212
Manz, Martha, 99
Martens, Elmer, 232, 290
Martens, Franz, 134
Martyrs, 148-150
Materialism, 75-77
McGavran, Donald, 255
McPherson College, 91, 102, 129
Mennonite Brethren Bible College, 182-185
Mennonite Brethren Biblical Seminary, 171, 185-186, 226, 274, 275, 308
Mennonites in Prussia/Poland, 4, 6, 10, 67, 121, 211
Meyer, Frederick B., 58, 124
Miles, Delos, 256
Mill, John Stuart, 252
Miller, Herman, 227
Minneapolis City Mission, 89
Mission Changes, 261-280
Mission Methods, 91-93
Missions in Africa, 60, 97, 98, 99, 100, 101, 161, 191, 192, 204, 262, 263, 271, 279
Missions in Brazil, 274-275
Missions in India, 60, 91, 92, 95, 101-105, 118, 128, 159, 174, 191, 204, 255, 262, 263, 265, 267, 271, 279, 280
Missions in Japan, 204, 267, 279, 280
Molotschna, 115, 116, 122, 134, 144
Moody Bible Institute, 191-193
Moravia Brethren, 9, 26, 83, 90, 116
Mullins, Edgar Y., 72, 182

Multiple Ministry, 61-65, 224-226
Murch, James DeForest, 186

# N

Nakamura, Takao, 280
Netherlands, 4, 26, 83,
Neu Kronsweide, 11, 14
Neufeld, Abraham H., 58
Neufeld, Elizabeth, 92, 102
Neufeld, Heinrich, 85, 89
Neufeld, J.J., 109, 110
Nikolaifeld Mennonite Church, 134
Nonresistance, 126-127, 140-142
Northwestern Bible Institute, 191, 192, 193

# O

Ohrloff, , 5, 116, 134, 189
Orenburg, 115

# P

Pacific District Conference of M.B. Churches, 173, 240, 291
Page, Kirby, 174
Palms, Roger, 302
Pankratz, Johann, 59, 130
Pankratz, John H., 91, 92, 102
Pankratz, Maria, 91, 92, 102
Pastoral Letters, 287-290
Pauls, Tina, 192
Penner, Anna, 91
Penner, John A., 91
Penner, Peter E., 59, 75, 109, 110, 112
Peters, Anna, 91
Peters, Frank, 232

Peters, Frank C., 183, 283, 290, 325
Peters, G.W., 240, 284
Peters, Isaak, 106
Peters, Peter, 9
Philips, Dirk, 9
Pietism, 9-12, 122-127, 136-137, 189-195
Pluralism, 209-210
Plymouth Brethren, 123, 124
Prairie Bible Institute, 193
Prieb, Wesley, 283
Principalities and Powers, 290-294

## Q
Quiring, J.H., 284

## R
Ratzlaff, Edna, 100
Ratzlaff, John C., 100
Ratzlaff, Vern, 284
Red River Valley, Man., 168
Redekop, Calvin, 211, 212, 325, 326
Redekop, John H., 170, 290, 307
Reeves, Richard, 207
Regehr, Heinrich, 159
Regehr, Henry, 232
Regehr, Johann, 130
Regehr, John, 232
Regier, Albert, 240
Regier, G.P., 65
Regier, Heinrich, 158
Regier, J.J., 59
Reimer, Adolf, 36, 88, 89, 146
Reimer, David, 36, 148
Reimer, Jacob, 12, 121, 127
Reimer, Jacob W. , 66, 110, 111, 112, 125, 126
Reimer, Katrina, 91
Reimer, Klaas, 8, 134
Reimer, Roland, 308
Relativism, 206-208
Rempel, Peter P., 59
Renewal, 1-12, 143-146, 162-164
Rice, John R., 193
Riley, William B., 192, 193, 194
Rimmer, Harry, 193
Ris, Cornelius, 17, 37, 197
Rufus, Vedulla K., 280
Russian Revolution, 139-152
Russländer, 156-160
Ruth, Paul, 173
Rückenau, 66, 122

## S
Samara, 115
Sample, Tex, 253
Sanctification, 72-74
Sandburg, Carl, , 327
Sattler, Michael, 21
Schatter, David, 5
Schellenberg, Abraham, 59, 130, 172
Schellenberg, David, 44, 66, 121, 122
Schellenberg, Katherine, 92, 102
Schellenberg, Peter E., 173, 174
Schlabach, Theron F., 190
Schleitheim Confession, 70-71
Schmidt, Christian, 68
Schmidt, Henry J., 208, 232, 250, 278, 303
Schools in Russia, 157
Schrag, Robert, 2
Schrank, Robert, 207

Schroeter, August A., 174
Scofield, Cyrus I., 110, 194
Scripture, 18-21, 200-201
Sectarianism, 152
Secularization, 208-210
Selbstschutz, 126-127, 140-145
Siberia, 115, 146, 148, 150
Siemens, Len, 284
Simons, Menno, 9, 14, 21, 32, 40, 82, 84, 108, 182, 189
Smucker, Donovan, 20
Spener, Philip Jakob, 83
St. Chrishona Bible School, 58
Steinbach (Russia), 49
Stockmayer, Otto, 58, 124
Stroeter, Ernst F., 58, 124
Strong, Augustus H., 182
Study Conference, 282-284
Suckau, C.H., 162
Sukkau, Heinrich P., 89
Support for Ministers, 60-61

## T

Tabor College, 59, 111, 130, 169, 171-174, 180, 190, 191
Theological Education, 180-185
Theological Trends, 284-287
Theology of Change, 210-216
Thiessen, Franz C. 158
Thiessen, Jakob, 144, 158
Tienou, Tite, 273-274
Toews, Heinrich, 158
Toews, Henry F., 111
Toews, Jacob J., 250, 283
Toews, Johann A., 65, 76
Toews, John A., 4, 7, 11, 58, 65, 112, 133, 183, 210, 215, 240, 325
Toews, John B., 6, 11, 139, 142
Toews, John E., 308
Toews, Paul, 169, 175-176, 178, 190
Torrey, Reuben A., 173, 182, 191, 194
Troeltsch, Ernst, 29, 300
Troutman, Charles, 278
Turkestan, 115

## U

Unger, Abram, 18, 85, 89
Unruh, Abraham H., 15, 17, 44, 49, 58, 65, 89, 111, 113, 127, 158, 181, 183, 199
Unruh, Anna, 91
Unruh, Heinrich P., 117
Unruh, Kornelius, 117
Unruh, Martha, 91
Urbanization, 164-165, 208-210
Urry, James 10

## V

Veron, Juan, 279
Viebahn, General Von, 58, 124
Volkskirche, 5, 37, 39, 136
Voth, A.B., 284
Voth, Heinrich, 59, 87, 88, 97, 101, 102, 104, 130, 161
Voth, Heinrich S., 130
Voth, Johann, 130
Voth, John, 104
Voth, Tobias, 9, 83, 84, 117

## W

Wagner, Peter, 256
Waldheim, Russia, 49
Warkentin, Cornelius, 9
Warkentin, Henry K., 191
Warkentin, Herman, 105
Wedel, Cornelius P., 86, 161
Wedel, Peter, 96, 97, 161
Wiebe, Henry D, 21, 174
Wiebe, J.J., 240
Wiebe, Jacob J., 192
Wiebe, Katie Funk, 163, 290
Wiebe, Waldo 240, 241
Wieler, Johann, 88, 89
Wiens, David, , 192
Wiens, Delbert, 176, 309
Wiens, Frank, 105
Wiens, H.G., 240, 241
Wiens, Heinrich, 9
Wiens, Helena, 91
Wiens, Johann, 58, 158
Wiens, John G., 160
Wiens, Leo, 192
Wiens, Maria, 91
Willems, Arthur, 283
Willems, Katherine, 99
Williams, George H., 82
Winkler Bible Institute, 83, 191
Winnipeg Bible College , 193, 308
Winrod, Gerald, 173, 193
Wirsche, David, 279
Women in the Church, 149-150
Wüst, Eduard, 10, 11, 84, 87

## X, Y

Yankelovich, Daniel, 252

## Z

Zabala, Emilio, 280
Zaire, 94, 98, 101, 265, 271, 279
Zinzendorf, Count, 83
Zionsbote, 21, 23, 33, 58, 68, 91, 94, 109-110, 114, 130, 194
Zorrilla, Hugo, 275-277